The **Rough Guide**

The Gambia

written and researched by

Emma Gregg and Richard Trillo

ROUGH GUIDES

NEW YORK · LONDON · DELHI

www.roughguides.com

Contents

Kora, drumming and dance colour section following p.168

Beaches and boat trips colour section following p.248

Introduction to

The Gambia

The Gambia is West Africa at its most accessible. Stable, peaceful, affordable and within comfortable flying distance of northern Europe, this former British colony has been a popular winter holiday destination for four decades, and its appealing tropical climate, lively beach resorts and friendly atmosphere are enough to keep sunseekers returning time and time again. You can fully immerse yourself in the real West Africa here, too, by travelling up-country, where you'll discover picturesque mud-built villages, rice fields and palm groves, vibrant markets where you can haggle over batiks and balafons, and local festivals – invariably exuberant displays of colour, energy and noise.

The country has a great deal to offer **nature** enthusiasts: it's well established as a top birdwatching destination, and its greatest natural feature, the River Gambia, is becoming a major draw for eco-tourists. There's a rich seam of **history** to explore too in the Gambia valley, with heritage sites dating from prehistoric times to the slave trading era and the later colonial period. And, while ancient customs and traditions are still widely practised, younger Gambians are blending the old with the new and adding their own effervescent spin to traditional **music and dance**.

The Gambia's unique charm lies in its **smallness**: even the largest settlements, where crowds jostle along narrow streets brimming with heat, colour and noise, have an overgrown-village atmosphere. Elitism is hard to maintain in this close-knit environment – there's a rapidly acquired feeling of knowing everyone, and you can find yourself in conversation with the likes of senior government officials at the hotel bar without even realizing it. For many visitors, it's the **friendships** they make during their stay which leave the most lasting impression. Gambians are generally multilingual, speaking English and a variety of West African languages, and they have a well-earned reputation for being unpretentious, accepting and approachable, and for making strangers feel completely at home.

Wherever you go, you're never far from the **River Gambia**, which gives the country its name and determines its bizarre, elongated shape. The river rises in the Fouta Djalon hills in Guinea, winds erratically through southern Senegal, crosses into The Gambia at its eastern limit, then cuts a five-hundred-kilometre swathe down the middle of the country to the Atlantic. Up-country in eastern Gambia, the river is freshwater and bordered by lush green tropical forest, while the lower reaches are mangrove-fringed. Long-distance boat trips allow you to enjoy the river environment at its peaceful best, watching the changing scenery unfold and listening to the different sounds at dawn, daytime and dusk. The fertile river valley, watered and drained by the daily cycle of tides and the annual swing of flood and

▲ Hibiscus flower in a hotel garden

Fact file

• At 11,300 square kilometres (about the size of Yorkshire or Connecticut), The Gambia is one of Africa's **smallest** and most **densely populated** countries. The population is more than 1.5 million, and growing rapidly, with a birth rate of between four and five infants per child-bearing woman. Ethnic groups include Mandinka (42%), Fula (18%), Wolof (16%), Jola (10%), Serahule (9%), other Africans including Serer and Aku (4%), Europeans and Lebanese (1%).

• The Gambia is one of the world's **poorest** countries, with an average annual income of less than £200 (€290 / $370). However, destitution is not as widespread as these figures might suggest: most Gambians are subsistence farmers or fishermen, and are self-sufficient for most of the year. The main export crop is groundnuts (peanuts), although tourism is also an important source of revenue.

• Since independence from Britain in 1965, The Gambia has been a **multiparty democracy**. The president, His Excellency Al-Haji Yahya AJJ Jammeh, is only the country's second; his predecessor, Dawda Jawara, was ousted by Jammeh's military coup in 1994.

• Formerly just "Gambia", the country's official name – *The* Gambia – was coined post-Independence to eliminate confusion with Kambia, in Sierra Leone, and Zambia.

5

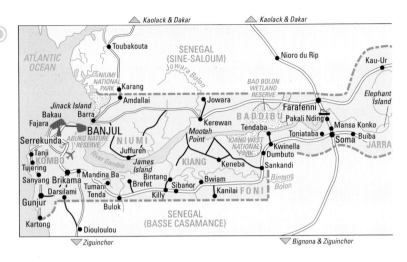

Kaolack & Dakar   Kaolack & Dakar

ATLANTIC OCEAN

Toubakouta

SENEGAL (SINE-SALOUM)

Nioro du Rip

Kau-Ur

NIUMI NATIONAL PARK

Karang

Amdallai

Jowara

BAO BOLON WETLAND RESERVE

Elephant Island

Jinack Island

Barra

Bakau

Fajara

BANJUL

NIUMI

Serrekunda

ABUKO NATURE RESERVE

Juffureh

Kerewan

Mootah Point

BADDIBU

Farafenni

Pakali Nding

Tendaba

Mansa Konko

Toniataba

Buiba

Soma

JARRA

KIANG WEST NATIONAL PARK

Kwinella

Dumbuto

Tanji

KOMBO

River Gambia

James Island

KIANG

Keneba

Sankandi

Tujering

Sanyang

Brikama

Mandina Ba

Bintang

Bwiam

Bintang Bolon

Tumani

Brefet

Sibanor

Kanilai

FONI

Darsilami

Tenda

Killy

Gunjur

Bulok

SENEGAL (BASSE CASAMANCE)

Kartong

Diouloulou

Ziguinchor   Bignona & Ziguinchor

drought, is a magnet for native and migrant wildlife species, including a remarkable profusion of birds.

The Gambia is a developing country in the poorest corner of the poorest continent and **tourism** here has always been inhibited by a lack of resources. While the choice of places to stay is growing every year – the country now has a number of luxury lodges as well as a good range of moderately priced resort hotels and guest houses – the infrastructure is struggling to keep up, particularly up-country. With rural highways in dire need of repair and both power cuts and water shortages a regular occurrence, hoteliers and travellers alike have to be resourceful. For some, this adds to The Gambia's appeal. Even the busiest resort areas still

▼ Fisherman mending his nets on Sanyang beach

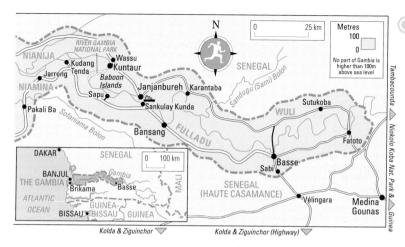

Kolda & Ziguinchor ▽   Kolda & Ziguinchor (Highway) ▽

have a down-to-earth, rough-edged charm that suits those who don't like their travel experiences too packaged.

For most visitors, the **beaches** are a major draw. With more than sixty kilometres of Atlantic coastline, the winter holiday brochures portray the country as a beach paradise. This is stretching the truth a bit – The Gambia's beaches certainly can't compete with those found in the Caribbean or on the Indian Ocean – but there are a few which come close to the broad, empty, palm-fringed ideal.

Although The Gambia lacks the scenic drama and conspicuously abundant game animals of Africa's great safari destinations, it's rich in **biodiversity**, with an unusually wide variety of natural habitats ranging from beaches to river, mangrove, tropical woodland and savannah, all crammed into a small area that's easy to travel around by a combination of driving, boating, cycling and walking.

With The Gambia's wilderness so accessible, far-sighted tour operators are beginning to appreciate the country's potential as an **ecotourism destination**. Low-impact holidays are growing in popularity, allowing visitors both to appreciate the natural environment and also learn about traditional Gambian society,

▲ Traditional singer, kora and tama players at Albreda near Juffureh

Baobab trees

Baobabs are commanding features of the African landscape, presiding over villages – and places where villages used to be – like wise old men.

The most ancient specimens are treated with the kind of respect normally reserved for historic monuments; legend has it that these mighty trees can live for thousands of years, and have supernatural properties.

In reality, it's difficult to age a baobab – there are no growth rings to count – but their sheer bulk, with their girth swelling to over 25m, is testament to their great longevity.

This tree is a survivor – deciduous, it can store enough water in the spongy tissues of its buttressed trunk to last right through the dry season, and if its fibrous bark is damaged, it regenerates. Gambians sometimes strip baobab bark to make rope. The bark, leaves and fruit also have several medicinal and dietary uses.

All the baobabs on mainland Africa belong to a single species, the African baobab, named *Adansonia digitata* after French botanist and explorer Michel Adanson who conducted an extensive study of the flowers and trees of Senegal in the mid-1700s.

by combining boat trips or bush drives with visits to rural villages or music and dance lessons.

You don't need to be a rugged adventurer to enjoy The Gambia to the full – in fact, if you've never been to **Africa**, it's one of the best places to start. Independent travel is reasonably cheap and straightforward, and there are plenty of day trips and longer expeditions which open up the interior to those who prefer guided tours. The Gambia also makes an ideal starting point for anyone wishing to explore West Africa in greater depth: it's within easy reach of Senegal, Mali, Guinea-Bissau and Guinea. The Gambia has much in common with its neighbours, and its hotels, guesthouses and restaurants, many of them right on the beach, allow you to acclimatize in comfort while getting to grips with the West African way of life.

Where to go

Most visitors to The Gambia base themselves in the string of Atlantic beach resorts in **northern Kombo**, the area closest to the capital, **Banjul**. Few visitors spend more than a day or so in the city itself; far more rewarding targets at this end of the country include **southern Kombo**, the southwestern region bordered by the Atlantic and the Casamance region of Senegal, between the fishing settlements of Ghana Town and Kartong. Here, the beaches, backed by lush countryside, are emptier and wilder than those in the resort areas.

If you have time to explore the **interior** of the country, you'll quickly find yourself deep in classic West African landscapes scattered with traditional villages and crisscrossed by red-earth roads. Here, women with their babies bound to their backs tend vegetable plots or stir spicy stews outside shaggy-thatched, mud-brick houses, and men clear fields with machetes or discuss village politics under shade trees. The up-country animal and birdlife is diverse and exotic; ornithologists will recognize many wintering migrants from Europe. There are also coconut groves and rice fields, and mangrove swamps and creeks plied by dugout canoes – and, of course, the mighty **River Gambia** itself to explore.

▲ Pirogues moored on the River Gambia near Janjanbureh

▼ Up-country airstrip, near Tendaba Camp

The most visited point on the north bank of the river is **Juffureh** which, along with nearby **James Island**, was once a colonial slave-trading station; both are now essential stops on The Gambia's heritage trail. The south bank market town of **Brikama** – home to many of The Gambia's most celebrated musicians – and the main centres further east offer an insight into up-country urban life, while the more far-flung **villages** can be fascinating places to learn about rural tradition. Both **Soma** and **Farafenni** are junction towns on the Trans-Gambia route between northern and southern Senegal, and each has a distinctive atmosphere: Soma is a bustling transport stop that benefits from the south bank's superior infrastructure, while Farafenni, on the less developed north bank, is a characterful rural town with a lively and colourful weekly market. Mid-river, **Janjanbureh Island**, location of the old colonial outpost of Georgetown, is an emerging ecotourism centre, well-placed for bird-watching and river-trips, as well as for visits to the **Wassu stone circles**, the country's most famous prehistoric site. **Basse**, a cosmopolitan trading town, is a good stopover on up-river explorations.

When to go

The Gambia's peak tourist season roughly coincides with the coastal **dry season**, which lasts around eight months from mid-October to mid-June, when the **rainy season** starts. Up-country, where temperatures are more extreme, the dry season lasts a few weeks longer. The **best month to visit** is November, when the rains are over, humidity has dropped, the dirt roads are passable, and the bush is still green

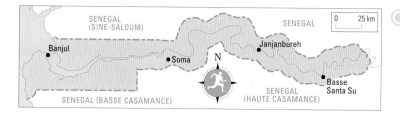

and busy with birdlife. December and January see the highest concentration of visitors. It's not unusual to have weeks of unbroken sunshine at this time, but there can sometimes be grey days and chilly nights. By March, the up-country landscape is a near-uniform golden brown and hazy with airborne dust; the last three months of the dry season are normally totally rainless.

While daytime **temperatures** in the resort areas vary little all year, **humidity** levels fluctuate considerably, rocketing at the end of the dry season and remaining high until October – nights can be very sticky from June to September. Some of the tourist hotels are closed from May to October, when there's a much reduced choice of charter flights. The country gets around 1300 millimetres (51 inches) of rain from mid-June to mid-October – nearly double London's yearly average – most of it falling at night, with August by far the rainiest month. The malaria risk is higher than usual during the rains, and some roads are waterlogged; however, birds, flowers and fresh vegetation are all abundant at this time, mangoes are in season, the resorts are pleasantly uncrowded, the sea is at its warmest, and, between the spectacular thunderstorms, the days are bright and clear.

Gambia climate (average temperature in °C)

	Jan	Feb	Mar	Apr	May	Jun	Jul	Aug	Sep	Oct	Nov	Dec
BANJUL												
daytime	31	32	34	33	32	32	30	29	31	32	32	31
night-time	15	16	17	18	19	23	23	23	23	22	18	16
days with rainfall	0.1	0.3	0	0	0.9	5	16	19	19	8	0.8	0.2
rainfall (mm)	3	3	0	0	10	58	282	500	310	109	18	3
sunshine (hours)	9	10	10	10	10	9	6	6	6	8	8	9

things not to miss

To help you get the most out of your stay in The Gambia, we have put together a personal selection of the country's highlights: special cultural events, historical sites and unspoilt stretches of wilderness. Arranged in five colour-coded categories indicating the best things to see, do and experience, each has a page reference to take you straight into the guide, where you can find out more.

01 Southwestern coast Page **156** • Along the palm-fringed bays between Brufut and Kartong, you can walk for miles and barely see another soul – though you may encounter cows, seabirds or even turtles.

02 Mandina Lodge Page **179** • Overlooking a beautiful creek, on the edge of Makasutu Culture Forest, this luxury bush lodge is a superb place to relax, right in the wilderness, and has one of the loveliest swimming pools in the country.

04 Microlight flights Page **112** • Get a bird's-eye view of snaking mangrove creeks and long-shadowed palm trees – an exhilarating experience, though not for the faint-hearted.

03 Makasutu Culture Forest Page **175** • Wild, green and beautiful, this well-preserved pocket of woodland is an excellent place to learn about forest fauna and medicinal trees and plants.

05 Kankurang dancers Page **288** • Colourful *kankurang* dancers and other masquerades have a crucial role in traditional rites, but they also entertain the crowds at major festivals.

06 **Long-distance river trips** Page **51** • Spend an adventurous few days cruising the River Gambia, enjoying the sights and sounds of the riverine wilderness, passing through the River Gambia National Park, and maybe spotting chimpanzees or hippos.

08 **Wassu stone circles** Page **237** • A tangible remnant of a mysterious ancient culture, Wassu is one of the most impressive megalithic sites in the Senegambia region.

07 **Jinack Island** Page **201** • A remote strip of land cut off from the mainland by a creek, Jinack Island is a haven for wildlife and an unspoilt beach retreat.

10 **Roots pilgrimage to Juffureh** Page **68** • The one-day pilgrimage to the up-country village of Juffureh, immortalized in Alex Haley's novel *Roots*, is one of the highlights of The Gambia's biennial International Roots Festival; the village itself has a small but thought-provoking museum of slavery.

09 **Sanyang beach** Page **163** • Sanyang has soft sand, sparkling sea and laid-back beach bars – it's a great place to chill out and watch the fishermen rolling brightly painted *pirogues* up the beach to unload the day's catch.

11 **Bao Bolon Wetland Reserve** Page **226** • The largest protected area in The Gambia is also the least explored, and a rewarding destination for the adventurous, with salt-flats, marshland, and well-preserved wetland areas that are excellent for birdwatching.

13 **Katchikali crocodile pool** Page **127** • You might never get closer to a crocodile than this. Charlie is The Gambia's most approachable reptile, and he resides at a sacred pool in Bakau.

12 **Country markets** Page **224** • The *lumos* (country markets) held once a week on the outskirts of rural towns like Farafenni are lively events, with fabric stalls, *juju*-makers, kola nut sellers and great heaps of seasonal produce.

14 **Creek trips by dugout pirogue** Page **51** • The Gambia's complex network of mangrove creeks is a haven for birds and a breeding ground for fish. To enjoy the tranquil environment to the full, take a trip through the narrowest waterways by dugout *pirogue*.

15 **James Island** Page **197** • With its atmospheric ruined fort and skeletal baobab trees, this bleak mid-river island is an essential stop for anyone tracing the history of the West African slave trade.

16 Janjang Bureh Camp
Page **246** • This quirky and charming riverside lodge is a friendly place to unwind after a long journey up-country; it also makes a perfect base for local birdwatching and river-trips.

18 Tumani Tenda ecotourism camp Page 180
• This rural camp surrounded by beautiful woods, farmland and mangrove creeks will appeal to anyone wanting to learn about local wildlife and traditional Jola lifestyles.

19 Abuko Nature Reserve
Page **143** • Only a short drive from the coastal resorts, Abuko's gallery forest and woodland savannah is easy to explore on foot, making it one of the best places in The Gambia to get really close to wild birds, reptiles and monkeys.

17 Chimpanzee Rehabilitation Project
Page **240** • Guests at the project's riverside Visitor Camp can view semi-wild chimps at close quarters – a unique and fascinating experience.

20 Albert Market, Banjul
Page **108** • The capital's main market is a bright, bustling place to browse, with a huge array of vividly patterned fabric, household goods, musical instruments, natural remedies, home-made beauty products and local fruit and vegetables.

Birds of The Gambia

The Gambia's remarkable diversity of accessible habitats
makes it an ideal birdwatching destination. Over 560 bird
species have been recorded in the country, including
Palearctic migrants which arrive in the late rainy season, and
for which The Gambia is the first vital belt of green after the
long flight south along the arid coast of northwest Africa.
This field guide provides a quick reference to help you
identify some of the most common varieties. It includes
a representative selection of native species and a few
migrants, presented in conventional taxonomic order. The
notes for each bird give you pointers about its usual habitat;
how widespread and common it is; typical songs and calls;
and general tips about seasonal variations in plumage.

❀ HABITAT   ✎ DISTRIBUTION   ♫ CALL   ✓ SIGHTING TIPS

Pink-backed pelican *Pelicanus rufescens*

🌼 Ocean, river and creeks.

✏ Common on the coast; breeds up-country in baobab trees, e.g. at Kwinella, near Tendaba.

🎵 Claps its bill, hisses and croaks noisily when nesting, otherwise silent.

✓ Large, stately bird, with pinkish back feathers visible in flight; perches on wrecks of ships in the Banjul area.

Hammerkop *Scopus umbretta*

🌼 Ponds, rice fields and creeks.

✏ Common throughout The Gambia.

🎵 Harsh guttural or cackling call; rowdy.

✓ All brown with an unmistakably shaggy, anvil-like crest, which it raises when alarmed; its famously large nests are used year after year, e.g. at Abuko.

Western reef heron *Egretta gularis*

🌼 Saltwater creeks, swamps and beaches.

✏ Common throughout The Gambia.

🎵 Harsh crow-like *kaw*.

✓ Blue-black with a white throat; follows other water birds and darts at fish that they miss.

Striated heron *Butorides striatus*

🌼 Mangrove creeks and swamps.

✏ Common, especially in the rainy season.

🎵 Forceful *tchack-tchack*.

✓ Brown when immature, blackish green and grey in adulthood; short tail; climbs through tangled vegetation.

Intermediate egret *Egretta intermedia*

🌼 Open coastal waters, flooded fields and creeks.

✏ Common throughout The Gambia.

🎵 Hissing call when breeding, otherwise silent.

✓ White plumage and yellow bill, which in both sexes turns bright red when breeding; often solitary.

🌼 HABITAT   ✏ DISTRIBUTION   🎵 CALL   ✓ SIGHTING TIPS

Marabou stork *Leptoptilos crumeniferus*

🌼 Widespread, but prefers semi-arid areas.

🪶 Common in central Gambia.

🎵 Claps its bill when breeding, otherwise silent.

✓ Massive bill and pink gular sac, bald head; gregarious; shares carrion with vultures.

Hooded vulture *Necrosyrtes monachus*

🌼 Urban tips, abattoirs, fishing beaches and bush.

🪶 Common, especially near human settlements.

🎵 Mostly silent but can emit a high-pitched squeak.

✓ Dark brown and scruffy-looking; omnivorous: food includes winged termites, oil palm fruit, insects and carrion.

Palm-nut vulture *Gypohierax angolensis*

🌼 Coastal woodland and mangrove creeks.

🪶 Common in western Gambia.

🎵 Mostly silent, but can growl and squeak.

✓ Brown when immature, black and white in adulthood; eagle-like; feeds on oil palm fruit and dead fish.

African jacana *Actophilornis africanus*

🌼 Freshwater ponds and rice fields.

🪶 Common throughout The Gambia.

🎵 Single screeches or loud rapidly repeated *kreep-kreep-kreep*.

✓ Carries its chicks under its glossy chestnut wings before they can fly; often eaten by crocodiles.

Whimbrel *Numenius phaeopus*

🌼 Beaches and mangroves.

🪶 Common Palearctic migrant, abundant in western Gambia Aug–April.

🎵 Seven-note tittering call as it takes flight.

✓ Largish brown wader, with distinctively striped crown; picks over mudbanks for insects and crabs.

🌼 HABITAT　　🪶 DISTRIBUTION　　🎵 CALL　　✓ SIGHTING TIPS

Egyptian plover *Pluvianus aegyptius*

🌸 Riverbanks, jetties and lakesides.

🖋 Migrant, common in eastern Gambia Sept–Dec, e.g. in Basse area.

🎵 *Chee-chee-chee* as it takes flight.

✓ Beautifully marked; usually seen in small groups; approachable.

Black-headed plover *Vanellus tectus*

🌸 Tussocky grassland.

🖋 Common in semi-arid areas, e.g. Fajara golf course, and in eastern Gambia.

🎵 Sharp *kiarr* or, when alarmed, high-pitched *kir*.

✓ Active at night, resting in the shade by day; staring golden eyes.

Senegal thick-knee *Burhinus senegalensis*

🌸 Riverbanks and creeks.

🖋 Common throughout The Gambia.

🎵 Staccato wailing call that rises and falls.

✓ Shelters in shady mangroves by day, active at dawn and dusk.

Senegal coucal *Centropus senegalensis*

🌸 Bush and gardens.

🖋 Common throughout The Gambia.

🎵 Sonorous, guttural *ouk-ouk-ouk* or pigeon-like *who-who-who*, like water glugging out of a bottle.

✓ Largish, and strikingly coloured in black, chestnut and cream, seen on perches or creeping through undergrowth.

Verreaux's eagle owl *Bubo lacteus*

🌸 Thickets and dry savannah.

🖋 Reasonably common throughout The Gambia.

🎵 Loud, grunting *whuuk-whuuk-whuuk*.

✓ Large owl, with pink eyelids and horn-like ear-tufts; seen roosting in trees; nests once every two years in baobab cavities; eats rats and hedgehogs, which it "peels", discarding the spiny pelt.

🌸 HABITAT   🖋 DISTRIBUTION   🎵 CALL   ✓ SIGHTING TIPS

Pied kingfisher *Ceryle rudis*

🏵 Beaches, cliffs, estuaries, rivers, creeks and pools.

📏 Common in aquatic habitats.

🎵 Very vocal, squeaky, chattering call.

✓ Africa's only black-and-white kingfisher, strikingly marked; unusually, hovers over water before diving for fish; approachable.

Giant kingfisher *Megaceryle maxima*

🏵 Coastal inlets, streams and ponds.

📏 Common in aquatic habitats in western Gambia, e.g. at the Bambo pool, Abuko, especially in the rainy season.

🎵 Loud crow-like *kek-kek-kek*.

✓ Large, heavy-billed kingfisher; favours particular perches, returning daily.

African pygmy kingfisher *Ceyx picta*

🏵 Thickets near pools and puddles.

📏 Common, especially during rainy season.

🎵 Thin, squeaky *seet-seet* or *chip-chip*.

✓ Tiny; seen on low shady perches or splash-bathing in pools; eats insects.

Abyssinian roller *Coracias abyssinica*

🏵 Open bush and grassland.

📏 Common, especially up-country in the dry season.

🎵 Raucous, guttural *kra-kra-kra*.

✓ Gorgeously coloured, with long tail streamers; conspicuous, often seen perched on trees, telephone wires or termite mounds by the roadside.

Little bee-eater *Merops pusillus*

🏵 Grassland, shrubbery and marshes.

📏 Common, the most widespread bee-eater.

🎵 Soft *sip* on taking flight; *siddle-iddle-ip-djee* on greeting.

✓ Contorts its body in order to sun its feathers; approachable.

Red-throated bee-eater *Merops bullocki*

Riverbanks (freshwater reaches) and gardens.

Reasonably common up-country, abundant in some areas, e.g. at Bansang quarry; often seen on high riverside perches.

Frequent *wip* call.

Highly gregarious; breeds in closely-packed colonies of burrows in vertical banks.

Northern carmine bee-eater *Merops nubicus*

Riverbanks, up-country mangroves and dry grassland.

Reasonably common in central and eastern Gambia, especially during the rainy season.

Short *tunk* on taking flight, or *chip-chip-chip*.

Large, strikingly coloured bee-eater.

Violet turaco *Musophaga violacea*

Forests and orchards.

Reasonably common, endemic to West Africa.

Resonant, guttural *kourou-kourou-kourou*.

Glossy purple plumage, with stunning red wing-feathers conspicuous when in flight; nearly always in pairs; eats figs.

Grey plantain-eater *Crinifer piscator*

Bush, dry open savannah and tall trees.

Common throughout The Gambia.

Loud, distinctive, laughing *kow-kow-kow* and *kalak-kalak-kalak*.

Grey, with a large conical yellow bill and a shaggy crest, which it raises when alarmed; white wing stripes conspicuous in flight; eats fruit and flowers.

Rose-ringed parakeet *Psittacula krameri*

Woodland savannah, thickets and gardens.

Common throughout The Gambia.

Noisy screeches and whistles.

Slim, long-tailed bird, all green with (in the male) black chin and pink collar; eats fruit and flowers; often seen in baobabs.

HABITAT   DISTRIBUTION   CALL   SIGHTING TIPS

Red-billed hornbill *Tockus erythrorrhynchus*

🌺 Open woodland, burnt savannah and large gardens.

🖋 Common throughout The Gambia.

🎵 Chuckling *kok-kok-kok-kokok-kokok-kokok*, rising in tempo and volume.

✓ Smallest Senegambian hornbill; found in pairs or flocks, often sunbathing on the ground; builds mud-nests in trees in the late rainy season; the entrance is plastered up with the female inside; characteristic "beak-heavy" flight.

Abyssinian ground hornbill *Bucorvus abyssinicus*

🌺 Open bush.

🖋 Reasonably common.

🎵 Deep, booming, repeated *uuh-uh-uh* from prominent bare branches.

✓ Huge black bird often seen walking through grassland; throat skin is pink in male, blue in female; conspicuous white primary feathers only visible in flight.

Bearded barbet *Lybius dubius*

🌺 Woodland and gardens.

🖋 Common especially in western Gambia.

🎵 Occasional crow-like *kaw* or bark.

✓ Large barbet with a massive yellow bill and bare eye-patches; heavy flight; eats ripe figs and pawpaws.

Fine-spotted woodpecker *Campethera punctuligera*

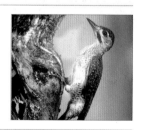

🌺 Woodland and palm groves

🖋 Common throughout The Gambia.

🎵 Loud ringing *wik-wik-whew-wee-yeu wee-yeu*.

✓ Often seen feeding on oil palms or on termite mounds; sometimes forages on the ground.

Beautiful sunbird *Nectarinia pulchella*

🌺 Farmland, bush and gardens.

🖋 Common throughout The Gambia.

🎵 Reedy chirps, then a shivering tumble of quick notes.

✓ The male is shiny emerald, with yellow and red breast, and long tail streamers; the female is drab olive; drinks nectar from flowers like a humming bird, often hanging at odd angles, even upside down.

🌺 HABITAT   🖋 DISTRIBUTION   🎵 CALL   ✓ SIGHTING TIPS   23

Yellow-crowned gonolek *Laniarius barbarus*

✿ Woodland, shubbery and gardens.

🖊 Common throughout The Gambia.

🎵 Pairs call in unison, a liquid whistle and rasping rattle *too-lioo ch-chacha*.

✓ Unmistakable black, red and golden plumage; often seen low down in shrubs; pairs are territorial.

Purple glossy starling *Lamprotornis purpureus*

✿ Savannah, woodland and open bush.

🖊 Common throughout The Gambia.

🎵 Squeaking, bubbling and wittering notes, or a scolding *shree*.

✓ One of several gregarious and noisy shiny-plumaged Senegambian starlings; short tail and staring yellow eyes; perches high in trees.

Village weaver *Ploceus cucullatus*

✿ Village trees, farms; breeds in colonies of knot-like nests in silk cotton trees or palms.

🖊 Very common throughout The Gambia.

🎵 Noisy, squabbling chirps.

✓ Yellow and olive plumage; the breeding male (Jun–Dec) is black-headed, with a chestnut nape; the head of the female and non-breeding male is yellow; very gregarious.

Northern red bishop *Euplectes franciscanus*

✿ Millet and sorghum fields, and open bush.

🖊 Common throughout The Gambia.

🎵 Constant stream of high-pitched squeaky notes.

✓ The breeding male (Aug–Dec) has spectacular scarlet and black plumage, which it puffs up when displaying; the female and non-breeding male are an inconspicuous straw-brown.

Red-cheeked cordon-bleu *Uraeginthus bengalus*

✿ Woodland, scrub and gardens.

🖊 Common throughout The Gambia.

🎵 Thin-toned piping call, or more elaborate *wit-sit-diddly-diddly-ee-ee*.

✓ Small, gregarious finches, often seen feeding on the ground with red-billed firefinches; the female lacks red cheek spot.

Exclamatory paradise whydah *Vidua interjecta*

✿ Dry savannah woodland.

🖊 Reasonably common in up-country Gambia.

🎵 Simple *chip* calls.

✓ The breeding male (Nov–Dec) has an extraordinarily long black tail, three times its body-length; perches high in leafless trees; the female and non-breeding male are drab brown.

✿ HABITAT   🖊 DISTRIBUTION   🎵 CALL   ✓ SIGHTING TIPS

Basics

Basics

Getting there

Flights to Banjul are around six hours from European capitals, and with The Gambia in a similar time zone, there's no jet lag. The alternative to flying, travelling overland, is a perfectly viable option if you have the time: The Gambia is a couple of weeks' steady driving from the UK.

The Gambia's **tourist season** runs from mid-October to late May, when a good choice of charter flight and hotel packages is available from the UK and several other European departure points. This is also the priciest time to visit, with peaks over Christmas and Easter and British school half-term weeks in November and February. The cheapest prices are available during the rainy season, June to October.

Even if you're planning on travelling independently during your visit, you may find it cheap and convenient to pick up a bargain **package** from a mainstream tour operator. If you're flexible about dates, you may even find a package for less than the price of a flight on its own, and you could simply use your hotel as a base for exploring further afield.

If you want more control over your departure and return dates and length of stay, you'll need to use a **scheduled airline**, either into The Gambia, which restricts the choice quite severely, or into Dakar, capital of neighbouring Senegal, which is much better connected to international flight networks. As an aid to selecting an airline, Ⓦwww.airlinequality.com is a useful peer to peer site.

Although The Gambia is little-visited for **specialist travel** in comparison with many countries in east and southern Africa, it is, nonetheless, extremely attractive to ornithologists, and there are several specialist **birdwatching** operators which include The Gambia as a prime destination. There are also several organized holidays for music and dance fans, plus a few "Roots" and **African heritage tours** aimed principally at African-Americans.

In the region, The Gambia is within relatively easy reach of Senegal, Mali, Guinea-Bissau, Guinea and Sierra Leone, either overland or by air, and as such makes a useful, low-cost, **entry point into West Africa**. Banjul is also a good exit point from an African overland trip: it's possible to get a one-way ticket on a charter flight from The Gambia either to London or to a UK regional airport, bookable either before you leave or after arrival, through The Gambia Experience (see p.29).

Flights from the UK and Europe

The most straightforward connections **from the UK** are **charter flights, with year-round** regular direct services to Banjul from London Gatwick and from Bristol, Manchester and Nottingham East Midlands during the tourist season (Oct–May). Prices range from £170–£500 return, depending on the season and the length of stay, with full price mid-season tickets typically around £400. Most charter seats are bookable only through the agents and tour operators that have block-booked allocations, rather than direct with the charter airlines, but special promotions are sometimes introduced to fill seats. There are

Airport arrival and departure taxes

Immigration authorities usually apply a D250/£5/$10/€10 **tourist arrival tax**. The Gambia's airport **departure tax** (£11/€16/$20, payable in any currency) is nearly always included in the price of charter and scheduled flights out of Banjul – but double check with the airline or their agent.

Climate change is a serious threat to the ecosystems we all rely upon, and air travel is among the fastest-growing contributors to the problem. Rough Guides regard travel, overall, as a global benefit, and feel strongly that the advantages to developing economies are important, as are the opportunities for greater contact and awareness among peoples. But we all have a responsibility to limit our personal impact on global warming, and that means giving thought to how often we fly, and what we can do to redress the harm that our trips create.

Flying and climate change
Pretty much every form of motorized travel generates CO_2 – the main cause of human-induced climate change – but planes also generate climate-warming contrails and cirrus clouds and emit oxides of nitrogen, which create ozone (another greenhouse gas) at flight levels. Furthermore, flying simply allows us to travel much further than we otherwise would do. The figures are frightening: one person taking a return flight between Europe and California produces the equivalent impact of 2.5 tonnes of CO_2 – similar to the yearly output of the average UK car.

Fuel-cell and other less harmful types of plane may emerge eventually. But until then, there are really just two options for concerned travellers: to reduce the amount we travel by air (take fewer trips – stay for longer!), and to make the trips we do take "climate neutral" via a carbon-offset scheme.

Carbon-offset schemes
Offset schemes run by ⓦclimatecare.org, ⓦcarbonneutral.com and others allow you to make up for some or all of the greenhouse gases that you are responsible for releasing. To do this, they provide "carbon calculators" for working out the global-warming contribution of a specific flight, and then let you contribute an appropriate amount of money to fund offsetting measures. These include rain-forest reafforestation and initiatives to reduce future energy demand – often run in conjunction with sustainable development schemes.

Rough Guides, together with Lonely Planet and other concerned partners in the travel industry, are supporting a **carbon-offset scheme** run by climatecare.org. Please take the time to view our website and see how you can help to make your trip climate-neutral.

ⓦ**www.roughguides.com/climatechange**

also charter flights to Banjul from **a number of European capitals**, bookable through European travel agents.

There are direct **scheduled flights** from Europe to Banjul with Astraeus from London Gatwick and SN Brussels Airlines, from Brussels.

You could also use scheduled flights via **other West African cities**, with or without a stopover en route. Most major European cities have direct flights to one or two West African capitals with onward connections to Banjul, though stopovers are sometimes lengthy. **Dakar**, capital of Senegal, is the most obvious. Senegal entirely surrounds The Gambia and is a good destination in its own right. There are flights to Dakar via Paris with Air France or Air Sénégal International; via Milan with Alitalia; via Frankfurt with Lufthansa; via Lisbon with TAP Air Portugal; via Casablanca with Royal Air Maroc; and from several European airports with the charter airline Condor. Direct flights from Dakar to Banjul take around forty minutes on frequent services and cost around £85 (€125) or you can do a surface connection with relative ease (see p.101).

There are no non-stop flights from **Ireland** to West Africa. Your best bet is to fly to Gatwick, Bristol or Manchester, then by charter to Banjul or by scheduled flight via another West African city.

Airlines

The following airlines fly into Banjul from the UK and Europe and accept direct bookings.

Astraeus UK ☎01293/819800, ⓦwww .flyastraeus.com. Twice-weekly flights from London Gatwick to Banjul, run in association with The Gambia Experience.

Condor Germany ☎0180 5 767 757, ⓦwww .condor.com. Flights from several European airports.

SN Brussels Airlines UK ☎0870/735 2345, Belgium ☎32/70 35 11 11, ⓦwww .brussels-airlines.com. Reliable and relatively frequent flights to Banjul via Brussels.

Thomas Cook UK ⓦwww.flythomascook.com. High-season flights from Bristol, London Gatwick, Manchester and Nottingham East Midlands.

Thomsonfly UK ☎0800/1900 737, ⓦwww .thomsonfly.com. Charter flights to Banjul, which can be booked as flight-only.

Specialist travel agents in the UK and Europe

Africa Travel Centre UK ☎0845/450 1520, ⓦwww.africatravel.co.uk. Helpful Africa specialists offering packages and overland tours.

The Gambia Experience UK ☎0845/330 2060, ⓦwww.gambia.co.uk. Mostly deals in Gambian package holidays, but also acts as a charter flight agent.

North South Travel UK ☎01245/608 291, ⓦwww.northsouthtravel.co.uk. Friendly, competitive travel agency, offering discounted fares worldwide – profits are used to support projects in the developing world, especially the promotion of sustainable tourism.

Responsible Travel UK ⓦwww.responsibletravel .com. Recommended operators for travel run on sustainable and ethical lines, with detailed customer feedback ensuring compliance.

STA Travel UK ☎08701/630 026, ⓦwww .statravel.co.uk. Worldwide specialists in low-cost flights and tours for students and under-26s, though other customers welcome.

Trailfinders UK ☎0845/058 5858, Dublin ☎01/677 7888, ⓦwww.trailfinders.com. One of the best-informed and most efficient agents for independent travellers.

TravelPoort Gambia Netherlands ☎31-71/589 32 00, ⓦwww.gambiatravel.com. Flights and packages from the Netherlands and Belgium.

usit NOW Ireland ☎01/602 1904, ⓦwww.usitnow .ie. Student and youth travel specialists.

Package holidays

Gambian **package holidays** are generally aimed at those looking for a relatively cheap tropical winter holiday. Most UK tour operators, and a many across Europe, offer winter sun brochures which include the Gambian resort area (departures Nov–May), while specialist tour operator The Gambia Experience (see above) also features year-round packages. Until the late-1990s, there was very little **luxury tourism** in The Gambia, but the mix is changing, with new top-end hotels opening and others improving their services. Facilities, atmosphere and value for money all vary a great deal, however, and a low-cost package is likely to feature hotels with very modest standards.

Flights from the US and Canada

Currently the only direct flight **from North America** to The Gambia is from **Baltimore/ Washington** with North American Airlines (☎1-800/359-6222, ⓦwww.northamericanair .com) – around eight hours to Banjul. Alternatively, flying to **London** (from as little as $300 on a discount deal) and then on to Banjul by charter (from around $350) is one of the least expensive ways to get to The Gambia from most North American departure points. You could, equally, plan a route **through Brussels**, using Belgium's scheduled airline, SN Brussels, or **through Amsterdam** or one of the other European hubs, several of which handle tourist traffic to Banjul by charter.

If you'd like to fly into another **West African city** and continue to Banjul by connecting flight or overland, you have a greater choice of European hubs, but not much more choice of direct flights from North America. South African Airways has services from New York to Dakar and Royal Air Maroc flies from Montreal and New York to Dakar via Casablanca.

If you do break your journey in Europe, remember that the "two pieces" **luggage limit** that applies on transatlantic flights becomes a 20kg (44lb) limit for the rest of the world.

Travel agents

Airtreks.com ☎1-877/247-8735, ⓦwww
.airtreks.com. Round-the-world specialist that can
provide multi-stopover flight tickets including Banjul.
Educational Travel Center ☎1-800/747-5551,
ⓦwww.edtrav.com. Student/youth discount agent.
STA Travel ☎1-800/781-4040, ⓦwww.sta-travel
.com. Worldwide specialists in independent travel.
Travel Cuts Canada ☎1-866/246-9762, US
☎1-800/592-2887, ⓦwww.travelcuts.com.
Canadian student-travel organization.

Flights from Australia and New Zealand

The only **direct flights** to Africa currently on
offer **from Australia or New Zealand** are
the Qantas/South African Airways flights
from Perth to Johannesburg. From there you
can pick up connections to West Africa, but
nothing direct to Banjul. The easiest option is
to get yourself to Europe and pick up a flight
to Banjul from there.

Travel agents

Adventure Travel Company New Zealand
☎09/379 9755, ⓦwww.adventuretravel.co.nz.
New Zealand agent for overland companies such as
Explore Worldwide.
Flight Centre Australia ☎133 133 or 07/3011
7830, ⓦwww.flightcentre.com.au, New Zealand
☎0800/24 35 44, ⓦwww.flightcentre.co.nz.
STA Travel Australia ☎1300/733 035, ⓦwww
.statravel.com.au, New Zealand ☎0508/782 872,
ⓦwww.statravel.co.nz.
Trailfinders Australia ☎1300/780 212, ⓦwww
.trailfinders.com.au.

Flights from other African countries

Banjul is well connected with other **West
African countries**, with direct flights from
Dakar (Senegal), Conakry (Guinea), Freetown
(Sierra Leone), Accra (Ghana) and Lagos,
Abuja and Port Harcourt (Nigeria). All other
West African capitals have connections to
Banjul via Dakar.

If you're starting your journey to the
Gambia from **North, Central, East or
Southern Africa**, you will not be able to fly
to Banjul direct. Ghana International Airlines
flies from London to Accra, from where you
can fly to Banjul with regional airlines. Other

options include flying to **Dakar** with South
African Airways or Royal Air Maroc, and
continuing to Banjul with another airline or
overland. South African Airways flies from
many African cities to Dakar via Johannesburg, and Royal Air Maroc flies to Dakar via
Casablanca.

Airlines

Air Guinée ⓦwww.mirinet.com/airguinee. Flights
to Banjul from Dakar and Conakry.
Air Sénégal International ⓦwww.air-senegal
-international.com. Daily flights from Dakar to Banjul.
Bellview Airlines ⓦwww.flybellviewair.com.
Flights to Banjul from Freetown, Lagos, Abuja and
Port Harcourt.
Gambia International Airlines ⓦwww.gia.gm.
No fleet as such, but sometimes leases aircraft.
Ghana International Airlines ⓦfly-ghana.com.
London–Accra on a good new private carrier.

Travel agents

Africa Travel Centre South Africa ☎021/423
4530, ⓦwww.backpackers.co.za. Local branch of
the London-based Africa specialist.
STA Travel South Africa ☎0861/781 781, ⓦwww
.statravel.co.za. Good for youth and student airfares.

Overland travel

With careful planning, sufficient time, and
some determination it's feasible to get all the
way from Europe to The Gambia **overland**
via Morocco, Western Sahara, Mauritania
and Senegal. This is an excellent way to
travel if you want to become fully immersed
in the identities and landscapes of West
Africa en route.

Driving yourself

The commonest overland route sees vehicles hugging the **Atlantic coast** on the way
south from Morocco and then continuing
on a new tarmac road through Mauritania
from Noudhibou to Nouakchott. This route is
relatively easy on vehicles, and many people
with no prior experience complete the journey in unmodified cars or on motorbikes.

Taking into account fuel, maintenance,
insurance and various bits of optional
special equipment such as a GPS system,
driving yourself can be a fairly **expensive**
business. Even if you have someone on

The holidays offered by the companies listed below are designed to appeal to travellers from all countries who want to join a group in pursuing a **special interest**, such as birdwatching, fishing, cycling, trekking, or exploring African music, culture and heritage.

While few of the long-distance adventure tours that cross Africa visit The Gambia, some pass through nearby Senegal, and their itineraries are often flexible enough to accommodate a detour into The Gambia. Some of these agents and tour companies can put together **tailor-made itineraries**. These trips don't generally include flights, but most companies can arrange flights for you on request. They're listed by region, but it's normally possible to join their trips from any point on the globe, either booking direct or through a local agent.

Operators in the UK and Europe

Avian Adventures UK ℡01384/372103, ⓦwww.avianadventures.co.uk. Offers small-group birdwatching trips to The Gambia and Senegal.

Batafon Arts ℡01273/605791, ⓦwww.batafonarts.co.uk. Drum and dance holidays in Guinea and the Gambia.

Birdfinders UK ℡01258/839066, ⓦwww.birdfinders.co.uk. Special interest tours for birdwatchers, including one- and two-week tours of The Gambia, and custom trips.

Drum Doctor Holidays UK ℡01462/711 842, ⓦwww.realafrica.net. Music-focused holidays, with daily drum tuition and accommodation in a simple Gambian compound a 10min walk from the beach in Bakau, with vegetarian meals.

Explore Worldwide UK ℡0870/333 4001, ⓦwww.explore.co.uk. Interesting small-group tours including an easy-going Gambia and Senegal trek by land and river.

Hidden Gambia ℡01527/576239, ⓦwww.hiddengambia.com. Design your own tour of The Gambia by booking your flight, driver, guide, and hotels through this imaginative operator.

Ornitholidays UK ℡01794/519445, ⓦwww.ornitholidays.co.uk. Experienced operator, offering trips to renowned birding destinations, including The Gambia.

The Travelling Naturalist UK ℡01305/267994, ⓦwww.naturalist.co.uk. Worldwide programme includes an annual fifteen-day tour of Senegal and The Gambia.

Yogabelle ℡07771/877587, ⓦwww.yogabelle.co.uk. Occasional yoga retreats in the southern Gambian wilderness.

Specialist operators in the US and Canada

Alken Tours ℡1-800/327-9974 or 718/856-9100, ⓦwww.alkentours.com. This company has a specialist division for flights and trips to Africa, including visits to the Roots Homecoming Festival.

Spector Travel ℡617/351-0111, ⓦwww.spectortravel.com. Roots and culture tours of The Gambia and Senegal.

---

board who knows the vehicle inside out, any serious breakdown can be costly and tedious. Travelling in a **convoy** of at least two vehicles cuts down on the chances of getting stranded. You'll also need time: a minimum of two weeks moving fast, or a month at a more comfortable pace.

The outstanding advantage of taking your own vehicle is that you can get right **off the beaten track**, if the vehicle is sturdy enough.

A good way to recoup at least some of the costs is to **sell up** on arrival in The Gambia, or on the way through Senegal; with the right type of vehicle, you could make a profit, but be prepared for a certain amount of red tape when selling any vehicle, and note that the recent influx of vehicles from the UK (see box "The Plymouth-Banjul Challenge") has seen customs authorities trying to restrict the import of right-hand drive vehicles. For more

The Plymouth–Banjul Challenge

Inaugurated in December 2002 and now an annual event, this slightly batty amateur **trans-Saharan race** was inspired by the famous Paris–Dakar Rally. It follows a different – rather straighter – route across the desert. Participants have to follow a few idiosyncratic rules – notably, no car may be worth more £100 at the outset, and all must be auctioned for charity at the end. This auction takes place in The Gambia, where all the banger-drivers gather for a triumphal celebration. For online information, visit ⍾www.plymouth-dakar.co.uk.

information on driving to West Africa, consult *The Rough Guide to West Africa*.

Local transport

Public transport on the **overland route** to The Gambia is scant for much of the way between southern Morocco and Senegal. Once in Dakar, it's straightforward to continue to The Gambia by **bush taxi**. Shared Peugeots drive from Dakar's *gare routière* (taxi garage) at Pompiers, via Kaolack, to the Senegalese border at Karang in about five hours. You go through Senegalese and Gambian formalities and then change again for the short journey to Barra, or the junction for The Gambia's north bank highway.

It's also easy enough to enter The Gambia overland from the south. The road from **Ziguinchor** in Casamance, southern Senegal, takes you to the hassle-free border post of **Séléti**, not far from Mandina

Ba and Brikama. Frequent bush taxis run from Ziguinchor's *gare routière* to Séléti, where you need to change onto a Gambian bush taxi. Note that occasionally outbreaks of violence and fighting in Casamance's sporadic, low-level rebellion against Dakar may close this route or make connections and border crossings slow or difficult, and potentially dangerous. Check for news on the Internet.

Travelling overland **from Mali**, the route to Banjul via eastern Gambia is more enjoyable, though slower and more expensive, than the dreary highway from Mali through Senegal to Dakar. Break your journey at Tambacounda, then make your way into The Gambia either via Vélingara, or the less-used crossing near Fatoto, and pick up a bush taxi to Basse; from here, you can take a bus to Banjul (two each morning), or bush-taxi-hop your way down the river.

Ethical tourism

Although The Gambia has been welcoming tourists since the 1960s, its holiday industry is still in the developing stages. The country's decision-makers are therefore in a good position to learn from mistakes made elsewhere, and encourage growth which minimizes cultural disruption and is socially and environmentally sustainable. At the same time, tourists themselves have an important role to play in shaping the country's future as a holiday destination.

The steady growth of tourism in the resort areas of The Gambia has been an economic boon to the country. The Gambia Tourism

Authority has expressed a hope that the country will soon be welcoming a million tourists a year, ten times the present number, and President Jammeh himself has substantial personal investment in tourism projects. With the country's ambitions running high, campaigners are working to encourage **environmentally responsible** and **culturally sustainable development**, with some degree of success: the country has formulated its own national Responsible Tourism policy. Sadly, however, ethical tourism is something that some tourism stakeholders either ignore, or just bandy about as a buzzword. The resort areas have already suffered social and cultural disruption and environmental degradation which could have been avoided through long-term practical policy-building. Meanwhile multinational **package tour operators**, which allow only minimal trickle-down of the benefits of tourism to the Gambian people, have a stranglehold over the whole Gambian holiday industry, making it hard for small, independent hotels and tour companies to survive.

The best hope for the future of tourism in The Gambia is that **tourists themselves** exert sufficient pressure to ensure that future development is sympathetic both to the natural environment and to the long-term interests of the Gambian people. If you're concerned about the impact of tourism, contact the organizations listed below.

Contacts

Association of Small Scale Enterprises in Tourism (ASSET) Bakau ☎ 449 7675, ⓦwww .asset-gambia.com. Gambian organization representing and supporting small tourism service providers such as guesthouses, ground tour operators and juice-pressers. Provides information about these and about sustainable tourism issues. Recognized in the 2005 Responsible Tourism Awards for its crucial contribution to poverty reduction.
Gambia Tourist Support (GTS) Kololi ☎ 446 2476, UK ☎ 0845/612 0261, ⓦwww .gambiatouristsupport.com. Non-profit Anglo-Gambian charitable fundraising organization which can provide information and advice on many issues relating to tourism in The Gambia, including responsible and sustainable tourism: has an informative and refreshingly candid website. Annual membership £12.50.
International Centre for Responsible Tourism-Gambia (ICRT-G) ⓦ www.icrtourism.org/gambia .htm. Hosts courses on responsible tourism, community-based initiatives and economic development led by Adama Bah of Tourism

Concern and Dr Harold Goodwin of the University of Greenwich, co-founder of the DFID Pro-Poor Tourism Project.
Responsible Tourism Parnership UK ⓦwww .responsibletourismpartnership.org. Not-for-profit organization working to help improve tourist destinations for both residents and visitors. The Gambia's Responsible Tourism Policy can be downloaded from their website.
Tourism Concern Gambia c/o Adama Bah ☎ 446 2057, 991 7343, UK ☎ 020/7753 3330, ⓦ www.tourismconcern.org.uk. Campaigns for the rights of local people to be consulted in tourism developments affecting their lives. The Gambian branch works closely with ASSET.

Environmental awareness and ecotourism

The Gambia is a small country with a rapidly expanding population, and awareness of the fragility of the **natural environment** is just beginning to hit home. Human requirements – for farming land, firewood and food – can sometimes appear to be in direct conflict with accepted conservation practice, and education programmes are seeking to encourage Gambians to explore eco-friendly ways of running their lives.

There's visible evidence of The Gambia's losing battle against environmental degradation everywhere in the country. **Refuse** is poorly managed, with beaches suffering from the litter washed up by the Atlantic breakers, and deliberate dumping on waste ground is a major problem. The Gambia has no heavy industry, and traffic is still not heavy enough to cause major **air pollution**, but rubbish fires emit toxic gases in residential areas. Tidal erosion continues to gnaw away at some of the Atlantic beaches, despite costly engineering programmes to combat this (see p.133) and, up-country, wind erosion has left chunks of deforested land barren. Bush fires, some of them started deliberately by farmers to clear land for crops, degrade the environment further every season.

As a visitor, you can do your bit to combat **environmental damage**. Try not to create litter, and try to take home everything you brought with you. Minimize your electricity consumption, and think about whether you really need your room to be air-conditioned

Guidelines for responsible tourism

Respect local **culture and customs**. Read "Culture and etiquette" on p.72, and try to be alert to messages, spoken or unspoken, from Gambians you encounter. Dress appropriately, be aware of a few key points of Gambian history (such as the slave trade, colonization, independence and the coup), respect Muslim sensibilities, and try to learn a few phrases in the local languages – greetings are a good start.

- Go **up-country**. At present, rural areas reap few of the benefits of tourism – Kombo district gets the lion's share. By visiting up-country communities you assist the process of alleviating rural poverty.

- Visit **national parks and reserves**. By doing so you are contributing to their upkeep and helping safeguard Gambian fauna and flora.

- Think about visiting **off-season**. Staggering the influx of tourists throughout the year would greatly improve The Gambia's tourism cash flow – many Gambian holiday industry workers are jobless during the rainy season.

- Consider travelling on a **flight-only** basis, rather than booking a package. Choosing your accommodation independently gives you complete freedom to move around the country, and more of the money you spend will go to local businesses. Gambian hotels sell rooms to foreign package-tour companies at a huge discount, little of which is passed on to the customer – the multinationals benefit most from package tourism.

- If you buy a **package**, don't buy a full-board or all-inclusive one. There has been a semi-successful campaign in The Gambia to have these banned, as they eliminate fair competition from local providers such as restaurants and bars. They also isolate tourists, culturally and physically, from the real Gambia. If you're on a tight budget, an all-inclusive is not the best option anyway – local restaurants and bars are very cheap.

- Choose products and services from **local suppliers**. Some tourist restaurants import ingredients to make international-style dishes. Many places use cheaper Dutch eggs (usually quality-control rejects), even though Gambian eggs can be excellent, and some supermarkets sell imported goods even when good Gambian alternatives are available. Seek out the places that sell and use Gambian produce – local (rather than tourist) restaurants use fresh ingredients straight from the nearest market.

- Don't buy **CDs** or **cassettes** from hawkers, "recording studios" or market stalls – they will almost certainly be pirate copies, which deny local musicians royalties.

- Don't flaunt your relative wealth, and respect the Gambians' right to expect locals and tourists to pay **different rates** for the same things, such as museum entrance fees. Taxi drivers are well-known for trying it on, but don't automatically assume that others are out to rip you off. Remember also that some workers, such as musicians and guides, rely on **tips** as a principal form of income.

- Don't break **promises** – if you take a photo of somebody and say you'll send them a copy, don't forget to do so; if you say you're going to raise funds for a village school when you get home, follow your pledge through.

- Remember that Gambians are entitled to their personal **privacy**, and may also restrict visitor access to areas which are not strictly private, such as holy sites and places of worship.

– if the answer is yes, don't leave it on when you're out, or when you have the door or windows open. Think, too, about your water consumption, and don't request items such as towels to be laundered if they've barely been used.

Consider your means of **transport**. Travelling on foot or by bicycle can be preferable to travelling by taxi. Never drive or permit yourself to be driven on the beach – Gambian beaches were once home to breeding turtles but human disturbance of their natural habitat has almost wiped them out.

Gambian tour operators are fully aware of the pulling power of the label "**ecotourism**", but not all of them follow ecologically sound practices as a matter of course. Check your tour operator's commitment to conservation issues carefully before committing to an excursion on the basis of its supposed eco-friendliness. If you're concerned about the behaviour of any hoteliers, tour operators, drivers or guides, consider making a formal complaint.

Health

There's no reason to expect to get ill in The Gambia if you're careful. The most likely hazards are stomach problems and sunburn. Nor do the Gambian immigration authorities require any vaccinations for travellers arriving direct from outside Africa. Malaria, however, is a real danger, and you should carefully follow a course of tablets.

The only health certificate that you are legallly required to have in order to enter The Gambia is **yellow fever** – but only if you're arriving in The Gambia from an infected zone (in practice from any other country in sub-Saharan Africa).

In the **UK**, the first source of advice and probable supplier of jabs and prescriptions – if you need any because of your itinerary or the length of your stay – is your **GP**.

Visitors from the **US or Canada** should not immediately head for expensive specialist travel clinics, where the cost of various jabs can easily run into hundreds of dollars. Local county or city health departments across the country offer inoculations at a far lower rate.

In **Australia and New Zealand** you can usually get vaccinations from your GP or at a local health centre, but you're likely to find more specialized information from the privately run Traveller's Medical and Vaccination Centres (☎1300/658 844, ⊛www.tmvc.com.au), which have clinics in 23 cities.

In The Gambia, moderate injuries and illnesses can be treated locally, but for major medical treatment, you're advised to return home: The Gambia suffers from a shortage of facilities. The Royal Victoria Hospital in Banjul is undergoing a programme of improvement, and up-country there are new **hospitals** at Farafenni and Bwiam as well as the older one at Bansang, but in all cases standards and equipment are limited. The coastal urban area has a choice of **private medical and dental clinics** (see p.149). By contrast, remote districts have only rudimentary **community clinics** where, however, charges are low and the treatment available is normally proficient.

Vaccinations

If you're visiting The Gambia for a couple of weeks and don't plan to spend time staying in rural villages or poor urban districts, or travelling by local transport, then no

---

Travel health information

For a book on your health in tropical countries, you couldn't do better than *The Rough Guide to Travel Health* by Dr Nick Jones. The website of the International Society for Travel Medicine – ⊛www.istm.org – has a full list of clinics specializing in international travel health. If you plan to live in The Gambia, get hold of the classic *Where There is No Doctor* by David Werner.

pre-departure **vaccinations** are necessary. For longer stays in places and situations in which there's a significant chance of exposure to infection, the following vaccinations are currently recommended: meningitis, polio, yellow fever, typhoid, tetanus, and hepatitis A. Your doctor will be able to advise whether your particular itinerary necessitates all or just some of these.

Plan ahead – some first-time inoculations need to be administered well in advance of your travels, and some can't be taken together. A complete course may need to be spread out over a few weeks.

Immunization against **meningitis** is a good precaution if you're planning extensive travels. Although there have been no recent outbreaks in The Gambia, other West African countries are affected from time to time. **Polio** is now more or less eliminated in the region, but it's still worth checking that you are covered.

Yellow fever jabs are good for ten years and confer high immunity. A yellow fever certificate becomes valid ten days after you've had the shot. Yellow fever is a monkey disease but it can be spread by mosquitoes to humans. Once contracted, there are no specific drugs to cure the illness, which takes a few days to develop into liver failure and kills about fifty percent of its victims. Epidemics are very rare, but the jab is nonetheless a wise precaution – recent outbreaks in Senegal and Guinea led to massive vaccination campaigns. If you're arriving in The Gambia from an infected area (essentially any other country in sub-Saharan Africa), you'll be required to show a yellow fever certificate.

You shouldn't consider major travels without a **typhoid** vaccination (which lasts three years) or a **tetanus** booster (ten years). Nor is there any reason not to get **hepatitis A** shots which protect you for up to ten years against this **serious liver disease,** which can be spread by contaminated food and water. Whether or not you have the hepatitis A shots, be very careful about cleanliness and watchful for contamination of water – tap water is usually safe to drink, but in a few remote locations domestic water supplies may be of poor quality.

Hepatitis B, like **HIV**, is caught through unprotected sexual contact or through the transfer of blood products, usually from dirty needles; combined immunization against hepatitis A and B is available.

Most doctors no longer recommend the **cholera** jab; it's relatively ineffective, and the risks of contracting cholera are negligible unless you're living in the middle of an epidemic. Some doctors will quite willingly provide a cholera certificate indicating you *have not* had the jab. It seems to do the job on those odd occasions when up-country border officials are checking absolutely everything.

Malaria

Malaria is caused by a parasite carried in the saliva of female *Anopheles* mosquitoes. Although curable, it causes more deaths than any other tropical disease, killing over a million people annually, of whom over ninety percent are Africans, mostly children under 5. Malaria has a variable **incubation period** of a few days to several weeks, so you can become ill long after being bitten. If you go down with malaria, you'll probably know: the fever, shivering and headaches are like severe flu and come in waves, usually beginning in the early evening. Malaria is not infectious but it can be highly dangerous if not treated quickly.

Despite a long-term programme of research into the disease, not least at the Medical Research Council in The Gambia, a vaccine has yet to be developed. And note that the Royal London Homeopathic Hospital explicitly advises against reliance on **homeopathic** "anti-malarial" preparations, none of which have been adequately tested.

As well as taking common-sense measures to avoid being bitten (see opposite), it's vital to be prepared with a course of **prophylactic tablets**. We've outlined below some of the drugs available, though it's important to discuss the various options with your doctor before deciding what to take. It's worth noting that the strain of the malarial parasite commonly found in West Africa, **falciparum**, is especially severe and widely resistant to treatment with chloroquine, the common drug that has been used for decades. **Pregnant women** are at particular risk from the complications of falciparum malaria and need to explore the issue especially carefully with their doctor when planning a trip.

Anopheles **mosquitoes** prefer to bite at dusk and at night and can be identified by their eager, head-down position when preparing to bite. Their prevalence varies between seasons and from location to location. As a rule of thumb, there are more mosquitoes in humid areas than in arid ones; the banks of the River Gambia and the mangrove creeks have far more mosquitoes than the beaches; Banjul has more than Serrekunda; shady woodland areas (including hotel gardens) have more than open areas. If you choose to stay in air-conditioned hotels and don't go out much, your risk of exposure is lower than if you camp or stay in bush lodges. Throughout the country, the worst time for mosquitoes is the **rainy season**: most incidences of malaria in The Gambia occur between June and December. By the end of the dry season, the mosquito population has dropped to a minimum.

It's possible for a single mosquito bite to infect you with malarial parasites, but, because the effects can be **cumulative**, your chances of going down with a fever increase the longer you spend in an area where it's hard to avoid being bitten.

Antimalarial drugs

Your doctor will advise which pills to take and what the various side effects can be. It's important to maintain a careful routine and cover the period **before and after** your trip with doses. If you're living in The Gambia for more than a few months, malaria tablets can be bought in small shops and from street vendors.

The old anti-malaria drug combination of Nivaquin (chloroquine) and Paludrine (proguanil hydrochloride) is now considered largely ineffective against Gambian malaria; instead, the commonly prescribed preventatives are: the controversial drug **Lariam** (mefloquin), which has a poor record for side-effects; the antibiotic **doxycycline** and the new drug **Malarone** (a single tablet of atovaquone with proguanil hydrochloride) which, while expensive, appears to have few if any side-effects in most people and is extremely effective. Malarone is handy, too, because it can be started a day before you travel and can be discontinued just

a week after you leave the malarial zone. However, it's not suitable for babies or for trips of over a month.

Mosquito nets and repellents

It's worth getting into the habit of applying **mosquito repellent** all over your body every evening. If you're staying in cheap accommodation, try to choose a reasonably bug-proof room: make sure the windows have mesh screens and that the door fits well in its frame. Sleep under a **mosquito net** when possible – if you're travelling for a while, it's worth bringing a small, lightweight net with you, as the locally bought nets tend to be bulky. Other precautions include burning mosquito coils at night (also on sale locally) and spraying your room with insect-killer (hotel staff will do this for you as a routine or on request).

Malaria treatment

If you think you might be getting a fever, the priority is to seek **treatment**. Delay is potentially risky; travellers who deal casually with malaria die of the disease every year. Ideally, confirm your diagnosis by getting to a doctor and having a blood test to identify the strain. If this isn't possible, take an appropriate remedy, which should be a different drug to the one you're taking as an anti-malarial. The recommended doses are: two Lariam tablets, followed by another two, six hours later; or one doxycycline capsule twice a day for seven days plus two quinine tablets three times a day for the first three days; or four Malarone tablets per day in a single dose for three days.

Be aware that the symptoms of malaria can be cyclic – after a day or two of improvement you may be knocked out again.

Schistosomiasis

Schistosomiasis – also known as **bilharzia** – is potentially very dangerous, though easily curable. Bilharzia comes from tiny flukes that live in freshwater snails and which, as part of their life cycle, leave their hosts and burrow into animal (or human) skin to multiply in the bloodstream. The snails themselves favour only stagnant water, though the flukes can be swept downstream. While it's possible to pick it up from one brief contact, the risk of contracting bilharzia is fairly low unless you repeatedly come into contact with infected water. If infected, you'll get a slightly itchy rash an hour or two later where the flukes have entered the skin. If you have severe abdominal pains and pass blood – the first symptoms after 4–6 weeks – see a doctor.

To avoid the disease, the usual **recommendation** is to steer clear of river water that's not been vouched for. Snail-free water that's stood for two days, or has been boiled or chlorinated, is safe, as is salt or brackish water.

Sleeping sickness

Sleeping sickness – **trypanosomiasis** – is mainly a disease of cattle and horses and, to a much lesser extent, people. It's carried by tsetse flies that crowd streams and riverbanks in deep bush areas. They're determined insects with a painful bite, attracted to large moving objects such as boats or Land Rovers, and often fly in the windows of vehicles driving through the bush.

Infection is rare among travellers – fortunately so, because the drugs used to treat it aren't very sophisticated. But a boil which suddenly appears several days after a tsetse fly bite might indicate an infection you should get examined. Untreated, sleeping sickness results in infections of the central nervous system and drowsiness.

Sexually transmitted diseases and HIV

The only other real likelihood of your encountering a serious disease in The Gambia is if it's **sexually transmitted**. **STDs** are widespread, particularly in the larger towns, and **HIV** infection is alarmingly prevalent and spreading all the time, despite its incidence being far lower than in many other African countries. It's very easily passed between people suffering relatively minor, but ulcerous, sexually transmitted diseases, the prevalence of which is thought to account for the high incidence of heterosexually transmitted HIV.

Heat-related complaints

Don't underestimate the strength of the **tropical sun**. Common-sense precautions

against **dehydration**, **heatstroke** and **sunburn** include drinking plenty of water, limiting intake of caffeine and alcohol, and wearing a high-protection factor sunscreen, even on overcast days. It's important not to overdose on **sunshine** – at least to start with; the powerful heat and bright light can mess up your system, so a hat and sunglasses are necessities.

Before acclimatizing, many people get a bout of **heat rash**, an infection of the sweat ducts caused by excessive perspiration which doesn't dry off. A cool shower, **zinc oxide powder** and cotton clothes should help.

Water and bugs

You should have no trouble finding safe **drinking water** in The Gambia. Bottled water is widely available; plus, in most places, any unbottled water you drink will have come from a tap and is likely to be clean. Gambian tap water is chlorinated and much safer than the tap water in most other African countries. There's no need to hesitate, therefore, about ordering ice. However, in remote rural areas with no mains supply, you should be cautious of drinking unpurified water, unless you know the source to be free from contamination: bad water, sourced for example from a dirty well, is a principal cause of **diarrhoea**.

In truth, **stomach upsets** don't plague many travellers badly, but everyone's constitution reacts differently to unfamiliar food and drink. If you're visiting for a short time only, and want to be able to drink water of uncertain origin, add a few drops of iodine tincture, use purifying tablets and/or boil water. If you want to be absolutely safe, **purification**, a two-stage process involving both filtration and sterilization, gives the most complete treatment.

For **longer stays**, and especially if you're travelling widely, think of re-educating your stomach rather than fortifying it. It's virtually impossible to travel in West Africa without exposing yourself to strange bugs from time to time. Simple local restaurants and street food sellers generally use fresh ingredients, and cook them well. The worst culprits are restaurants that don't take proper care over freezing and thawing food.

If you do have a **serious attack of diarrhoea**, 24 hours of nothing but plain tea, flat
Coke, or just boiled water may rinse it out.
While most upsets resolve themselves, it's
vital to replace lost fluids; you can make up a
rehydration mix with four heaped teaspoons
of sugar or honey and half a teaspoon of salt
in a litre of water. If the diarrhoea seems to
be getting worse, or you have to travel a
long distance while stricken, any pharmacy
should have name brand anti-diarrhoea
remedies. These shouldn't be overused;
restrict yourself to a day's worth.

Avoid using **antibiotics** at the first sign
of trouble. Antibiotics and anti-diarrhoeal
drugs shouldn't be used as preventatives: they annihilate your gut flora and
will not work on viruses; it's better to seek
a doctor. If you have blood in your diarrhoea, however, and it's impossible to see
a doctor, take a course of ciprofloxacin as
a last resort – arrange this on prescription
with your GP before leaving home.

Lastly, two common gynaecological problems. **Cystitis** can be relieved, if not eradi-
cated, with plenty of water, vitamin pills and
acidic fruit juice: oranges and pineapples
are available in abundance during the dry
season. As a last resort, the broad-spectrum
antibiotic amoxycillin, available on prescription, is useful against this (and many other
infections). **Thrush** responds well to a good
dose of yogurt, both eaten and applied.

Injuries, bites and wildlife

Take more care than usual over **minor cuts**
– in a tropical environment the most trivial
scratch can become a throbbing infection if
you ignore it.

As for **animal attacks**, Gambian **dogs**
are usually sad and skulking and pose little
threat, though like captive **monkeys** they
may carry rabies: if bitten, see a doctor
without delay. The Gambia's other large and
potentially dangerous animals are the relatively common **Nile crocodile**, which rarely
grows beyond three metres here, but should
always be treated with respect, and the
unpredictable **hippopotamus**, close proximity to which should always be avoided (for
more information on wildlife, see p.292).

Apart from mosquitoes, **insects** are less of
a problem here than in many other tropical
countries, but **tsetse flies** and **sandflies** can
sometimes be a nuisance, and you should
pack insect bite relief cream, since scratch-
ing may lead to an infection. If, while staying
in cheap accommodation, you wake up with
a neat row of small, red, very itchy bites then
bedbugs may well be the cause – they are
harmless.

Scorpions and spiders abound, but are
hardly ever seen unless you go turning over
rocks or logs. Scorpion stings are rarely serious and spiders are mostly quite harmless.

Snakes are common but, again, the vast
majority are harmless and rarely seen – walk
heavily and they obligingly disappear. In the
very unlikely event that you are bitten by a
poisonous snake, you will certainly know all
about it: kill the snake if you can, for identification, and try to stay calm. Send someone
for medical help, and don't try any heroics
with tourniquets or razors.

Sea anemones, sting rays and jellyfish
are occasionally found in shallow tidal water;
the varieties found in The Gambia are not
dangerous, but it still pays to be vigilant.

Costs, money and banks

The rapid inflation that dogged the Gambian economy in the late 1990s and early 2000s has slowed right down, and the local currency, the dalasi, is now relatively stable. While many locals are left wondering how to afford the basics such as rice and transport, tourist services such as day-trips, accommodation, drinks and restaurant meals remain competitively priced in real terms. This is likely to remain the case for some time as, with new tourist-friendly supermarkets, hotels and self-catering apartments popping up all over the resort areas at a rate that outstrips demand, competition between rival businesses is fierce. Many businesses and banks still don't accept plastic, though, so it's wise to come equipped with a fist-ful of cash and travellers' cheques to exchange for dalasis.

Costs

It's perhaps surprising to find that, compared to other developing countries, West African nations can be **expensive** to visit, and the cost of living in The Gambia is high for the region – anything like a Euro-American life-style costs almost as much as in Europe or America. Despite this, mere survival can be dirt cheap and it's perfectly possible to have a comfortable and enjoyable holiday in The Gambia on a modest budget.

If you're visiting The Gambia on a flight-plus-bed-and-breakfast package, and plan to minimize costs by using cheap transport, eating market food or at local restaurants, and possibly spending a few nights away from your hotel either camping in the bush, staying with people, or in budget hotels, it should be just about possible to get by on **£100/€150 a week** (though £200/€300 split between two gets you more value for money). It's clearly much harder to keep costs down in the resort areas, where tempting comforts and consumables are available, and it would be easy to get through double the above amount. If you arrive on a flight-only deal and choose to stay in a **tourist hotel**, the cost of accommodation is likely to be your biggest single expense: typically £20–50/€30–75 per night for a double room.

If you'd like to see more of the country than just the resorts, a good way to keep costs really low is to **cycle** (see p.47), which not only saves on fares but also enables you to seek out inexpensive accommodation or tent space. A cycle tour of The Gambia need not cost more than £10/€15 a day.

As a very general guideline to budget planning, a twin room in a cheap hotel can usually be had for under £10/€15 and very occasionally for less than half this amount. Short hops by **shared taxis** in urban areas have fixed fares of around £0.10–0.20/€0.15–0.30c; **local taxi hire** starts from around £1/€1.50; and long-distance road transport by **bush taxi** works out, on average, at £1.50–2/€2.25–3 per 100km, though it varies with the quality of the road and the speed of the vehicle. River trips tend to be more expensive. As for **food and drink**, you can eat your fill for well under £1/€1.50 if you eat street food or sit at a market or taxi garage chop house. Main courses at the more reasonable tourist restaurants are around £2–5/€3–7.50). A 1.5-litre bottle of water costs £0.40–1.20/€0.60–1.80, a 330ml bottle of Julbrew beer is £0.60–1.20/€0.90–1.80 and a soft drink £0.20–0.65/€0.30–1. You'll quickly discover that prices vary a great deal between the tourist places and those with a more local clientele, and that small shops and supermarkets are much cheaper than hotels and bars.

Travelling on a higher budget, **tourist taxi fares** are relatively steep (starting at £3/€4.50 for a short hop), **car rental** rates can be high at £16–50/€24–75 per day plus fuel and insurance, and the **top-flight hotels** are expensive at over £100/€150 per night for a double room. The cost of fuel – in mid-2006, D30/£0.60/€0.90 per litre for

Tipping

If you stay in tourist hotels, and go on organized excursions, you will be expected to **tip** staff, but it can be a problem to know how much to give, and when. Many staff will only be paid around £1/€1.50 per day, while those in business for themselves, such as taxi drivers, might make ten times this. For most **minor services**, a small-denomination banknote is adequate – about the price of a soft drink or a packet of green tea from a shop. For **waiters** in tourist restaurants, around five percent of the bill is fine. For hotel waiters and domestic staff who look after you every day, think about giving something up to £2/€3 at the end of each week. Many tourist hotels have a staff box, so gratuities are shared equally. If you'd like to give a special gift to somebody, it's a good idea to enclose a note explaining it's a present from you, so there's no chance of misunderstanding.

In the humblest establishments, tipping is not very common, so the owners of **local restaurants** will be delighted if you tip them. Gambian **taxi drivers** do not normally expect tips. On organized excursions, the **guides** and **drivers** consider tips at the end almost as part of their pay: everyone on a group trip should give around £1/€1.50 per day for each crew member.

---

petrol, or D28/£0.56/€0.84 for diesel – has been rising steadily.

Bargaining

You'll need to get into **bargaining** quickly, as it's the normal way of conducting business. Moreover every time you pay an unreasonable price for goods or services you contribute to local inflation. There's a danger, however, that by bargaining over-hard you could cause offence, so if you're in any doubt about what constitutes a fair price, ask a disinterested local, and remember that good humour counts for much.

Bitikos (small general stores) and supermarkets invariably have **fixed prices**, as do the itinerant sellers of fruit, nuts, bags of water and suchlike who mainly sell to locals (as opposed to the beach hawkers who target tourists). Fares on shared public transport are subject to state control and are fixed, but baggage fees can be haggled over. Tourist taxi fares are officially fixed but in practice there may be some room for negotiation. Fares for "town trips" by local taxi (see p.44). are more flexible. Pretty much every other item or service (including, sometimes, hotel rooms) can and should be bargained for. Don't make any offer you're unwilling to commit to, though, as to refuse to pay once an offer has been accepted can cause grave offence.

In **negotiations** there's generally a "last price" which the seller has in mind from the outset. You can assume the one you're quoted is more, but a few good-natured offers will establish the fact. Don't automatically assume you're in the clutches of a rip-off artist: concepts of **honour** are very important. Try offering a bulk price for several items or services at once, or ask for some "presents" to be added to the thing you're negotiating over. You could consider throwing items from home into the deal as well – bartering is accepted practice, particularly in tourist markets.

For men, it's normal to make **physical contact** – clasping hands with the trader is usually enough to emphasize a point. Be as jocular as possible and don't be shy of making a big scene – the bluffing and mock outrage on both sides is part of the fun. Women can't pursue these negotiating tactics in quite the same way, except when buying from women – invariably much tougher.

Try to **delay** the moment when you have to name your first price. The seller's price may drop way below your expectation before you've made any offer, so forget the standard "offer-a-third-come-up-to-a-half" formula. If you do arrive at an impasse you can always drop the matter and come back later. With stalemates, a disinterested companion tugging your sleeve always helps.

Currency

The Gambian currency is the **dalasi**, which comes in 5, 10, 25, 50, and 100 dalasi notes, and one-dalasi coins. Various denominations of bututs exist (there are 100 bututs to the dalasi), but are now rarely used.

The days of the dalasi are numbered, since Ghana, Nigeria, Sierra Leone, Guinea and The Gambia are in the process of forming a new monetary union, the **West African Monetary Zone (WAMZ)**, with a common currency. The new currency is due to be introduced by 2009, and is likely to behave similarly to the **CFA franc** (pronounced "seffa"), which you will encounter in The Gambia from time to time and will need if you're travelling from The Gambia into neighbouring Senegal. The CFA franc is the common currency of eight West African countries including Senegal, and is a hard currency with a fixed exchange rate pegged to the euro.

In mid-2006, the following **official exchange rates** (approximate) apply: £1 = D52; $1 = D28; €1 = D36. You can check current exchange rates and convert figures on Ⓦ www.xe.com.

Cash and travellers' cheques

While a few European exchange bureaux deal in dalasis, you'll get better rates in The Gambia. If you're spending more than a few days, you're best off carrying funds in sterling or euro **travellers' cheques**, which are equally widely accepted. Danish and Swedish kronor are also often accepted in the resort areas. US dollars are less widely accepted and tend to be exchanged at unfavourable rates.

Hotels and some shops and traders will take travellers' cheques as payment, but it's essential to have some sterling or euros in **cash** as a stand-by. If you're in The Gambia for a short stay and you're on a budget it's worth considering carrying all your hard currency in cash and changing money as often as suits you. You will get a better exchange rate for cash than for travellers' cheques.

Denominations of travellers' cheques and cash should be as small as you can manage, bearing in mind the bulk that a large sum of exchange will amount to. A small stash of low-value hard-currency notes (£5 and €5) is always useful.

The usual **fee** for travellers' cheque sales is one or two percent, though this may be waived if you buy the cheques through a bank where you have an account. Keep the purchase agreement and a record of cheque serial numbers safe and separate from the cheques themselves. Some banks may not cash your cheque without the original receipt. In the event that cheques are lost or stolen, the issuing company will expect you to report the loss immediately to their nearest office; most companies claim to replace lost or stolen cheques within 24 hours. **American Express** and **Thomas Cook** are the most widely recognized brands, and also the fastest to replace lost cheques.

While you're on the move, it's wise to keep cash, travellers' cheques and airline tickets in **small plastic bags** (to protect them from sweat) somewhere secure and invisible. Tourist hotels usually have room safes rentable by the day.

Debit and credit cards

Debit cards are a handy backup source of funds, and can be used either in ATMs (if you can find one that works) or over the counter in banks, some shops, and in payment for tourist services such as major hotels, restaurants, tours, car rental and flights. Gambian ATMs only let you withdraw D2000 per transaction. You can make as many withdrawals as you like, funds permitting, but your bank is likely to charge you a flat transaction fee each time, making this a relatively expensive way to obtain dalasis.

Credit cards can be used to pay for some items and services – Visa is the most recognized – but can't normally be used to obtain cash advances. Businesses which accept plastic typically charge a commission of around ten percent.

A compromise between travellers' cheques and plastic for American travellers is **Visa TravelMoney**, a disposable pre-paid debit card with a PIN which works in all ATMs that take Visa cards. You can load up your account with funds from your bank account at any time, by phone or online, and when they run out you simply throw the card away. You can buy up to nine cards to access the same funds – useful for couples or families travelling together. It's wise to buy at least one extra as a back-up in case of loss or theft. Since the cards cannot be used without the PIN, your funds are secure. You can find a local card issuer online at ⓦhttp://usa.visa.com.

Banks and exchange bureaux

The most useful **bank** is Standard Chartered, most branches of which have ATMs. At the time of writing, the only ATMs in the country are on Nelson Mandela Street in Banjul, on Kairaba Avenue near the Westfield junction, on Bertil Harding Highway near the traffic lights, on Atlantic Road in Fajara and on Senegambia Road in Kololi. There's no ATM at the airport.

Other banks you'll come across include Trust Bank, First International and IBC. The charges for foreign exchange differ from bank to bank. In Kombo district, there are banks in Banjul, Serrekunda, Bakau, Fajara, Kololi, Brikama and at the airport. Up-country, Farafenni and Basse are currently the only towns with banks.

If all you need to do is change money, and you don't want to suffer the premium rates set by the hotels, it's worth seeking out an **exchange bureau**, generally found only around the resort areas. Bureaux are quicker and more efficient than the banks, and sometimes offer slightly better rates, usually with no commission. Their rates are not always fixed, so it's worth striking up a friendly relationship with one and seeing how far negotiations can take you.

The parallel market

An unofficial, **parallel exchange system** (effectively a black market) operates for the benefit of locals who can't obtain hard, foreign currency through official channels. However it's illegal, and travellers are advised to steer well clear. Moneychangers, once conspicuous, have all but disappeared from Gambian towns; a few still operate clandestinely at transit points such as Barra, though, and if you're really stuck, businessmen who trade in imported goods may be open to offers.

Wiring money

Having money **wired from home** is not particularly convenient or cheap, and should be a last resort. Money is only paid out in dalasis. It's better to bring with you on your trip all you'll need, and more, in travellers' cheques, or to make cash withdrawals with a debit card, even if this means waiting for somebody back home to pay the funds into your account first.

Money-wiring companies with connections in The Gambia include: Bayba Express (ⓦwww.bayba.com), which is relatively efficient and has good rates, and Western Union (ⓦwww.westernunion.com), which has many agents, but can be pricey and slow.

Getting around

The Gambia has no railway lines, and no internal flights except by private arrangement. The most common way to get around is by road, which is often a slow, dusty and bumpy experience. The most satisfying ways to get around the country are by rented Land Rover (if you can afford it), by bicycle (if you have time) or by double-decker *pirogue* on the river.

Internal communications within The Gambia are severely hampered by the state of the country's **roads**. The major artery which runs all the way along the south bank of the River Gambia from Banjul to Basse, via Serrekunda, Brikama, and Soma, was sealed in the 1970s, then neglected so badly that a few stretches (most notoriously the 100km or so west of Soma) are currently a nightmarish mess of potholes. Although a rebuilding programme is underway, it has been hampered by serious delays, and at the time of writing there is no definite end-date in sight. The main road on the north bank of the river has become the route of choice for most up-country journeys; this once-rugged highway is now either newly sealed or newly graded all the way to Janjanbureh.

The main roads around the resort areas are generally well maintained, with good tarmac stretching from the airport to the coast, and right down to Kartong in the south. The Banjul–Serrekunda–Brikama road is mostly in very good condition, and the section from Soma to Basse is a blessed relief after the rigours of the stretch west of Soma.

Hitting the **backroads** can be a relaxing and rewarding way to travel. By vehicle, even in the dry season, you'll need a **4WD** to tackle the tougher laterite and sand tracks; in the rainy season many back roads become impassable.

If you're thinking of **hitching** around The Gambia for free, think again. The majority of rural people in West Africa get around by waving down vehicles (not thumbing, which may be considered rude), but they invariably pay. Private vehicles are scarce up-country, and there's a reluctance to deny trade to the bush taxi drivers; off their routes, you may get lifts but you'll usually end up paying a contribution to the driver.

If you're hardy and not tied to any schedule, you could simply **walk**. All over the region, you'll come across local people walking vast distances because they have no money at all to pay for transport. Many schoolchildren have to walk several kilometres to and from school every day. If you're hiking for a few days you can fall in with them – they'll enjoy trying out their English on you.

By tourist taxi

Tourist taxis are painted green, with white diamonds on the sides and bonnet. They're fully insured and have to pass an annual inspection. They offer trips at **fixed prices**, including waiting time and a return journey if required, and these prices are posted up on boards at the taxi ranks in the resort areas, so you know exactly where you stand. though there is usually room for a little negotiation. They also have access to the (few) restricted areas within the resorts that are out of bounds to local taxis, such as the Senegambia, Kotu and Cape Point turnarounds.

The main **disadvantage** of tourist taxis is that their prices are way above those of local taxis (roughly three times as much as "town trips"). And, as they're beyond the means of most Gambians, you'll have only limited contact with local people if you always choose tourist taxis over equivalent local transport.

By bush taxi

The alternative to taking a tourist taxi is to take a **local taxi** or **bush taxi**, which will cost just a few dalasis if you're happy to get on and off at points along a standard route, or something closer to the price of a tourist taxi if you'd like to charter the car for your own trip.

The **bush taxi** is the classic form of West African public transport, providing an essential public service in both urban and rural areas. Bush taxis can be cars, minibuses or vans. They function like buses, in that they follow standard routes and are shared between a number of passengers who each pay a fixed price for their seat and, usually, their luggage, according to how far they're travelling; unlike buses, however, they don't normally run to a timetable, and passengers can get on or off anywhere along the fixed route.

In urban areas bush taxis are usually either small **minibuses** (sometimes called *tanka-tankas*), converted to squeeze in the maximum number of passengers, complete with narrow benches and lino on the floor, or **yellow and green four-door saloon cars**, shared between up to four passengers.

Up-country bush taxis can vary from a reasonably comfortable **Peugeot estate** (station wagon) seating five, six or seven plus driver in reasonable comfort, to a brightly painted **passenger van** (known as *gelleh-gellehs*), big enough for 15–25 passengers. A basket of chickens stuffed under the bench, and maybe a goat or two tied to the roof are regular fare-paying additions. Most vehicles have roof-rack luggage carriers and one or two coveted seats at the front, next to the driver, for which you often pay a surcharge. In rural areas, **carts** – basically wooden platforms on two wheels, drawn by horses, donkeys or oxen – operate as slow bush taxis.

The chaos that seems to accompany bush taxi journeys is an illusion. They are nearly all licensed passenger vehicles, serving approved routes at fixed rates. In busy areas they run frequently all day. On quieter routes, however, there may well be only a couple of vehicles a day, and these won't leave their starting point (generally an open area or section of roadside known as a bush taxi garage) until they have a full complement of paying passengers. There may be occasions when you want to pay for more than one seat, either to give yourself extra room, or to get the taxi on the road if it's taking a long time to fill up. There's no point in trying to pick up a bush taxi down the road from the garage on a route like this as they will all cruise past you full.

To flag down a bush taxi, hold out your arm and wave up and down. Bush taxis with spaces to fill may well try to flag *you* down, by decelerating and hooting as they approach. Once you're near your destination, the driver (if it's a car) or fare-collector (if it's a minibus or van) will collect the fares – known as *pass* in Wolof. You're very unlikely to be overcharged. When you want to get off, indicate to the driver or fare-collector. If the taxi is crowded and it's hard to get their attention try yelling "*Fi!*" ("here!" in Wolof). There are a few places, usually specific junctions, where taxis are not permitted to stop; otherwise you can get off anywhere.

All bush taxis are available for **private hire**, and if you get into an empty taxi, the driver may assume you want to charter the whole vehicle unless you say otherwise. A journey to an address you specify (which may be off the standard bush taxi routes) is known as a **town trip**; you have the car to yourself. Taxis are unmetered, so you negotiate **fares** in advance. Ask the advice of a local you trust if you're not sure what you should be paying; some tourists pay far too much because they don't realize that town trip fares are far lower than tourist taxi fares (see opposite). As a guide, work out how much a similar distance by shared taxi would cost if you paid for all the seats – this is the absolute minimum you can expect to pay, though in practice you may end up paying double this. It's best to equip yourself with directions to your

Bush taxi survival

Bush taxi **drivers** are generally competent and experienced, but their vehicles are among the most dangerous on the roads. Don't be afraid to make a big fuss if the driver appears to have lost all sense. Ask and then shout at him to "Slow down!" and try to enlist the support of fellow travellers – though to many Gambians being hurtled along in a rickety vehicle is a routine experience.

You'll be in close bodily contact with fellow passengers throughout. On long distance journeys, sharing some kola nuts goes down well (see p.73). As ever, it's a good idea to bring **water** with you, but there are always plenty of fruit-, nut- and drink-sellers keen to strike a deal through the windows whenever taxis make routine stops.

You won't have much opportunity to enjoy the scenery, unless you're in one of the prized **front seats**: the windows inside the minibuses and vans are often curtained against the sun. Nor is this the most flexible way to travel – up-country, you may be reluctant to get off a taxi anywhere that doesn't have a bush taxi garage, for fear of getting stuck.

On the plus side, travelling by bush taxi can be a colourful, even enjoyable, experience, allowing you to meet Gambians in an ordinary context. You won't be hassled on a vehicle, and it's up to you whether to chat or just lose yourself in your own private space – a relief for anyone weary of the intrusive attention foreigners often attract elsewhere.

Choosing your seat

When travelling by bush taxi, it's worth considering your general direction through the trip and **which side to sit on** for the shadiest ride. This is especially important on dirt roads when the combination of slow, bumpy ride, dust and fierce sun can be horrible. On a busy dirt road with lots of other traffic, try to avoid sitting on the left of the vehicle, or you'll be inhaling fumes.

Bush taxi seats vary greatly in leg-room, and the best **views** are from seats near the front, which is also the safest place.

destination as the driver may have no clue. If you find a good driver based in a convenient location, it's worth taking his mobile phone number for future bookings.

Most towns have a **taxi garage**, not a building as such, but an area where vehicles assemble to fill with passengers. Some large towns, like Banjul, Serrekunda and Soma, have several garages, each serving different destinations and usually conveniently located for the appropriate route out of town (though not always conveniently located for you). They sometimes double as, or adjoin, market places, and they're good places to pick up street food.

The **smaller taxis** generally sell their seats and drive straight from A to B, if possible without stopping. They often do the trip in half the time it takes a more beaten-up minibus, *gelleh-gelleh* or *tanka-tanka*, which may drop people off and take fares en route. But the latter options are often the only way to get to more obscure destinations, or to travel on the roughest roads. And not surprisingly they're cheaper.

In the busiest taxi garages, such as those in Serrekunda and Barra, you'll find you're quickly surrounded by **taxi scouts** trying to get you into their vehicle, which can be a hassle. It pays to behave robustly and to know exactly where you're going, plus the names of any towns en route or beyond, as you may have to change vehicles.

Up-country, the ideal **time to travel** is early in the morning. By a couple of hours after sunrise the best vehicles have gone, and on some routes, there won't be another that day.

Before long, you'll run into a situation where you seem to be the only passenger in a **stationary vehicle** you were assured was about to leave. When this happens, it's better to forget over-ambitious travel plans (especially after midday) or to take a shorter journey with a vehicle that's nearly ready to go. In order to guarantee you'll stay and attract others, drivers, owners and scouts will often try to get you to pay up front. Your luggage tied on the roof generally ought to be sufficient sign of your good faith and, unless you see others paying, it's always best to delay payment until you've set off. Make sure you pay the right person when you do.

The only occasion on which you're in danger of being **overcharged** is when you're only travelling part of a long-distance route, when you might be asked for the full fare. The charges made for hoisting your **luggage** onto the taxi roof may be up for debate, too, and you might have to argue about how small, light and streamlined it is – don't be afraid to make a scene, but remain good-humoured. You shouldn't have to pay more than one-third of your fare for a backpack or large bag, and normally less.

During **long waits**, keep an eye on your luggage. Anything tied on the roof is safe, but bags very occasionally get grabbed through open windows. Don't worry unduly, however, if the vehicle, while waiting to fill, and with booked passengers scattered around, suddenly takes off with all your gear on top. While it's obviously a good idea to make a mental note of the vehicle registration, you should avoid offence by not appearing suspicious. They've probably gone to fill up with fuel, and will be back.

By car

Car rental is not highly developed. You can pick up a car at the airport or in the resorts (see p.149), but elsewhere in the country the possibilities are effectively zero. Rates, including mileage and insurance, start at around D1000 (£20/€30) per day for a car, and £28/€40 for a 4WD, but can be astronomical. Petrol costs D30 (60p/€0.90c) per litre, and rising, with fuel shortages a regular occurrence.

There are several general points to bear in mind. First, rented cars cannot, as a rule, be driven out of The Gambia into Senegal. Some firms insist on **four-wheel-drive** if you'll be departing from surfaced highways, even in the dry season. It's normal to have a **driver** (self-drive is less common), and it's important to be clear in advance about his daily pay, lodgings and subsistence. If you're driving, you'll need an **international driving licence**, and will normally need to be over 23.

An alternative is to simply rent a **taxi** on a daily basis. Buy the fuel separately, and settle every other question – the driver's bed, board, cigarettes – in advance too. However good the price, don't take on a vehicle that's unsafe, or a driver you don't like and can't communicate with.

Driving

Don't automatically assume the vehicle is roadworthy. **Before setting off**, have a look at the engine and tyres and don't leave without checking water, battery and spare tyre (preferably two and the means to change them) and making sure you have a few tools. It's also a good idea to keep jerry cans of water and fuel on board. As for breakdowns, local mechanics are usually excellent and can apply creative ingenuity to the most disastrous situations. But spare parts, tools and proper equipment are rare outside the Kombo coastal area.

When **driving**, beware of unexpected rocks, ditches and potholes – not to mention animals and people – on the road. It's usual to honk your horn stridently to warn pedestrians and cyclists. Never pass a roadside checkpoint or barrier without stopping and waiting to be waved on, and don't drive anywhere without all your documents.

The Gambia drives **on the right**, though in reality vehicles keep to the best part of the road until they have to pass each other (potholes account for many head-on collisions). Right- and left-hand **signals** are conventionally used to say "Please overtake me" or "Don't overtake me!", but you

shouldn't assume the driver in front can see that the road is safe for you to pass, and many drivers never look in their mirrors. Don't assume anything about the behaviour of other drivers – road death statistics are horrifying, especially considering how few vehicles there are in the country.

By bicycle

In many ways **cycling** is the ideal form of transport in The Gambia. It gives you total independence; you can camp or take your bike into hotel rooms with you. If you get tired of pedalling you can transport your bike on top of a bush taxi or bus (reckon on paying about half-fare for it).

A bike allows you to explore well off the beaten track. Routes that can't be used by motor vehicles because they're too rough, or involve crossing creeks, are all accessible. With a tough bike, you can follow **bush paths** – though remember to give ample verbal warning to people walking ahead of you, who may otherwise be frightened by your sudden arrival behind them. If your tyres are up to it you can also ride along the beach at low tide (leaving the bumsters standing).

You can **rent** bicycles from a number of bike rental stalls on the coast, mostly near major hotels. The quality varies hugely. The going rate is reasonable at around D200-300 (£4–6/€6–9 per day), with discounts negotiable for longer periods.

Rental bikes are not usually well-adapted for long-distance touring, although they often have carriers. For long trips you could bring a bike from home to The Gambia, or buy one there: there are dealers in most towns. Serrekunda has the greatest choice, with good secondhand machines from about D2500 (£50/€80) and new ones for under D6000). Remember to take powerful battery-powered **lights** – the front light can double as a torch and getting batteries is no problem, and it's surprising how often you will need to cycle after 7pm. A rear-view mirror is very useful for main roads, but when it comes to predicting the movement of the traffic around you, don't take anything for granted. Cycle locks and sturdier padlocks and chains are sold in markets.

Depending on your fitness and enthusiasm, expect to cycle around 50–100km per day. The going in The Gambia is generally flat and gentle and, with breaks, you could cover the whole country from west to east and back again in a fortnight.

By ferry, river cruiser and pirogue

While it's unbeatable for sightseeing, the **River Gambia** has no regular public services. In practical terms, it can't be considered a significant transport route, and what should be one of The Gambia's major transport arteries is instead a hindrance to north–south communications. There is a plan to build a bridge between Bambatenda and Yelitenda near Farafenni and Soma, providing a crucial link in the Trans-Gambian highway, but at present there are no bridges, and only small, hand-hauled or spluttering **diesel ferries** pulling people and vehicles across the river at key points up and down the country. The most significant of these is the vehicle ferry across the mouth of the river from Banjul to Barra (see pp.102–103). There are also **vehicle ferries** linking Janjanbureh Island to the north and south banks of the river at Lamin Koto and Sankulay Kunda;

a Bambatenda–Yelitenda ferry; and ferries at Bansang, Basse and Fatoto. Elsewhere, the river can be crossed by **hand-paddled passenger boat**.

You can also travel on the river by small motorized fishing **pirogue** (a long, narrow traditional wooden canoe), motorized launch, larger *pirogue*, or powerboat. These are excursions rather than public transport services. For more details, see p.147.

By microlight and light aircraft

The Gambia has no internal flights and no up-country airports – just a few landing strips. It is, however, possible to get around **by air**, though only by private arrangement.

Madox Airsports (☎770 2119 or 702 1167, ⊛www.madoxairsports.co.uk), primarily a **microlight**- and light aircraft training centre, take people out as passengers on request – an unforgettable way to experience the country. By **light aircraft**, you can be flown up-river to Tendaba or Janjanbureh in a fraction of the time it takes to bump along by road.

Tours and guides

Organized tours in The Gambia are the equivalent of group safaris in East or southern Africa – you don't have to participate, but if you don't, you might miss out on a great deal of what the country has to offer. They're a great way to get your first taste of the country outside the resorts, and highly recommended if you're new to West Africa. As a way of getting out and about, without the hassle of organizing everything for yourself, the idea can have great appeal.

If you'd like a more tailor-made feel to your adventures, or you prefer to travel in a very small group, talk to one of the **ground tour operators** (local tour companies running organized trips) about arranging a bespoke trip: their guides, drivers and vehicles can be hired by the day for this purpose. There are also **specialist guides** and operators who

can accompany you birdwatching or fishing: it pays to select these carefully according to the level of expertise you require. Alternatively, you could hire one of The Gambia's posse of freelance **Official Tourist Guides** (OTGs); this is likely to work out cheaper than hiring a guide from a ground tour operator or a specialist guide, but most OTGs don't have a comparable level of knowledge and experience. Finally, there are **bumsters**: ubiquitous in the tourist areas, these young Gambians make their money by offering various services to tourists on an informal basis, using extremely intrusive sales tactics. While many are totally unreliable, some bumsters are very good at introducing visitors to off-beat places and people they wouldn't encounter by other means.

Ground tour operators

Ground tour operators offer programmes of standard tours (see p.51), some of which overlap: several companies run similar excursions to popular destinations. Other trips are unique to individual operators.

Most operators can also tailor-make **private trips** on request. On the simplest level, these can amount to just hiring a Land

Birdwatching trips

Many of The Gambia's native bird species are so brightly hued, noisy and conspicuous that even the most inexperienced birdwatchers can spot them easily. However, if you'd like to study the country's birdlife in detail, or seek out particular species, a **professional guide** can be invaluable – without their assistance, you may find it hard to spot the birds that interest you most.

Keen birdwatchers can visit a variety of the best habitats by joining a **group tour** designed specifically for wildlife enthusiasts, or by hiring a **freelance bird guide** by the day. Most group birding trips organized by special interest tour operators (see p.31) promise sightings of hundreds of species; a well-run trip should also be able to accommodate requests to study the behaviour of a handful of key species in greater detail.

A good guide will know exactly which species are most likely to be feeding or roosting in which location, and how to get you there. Of course, guides with in-depth ornithological knowledge charge higher fees. The best can mimic many bird calls, summoning a particular species within minutes, and can throw calls back and forth with the bird in a conversational manner. Bear in mind when choosing a guide that they have to be able to communicate well with you too – some guides are brilliant birders but poor English-speakers.

Guides sometimes meet and wait for clients at the WABSA (West African Bird Study Association) shelter near Kotu Stream Bridge, Kotu, or at the Education Centre at Abuko Nature Reserve. The Gambia Birding Group (ⓦ www.gambiabirding.org) is a good source of **information and advice** on guides and ornithological matters, while the detailed reports of bird sightings posted by enthusiasts on websites such as Bird Tours (ⓦ www.birdtours.co.uk), Fat Birder (ⓦ www.fatbirder.com) and Travelling Birder (ⓦ www.travellingbirder.com) can also help a great deal in planning an itinerary.

Recommended guides include:

Modou and Yaya Barry c/o Kombo Beach Hotel ☏ 117 5112. Offers Kombo-based and up-river birding excursions, including all accommodation and transport.

Birds of The Gambia ☏ 993 6122, ⓦ www.birdsofthegambia.com. Private birdwatching safaris for specialists and keen beginners, run by the renowned British ornithologist Clive Barlow, author of the region's most authoritative field guide, from his base in The Gambia.

Mass Cham ☏ 992 4763. Independent bird guide who works mainly in Kombo district.

Modou Colley ☏ 990 8916, ⓔ mcolley99@yahoo.com. Experienced guide and secretary of WABSA.

Wally Faal Serrekunda ☏ 437 2103. Established independent guide.

Habitat Africa Lamin ☏ 992 1551, 990 7694, ⓔ habitatafrica@hotmail.com. Network of a dozen Gambian bird guides coordinated by experienced and highly respected local birder Solomon Jallow.

Rover with a driver and possibly a guide. This kind of travel enables you to get to places that public transport doesn't reach – without the hassle of lugging your bags around on your back – particularly appealing if you're visiting national parks. Getting more detailed, you could ask the company to prearrange an itinerary including overnight stops, special events or ceremonies, visits to stone circles or meetings with musicians or healers. The best ground tour operators may be able to **recommend a guide** who knows your target area inside out, and can act as your interpreter, wildlife expert and cultural guru – you're likely to experience far more with their assistance than you could ever hope to on your own.

African Adventure Tours Bakau ☏ 449 7313, ⓦ www.africanadventuretours.com. Works closely with Dutch tour operator Olympia, offering standard itineraries plus a more unusual "Roots by land" trip.

Alkamba Travel & Tours Banjul ☏ 420 2059, ⓔ alkamba@gamtel.gm. This Gambian-run operator often runs Roots and heritage tours.

Discovery Tours Bakau ☏ 449 5551, ⓦ www.discoverytours.gm. Professional outfit with a good

Fishing trips

The Gambia is still a top **fishing** destination for beginners and experts alike, even though its waters have been over-fished by illegal trawlers in recent years. The country attracts serious enthusiasts, including the celebrity angler **John Wilson**, and the unofficial world record for the heaviest line-caught Atlantic tarpon (38kg and well over 2m long) was made here. The **West African Shore Fishing Festival** is held in The Gambia every year in November, a major competitive event with a £40,000 prize fund; for details contact World Sport Fishing in the UK (☏ 01480/403293, ⓦ www.worldsportfishing.com).

For **inexperienced anglers**, a number of tour companies and one-man-and-a-boat operators can arrange **fishing trips** lasting from a couple of hours to a day, usually launching from near Denton Bridge, Oyster Creek, to explore the mangrove-lined waterways near Banjul (see p.147). Rods, bait and lures are provided and you stand a good chance of catching some of the commonest fish, such as ladyfish, snapper, catfish or mullet – some trip operators promise "no fish, no fee".

Experienced anglers will probably prefer the assistance of a specialist **fishing charter company**, who can provide fully equipped boats, tackle, bait and expert guides as required. You can choose between high-adrenaline **Atlantic sport fishing** for sailfish, dorado, tuna, barracuda jacks and tarpon (generally on a catch-and-release basis); **creek fishing** in the Tanbi Wetlands (sailing from near Denton bridge) for smaller saltwater species; and **freshwater fishing** up-river (notably at Janjanbureh) for prize species such as tigerfish and arius and clarius catfish. Boat fishing is possible all year round, conditions permitting; tarpon are caught during the rainy season.

You can also fish from the **beaches** anywhere along the Atlantic coast for tarpon, guitarfish (like sand sharks), captainfish, groupers and rays. October to May is the best time of year for this, particularly November and December. When on the beaches you should be prepared to deal with bumsters. Sanyang is a favourite beach-angling spot, as the hassle here is far less than in the northern Kombos, the fishing is decent, and there are some great beach bars.

Recommended fishing charter companies include:

Gambia Sport Fishing Gambia Watersports Centre ☏ 777 4777, 778 3400 or 779 1799, UK contact ☏ 01509/569963, ⓦ www.gambiasportfishing.com. One of the best fishing operators in The Gambia.

Hooked on Gambia ☏ 777 4728, ⓦ www.hookedongambia.co.uk. British-run outfit offering low-impact fishing trips using small, well-equipped boats (suitable for two anglers).

Janneh Boating Fishing and Limo Hire Bakau, ☏ 449 7630 or 990 5894, ⓦ gambiafishing.tripod.com. Fully equipped boats available for private charter.

choice of group tours, including "Roots" river cruises and "Bush and Beach" safaris.

Faces and Places Kololi ☎ 446 2057 or 991 7343. Small, enlightened tour company promoting responsible and sustainable tourism in The Gambia.

Gambia River Excursions Bakau ☎ 449 4360, ⓦ www.gambiariver.com. Ground tour operator specializing in up-river boat trips. Also runs *Lamin Lodge*, and the "Birds and Breakfast" and "Sunset Cruise" boat trips.

Gambia Tourist Support Kololi ☎ 446 2476, ⓦ www.gambiatouristsupport.com. This enlightened charitable organization can organize tailor-made trips with an informal, personalized feel.

Gambia Tours Kololi ☎ 446 2601, ⓦ www .gambiatours.gm. Large company with a comprehensive list of group excursions, including "Roots", Janjanbureh, Tendaba, and shorter trips.

Gamtours Kanifing ☎ 437 2194, ⓦ www .gamtours.gm. Long-established Gambian-owned company with a standard selection of trips; can also take groups into Senegal to explore the Sine Saloum National Park or Dakar.

Paradise Tours Fajara ☎ 449 4088, mobile ☎ 992 0201, ⓦ www.paradiseisland-gambia.com. Arranges visits to *Madiyana Lodge* on Jinack Island, by *pirogue*.

RM Tours Kotu ☎ 446 2226, ⓦ www.rmtours.gm. Group excursions, including fishing, dolphin-spotting, and a "Gambia By Night" tour, plus tailor-made trips.

Tilly's Tours Kololi ☎ 770 7356. British-run company offering tailor-made trips.

West African Tours Bakau ☎ 449 5258, ⓦ www .westafricantours.com. A large, well-established and reliable operator, with excellent drivers and guides. Extensive programme of popular standard group excursions, including Roots, Treasure Island (Jinack), Makasutu, Janjanbureh, and Tendaba, plus some more unusual ones. If you'd like to plan a bespoke trip, they're an ideal first port of call.

Standard tours

Off-the-peg group tours from the resorts to The Gambia's attractions run every week (sometimes more than once a week) during the tourist season. They're aimed at the **average tourist** who wants an interesting and enjoyable trip that's not too arduous, and doesn't require special background knowledge or equipment. You'll be **collected** from your hotel or another pre-arranged spot, and driven back there at the end of the trip. **Tour groups** vary in size but are typically 12–25 in number; organizers try and plan things

so that all the members of a group speak a common language.

These tours are not for everybody of course – they can give you a quick, fun look around, but won't generally give you an in-depth insight into Gambian ecology, tradition or lifestyles. And the size of groups makes one-to-one discussion with the guide difficult. Guides are for the most part trained not to be over-pushy, sticking instead to a pre-planned patter, so it's only the most inquisitive groups that end up extracting detailed information from them. The trips will, however, answer at least some of your questions (plus a few that hadn't yet occurred to you), and possibly inspire you to plan your own, more personalized, travels in due course.

Trips **vary in length** from a couple of hours to a few days, and guides will cheerfully announce that all timings are GMT – "Gambia Maybe Time" – preparing you for unexpected delays on route. Having said this, most trips are very efficiently run – the guides and drivers follow tried and tested schedules, and you may, if anything, be left wishing there'd been more time to dawdle. **Payment** for the trip is generally made in hard currency, in advance, but not normally before you arrive in The Gambia. Most tourists **book excursions** through tourist hotel reps – who earn a commission on the sale – but there's nothing to stop you approaching one of the operators direct, particularly if a tour that interests you doesn't feature on your rep's day-by-day programme. You're likely to pay the same price however you book. Depending on the length of trip, meals may be included. Your only **expenses** during the trip will be drinks, souvenirs, and tips for the driver and guide. The prices below are approximate.

Abuko Nature Reserve Half-day; £15/€22. A short guided walk around the forest, with time to admire the trees and plants, and hopefully spot monkeys, birds and crocodiles. See p.143.

Banjul Highlights (Orientation and City Tour) Half-day; £15/€22. A brief introduction to Banjul and northern Kombo district, the idea being that you can come back under your own steam later for a longer look at anything that appeals. Stops include Banjul's Arch 22, National Museum, and Albert Market, plus possibly a local school, Banjul Brewery, a batik "factory", and the Katchikali crocodile pool. See p.98.

Birds and Breakfast or **Sunset Cruise** Morning or late afternoon; £23/€34. Enjoyable cruises by dugout canoe and/or double-decker cruising *pirogue* through the mangrove creeks of the Tanbi Wetlands, near Banjul, with a stop at *Lamin Lodge*, a wonderful rickety timber bar-restaurant on stilts. See p.148.

Bush and Beach (4WD Adventure) Full day; £30–34/€45–51. Thoroughly recommended, these trips pack a lot of experiences into a day, driving round the Kombos in a safari truck. You'll get to see a slice of real-life urban and rural Gambia, meet people living in a family compound, and visit a village school; you'll get driven through the bush and have lunch on the beach, plus a visit to the excellent Tanje Village Museum and the village's busy fishing centre. See p.166.

Camel Safari and Beach Barbecue Half-day; £25/€36.50. A very touristy option – you'll head down to Tanji where camels will take you along the beach for half an hour or so, two punters per beast. Humans and camels then lunch and relax before lumbering back again. See p.167.

Champagne and Caviar Full day; £27/€40. A luxurious way to explore the Tanbi wetlands, near Banjul in a double-decker *pirogue*. The caviar may or may not materialize but you'll certainly be well looked after. See p.145.

Creek Fishing Half-day; £23/€33.50. A chance to mess about in boats and haul something wriggly out of the mangrove creeks near Banjul. See p.145.

Gambia River Excursions One to three days, from £45/€66. Cruising by river from Tendaba to Janjanbureh, or from Janjanbureh to Basse, you travel by rustic double-decker *pirogue* past lush riverside jungle, stopping at remote villages and markets. Nights are spent mid-river, sleeping on deck under the stars on mattresses with mosquito nets. Highly recommended. See Chapters 4 & 5.

Janjanbureh Two days and one night; £75/$120. A whistlestop visit to Janjanbureh Island. Groups usually stay at either *Janjang Bureh Camp* or *Bird Safari Camp*, both good bases for birdwatching and river swimming, with campfire entertainment from local drummers and dancers. See p.241.

Jinack Island (Paradise or Treasure Island) Full day; £38/€55. After taking the ferry to Barra on the River Gambia's north bank, you visit a remote rural village near the Senegalese border, then cruise the waterways of the southern Saloum Delta to Jinack Island, with lunch on the beach. See p.201.

Juffureh, Albreda and James Island (Roots) Full day; £24–37/€35–54. Very popular excursion. Most tour groups get to Albreda, Juffureh and James Island by river cruise from Banjul, but it's also possible to cross from Banjul to Barra by ferry and continue overland. You visit the village, meet members of the Kinte family (made famous by Alex Haley's novel *Roots*), and visit the slave trade museum and Fort James. See p.193.

Makasutu Culture Forest plus Brikama craft market or jam-making centre Full day; £35/€51. Includes a guided woodland stroll and quiet cruise by dugout *pirogue* along the beautiful Mandina Bolon. After an African buffet lunch, there's spirited singing and dancing from local women. The visit to Brikama is basically a souvenir stop. See p.175.

Makasutu Bushtrackers' Breakfast Morning; £27/€39. With an early start and a limit of six people per guide, this woodland walk offers far better wildlife-watching opportunities than the standard Makasutu excursion. Includes a campfire breakfast. See p.178.

Makasutu Evening Extravaganza Evening; £35/€51. In the atmospheric surroundings of Makasutu's Base Camp, deep in the bush, guests are treated to a generous barbecue with spirited entertainment from jugglers, acrobats, drummers and dancers – and are invited to join in. See p.178.

Sport Fishing Full day; £25/$40. Aimed at experienced anglers, sport fishing trips take you out into the mouth of the River Gambia or to the Atlantic reefs, fishing for jacks, ladyfish, butterfish, red snapper and barracuda. See p.147.

Tendaba Two days and one night; £60/$96. A trip to *Tendaba Camp*, a large riverside lodge with a swimming pool, around four hours' drive from the coast along bumpy roads, with opportunities to visit Kiang West National Park and Bao Bolon Wetland Reserve. See p.217.

Working Day Half day; £15/€22. Offering an insight into a few of the tougher realities of urban life in The Gambia, this illuminating tour takes in Serrekunda, with a visit to the batik "factory", then moves on to the SOS Children's Village in Bakoteh and the Sukuta Health Centre and Maternity Clinic. See p.134.

Official tourist guides

Official tourist guides (OTGs) are badged and uniformed freelance guides who have gone through a selection and training procedure, and abide by a code of conduct. The OTG scheme arose partly as a solution to the bumster problem (see opposite); a number of bumsters were selected to be trained up to be OTGs, thus "legalizing" a role they had already adopted for themselves.

You can book one for anything from a simple assignment like showing you around

The Gambian term "**bumster**" refers to touts, fixers, chancers, gigolos, wheeler-dealers, informal guides and guardian angels – you'll find them wherever you find tourists, unless they've been specifically banned or driven away. Their **services** range from showing you around, fixing up deals on taxis, trips and foreign exchange, and general chaperoning, to being your best friend (and more) throughout your stay, barely leaving your side.

Gambian bumsters tend to be a dignified lot, with a highly developed sense of self-worth: they believe they are offering an honest and useful service, and as such should have the same rights as any tourism workers. The truth is that most are **school drop-outs** who are smart enough to realize that there's far more money to be made out of offering services to tourists than from any of the other options available to them. Some see "bumstering" as a way to accumulate enough capital to enable them to start their own business; others hope that it's only a matter of time before they meet the European or American benefactor who will make their dreams come true; others are simply desperate for quick cash to fund a drug habit.

The classic **bumster-tourist relationship** is the partnering of young, attractive rastas with middle-aged white women. Some of these liaisons are innocent and completely genuine, but some are founded on a basis of pre-arranged mutual exploitation, for sex and money. The Gambia has plenty of stories of European women who have fallen in love with Gambians and arranged their passage to Europe, only for them to turn abusive or disappear without trace, or of young Gambians (male and female) who have been promised the world by a tourist, who in the end fails to deliver.

If you take on a bumster, you are guaranteed an adventure of sorts. Sometimes their **assistance** can be useful; they can be great company, and will ensure you're not hassled by others. Yet, however friendly bumsters may seem, some completely fail to deliver (many, for example, are worse than useless as guides) and they're all in it for the money. Get all the **negotiation** done in advance to avoid misunderstandings later, and be cautious – not all bumsters are as honest as they make out.

Visitors who have no interest in hiring a bumster can find them **intimidating** and manipulative. Bumsters on the make will barge up to tourists, butt into conversations, and start hustling, using a catalogue of standard chat-up lines. A favourite is to feign recognition, hoping the tourist will be too embarrassed to admit they don't remember them. Annoying though this may be, bumsters are **rarely dangerous**, and it doesn't take long to devise your own strategy for dealing with them. If somebody invades your space, tell them plainly that you didn't invite them and you have no work for them: in Gambian society it's rude to impose yourself on somebody uninvited. You may have to harden yourself to a little verbal abuse – many bumsters are quick to call anyone who rebuffs them a racist – but it almost certainly won't lead to anything.

Some visitors have said that they will never return to The Gambia because they found the bumsters so enervating. With passions boiling about the threat this poses to the Gambian tourist industry, the government has over recent years been engaged in a **major crackdown** targeting anyone caught hassling tourists or suspected of doing so. Uniformed members of the Tourism Security Unit patrol all the main tourist areas. Treatment of offenders tends to be harsh in the extreme – once arrested by paramilitary guards they may be subjected to severe verbal and physical abuse followed by a spell behind bars or in community service. Once-bitten bumsters who, through sheer defiance, continue to ply their trade are well aware of the risks and will quickly slope off if you reproach them with a stern "Don't bumster me."

the local market, to something more involved such as accompanying you on an up-country trip lasting several days. Their fees are fixed at D250/£5 per half day or D400/£8 per full day; it's best to negotiate incidental expenses in advance.

OTGs can be invaluable, taking you to places you may not otherwise have discovered, introducing you to local customs, and acting as a **translator**. On the other hand, going around with a uniformed OTG makes it all-too-obvious you're a tourist. Furthermore, their training is not exhaustive – your guide's knowledge of history and culture may be as sketchy as the average untrained bumster's.

Most OTGs are based at the **OTG station** in Kololi (near the *Kairaba* and *Senegambia* hotels). There's another station in Juffureh/ Albreda, and more are planned for elsewhere in the country. One particularly enterprising OTG has compiled a website, ⊛www.gambia tourguides.co.uk, with plenty of suggestions for trips and activities plus contact details for himself and many of his colleagues.

National parks and reserves

The Gambia is not a safari destination in the same league as East or southern African countries. It does, however, have large stretches of unspoilt wilderness, and several national parks managed by the Department of Parks and Wildlife Management that are worth taking in if you're interested in seeing West African fauna.

There are a number of good wildlife-watching locations, such as the protected areas at Abuko and Bijilo, within walking, cycling or taxi-ride distance of the resort hotels. Elsewhere, you'll need to have your own transport, or be part of a guided tour, to reach the best areas. Once you're there, there are plenty of opportunities for exploration without a vehicle (avoiding disruption and noise), either on foot, walking through the bush, or by boat, exploring the river or the miles of mangrove creeks. Most of the reserves have very little in the way of visitor infrastructure, though – their primary purpose is conservation, rather than tourism.

Growing awareness in the 1960s and 1970s of the long-term detrimental effects of hunting and deforestation led to the establishment of The Gambia's first **reserves**. None of the reserves has much in the way of tourist infrastructure, and only Abuko receives more than a trickle of visitors. However, each reserve has a distinctive character, and visitor numbers are likely to increase when the roads are improved, making them more accessible.

All of The Gambia's government-managed protected areas have the same fixed **entrance fee** (D31.50), and all are open daily from 8am–6pm; special permission may be requested to visit outside these hours (visiting at dawn, at dusk and at night yield different experiences). For further information on parks and reserves, contact the Department of Parks and Wildlife Management, ☎447 2888, ✉wildlife@gamtel.gm. A growing number of smaller woodland and wilderness areas are now being managed as community-run reserves, some of which, notably Pirang Forest Park, Brufut Woods and Kunkilling Forest Park, provide first-class birdwatching. There's also a plan in the

For information on guides and organized wildlife tours, see p.48. For more on habitats and species, see pp.292–295, and p.17.

pipeline to create a major new community-run protected area in Kombo district, the Ballabu Conservation Area, running all the way from the Tanbi Wetlands down to Pirang.

Abuko Nature Reserve The Gambia's first protected area, Abuko is close to the resorts and small enough at well under two square kilometres to be explored comfortably on foot, and it includes dense evergreen gallery forest and Guinea savannah, with an impressive population of birds, monkeys and reptiles (see p.143).

Bao Bolon Wetland Reserve At around 220 square kilometres, this is The Gambia's largest protected area and one of the least-visited, with a fascinating range of habitats, including desert-like salt marshes and beautiful, bird-rich creeks forested with towering mangroves. It can be visited by boat from Tendaba, or by private vehicle from the Kerewan–Farafenni road (see p.226).

Bijilo Forest Park Very close to the Senegambia area hotels and easily strolled around on foot, this tiny park (half a square kilometre) is a good place to spot monkeys (see p.134).

Kanilai Game Park A small park holding a number of species, run by President Jammeh outside his home village in Foni District (see p.214).

Kiang West National Park Riverside woodland habitat, 115 square kilometres in extent, with baboons, bush pig, various antelope and a host of bird species, commonly explored by vehicle from Tendaba (see p.219).

Niumi National Park Situated on The Gambia's northern Atlantic coast, and including Jinack Island, this RAMSAR-recognized park is noted for its untouched stands of mangroves, explored by boat from Banjul or Jinack (see p.201).

River Gambia National Park Formerly known as Baboon Islands National Park, this is a group of five lushly forested, protected midriver islands, downstream from Janjanbureh. The islands are home to a colony of rehabilitated chimpanzees; if you're passing by boat, you may catch a glimpse of the primates from the river. To enjoy the river environment to the full, a stay at the Chimpanzee Rehabilitation Project Visitor Camp is highly recommended. This is an excellent area for birdwatching, and you may also spot hippos and even manatees (see p.240).

Tanji River (Karinti) Bird Reserve In a country famed for its birdlife, this walkable area of just over six square kilometres is the only officially protected bird reserve, and it includes the offshore Bijol Islands, an important breeding colony for birds and turtles, which can only be visited by DPWM boat (see p.167).

Accommodation

Most tourist visitors to The Gambia have hotels pre-booked for the duration of their stay, as part of a flight-plus-accommodation package, but it's perfectly possible to take an ad-hoc approach to finding accommodation, allowing your itinerary to be flexible. At certain times of year (particularly at the peak holiday times of Christmas, New Year and Easter) the busiest tourist hotels are all booked in advance – and the most popular places may be completely sold out throughout the season – but it's always possible to find somewhere to stay if you're happy to look a little off the beaten track, and not limit yourself to the hotels used by the tour operators.

The vast majority of **tourist hotels** are concentrated in the resort area in **Kombo district**, west of Banjul and Serrekunda. Despite this high density of accommodation, even the busiest resort areas are low-key and uncrowded, and development has, for the most part, been sympathetic to the environment. The Gambia doesn't have any towering concrete monstrosities; even the largest hotels (accommodating well over four hundred people in the high season) are well-landscaped, with tropical trees and flowering shrubs.

The area of fastest tourist development outside the resort areas is the **southwestern coast** – the stretch of empty beaches running from Bijilo down to Kartong, near the Senegalese border. Even here, development has progressed at a gentle pace, with rustic **guesthouses** and **lodges**, their sophistication partly limited by the shortage of services in this area. This is now changing, and options are likely to increase greatly.

In addition to the coastal resorts, there's a small number of **riverside lodges** and **up-country hotels** catering for adventurous, ecologically aware visitors.

At the budget end, on the fringes of the resort areas and up-country, you'll find a few **tourist guesthouses** catering for backpackers and independent travellers looking for a down-to-earth place to stay which feels distinctively African.

It's also possible to find **informal lodgings with local people**, useful if you're really travelling on a shoestring, and a good way to experience local life. If you have appropriate connections (or are prepared to make some), you can also stay in mission houses and NGO or volunteer rest houses.

Finally, **camping** is a viable option if you're fully equipped, although there is only one formal campsite as such, in Sukuta near Serrekunda.

Major tourist hotels

Most of The Gambia's **major hotels** are designed to appeal to tourists visiting for a week or two's relaxation in the sun. As such, they're fun, informal places, where the rooms themselves may be nothing special but plenty of thought has gone into creating appealing pool, bar, restaurant and beach areas – the places where you'll spend most of your waking hours.

Facilities and levels of service tend to be modest by international standards, so tour operators use their own locally specific grading systems to distinguish between the top-end, mid-range, and budget hotels. All have swimming pools, restaurants, bars, and rooms with private bath or shower. In some, extras such as air-conditioning (AC), TV and the use of a safe are not automatically included without additional payments, and payments for AC can be up to about £5 (€7.50) per day.

The **atmosphere**, style, and nationality mix of the hotels varies greatly. One subtle factor to bear in mind is how "African" you'd like your stay to feel. Some hotels have gone so far to cater for Western tastes that they've lost all sense of their surroundings, while others have a distinctively African atmosphere, in their decor and the attitude of the staff.

If you're booking a short break in The Gambia, it's worth considering just going for the **cheapest possible option**, staying there for your first night, then, if it's not to your taste, writing off the cost of the other nights and moving on somewhere else, possibly to a small independent hotel or an up-country lodge.

Accommodation price codes

Accommodation prices in this book are coded; the prices refer to the rate you can expect to pay for a double or twin room for two people. Single rooms, or single occupancy, will normally cost at least two-thirds of the twin-occupancy rate, but bear in mind there's often a chance to negotiate a better deal.

In the resort area, you can often get a fairly basic place, usually without air-con and certainly without hot water, for under D500 (£10/€15). For a simple but decent twin room with clean sheets, air conditioning and self-contained, private shower room, expect to pay D750–1000 (£15–20/€22–30). A night at a tourist hotel with air-con and good facilities is likely to start at £20/€30. The top-end places, at well over £50/€75 per night, offer international-class luxuries – Gambian style.

- ❶ Under £10/€15
- ❷ £10–15/€15–22
- ❸ £15–20/€22–30
- ❹ £20–30/€30–45
- ❺ £30–40/€45–60
- ❻ £40–50/€60–75
- ❼ £50-80/€75-120
- ❽ Over £80/€120

Some tourist hotels are **block-booked** by tour operators, but others are available to independent travellers, and discounts are sometimes on offer to walk-in clients. Tourist hotels that stay open off-season (June–Oct) generally operate lower tariffs at these times.

Small independent tourist hotels

If you're travelling independently, rather than booking a package, you'll discover that most of the tourist hotels ignored by the tour operators are much more affordable than those splashed across the glossy brochures. Some of the small **independent tourist hotels** in Bakau, Fajara, Kotu and Kololi are among the most pleasant and interesting places to stay in the whole country. Sometimes tour operators don't send their package tourists to these places merely because their pool is small, or they're not right on the beach (a drawback shared by several of the big package places incidentally).

Small independent hotels tend not to have extensive activity programmes but they're generally much more **tourist-oriented** than urban hotels and hostels. They attract a mixture of locals, expats and discerning independent travellers and make a very good choice if you're looking for a place that's relatively quiet.

Self-catering accommodation

Self-catering accommodation is really taking off in the resort areas. Some places have a pool, restaurant and bar; others are aimed at those for whom the extras laid on by the tourist hotels have no great appeal. A self-catering mini-apartment tends to be much more spacious than a hotel room, and even if you end up eating out all the time rather than cooking for yourself, having a fridge is useful. When choosing self-catering accommodation, check how close it is to shops, markets, restaurants and local transport routes.

Tourist guesthouses

The Gambia's **tourist guesthouses** cater for independent travellers looking for a good-value, down-to-earth place to stay which feels distinctively African. They tend not to

be located in the prime resort areas, but are mostly found on the fringes of the resorts, a walk away from the beaches, or on the less-developed southern Atlantic coast.

Some guesthouses are in **blocks** like West African urban compounds, or in **thatched roundhouses** in a garden compound. Furnishings are simple (a mattress on a built-in platform for a bed, possibly some locally made cane chairs and batik fabrics). You may or may not have private washing facilities and electricity. Hot water is rare, but at most times of year you're unlikely to miss it.

Urban hotels

Every large Gambian town has simple **urban lodgings** aimed at locals rather than foreign tourists. Standards vary a great deal but the good ones can be excellent places to stay and offer a much more grass-roots experience of The Gambia than the tourist hotels.

Outside Banjul and the resorts, there's not much local market for Western-style hotels. **Small-town hotels**, particularly the cheapest dives, are usually equated with drinking and prostitution. Rooms are often taken for a few hours only, and there may well be a gang of women and toddlers permanently in residence. Don't be put off unduly; these can be lively places, and by no means all are intimidating for female travellers – though you may have to pick a room carefully for anything like a quiet night.

Although there are no internationally affiliated youth hostels in West Africa, you'll find a YMCA **hostel** in Kanifing, near Serrekunda.

Up-country riverside and bush lodges

It's much easier to find people and places unaffected by tourism up-country than on the coast. If you have time, an up-country stay is highly recommended. You can enjoy the River Gambia to the full by staying at one of the **up-country riverside lodges** catering for birdwatchers, fishing enthusiasts, and anyone keen to spend time in the bush. There are also **bush lodges** away from the river; their facilities vary from simple to luxurious, but all have bags of character, and can be memorable places to stay.

At present, the **choice** of up-country tourist accommodation is very limited; this

Cheap hotel practicalities

Ask to **see the room** first. Check the essentials, such as the mosquito screening on the windows and state of the bathroom, and keep asking to see more rooms until you're satisfied.

It's worth **haggling** over the price of a room. If there's AC or a fan but no electricity, or if you'll be staying for a few days, ask for a discount. Check there'll be no tax on top. You usually pay on taking the room and may have to leave your passport with the person in charge if there's no registration card to fill out.

During the **cold weather** of the harmattan (generally Jan–Feb), ask for a bucket of hot water to supplement the cold tap.

should change as the road network improves and The Gambia's popularity as an ecotourism destination takes hold.

Staying with locals

If you have friends in The Gambia, or are happy to scout about for an invitation, **lodging** in a **family compound** is a great way to experience Gambian daily life. As a holiday option, such experiences can vary enormously, and depend as much on the outlook and expectations of the guests as on the hosts. All over the country you'll run into people who might want to put you up for the night. A warm, but more noticeably, a *dutiful* **hospitality** characterizes most of these contacts: to Gambians it would be unthinkable not to treat a stranded traveller royally. Single travellers who get into conversation on public transport are most likely to receive invitations. Your hosts are typically a low-income family, and you'll be expected to correspond later and send photographs.

It's sometimes difficult to know how to **repay** such hospitality, particularly since it often seems so disruptive of family life, with you set up in the master bedroom and kids sent running for special things for the guest. In the resort areas it would be normal to offer a daily payment roughly equivalent to the price of a room in a basic local guest house in exchange for bed and board; in rural areas you might like to offer the whole family something special. While it's impossible to generalize, for female guests a trip to the market with the woman or women of the household is an opportunity to pay for

everything. Men can't do this, but buying a sack of rice (get it delivered by barrow or porter) makes a generous gift.

Camping

Away from the coastal resorts, **pitching a tent** is unproblematic if you have your own transport. Despite a fairly high population density, you can find secluded spots off the main roads where you can camp for a night and enjoy the bush. Don't assume you can always do this anonymously, though, particularly with a car: a vehicle in the deep bush is unusual and noisy and people will flock round to watch you.

Bush-camping is easier if you're cycling or walking. Bring the lightest tent you can afford. You may still be visited by delegations of machete-wielding villagers, but satisfaction that you're harmless is usually their first concern. Some cigarettes or a cup of tea breaks any ice.

In more heavily populated or farmed districts it's best to **ask someone** before pitching a tent. It's safe to assume that every plot of land belongs to somebody; approaching them may well lead to an invitation to stay in their compound. Out in the wilds, hard or thorny ground is likely to be the only obstacle. Fill your water bottles from a village before looking for a site.

If you're travelling by **public transport**, it's a lot harder to camp. Vehicles go from town to town and it's hard to arrange to be dropped off at just the right spot in between. Heading out of town to find a place to camp, you could end up walking for miles.

Eating and drinking

If you're staying in the resort area for most of your time in The Gambia, you'll find no shortage of places to eat and drink, but you may have to search around to find traditional Gambian cooking.

Most of the **tourist restaurants** aim to appeal to the broadest possible clientele by offering "international" menus, and the results are often disappointing. By far the best way to sample authentic Gambian food is to be invited to a Gambian home. Alternatively, you could do as the locals do when they're away from home in the daytime, and eat at one of the inconspicuous **local restaurants** or streetside stalls found in the commercial districts of every town. It helps to know where to look and what to ask for, so going with a guide or a Gambian friend can help you find very inexpensive food that's fresh, tasty and nutritious.

The Gambia lacks a well-defined **cuisine**, partly because supplies can be erratic, and recipes aren't written down, so no two meals ever taste quite the same. Even so, there's a considerable variety of culinary pleasures, and a huge range of intoxicating drinks.

The resort area **bar scene** is growing rapidly, with many different tastes catered for, from conventional hotel bars and relaxed poolside bars to English-style pubs, intimate cocktail bars and pre-club joints with loud music and a flashy clientele.

Traditional Gambian food

The great thing about **Gambian food** – if you're hungry – is its massive calorific value. Although less bulky alternatives are usually available, most meals consist of a pile of the staple diet plus a sauce or stew. By far the Gambians' favourite **staple** is **rice**, but **couscous**, tiny grains of durum wheat flour known locally as **coos**, is also common, as are root crops such as **cassava**.

Sauces can be based on **palm oil** (thick, copper-coloured and harvested from the oil palm trees found all along the Gambian coast and in the better watered areas up-country), on **groundnut paste** (local peanut butter), **okra** (five-sided, green pods with a high slime content which is much appreciated), various **beans**, and the **leaves** of sweet potatoes and cassava among others. All are usually spiced, often with **chillies,** and seasoned with stock cubes. The more expensive, or festive, "sauces" contain **fish**, **beef**, **chicken** or **mutton**. Beef and chicken, being relatively pricey, may be reserved for special occasions; **eggs** are always available. Wild boar ("bush pig") and large, herbivorous rodents ("bush rat"), the commonest varieties of bush meat, can be delicious, if carefully prepared.

Most tourist hotels have a weekly Gambian **buffet evening** which is a great opportunity to try out a range of Gambian specialities. One standard is **chicken yassa** – chicken marinaded with onion, lime, garlic and chilli served with rice – delicious when prepared well, but sometimes just casseroled fowl with a searing sauce. **Domodah** (in Mandinka) or **mafe** (in Wolof) is invariably good, a rich peanut stew often made with palm oil, bitter tomatoes and chicken or beef, again served with rice.

Jollof rice is a rice and palm oil dish usually cooked with beef (or sometimes fish), tomato puree and vegetables – peppers, aubergine, carrots and squash. **Benachin** (which means "one pot" in Wolof) is a chunky fish stew, essentially fish and rice, sometimes with vegetables. **M'bahal rice**, another Wolof rice dish, is made with dried fish mashed together with groundnuts and peppers – dry, hot and spicy. **Plasas** is a tasty okra- or cassava-leaf and palm-oil sauce with dried fish and sometimes meat.

The best feature on the coast is quantities of fresh **fish and seafood**: shrimps, ladyfish (like sole), butterfish, meaty barracuda if you're in luck, and excellent chowders and bisques in a few places. Gambians are keen on grilling food over charcoal, and some of their most delicious meals are the simplest – such as grilled barracuda steak with salad, or seafood kebabs. The commonest Gambian fish is the **bonga**, which doesn't often appear on tourist menus because it's so bony, but, once smoked, can be ground to make a delicious paté.

You'll find quite good French-style **bread** all over, the two commonest varieties known locally as *tapalapa* and *senfour*. **Pies** – resembling Britain's Cornish pasties, but fried like samosas – seem to be a leftover of colonial influence; they're found in meat and fish varieties, and are often surprisingly tasty. **Fruit** you can get just about everywhere (see p.62).

Where to eat

Bakau, Fajara, Kotu and Kololi all have a variety of **restaurants**; Fajara has the greatest concentration of quality places, and the Senegambia area of Kololi is the busiest, brashest strip. All of the major hotels, and many of the small independent places, have at least one restaurant.

There's a far greater choice of eating places in the Gambian **resort area** than anywhere else in the country. If you leave the coast and head up-river, you will find virtually no tourist restaurants except at the hotels (which are few in themselves). Even Banjul has very few restaurants, since eating out does not figure prominently in typical Gambian family or business life. Every town has **local eateries** that are cheap enough for the pockets of most Gambians, but these are aimed largely at people on the move, and local workers who don't have the opportunity to go back to their compound for lunch.

An alternative source of quick and tasty calories when you're in a town is to eat **street food**, which is sometimes superb. But if you're ever invited to eat in a **family compound** then all previous experiences of Gambian food are likely to pale into insignificance – home cooking can be truly excellent.

Tourist restaurants

Few Gambian **hotel** and **tourist restaurants** qualify as anything better than mediocre, but a handful are excellent. In the resort area, you'll never be more than a short taxi ride away from the better places, most of which are in Fajara and Kololi. Styles of food represented – with varying success – include American, Chinese, Thai, Japanese, Indian, Lebanese, Italian, traditional international and modern international. Most concentrate on tried-and-tested standards like steaks, pizzas, curries, grilled fish, salads, and chips with everything. Very few tourist restaurants make a big feature of traditional Gambian food.

A main course at a modest tourist restaurant is likely to be priced around D100–250 (£2–5/€3–7.50) and the most expensive places charge D300-500 (£6–10/€9–15).

Beach bars

Beach bars tend to be rustic, bohemian places serving simple, fresh **food**, typically grilled fish and chips. In a country where the vast majority of meals served to tourists use at least some frozen ingredients, it's refreshing to go to a beach bar and know that you can order fish that was caught only hours earlier. You may, of course, have to wait a while for it to arrive.

For more about beach bars in Kombo district, see p.133 and p.164. A plate of fish and chips is likely to set you back less than D150 (£3/€4.50).

Local restaurants

Most towns, even the smallest, have at least one or two **basic restaurants** or **chop shops**. However unpromising these may look from the outside, it's definitely worth checking some of them out. Some are inconspicuous, others more obvious with jaunty hand-painted signs, but they all offer a genuine African experience, with simple, but often excellent food at rock-bottom prices – typically less than D50 (£1/€1.50) for a plate of whatever is on offer that day.

If they have a **menu** at all, it might be a blackboard with a list of choices of which most are not available on the day of your visit. But don't be put off – it's normal for such places to just serve one or two dishes of the day, and they do them well. It's natural to feel hesitant over what you eat in small restaurants where you can't be certain of the freshness or provenance of your food, rather than at street stalls where it's all cooked before your eyes. Places packed with locals are usually a good bet.

Local restaurants sometimes have a few **tables** in a courtyard, or **benches** outside at the front, but Gambians in general prefer to eat in seclusion rather than in public, so it's normal to be seated on a bench inside one of these hot, dark, smoky boxes, at a shared, plastic-covered table.

The Gambia has local **fast-food joints**, too. Some are as forgettable as fast-food joints anywhere (the international chains are, to date, still absent), but some are pretty good. **Lebanese places**, providing snacks and sandwiches, especially *chawarma* – spit-grilled mutton in pitta bread – are almost as common as burger franchises in the US.

Afra barbecues

Gambians everywhere love **afra**. It's a simple formula common to many African countries – you choose a cut of meat from a joint hanging from a hook in the shop. It's chopped up in front of you, seasoned, flung on a grill to sizzle over hot embers in a wood-fired furnace, then, when done, doused with mustard and/or sauce and wrapped up in brown paper, for you to eat in your fingers, with fresh *tapalapa* bread. The price depends on the quantity of meat you order, typically starting at under D50 (£1/€1.50). Though essentially fast food, there are *afra* places that have benches and tables and something of a restaurant feel. *Afra* is almost exclusively a **late-night** habit for Gambians, especially after a night out clubbing.

Street food

Gambian street food is certainly worth trying, but you won't normally find much in the resorts. The best hunting grounds are the busy commercial and market areas of any town.

The secret is to **eat early** (11am–noon) and dusk (5–6pm), when most people eat and food is fresh. Street food isn't usually a takeaway – there's often a table and benches, plastic bowls, spoons and cold water. Sometimes, though, you'll just find women with covered enamel bowls waiting

by the roadside or in the market for custom-ers. They may well have a different type of **stew** or **sauce** every day, to pour over rice or into bread to make a sandwich. You'll also find little **fritters** made from millet or rice flour, sometimes spicy, sometimes sweet. One snack that's pretty well universal is sticks of kebabed meat, often eaten as a sandwich in a piece of bread. Everything is extremely cheap: just a few dalasis. Anything extra you want – soft drinks, instant coffee – can be fetched for you from nearby.

If you're travelling you're likely to adopt the habit of eating **breakfast** in the street. At roadside coffee stands you'll get excellent hot Nescafé, shaken up to give it a cappuc-cino-style froth, with margarine-smothered bread or omelette. But be ready to say so promptly if you want your coffee black or – big shock to local people – without sugar. As it's sometimes made with sweetened condensed milk, white-no-sugar can be a problem.

Vegetarian food

Traditionally, The Gambia makes no concessions to **vegetarians**, for whom eating ready-prepared food, whether on the street or in all but a few restaurants, is unrewarding. Animal protein is the focus of most dishes, and even where it's apparently absent (for example, in vegetable *domo-dah*) there's likely to be some meat or fish stock somewhere – rice is often cooked in it. This means, if you're strictly vegetar-ian, you're mostly going to have to choose your restaurants carefully, or stick to eggs, market fruit and veg and any food you cook for yourself.

Peanuts, boiled or roasted, and locally ground peanut butter are a good source of vegetable protein. **Cheese** is hard to find, except, imported, in supermarkets, but even when you're away from the resort areas, where the supermarkets are concentrated, bread, margarine, canned **milk** in various forms (and milk powder) and **hard-boiled eggs** are always easily obtainable, as are, often, delicious **soured milk** and **yoghurt**.

Vegetarians who are the **guests** of Gambian families have a hard time – with such status attached to meat, vegetarianism is regarded as an alien philosophy.

Communal eating

If you're lucky enough to be staying **with a family**, or just visiting for the day or for a special ceremony, you're likely to experience well-prepared and tasty food – though according to their means this may depend on how much you contribute.

In homes or at work, people eat around a **communal dish**. In strictly Islamic families it's always males at one, females at another (although foreign women tend to be treated as honorary men). Everybody **washes their hands** first, generally with water poured from a kettle, and the bowl or bowls are placed on a mat on the floor. These will contain mounds of rice or couscous with sauce poured on top and vegetables, meat or fish balanced in the middle.

Take off your shoes (it's polite to do this before stepping onto any mat in a Gambian home) and sit down by the bowl, following the example of your hosts. Even if you're not hungry, it's impolite to refuse an offer of food, so you should at least taste a little. You may be offered a spoon; if not, you eat with your right hand only (this is a strict rule), helping yourself from the part of the bowl nearest you, mashing some rice or couscous into a ball in your fingers and rolling it in a little sauce. You may find that your hosts politely nudge the choice bits of meat or vegetables from the centre of the bowl towards you.

It's normal to eat in silence (punctuated by the occasional polite belch and compliments to the host, remarking how wonderfully "hot" or "sweet" the food is), and for everyone to finish in order of age, the eldest first. You get up and leave the bowl as soon as you're finished.

Communal eating is such an integral part of Gambian social interaction that it's no great surprise that restaurants, where someone goes and buys a meal for themselves and eats separately from their companions, are not all that common away from the tourist areas.

Fruit and nuts

Fruit and nuts make for satisfying eating in The Gambia. Most hotels make a big feature of fruit at breakfast time, but, unfortunately, only a few bars serve fresh juices, sticking instead to bottled soft drinks or imported juice from cartons. There are plenty of juice-sellers serving made-to-order concoctions from stalls on the resort beaches, but these are all too often watery and over-sweet.

It's very easy to find fruit, peanuts and cashews at **markets** and **on the street**, from itinerant traders with trays on their heads, and on the beach at stalls. Some stalls sell **coconuts**, in slices or whole, with the top lopped off for you to drink the juice. Locally-grown bananas, coconuts and pawpaws are available all year round, but other fruit is seasonal: mangoes are everywhere from June to September, and most other fruit ripens in the dry season.

Local **bananas** come in several varieties, all wonderfully flavoured, including the thin-skinned dwarf ones sometimes called "apple bananas". **Pawpaw** trees are common

although Gambians don't eat pawpaws much. They're very good (and good for you) with lime juice. Gambian **mangoes** are delicious and come in many varieties, but most tourists miss them as they ripen in the rainy season. African varieties of **citrus fruit** are very sweet, particularly **grapefruit** and **limes**. From December to the end of the dry season, **oranges** (bright green when ripe) are abundant and available for next to nothing from women with trays or men with barrows and sharp knives. Gambians like them peeled with the pith left on so they can suck out the juice. Also easy to grow in the Gambia are **watermelons** – you'll see mountains of them for sale by the roadside from November to January – sweet and thirst-quenching. **Pineapples**, however, are usually imported from other West African countries.

You'll come across several different grades and varieties of **dates**, especially during Ramadan, when they're a favourite part of breaking the fast after sunset. You'll also come across fruit which is more often used to make juices and cordials than eaten. There's the **ditah**, a little brown fruit with tasty, bright green juice, and the **tamarind**, available from January to March, and crushed to make *daharr* juice, which has a dark, treacly, sweet-sour flavour, and is sometimes added to *benachin* (see p.59).

Wonjo, not actually a fruit, but the flower-like crimson pods of the sorrel plant, is commonly cultivated in fields and gardens, and sold fresh or dried, to be steeped in water with sugar and (sometimes) mint to make a refreshing bright red cordial. The fruit of the **baobab** tree, ripe from around January, contains white seeds, which, when dried, are used as a sherbet for making *bwi* cordial or sorbet. The juice, naturally tart, is sometimes sweetened with sugar and flavoured with vanilla or banana essence.

Known locally as **groundnuts**, **peanuts** are harvested from November, when you'll see stacks of plants piled up in the fields. They can be eaten raw, fresh from the field, but are more commonly shelled and boiled or roasted then sold by the tin cupful (wrapped in paper) or small bagful as a snack. They're a primary ingredient in Gambian cooking. Look out for Gambian peanut brittle, sometimes sold by market, street and beach vendors.

Cashew nuts are sold in little bags by vendors everywhere, and cashew fruit are available in June and July. A single nut grows at the apex of each cashew "apple" which is too bitter to eat, but can be chewed for its delicious, light juice. In some parts this stuff is made into a potent hooch. It's best not to feast off cashew trees – they only have a small number of valuable nuts each and owners get very upset. Beware, too, of the staining properties of the juice.

Drinking

Gambian **tap water** is usually safe to drink (see Health p.38), though tour reps may try to convince you to drink nothing but **bottled water**. Supermarkets and some general stores carry large bottles of mineral water – The Gambia has its own quality brand called *Naturelle*, which is filtered, ozonized and bottled in Kanifing – but it's less common to find this in village shops.

For locals, probably the most widely consumed beverage in The Gambia – after water – is **green tea**, known locally as

attaya (see box, p.64). Apart from Nescafé, which is ubiquitous (the variety available in West Africa is strong and good), **coffee** is less popular, and real coffee rare except in some hotels and a few cafés in the resort areas. Various tea-like **infusions** are locally common. If you're drinking at a local coffee stand, you might come across one which is widely popular in West Africa (as a base for mixing in a lot of sweet concentrated canned milk): *kinkiliba*. It's reasonable on its own straight from the hot bucket or kettle, but don't mistake it for water and have Nescafé added, when it tastes disgusting (this would, however, raise no eyebrows as Gambians sometimes drink it this way).

When you can't get cold water, **soft drinks** (known as "softs") – especially Fanta orange, Sprite lemonade and Coke, all manufactured and bottled locally – are permanent stand-bys. In remote areas any establishment with electricity is almost bound to have a fridge of battered bottles (bottles are always returned to the wholesaler: *never* take the bottle away – this is serious theft!). Less-regularly available bottled sodas include fruit cocktail (which contains some fruit juice), Vimto, VitaMalt, tonic water, bitter lemon, soda water, and Malta (a very sweet non-alcoholic beer).

On the street, particularly in market and bush taxi garage areas, you'll often see vendors carrying trays of cold water in sachets, and locally made **fruit juices** (cordials) and **ices**, also in plastic bags, sold by children from cooler buckets. They're all made with tap water: ginger (light brown) is refreshing, as too are *wonjo* (red, from sorrel flowers) and *bwi* (white, like sherbert, from baobab fruits).

Beer and spirits

The most obvious drink in The Gambia is **JulBrew lager**, which is 4.7 percent ABV and fairly palatable. Although many Muslim Gambians don't drink, they are tolerant of those who do, and alcohol is widely available in the resort area and in major towns. However, this European-style beer is extremely expensive to the majority of local people and it can therefore sometimes be difficult to find in smaller villages.

Most of the time, JulBrew is served cold, in 330ml bottles, as is **Guinness**, also

Attaya

Brewing and sharing **green tea** (*attaya* in The Gambia) is a quintessentially West African ritual. It's a procedure that demands a certain amount of artistry and skill, giving the tea-maker an opportunity to show off and share a little downtime with companions. *Attaya*-drinking does not form part of a meal, but is an **event** in its own right. The sharing involved expresses appreciation and cements and reinforces friendships, and the whole ritual takes time, constituting a lengthy but hotly defended break in any working day. *Attaya*-making is particularly big with youths; friends take it in turns to brew, and tease each other as to who's the expert.

The *attaya* ritual traditionally has three rounds. The **recipe** is a packet of tea (always bitter Chinese Green Gunpowder), boiled up over a charcoal burner with a small amount of water and a large amount of sugar in a little enamel teapot. Brewers with flair may add something extra, like fresh mint or vanilla. The brew is poured repeatedly, and with a flourish, between two small Maghrebian-style glass tumblers until the glasses contain half liquid, half foam. It's then sipped, loudly, as a mark of approval.

For the **second round**, more sugar and water is added before steeping; the third round is even sweeter. Supposedly, the **third round**, sweet and mild, is for children and the elderly, the second, full-bodied, for women, and the first, strong and bitter, for "real men". But, as in everything Gambian, form doesn't have to be followed. As a **hot tonic**, it has a real kick, which explains why it's apparently required drinking for night watchmen – you'll spot the glow of charcoal burners on compound doorsteps when you're out at night.

Attaya is so **popular** that whenever you're in Banjul you're likely to see merchants unloading crate after crate of green gunpowder tea, freshly imported from China. A packet of *attaya* and a bag of sugar, found at any local shop – or *bitiko* – makes a good small gift.

brewed locally. It's worth tracking down the bars which serve JulBrew on **draught**, particularly those with a high enough turnover to keep it fresh.

Palm wine, a coastal West African speciality, is produced from palm sap which, after tapping, ferments in a day from a pleasant, mildly intoxicating juice to a ripe and pungent brew with seriously destabilizing qualities. The flavour is aromatic and slightly acidic. It can also be distilled to produce a colourless firewater with various jokey names including "Kill-me-quick". The most common palms tapped are oil- and raffia palms. Palm-tapping is a speciality of the Manjagos, a non-Muslim ethnic group, who sell palm wine from informal drinking dens known as palm wine ghettoes – either a compound, or just a clearing in the bush.

The Gambia has its own home-produced variety of fruit liqueurs, made by King Kombo in Kombo district. **Imported spirits** are common enough in the resort area bars, restaurants and supermarkets, some of which also sell **imported beer and wine**, often at very reasonable prices.

The media

English tends to predominate over Gambian languages in public life: education and parliament operate almost exclusively in it, and the media uses it heavily. Although there are TV and radio broadcasts in Wolof, Mandinka and, occasionally, other African languages, Gambian newspapers are in English. The Gambian press is pretty lively, though very parochial; for international news and sport, CNN, the BBC, and European sports stations are increasingly available on satellite TV, and you can find imported newspapers in the main urban areas.

Gambian **newspapers** and radio and television **news bulletins** are not only overwhelmingly Gambia-centric, they're also subject to government censorship and constricted by a National Media Commission with the power to silence writers who won't reveal their sources, and to shut down unlicensed media operations.

For all this, Gambian **journalists** can be intrepid and forthright, and the country has a thriving press. Gambian newspapers are far from sycophantic towards the government and they are stridently opposed to what they perceive as infringements of press freedom. Their **news coverage** may be patchy, with occasional lapses into grandiose prose, but they're still an excellent window onto local preoccupations and concerns. They sometimes carry adverts for **forthcoming events** (the *Daily Observer* is best for this). All are flimsy tabloids which can sometimes be hard to track down, especially upcountry. There are usually vendors selling copies at the Kairaba Avenue traffic lights in the mornings. Shops in Kombo district that stock newspapers include Timbooktoo bookshop in Fajara and a few supermarkets and hotel shops.

The availability of **imported English-language newspapers** and magazines is slowly improving, but again you're unlikely to find any outside northern Kombo. A few supermarkets regularly stock British and European titles, plus the *Herald Tribune* and *USA Today* and sometimes *Time* and *Newsweek*. You'll also see *New African* and *BBC Focus on Africa* magazines.

Gambian radio stations have blossomed in recent years, though like the print media they're subject to harassment. They're a good way to tune into the mood of the country, music-wise, and also act as bulletin boards for local live events. Unfortunately for visitors, many adverts are in Wolof only.

If you're travelling for any length of time, it's a good idea to invest in a small short-wave radio in order to listen to the **BBC World Service** – quite an institution in West Africa.

The Gambia's single national **television channel**, Gambia Television, run by the state-owned broadcasting corporation GRTS (Gambia Radio and Television Service), is still young (The Gambia had no television until 1995). Its comprehensive coverage of presidential goings-on can make it seem like a APRC propaganda vehicle, but it also broadcasts magazine programmes and cheesy imported soaps (which, inevitably, have cult following) plus classified ads (birth, marriage and funeral announcements against a background of tasteful muzak). It's hard to find programme listings anywhere.

The station broadcasts nationwide, with the potential to reach sixty percent of the population. Both up-country and in the Kombos, families which can afford a television often set it up outside in their compound in the evening for themselves and their neighbours to watch – so long as there's electricity. Expats generally prefer **satellite TV** or rented **videos** – video shops abound. Many of the tourist hotels have satellite TV, some tuned permanently to CNN.

Newspapers and magazines

Daily Observer and **Sunday Observer** Ⓦ www .observer.gm. The most popular daily, with unadventurous reporting; good for occasional "what's on" news and ads.

Foroyaa Leftist alternative newspaper, published bi-weekly.

The Gambia Daily Good editing and writing, with well-balanced reporting.

The Gambia Echo ⓦ www.thegambiaecho .com. Outspoken online newspaper compiled by established local journalists.

The Independent One of The Gambia's more opinionated papers, pulling no punches in criticizing the government.

The Point ⓦ www.thepoint.gm. Newspaper appearing three times a week, featuring news and entertainment reviews.

Radio stations

BBC World Service 6.005MHz (49m), 11.765Mhz (25m), 15.400MHz (19m) and 17.830MHz (16m) at different times of day, ⓦ www.bbc.co.uk /worldservice. General BBC World Service coverage, plus excellent Africa Service programmes including the morning magazine *Network Africa* (7.30am GMT) and *Focus on Africa* (5.05pm GMT).

City Limits 93.6FM. A Dutch-run music and chat station, with similar sounds to the more popular West Coast Radio, and reggae at weekends.

Radio 1 FM 102.1 FM. Commercial station broadcasting in Wolof and other languages and playing West African music.

Radio France Internationale 89.0 FM, ⓦ www.rfi.fr. African and international news bulletins and magazines in French, with some items in English.

Radio Gambia 648MHz AM, 91.4 FM. Anodyne national broadcast service from GRTS, in English, French, Wolof, Mandinka and other local languages. News, announcements ("will all members of the national football squad please get in touch with the coach..."), endless request shows and phone-ins.

Sud FM 92.1 FM. Senegalese station playing *ndagga* music and current affairs shows in Wolof and French.

Voice of America various short-wave frequencies, ⓦ www.voa.gov. Less wide-ranging output then the BBC and not such good reception.

West Coast Radio 95.3 FM, ⓦ www.westcoast .gm. Popular independent radio stations, with good reception, mostly broadcasting in English and Wolof, and playing reggae, soul and R&B, plus chat and news of gigs and other events.

Festivals and public holidays

In addition to the main Christian and Islamic religious festivals, The Gambia has its own national holidays and festivals. These are rarely as established as you would find, for example, in Europe. Holidays commemorating no longer respected events are quietly ignored, and new holidays are declared whenever the president deems it appropriate. Traditional Gambian festivals are joyous occasions, featuring plenty of music, dance and song, and the highlight of the secular festival calendar is the unmissable biennial International Roots Festival.

Public holidays

January 1 New Year's Day
Feb 18 Independence Day
March/April Easter Sunday
March/April Easter Monday
February/March (at present) Maolud Nabi
May 1 Labour Day
Aug 15 Feast of the Assumption
July 22 Revolution Day/Anniversary of the Second Republic
Sept/Oct (at present) Koriteh

Nov/Dec (at present) Tobaski
Dec 25 Christmas Day

It's business as usual at the **markets,** most **restaurants** and many **shops** on Gambian public holidays. Even if you can't find a bank or post office open, you'll have no trouble finding **public transport**. It's a different story, though, on **Clean The Nation Day** (Set-setal), a relatively recent government initiative which takes place on the first and/or last Saturday morning of every month. Entire

Tamharit – Islamic New Year	Beginning of Ramadan
(1st Moharem)	(1st Ramadan)
Jan 20, 2007	Sept 13, 2007
Jan 10, 2008	Sept 2, 2008
Dec 29, 2008	Aug 22, 2009
Ashoura (10th Moharem)	Koriteh – Id al-Fitr (1st Shawwal)
Jan 29, 2007	Oct 13, 2007
Jan 19, 2008	Oct 2, 2008
Jan 7, 2009	Sept 21, 2009
Maolud Nabi – The Prophet's	Tobaski – Id al-Adha (10th Dhu'l Hijja)
birthday (12th Rabia)	Dec 20, 2007
March 31, 2007	Dec 9, 2008
March 20, 2008	Nov 28, 2009
March 9, 2009	

communities are expected to throw themselves into cleaning up their local environment; shops, banks and markets are closed and all traffic, bar emergency services, is banned from the roads.

Islamic festivals

Like other West African countries, The Gambia has a significant **Muslim** population. Muslim holy days are observed devoutly in strictly Muslim districts, less formally elsewhere. Transport services are reduced during these festivals, and most other services grind to a halt, except for tourist restaurants and hotels.

The **principal events** to be aware of are the ten days of the Muslim New Year at the beginning of the month of Moharem (**Ashoura** on the 10th of Moharem celebrates, among other events, Adam and Eve's first meeting after leaving Paradise); the **Prophet Muhammad's birthday** (known as *Maolud Nabi*); the month-long fast of **Ramadan** and the feast of relief which follows immediately after (sometimes known as *Id al-Fitr* but best known in The Gambia as *Koriteh*); and the **Feast of the Sacrifice** or *Tobaski*, which coincides with the annual *Hajj* pilgrimage to Mecca, when Muslim families slaughter a sheep.

The days surrounding Tobaski can be lively, with clubs and live-music venues laying on special events for a few nights in a row. **Ramadan** isn't an entirely miserable time either, although some businesses close during the daytime, service can be slow, tempers short, and you won't hear much music anywhere. **Fasting** applies throughout the daylight hours, and covers every pleasure including food, drink (even water), tobacco and sex. While non-Muslims are not expected to observe the fast, it's offensive in strict Muslim areas to contravene publicly. Instead, switch to the night shift, as everyone else does, with dried dates, iced water, fresh fruit and sweet tea to break the fast at dusk, and applied eating and entertainment through the night.

Both Tobaski and Koriteh are occasions for massive **family celebrations**, with plenty of eating, drinking and parading of new clothes. The pressure can be great to provide a spectacular spread, and to dress fabulously. The weeks preceding major festivals can be tense times, with Gambians from all walks of life trying to up their income however they can, and tailors working shifts round the clock. When the festival arrives, **charity** is expected, and you may be approached for "saliboo" – a gift in honour of the festival.

The **Islamic calendar** is lunar, divided into twelve months of 29 or 30 days (totalling 354 days), thus festival dates shift forward by about eleven days each year, their precise dates dependant on official sightings of the moon. For more about Islam in the Gambia, see p.285; for greetings used at festival times, see p.313.

Christmas and New Year in The Gambia

Christmas, like Easter, is observed as a religious ceremony in Christian areas and, on a more or less secular basis, all over the country. Christmas and New Year are major events in the resort areas, where the Western influence is greatest, and in Banjul, where there's a sizeable population of Akus and other Christians. From early December, hawkers sell tinsel in the streets, and resort hotels really go to town on Christmas lights, music, gala menus and firework displays. Hotel Christmas dinners can be extravagant, while restaurants and clubs also lay on special entertainment.

The Gambia's most idiosyncratic Christmas tradition is its **fanal processions**, unique to Kombo district. *Fanals* are large model boats, often over three metres in length, made from paper lace stuck over a bamboo frame; by night, they are beautifully lit from inside with small lights or candles. They're paraded from compound to compound in urban areas by *fanal* societies, with much drumming and singing. The societies collect donations from each compound head, which go towards a big party. The *fanals* themselves end up on display at the compound of their most generous sponsor. The Gambia Tourist Authority, keen to keep the tradition alive, organizes *fanal*-making competitions. There's an example of a *fanal* at the National Museum in Banjul.

Another popular and noisy Gambian Christmas and New Year tradition is the hunting devil **kankurang**. Gaggles of singing Mandinka kids or youths with seed-pod shakers, jerry-can drums and other home-made instruments tour the streets collecting money, in the company of the *kankurang*, a masked dancer dressed in a costume made of red rag, sacking and fur-fabric, with various gourds and bells hanging down his back, and horns on his head. Similarly, Jola **kumpo dancers** (see p.214) also make an appearance at Christmas and New Year. The Wolof contribution to the fun is the **simba** or **zimba** (lion dancers), impressive in their cow-hair head-dresses, yellow and black face-paint, and spectacular suits of fur fabric embellished with *jujus* and cowries. The *simba* have a stomping, kicking style of dancing, and fix onlookers with a fierce stare until they dance too; if the *simba* is not satisfied, the victim has to pay a cash tribute, which the dancer clamps between his teeth.

Sometimes there'll be a Christmas **street carnival** in The Kombos, when the whole district explodes with music and dancing – you may even see a Gambian Father Christmas on horseback. Events like this are not always well-publicized, so ask around locally to find out what's on when.

International Roots Festival

The Gambia's most important cultural event is the **International Roots Festival**, held biennially in various locations over a week in June. Inaugurated in 1996, the festival's original target audience was black Americans keen to reconnect with their roots in a joint celebration of African cultural heritage. Now devised with **all nationalities** in mind, but especially individuals of African descent, it attracts Gambians of all ethnicities, resident and expatriate, plus other Africans and people from the African diaspora. Its underlying agenda is to **court foreign patrons** willing to get involved in The Gambia, long-term, by buying property, starting businesses,

sharing skills and resources, or contributing to development projects, but everyone, whatever their interests, is welcome to join in the festivities. The organizers hope to make the Roots festival as big on the world stage as the Notting Hill Carnival. It's a long way off achieving this kind of fame, and some of its events are rather haphazard, but it's still a superb event.

Festival-goers can choose between attending a few individual events (some of which are free), or paying a **registration fee** for the whole programme of cultural shows, visits, concerts, seminars and parties. The centrepieces of the festival have in previous years been a one-day **Roots pilgrimage** to Juffureh, Albreda and James Island, and a two-day event held at **Kanilai**, President Jammeh's home village (see p.212). The pilgrimage is similar to standard Roots trips (see p.198), except that participants are met and entertained by a welcome committee of hundreds including chiefs, *jalis* and local schoolchildren. At Kanilai, "Homecomers" from the diaspora have the opportunity to undergo a scaled-down version of the *futampaf*, the traditional Jola tribal initiation rites associated with circumcision (but without the surgery). Traditional "bush school" is not common nowadays, and traditional values are being eroded, so part of the purpose of the Roots *futampaf* is to serve as a tangible reminder of the past. After their instruction, the initiates are dressed in beads and cloth and presented to the tribe, in a ceremony with much music, dance and noise. Saplings are planted on their behalf, they are presented with a ritual spouse, and a chicken is sacrificed for each of them. Other events at Kanilai include **wrestling** bouts, **fire-eating**, and **cultural shows** of music and dance with troupes from all over The Gambia and beyond, accompanied by ear-splitting ritual **cannon fire**.

The range of events staged during the Roots festival changes from year to year but the variety is excellent. Big-name musical stars such as Youssou N'Dour, Viviane and Jaliba Kuyateh have, in the past, performed onstage at gala dinners and massive stadium shows. One of the most outstanding events is the Banjul regatta, with rowing teams from fishing communities competing in speed trials, and wrestlers whacking each other with pillows on a greasy pole held horizontally over the dock. Equally entertaining are the parties and carnival processions; practically every event is accompanied by exuberant singing, drumming and dancing.

For more information, see Ⓦwww.rootsgambia.gm.

Other festivals

Independence Day (Feb 18) celebrates The Gambia's declaration of independence from Britain in 1965. Most communities stage events at stadia and football fields. These involve military parades, uniformed schoolchildren marching past in impeccable uniforms, military and traditional bands, and cultural troupes.

In northern Kombo, where reggae is a way of life for huge numbers of young Gambians, **Bob Marley Day** (May 11) is celebrated with tribute nights at the clubs and bars, decked out in red, gold and green.

The **Kanilai Cultural Festival**, a recent addition to the Gambian calendar, takes place in odd-numbered years around the time of President Jammeh's birthday (May 25). The whole community celebrates with music, dance and wrestling bouts, and visitors are welcome.

Carnival Parade (June) is a spirited one-day carnival of floats, costumed dancers and music in the Kairaba Avenue and Bertil Harding Highway area, culminating in a music and dance show at the National Stadium, Bakau, or the football field, Kololi. In years when the Roots festival is held, the carnival is incorporated into the programme.

Liberation Day (July 22) is the anniversary of the 1994 coup which brought Jammeh to power. In recent years it has begun to overshadow Independence Day, and has been marked as a political occasion, with forthright speeches from the President, and a national celebration.

Finally, **National Tourism Week** (Nov) and the **ASSET Showcase** (Dec) are held in the resort area towards the beginning of the tourist season. Their aim is to encourage cultural tourism and promote local businesses and craftspeople through music, dance, traditional Gambian cooking, stage shows, parades, craft stalls and visual arts.

Sports and entertainment

The Gambia's national sport is traditional wrestling, but in recent years football fever has been sweeping the country. With no film industry and very little theatre of any sort, The Gambia's entertainment programmes tend to focus on live music and dance.

Spectator sports

Visitors are welcome at the Senegambian **wrestling** tournaments that are staged in various locations from time to time. Unfortunately, popular interest in the sport has declined somewhat. Weekend bouts used to be held in many Gambian towns and villages throughout the dry season, drawing enthusiastic crowds of onlookers. Today, such events are rarer, except in the President's home village of Kanilai, which regularly hosts international events (see p.215).

The Gambia is too small a country to have much international sporting success, and, when it comes to **football** (soccer), Gambians tend to support the successful Senegalese national side as much as their own. The game is enormously popular, especially among young Gambians, both as a pastime and as a spectator sport, and now that more Gambians have access to satellite television – every town has "video clubs" where you can pay a few dalasis to gather round a big screen – the international football scene has become a favourite topic of conversation. It has also hit the political agenda – when President Jammeh tried to ban the *nawettan* (the annual country-wide rainy season tournament), as it distracted people from the crucial business of seasonal farming work, a passionate public debate ensued. Major **matches** are held at the National Stadium in Bakau, typically at weekends during the dry season, and are noisy, spirited events, with plenty of drumming and chanting. The most popular fixtures sell out so it's best to arrive well in advance of kick-off.

Sports facilities

The Gambia's only eighteen-hole **golf** course is at the Fajara Club (see p.129), an old-fashioned sports complex that's popular with expats. The golf course is between the beautiful grove of palms that lines Kotu Stream, and the beach. It's famous for its lack of grass in the dry season, when the greens are effectively "browns". It's a good birdwatching location, so golfers need to be on the lookout for birders straying off the paths.

The Fajara Club also offers **tennis**, **squash** and **table tennis**, as do some of the resort hotels. Watersports on the Atlantic coast are limited due to dangerous currents. **Body boarding** and **swimming** is possible, but can be hazardous at times – it's essential to pay heed to the lifeguards' flags. For **catamaran hire**, **wakeboarding**, **windsurfing** and **waterskiing**, contact the well-equipped and highly professional Gambia Watersports Centre (℡777 3777), based near Denton Bridge on the outskirts of Banjul. They also hire out **jetskis** but it's important to be aware of the dangers and of the noise pollution these cause. The currents and lack of underwater visibility make snorkelling or scuba diving a non-starter in The Gambia.

Live music and cultural shows

While for the majority of visitors entertainment means the hotel formula-mix of "cultural dance troupes" and home-style discos, it's easy enough to escape the dross and find real Gambian **musical entertainment**. To be fair, the hotels do sometimes host worthwhile gigs – some of The Gambia's best *kora* players have played to tourist audiences.

A good time to be in Kombo district is during a festival, or at the end of the month, when people can afford tickets for the bands that occasionally visit from abroad, usually Senegal. Visiting stars may perform two or three gigs on subsequent nights in different venues, the biggest by far being at the **National Stadium**,

Music lessons

One way to become involved in Gambian culture is to spend time with a **jali** or *griot* – a traditional musician – learning the art of the *kora*, *balafon*, or drums (*djembé* or others), or singing and dancing. Brikama is a good place to make enquiries, especially about *kora* lessons, as this town is home to many talented *jalis*; you may also be able to stay in your teacher's family compound. The following contacts can provide lessons, or put you in touch with musicians:

Drum Doctors UK ☏01462/711842, ⊛www.realafrica.net. Residential music workshops or daily individual *djembé* tuition in Bakau, with a UK-based musician who teaches and plays in Britain, Europe and Africa.

Drum factory Manjai Kunda (no phone). A compound where craftsmen build and carve drums; you can try them out or enquire about lessons here.

Jali Sherrifo Konteh Brikama c/o Compound Sounds, ⊛www.compoundsounds .com. Sherrifo, the son of mighty *griot* Alhaji Bai Konteh, is a regular performer at the *Kombo Beach Hotel* and has toured the UK. He gives *kora* lessons in Kotu, Brikama or elsewhere in Kombo.

Jobarteh Kunda Brikama ☏448 4143, The pleasant and peaceful family compound of renowned *kora* player Malamini Jobarteh in Brikama. Malamini's son Tata Din Din and other members of the extended family including Mamoud Jobarteh (*kora* player) and his colleague Modou Diouf (*sabar/tama* drummer who performed at Live 8 Africa Calling and WOMAD in 2005) all offer tuition when they're around. It's possible to stay in the compound as a guest of the family.

Kounta Kinté Association Juffureh ⓔamadoujuffure@yahoo.fr, ⊛www.kounta -kinte.com. French-run music and dance classes and workshops in Juffureh, with master musicians from Senegal and Mali.

Alagi M'Bye Nema Kunku ☏995 0030. The *kora* player who runs Maali's Music School in this village between Serrekunda and Sukuta offers *kora* lessons to visitors. The music school itself is a ground-breaking project whereby the children of non-*jali* familes (traditionally barred from music tuition) can learn music.

Safari Garden Hotel Fajara ☏449 5887. The hotel can recommend good *djembé* and dance teachers in Fajara, and has Gambian dance-aerobics sessions.

Bakau. International masters of *ndagga* and *mbalax* (distinctive styles of the Senegambian region), sometimes play here. Arrive early to get a seat or you'll never see the musicians, but don't expect the main act on stage until well after midnight.

Currently the biggest vogue among young Gambians is for **reggae** and **ragga**. The Gambia however is more distinguished for its Mandinka **kora musicians**. The most famous talents – Dembo Konteh, his brother-in-law Kausu Kouyaté, Foday Musa Suso, Jaliba Kuyateh, Malamini Jobarteh, Ebrima Jobarteh, Tata Din Din and junior Pa Jobarteh – are as likely to be playing in a British folk festival or with American musicians as in a compound in Brikama or at a wedding in Serrekunda. Wolof drummers often perform at "private" functions too – keep your ears open and drop in politely.

Culture and etiquette

You can't hope to avoid social gaffes completely in The Gambia, but humour and tolerance abound, so you won't be left to stew in embarrassment. Getting it right really takes a West African upbringing but people are delighted when you make the effort. Gambians are generally swift to include strangers into their lives with smiles and salutations; you'll have to get used to saying hello countless times a day.

Greetings

Greetings have a crucial part to play in everyday social interactions: no conversation starts without one. This means a handshake followed by polite enquiries, even as you enter a shop. A simple "Hello, how are you?" before you launch into your request is the very least you should say. Ideally, in English or an appropriate local language, you should swap something like "How are you?" "Fine, how's the morning?" "Fine, how's business?" "Fine, how's the family?", "Fine, thank God". Questions about your name, where you're from, and where you're going are all standard elements of routine greetings. Traditionally, such exchanges can last a minute or two, and you'll often hear them performed in a formal, incantatory manner between two men. While someone is speaking to you at length, it's considered polite to murmur in the affirmative, or say thank you at short intervals. Breaks in conversation are filled with more greetings. For local language examples, see p.308.

Shaking hands is normal between all men present, on arrival and departure. Foreign women, in most social situations, are likely to be treated by Gambians as honorary men. Gambian women shake hands with each other, but not normally with men. Soul brother handshakes and their variations are popular among young males. Less natural for Westerners (certainly for men) is an unconscious ease in **physical contact** between members of the same sex, but a studied lack of public contact between men and women. Male visitors need to get used to holding hands with Gambian men as they're shown around the compound, or guided down the street.

Social norms

Be aware of the left hand/right hand rule, which, like many **rules**, is sometimes broken. Traditionally the **left hand** is reserved for unhygienic acts, so to give something with the left hand amounts to an insult. Never use your left hand when eating from a communal bowl. Don't be put off by apparent shiftiness in **eye contact**, especially if you're talking to someone much younger than you, as it's fairly normal for those deferring to others to avoid direct looks. **Hissing** ("Tsss!") is an ordinary way to attract a stranger's attention, and you'll get a fair bit of this.

Answering anything in the negative is often considered impolite. Try to avoid asking yes/no questions, and avoid phrasing things in the negative ("Isn't the taxi leaving?") because the answer may well be an ambiguous "Yes…" Be on the look out, too, for a host of **unexpected turns of phrase** which often pop up in Gambian English, and can be amusing. "I am coming", for example, is often said by someone just as they leave your company – which means they're going, but coming back. Confusingly, "he" and "she" are used interchangeably when referring to either males or females, since Mandinka and Wolof do not have separate pronouns for the genders.

Gifts

It's a great privilege to be invited into a Gambian **family compound**, especially to join in a celebration, and if you accept an invitation, it's normal to take your hosts a **gift**. While money is always appreciated and a major celebration might merit a gift such as a bag of rice, it's also very useful to have some tokens to give to people. **Postcards** of sights from home and pictures of you and

Kola nuts

Giving and receiving **kola nuts** is a traditional exchange of friendship and respect. Kola nuts also have a crucial ritual function as a symbolic gift in social and business transactions such as marriages and the purchase of land.

Kola nuts are the pink and white chestnut-sized fruit from the pods of the indigenous kola tree, cultivated and traded on a grand scale throughout West Africa. Before the arrival of tobacco, cannabis, tea and coffee, kola – an appetite depressant and a mild stimulant when chewed for the bitter juice – was the main non-alcoholic drug of the region.

Buy a handful for **long journeys**, as much to share among fellow passengers as to stay awake. If you're visiting a village, a little bundle of nuts makes a **good present** to offer the *alkalo*, or village chief, when you first meet him or her.

---

your family are appreciated by Gambians who are generally passionate about photos of friends and family but may only have a few of their own. School kids are also delighted with school materials – exercise books or paper and pencils (more useful than ballpoint pens if paper is scarce, as pencil can be rubbed out).

When **visiting villages**, think carefully about how you are going to distribute any gifts you may have brought, and to whom. For example, it's better to give gifts for children to a parent or teacher, who knows who needs what, than to hand stuff out at random, which usually means it's the pushiest that end up with the most. You might also consider making an appointment to **visit a school**, to get a first-hand opinion of what would be most useful to the majority of students. Never **throw gifts** to children for them to scrabble over – even if you see Gambians do this – and never give gifts from vehicles, as this encourages chidren to tear after the wheels of cars and trucks, heedless of the hazards.

Time-keeping

People and things in West Africa are often late and Gambians like to joke about "GMT" (Gambia Maybe Time). That said, if you try to anticipate **delays** you may be caught out. Scheduled transport does leave on time at least some of the time – or even early if it's full. Even planes have been known to take off before schedule. Outside the urban areas, however, notions of time and duration are pretty hazy: dusk and dawn are the significant markers. Note also that in remote

areas, if a driver says he's going somewhere "today", it doesn't necessarily mean he expects to *get there* today. Always allow extra time – there's no better way to ruin Gambian travel than to attempt to rush it.

Appearance

West Africans set great store by their **style of dress**, and find it hard to respect those who, in their opinion, dress inappropriately or shabbily. Traditional Gambian dress for both men and women is long and loose, covering the torso, legs and head, and often the shoulders and arms as well. Covering up with cotton is generally cooler than exposing bare skin to the African sun.

Women should cover their legs, at least down to the knee, and **men** shouldn't go bare-chested. If you're cycling, however, or engaged in any sporting activity, then shorts are normally acceptable. It's useful, however, for women always to have a wrap available to tie round the waist.

Female travellers' **clothes and behaviour** will be noticed by everyone, and they're more important if you don't appear to have a male escort. Long, loose **hair** is seen as extraordinarily provocative and doubly so if blonde. Women can avoid sending out the wrong messages by keeping hair fairly short or tied up (or wearing a scarf) and wearing long skirts or loose trousers. If you find it's too hot to wear a **bra**, it's not going to interest anybody, but if you'll be travelling much on rough roads, you'll need a bra for support. Seriously.

While **topless sunbathing** (though not nudity) is acceptable around hotel pools and

Toubab! Toubab!

Nobody really knows how white people came to be known as **toubab** in West Africa – some say it's a corruption of a word meaning "doctor"; others (less plausibly) that it's derived from "two-bob", meaning two shillings, a tip paid to Africans by Europeans for errands run. These days the label *toubab* is applied indiscriminately in referring to any non-black. It's not a racist term, although, in some Gambians' eyes, it's a defining term – long after a Gambian has learnt a white individual's name, or profession, or country of origin, they'll still be calling them the *toubab* rather than the American, or the engineer, or John.

Children can get become quite over-excited when they spot a white visitor, particularly in rural areas, running full tilt towards tourist vehicles, regardless of the danger, screeching "Toubab! Toubab!" at the tops of their voices. Black tourists can, of course, provoke just as much interest. Visitors to The Gambia quickly discover that behind all the smiles, yells and rapt attention, the local children can often be shameless **beggars**. Children teach toddlers the catchphrase, "Any pen?" quickly followed by "Any mintie?" and, more aggressively, "Gimme money!", and some kids bunk off lessons in order to harangue passing tourists. Don't encourage begging by dishing stuff out in the streets like Santa Claus – if you want to help children who are genuinely in need, give your gifts direct to a school or a recognized charity (see p.82).

Of course, some children and adults have less mercenary intentions, and simply want to **chat** – many Gambians are genuinely interested in people from other countries. You will frequently be bombarded by a string of questions: "Hello – what is your name? – where is your husband/wife? – from which country? – from which hotel?" and so on. Remember that these are standard forms of address Gambians use on each other (see p.72), and the kids are just trying out sentences learnt during their English lessons at school. Bear with them – as more and more youngsters begin to speak English with as much confidence and flair as they speak multiple African languages, the brighter the future of The Gambia is likely to be.

on the tourist beaches (as opposed to the fishing beaches), **beachwear** is entirely inappropriate anywhere else.

Religious practice

The vast majority of Gambians are **Muslim**, and a well-balanced, tolerant attitude to religious differences characterizes the country. Gambians generally find it far harder to empathize with an atheist than with those with non-Muslim beliefs.

One of the requirements of Islam is that Muslims should **pray** five times a day, so you should take this into account if you're spending a day in the company of Muslims. Prayer may take place in a public place. On Fridays, Gambian Muslims wear their best traditional clothes for (in the case of men) their visit to the mosque for Friday prayers, or (for most women) prayers at home. Friday prayers normally take place around 2pm. If visiting a **mosque** you should take off your shoes. Women should be modestly dressed, with

body and head covered. Some mosques are closed to women, and menstruating women cannot enter any mosque. Non-Muslims are never allowed in during prayer times.

Muslims are forbidden from eating **pork** or drinking **alcohol**. Some choose not to abide by these rules, but it's still advisable to be judicious about drinking in strict Muslim areas. During the lunar month of **Ramadan** a fast is strictly observed by practising Muslims during daylight hours. Another requirement of Islam is the giving of **alms**, and many people give to the same beggar on a regular basis.

For more information on Islam in The Gambia, see p.285.

Photographing people

The Gambia is immensely photogenic, but to get good pictures takes great cultural sensitivity. There are two options if you want to get **photos of people**. You can take pictures before anyone knows it's happening, and deal with the problems after the event, or you can take your time and reach an agreement. The first approach will almost inevitably cause offence or get you into trouble – it's far better to ask people first, and to accept refusal with good grace. Shooting with a **digital** or **polaroid** camera means you can show your subjects their picture as soon as you've taken it; many people are delighted by this, especially if they have never had a photo of themselves.

Be prepared to **pay** a few dalasis or to send a print if your subjects have addresses. A family you've stayed with is unlikely to refuse a photo session, and may even ask for it. The same people might be furious if you jumped off the minibus and started taking photos.

Sexual attitudes

Sexual attitudes tend to be liberal, with sexual expression an important part of the social fabric in most communities, even though you'll rarely see public displays of physical affection between partners. Sex is openly discussed except in the presence of children, and it's rarely the subject of personal hang-ups. You're likely to be treated as a sexually available person even if you travel with a companion of the opposite sex, although being seen as half a couple may insulate you from advances to some extent.

Flirting is more or less universal and this is particularly true for female travellers, who may find the frank scrutiny from men unnerving. If a man asks a woman to "come and see where I live", or some similar euphemism, he means you should come and see where you are going to sleep together. Of course, sexual interest is by no means exclusively one-sided, and plenty of visiting women do engage in casual affairs, which can make things awkward for women not out for adventures.

Both men and women are likely to have no shortage of friendly amateur **offers** while visiting The Gambia. These are usually easy to turn down if you refuse as frankly as you're asked. Unwanted physical advances are rare. But it always helps to avoid offence if you make your intentions (or lack of them) clear from the outset. If you're not with a partner, a fictitious spouse in the background can be useful; having a photo with you might help.

This may, of course, be met with responses such as "But you're here on your own? In that case, I'd really like us to know each other...", so bolster your arsenal of rejoinders.

All this can be fun – there's no reason you can't spend an evening dancing and talking and still go back to your bed alone and unharassed. However, if you're uncomfortable, don't fear **causing offence** by being over-cautious, as long as you're polite at all times. Women should be wise to the tactics of bumsters (see p.53) and be wary of big men in small towns. Don't accept an invitation to the disco from the local chief of police unless you're on very firm ground, and don't feel obliged to meet someone as arranged if you've had serious second thoughts. Always lock your door at night.

For **male travellers**, questions of personal safety and intimidation don't arise in quite the same way. However, it's common for Gambian women, and especially unmarried girls, to flirt with strangers, and many town and resort bars and hotels are patronized by **prostitutes**. This is not the secretive and exploitive transaction of the West and pimps are generally unknown. There are plenty of cheap hotels happy to rent out rooms by the hour, and this even happens in some tourist hotels from time to time. However, premises suspected of operating as brothels, and women suspected of being sex workers, have recently been the subject of a sweeping clampdown by the Gambian government, enforced by the military police, as part of Jammeh's crusade to make his country a morally irreproachable Muslim nation.

Sexually transmitted diseases, and the AIDS virus, are on the increase, although their incidence in The Gambia remains lower than in many African countries. People are beginning to wake up to this reality, but you should be aware of the very real risks – and prepared for the occasion – if you accept any propositions. Both men and women should always carry, and use, **condoms** – the chances are local men won't have any.

One final word of warning: in the light of recent unearthing of what are alleged to be **child prostitution** rings in the Gambia, it's imperative that you make sure any friendships you strike up with Gambians and their children could never be in any way misconstrued.

As a **gay male visitor**, you're most likely to find like-minded company in the resort areas, where there are a few low-key hangouts. But beyond these areas, **homosexuality** is more or less invisible. People from a more traditional African background usually deny it exists, find the notion laughable, or describe it as a phase or a harmless peculiarity; others are more condemning. Gay sex is still illegal in The Gambia – though prosecutions are extremely rare. **Gay women** can't, as yet, expect to find any hint of a lesbian community anywhere.

Women travellers

In **up-country** areas, foreign women travelling alone are a rare sight and a source of curiosity. You might suffer occasional bouts of hassle because of your gender, but male egos here are normally softened by humour, and women travel widely on their own or with each other without major problems. Still, you're likely to feel very conspicuous and this can be tough if you value your personal space. On the plus side, female travellers get offers of hospitality more often than men, most without strings attached.

On **public transport** a single woman traveller may cause quite a stir. Fellow passengers won't want to see you badly treated: they'll speak up on your behalf and get you a good seat or argue with the driver over your baggage payments. Male passengers may assume protective roles. This can be helpful but is sometimes annoyingly restrictive, and can lead to misunderstandings. Speak your mind and be polite but direct.

Meeting local women in The Gambia is easy enough, but it's often more difficult to get to know them well. Most contact is mediated through male relatives, with whom you'll take on the social role of honorary man. You might want to take cosmetics in small containers, or earrings and necklaces, to give as **small presents** to female friends (every woman has pierced ears).

In the villages women are usually less educated than men, often don't speak English and are much more often to be found in their compounds, fields or vegetable gardens working to make ends meet. For their part, most Gambian women will find it hard to picture themselves in your position,

travelling around *your* homeland. **Family obligations** are everything. Conveying the fact that you, too, have a family and a home is a good way of reducing the barriers of incomprehension but, assuming you're over 15, explaining the absence of husband and children is virtually impossible. You can either invent some or expect sympathy – or even the offer of fertility medicine.

Women's rights in the The Gambia

Despite widespread paper commitments to **women's rights**, and a few women holding prominent positions in government and commerce, The Gambia remains a powerfully **male-dominated** country. Women do the vast proportion of productive labour and there are non-governmental women's organizations working to improve the lot of mothers, agricultural labourers and crafts workers. Professional market women usually run their own informal unions in towns. In The Gambia, current major women's issues, apart from labour rights, are primarily concerned with legal inequalities, and prescriptive religious and traditional cultural practices.

The Gambia has **three parallel legal systems**: modern sector law (based on English common law); customary law (based on ethnic tradition); and personal law (based on Islamic shari'a law). Both customary and personal law may be applied to cases regarding divorce and inheritance, and both tend to favour men over women. While mildly violent disciplinary behaviour towards women and children is socially accepted practice in The Gambia, harmful violence of any kind is a criminal offence. Nevertheless, actual prosecutions for violence against women are extremely rare.

Probably the most controversial traditional practice in West Africa is **female circumcision**, also known as **female genital mutilation** (FGM) – the surgical removal of parts of the outer genitalia. It's widespread in The Gambia: around eighty percent of women have had it performed. There have been worldwide campaigns to ban it, but in The Gambia President Jammeh has been unwilling to outlaw what he sees as a strong cultural tradition. Also controversial is **polygamy**, a common practice in Muslim communities, which, while sometimes benefitting the women concerned, more usually results in emotional and financial hardship. For more on traditional practices, see pp.280–290.

All these issues are complex and sensitive and it's perhaps wrong to make **assumptions** about Gambian women's own perceptions of their status and rights, or to attempt to raise them in casual conversation.

Crime and personal safety

It's easy to exaggerate the potential hassles and disasters of travel in The Gambia. Many visitors feel safer in The Gambia (which has the lowest crime rate in sub-Saharan Africa) than in their home country. True, there are a few urban locations, easily enough pinpointed, where snatch robberies and muggings occur from time to time. But most of the country carries minimal risk to personal safety compared with Europe and North America. The main problems are sneak thieving, "bumstering" (see box on p.53) and corrupt people in uniforms. The first can be avoided; the second is more an irritation than a danger, and dealing with the third can become a game once you know the rules.

Obviously, if you flaunt the trappings of wealth where there's **urban poverty**, somebody may want to remove them. There's always less risk in leaving your valuables in a securely locked hotel room or, judiciously, with the management. If you clearly have nothing on you (this means not wearing expensive-looking jewellery or wristwatches), you're unlikely to be threatened.

On arrival in The Gambia, it's wise to be cautious at first. It's important to distinguish harmlessly robust, up-front interaction from more sinister preludes that might lead to you being "bumstered". In the resort areas, **scams** include people spinning you a hard-luck story in order to cadge money. Don't feel unnecessarily victimized, but be rationally suspicious of everyone until you're more confident. Lastly, remember that impoverished **fellow travellers** are as likely – or unlikely – to rip you off as anyone else.

Apart from the standard of driving, Gambian **public transport** is fairly safe – The Gambia has none of the banditry that makes some parts of the developing world hazardous to travellers.

Theft

Hotel room **burglaries**, car break-ins and **muggings** do occur, but they're rare, and vary with the seasons: the rainy season and the weeks before major festivals, when people need cash, are the most likely times for opportunistic thieving. If you shout "Thief!", be swift to intercede once you've retrieved your belongings: robbers and pickpockets caught red-handed are usually dealt with summarily by bystanders, who generally assume the culprit is a foreigner who deserves swift punishment.

Pickpocketing can happen anywhere – usually the work of kids hanging around in markets, ferry terminals, or other crowded places. Make sure your valuables are secure.

More serious attacks are rare, but sometimes take place in specific areas of Kombo district. Black spots change regularly so listen to local advice. The least threatening districts include bush taxi garages (full of tough young transport workers on the lookout for threats to their passengers) and, surprisingly perhaps, the lower income suburbs and slums where people aren't used to travellers.

Drugs

Drug possession can easily land you a large fine or worse, and possibly deportation. Don't expect to buy yourself easily out of this kind of trouble.

Grass (marijuana, cannabis, *djamba, niamo, kali*) is the biggest illegal drug in The Gambia, much cultivated (clandestinely) and as much an object of confused opprobrium and fascination as anywhere else in the world. Many social problems are routinely attributed to smoking the "grass that kills" and it's widely believed to cause insanity. The usual result of a fortuitous bust is on-the-spot fines all round.

An altogether different state of affairs exists with **heroin** and **cocaine**, which are smuggled though West African airports en route to Europe (often inside hapless female "swallowers"). Some of the consignments get on to the streets, however – stay well clear.

If you're **walking** in an area you're not sure of, keep a destination in mind and stay alert: look ahead, and don't dawdle. Steer clear of creepy looking street sharks in jeans and running shoes (every robbery ends in a sprint). And never allow yourself to be steered down an alley or between parked cars.

The police

Unless you've lost a lot of money or irreplaceable property, think twice about going to the **police.** They're thought to be the nicest in West Africa (faint praise indeed), but they rarely do something for nothing – even stamping an insurance form may cost you. You will inevitably come into a fair amount of contact with authority; **checks** on the movement of people (police, security services and immigration officers) and goods (customs officers) take place at junctions and along highways. Never go anywhere without **identification** – you don't have to carry a passport at all times, but a photocopy of the ID pages in a plastic wallet is very useful.

Be warned that failure to observe the following points of general **public etiquette** can get you arrested or force you to pay a bribe. Never destroy banknotes, no matter how worthless they may be. Stand still on any occasion the Gambian national anthem is played or a flag raised or lowered; if you see others suddenly cease all activity, do the same. Pull off the road completely, or stand still if motorcycle outriders, armoured vehicles, and limos appear.

Finally, the police and security forces will often hassle you if they see you filming or taking **photographs** – usually on the pretext that you are taking pictures of them, or of "sensitive" buildings. You shouldn't take photos of anything that could be construed as strategic or military – including army or police buildings, vehicles and uniforms, prisons and, in theory, the President. Officially, this is seen as a "risk to state security". In practice, the president is far from camera shy and you're likely to get the chance to take a snap if you see him at a festival or state occasion. For more on camera etiquette, see p.74.

Bribery and corruption

If you find yourself confronting an implacable person in uniform, you don't have to give in to tacit demands for gifts or money; the golden rule is to **appear respectful** and **keep talking**. Most laws, including imaginary ones, are there to be discussed rather than enforced. If you reach a deadlock and you haven't got all day, a "**small present**" – couched in exactly those terms – is all it usually takes. If you're **driving** and your vehicle and papers are in order, you shouldn't have to pay bribes, except sometimes on entry to or exit from the country. If you're travelling by lorry or bush taxi, it's the driver who pays. Be patient and good-humoured; aggressive travellers always have the worst police stories.

Shopping

You'll have no shortage of opportunities to shop for souvenirs in The Gambia if you're staying in the resort area: every tourist hotel has a boutique of some sort, craft markets and hawkers sell locally made bits and pieces, and there are a few gallery shops. Local markets mainly sell produce and household goods but they're good for fabric and are colourful and lively to visit. Up-country there are far fewer places to browse.

European cottons printed with African designs (known as **"wax"**) and plain or patterned **damask** are to be seen everywhere, and can be both high-quality and good value. You'll also see plenty of tie-dye and batik, used for clothing and furnishings – fabulous creations are worn by both women and men, particularly at festivals or celebrations, or just because it's Friday, and Gambian tailors are adept at copying items or creating originals. Cotton is generally sold in six-yard dress lengths. **Bespoke items** of all sorts, not just clothing but also leather bags and shoes, silver jewellery, or items forged from steel or carved from wood, are often the best bargains in The Gambia.

The resort areas have **craft markets** known as *bengdulas*, where you'll find masses of items made specifically for tourists. Don't dismiss these places out of hand – look carefully, and you may spot some gems among the hastily carved wooden elephants (supremely un-Gambian) and cheap bangles made from wire and plastic strips.

Gambian **jewellery** and **belts** have always featured leather, beads and cowrie shells, so it's surprising that Gambians haven't latched onto the fact that these are fashionable in Europe and the US, and jazzed up their designs accordingly. If you'd like a genuine *juju*, rather than just a bit of stitched leather with a cowrie shell fixed on it, then you'll need to visit a marabout or one of the market medicine men. **Basketware**, woven not only into baskets but also trunks, lampshades, fruit bowls and other items, is generally good quality; craftsmen work on the beach and at roadside stalls.

If you hunt about in the *bengdulas*, Albert Market in Banjul, the Woodcarvers' Market

in Brikama and in the shops on Sayerr Jobe Avenue in Serrekunda, you'll find a few places selling **antique African carvings** and **masks**, imported from as far afield as Mali, Togo and Côte d'Ivoire. It's very unlikely these objects will ever have been used for ritual purposes (those that are, and have not been destroyed in the process, are guarded jealously by their owners), and their antiquity may be entirely artificial (a combination of rough treatment and judicious application of cobwebs and dust), but you may well find something made to a traditional design and with far more spiritual resonance than the shiny new teak objects churned out by the Gambian carvers. Similarly, beads described as **"trade beads"** are almost certainly not the genuine article – the beads that the eighteenth-century European explorers exchanged for slaves and other commodities have long since been sold, lost or consigned to museums – so judge them on their aesthetic appeal.

Places selling antiquities often also sell **musical instruments**, including *djembés*, *koras*, *balafons* and all sorts of percussion. However, if you're taking music lessons (see p.71) during your stay in The Gambia then your tutor, or his associates, is likely to be the best source of instruments: you can have the pleasure of watching an instrument being made for you to your own specifications.

Some *bengdulas* and hotel boutiques sell local **honey** (a prohibited import into the UK), jam, beeswax candles, and royal jelly beauty products packaged as souvenirs; the National Beekeepers Association of The Gambia, in Banjul Nding, near the airport approach road, sells these direct. It's also worth looking out for the beautiful **handmade albums**, books and stationery made

Art and craft shopping in The Gambia

Africa Living Art Centre Bakau. Fabulous, eclectic collection of art, antiquities, textiles, jewellery, and designer clothing. See p.130.

African Heritage Gallery Bakau. A good selection of old masks and bronzes, clothing and books. See p.126.

Albert Market Banjul. Wax prints, damask, souvenirs, musical instruments, bootleg cassettes, antique West African masks and carvings – plus vast quantities of food and household goods. See p.108.

Atlantic Road Craft Market Bakau. Watch carvers at work making *djembés* and wooden animals; also plenty of batik clothing and souvenirs. See p.126.

Gaya Kololi. A highly attractive selection of homewares and gifts, with a café attached. See p.134.

Glimpse of Africa Fajara. Textiles, pots, furnishings and decorative objects from all over the continent. See p.126.

Lemonfish Art Gallery Kartong. Original work from Gambian and West African artists. See p.169.

Senegambia Craft Market Kololi. Clothing, shoes and bags made from batik, tie-dye and leather. Dolls dressed in Gambian costumes. Beads, carvings, jewellery and souvenirs. See p.132.

Serrekunda batik factory Dippa Kunda. Garments, hangings and lengths of cloth. See p.135.

Tanje Village Museum Tanji. The museum has a small gift shop with an interesting selection of crafts, some made on the premises. See p.168.

Timbuktoo Bead and Mask Shop and **Art Collections** Serrekunda. A pair of nearby shops selling musical instruments, antique masks and beads, and Malian *bogolan* (mud cloth). See p.135.

Traditions Basse. Local weaving and West African artefacts. See p.253.

Village Gallery Kololi. Paintings, photography and sculpture by West African artists. See p.134.

Woodcarvers' Market Brikama. The biggest concentration of woodcarvers in The Gambia. See p.173.

---

from recycled materials by The Gambia's Paper Recycling Skills Project (see p.136); they're stocked by several boutiques.

Literacy levels in The Gambia are low, and **books** do not play much part in most people's lives, but you'll find a few titles in supermarkets and hotel shops and there's an outstanding bookshop in Fajara, Timbooktoo (see p.130). Most other Gambian "bookshops" are in fact stationers which also sell school textbooks. While you'll hear fabulous music everywhere in The Gambia, good quality **CDs** are hard to find – partly because pirating is rife (see p.302).

Travelling with children

Wherever you go in The Gambia, the reaction of local people to families and their children is exceptionally welcoming. However, travelling with young kids can be extremely hard work. The following is aimed principally at families with babies and under-5s.

Children's health

Health issues figure prominently in most parents' minds. With the exception of malaria, however, you can discount fears about your children getting tropical diseases in The Gambia.

Breast-feeding babies will be as protected against malaria as their mother, but it can be very difficult to persuade small children to take **pills** under any guise. With toddlers you may have to choose between ramming pills down their throats or giving in and risking it. In the latter case, the coast is much safer than up-country, but you should be extremely careful to cover them with Deet (diethyl-meta-toluamide) repellent early each evening and be sure they sleep under secure nets (take small nets for babies). For more on malaria, see p.36.

You can buy **disposable nappies** in The Gambia, but they are expensive and hard to find except in northern Kombo. **Baby foods** are also available in supermarkets in Kombo. You'll have few catering problems if you're staying in hotels: there's usually a good variety of fresh food, and staff will be happy to prepare it to infants' tastes, given some warning.

Unless you're visiting during the rainy season, bring some **warm clothing** for chilly mornings and evenings. Temperatures can drop considerably in December and January and hotels are not heated. Swimming pools, focus of attention for most children, are invariably unheated too and are often very cool in the mornings until the sun warms them up.

If you take any **excursions by water** – creek trips are popular and tremendous fun for kids as you skim through the mangroves – be aware that life jackets are rarely supplied. If your children are not confident swimmers, you should hold onto them.

Probably the most important health concern is the **sun** – in the tropics, the effects of ultra-violet on delicate skin can be severe. Keep children covered in sunblock and insist they wear hats; they should also wear T-shirts when swimming. Sunglasses, too, are a good idea, even for babies, to reduce the intense glare – you can always find little novelty ones that will fit. Also, make sure they drink plenty of clean **water**.

Travelling

Air travel with under-2s (who get no seat for their ten-percent fares) can be a nightmare. Make every possible effort to get bulkhead seats and a baby bassinet (hanging cradle). When you reconfirm 48 hours before flying, double-check you still have them. If you have lively children who won't easily settle, consider sleeping-tablets: trimeprazine can be obtained on prescription and they'll sleep right through the flight.

For a young family, standard group excursions are probably not on. Renting a **private vehicle** is quite feasible, however, and gives you the flexibility and privacy you need for changing nappies, toilet stops and so on. For babies and children too small for seat belts, you'll need a **car seat** which, if you have the right model, also works as an all-purpose carrier, pool-side recliner and picnic throne. If you have a light, easily collapsible **buggy**, bring it; many hotels and lodges have long paths from the central public areas to the rooms. A **child-carrier backpack** is also useful. For flying with all this baggage, remember you have a full **luggage allowance** only for every passenger with a seat.

Accommodation

Only one or two **hotels and lodges** specifically exclude children of any age. The most child-friendly hotels are those situated on good sandy beaches, such as at Cape Point, Bakau, and one or two excellent eco-lodges on the coast. Very few places offer **babysitters as standard**, but, with a few hours' notice, the management can usually find somebody to come in, and they're likely to leave the question of payment up to you. Alternatively, if the children are asleep, speak to the manager about arranging for a night watchman to sit outside. With mobile phones in wide use, it's not difficult to stay in touch and be back at your room in a few minutes if necessary.

Charity projects

Gambian tradition fosters a culture of self-help within the family, and Gambians aspire to being totally self-sufficient. Nevertheless, The Gambia is a developing country and it welcomes help from charities and NGOs specializing in poverty alleviation, education, healthcare and conservation, which in turn depend to a great extent on donations.

Apart from cash, skills, and training, charities also welcome **donations** of medical supplies, old but useable crutches, spectacles and wheelchairs, school supplies (exercise books, text books, readers, encyclopaedias, computers, pencils and pens), sports equipment like footballs and tennis balls, and children's clothing.

If you'd like to distribute your own donation of skills, funds or supplies to Gambians in need, rather than channel it through a charity, it's essential to seek local advice first, in order to make sure your contribution ends up in the most appropriate hands. The non-profit organization **Gambia Tourist Support** (GTS) is an excellent source of advice on this (see below).

If you book your holiday through **The Gambia Experience** (see p.29) you will automatically trigger a small contribution to their school-building fund by filling in one of their holiday questionnaires. They can also advise about making your own donations.

Charitable organizations

Action Aid Africa regional office (Nairobi) ☎ +254 20 425 0000, ⊛ www.actionaid.org. NGO concerned with reducing poverty worldwide, with long-running practical projects in up-country Gambia.

Concern Universal Head office (Hereford, UK) ☎ 01432/355111, ⊛ www.concern-universal.org. Has been working in The Gambia since the early 1990s, specializing in sustainable agricultural and horticultural development, enabling communities to be self-sufficient.

Friends of Gambian Schools (FROGS) UK ☎ 01373/641659, 01622/882395, ⊛ www .friendsofgambianschools.co.uk. Raises funds to improve educational facilities in The Gambia.

Friends of The Gambia Association Head office (Morden, UK) ☎ 020/8337 2103, ⊛ www.fotga.org .uk. Organizes schoolchild sponsorship and supports Gambian medical facilities.

Friends of the Gambian Organization for the Visually Impaired Chairman (Norfolk, UK) ☎ 01493/721506, ⊛ www.friendsofgovi.org.uk. Tackling blindness and sight-impairment in The Gambia.

Gambia Education and Teaching Support (GETSuk) Kololi ☎ +220 446 2476, UK ☎ 0845/612 0296, ⊛ www.getsuk.org. Founded by Gambia Tourist Support (see below) to raise funds for the education of needy children in The Gambia.

Gambia Horse and Donkey Trust (Ockley, UK) ☎ 01306/627568, ⊛ www.gambiahorseanddonkey .org.uk. Runs educational programmes in animal welfare and offers veterinary care in order to improve the health, well-being and productivity of working horses and donkeys in rural Gambia.

Gambia Tourist Support (GTS) Kololi ☎ +220 446 2476, UK ☎ 0845/612 0261, ⊛ www.gambiatouristsupport.com. Acts as a point of contact for various initiatives which create employment, education and training opportunities. **Makasutu Wildlife Trust** Abuko ☎+220 778 2633, ⓦwww.darwingambia.gm/mwt, ⓔdrumohq@qanet.gm. Aims to protect and preserve wildlife in The Gambia and raise awareness of conservation issues (see p.144).

SOS Children's Villages Sponsorship office (SOS-Kinderdorf International, Vienna) ☎+43 1 368 6678, ⓦwww.sos-childrensvillages.org; Coordination office, Gambia: ☎+220 446 0836, ⓦwww.sosgambia.org. Offers shelter and support for orphaned and destitute children.

Travel essentials

Background information

The best way to get up-to-date **information** on The Gambia is to keep an eye on news websites and talk to tour operators, hoteliers, and independent organizations with interests in Gambian tourism. For more in-depth background reading, try specialist bookshops and the libraries of universities running African Studies courses; recommended books are detailed in Contexts (see p.296).

The Gambia's **internet** industry is still in its infancy, its output unreliable; some of the most interesting online information about the country is presently generated in Europe and the US or by foreign volunteers temporarily resident in the country. This situation is likely to change, as internet literacy begins to gather pace locally. One or two Gambian newspapers are trying to assert an online presence (see p.65), but by far the best source of online news is AllAfrica (see p.84).

Tourist offices

The Gambia Tourism Authority is a policy-making body; although it's not really geared up for providing advice for tourists on demand, its staff can provide brochures, handouts and basic information.
The Gambia Yundum International Airport and Kololi, Mon–Thurs 9am–4pm, Fri 9am–12.30pm, ☎446 2491, 446 2493, 446 2494, ⓔinfo@gta.gm, ⓦwww.visitthegambia.gm.
UK 57 Kensington Court, London W8 5DG ☎020/7376 0093, ⓔoffice@ukgta.fsnet.co.uk,

Mon–Thurs 10am–4pm, Fri 10am–noon. Downstairs from the Gambia High Commission.
Germany Feuerbachstrasse 26, 40 223 Düsseldorf ☎+49 211 493 9584, ⓔbadjie@bap-consulting .de, ⓦwww.visitthegambia.gm.
Sweden Gambias Turistbyrå, Drottninggatan 35 1tr, 411 14 Göteborg, ☎+46 31 13 66 50, ⓔinfo @gambiainfo.com, ⓦwww.gambiainfo.com.

Websites

Travel advice

The following government websites provide up-to-date safety and security advice for travellers, country by country.
Australian Department of Foreign Affairs ⓦwww.smarttraveller.gov.au.
British Foreign and Commonwealth Office ⓦwww.fco.gov.uk.
Canadian Department of Foreign Affairs ⓦwww.voyage.gc.ca.
Irish Department of Foreign Affairs ⓦwww.foreignaffairs.gov.ie.
New Zealand Ministry of Foreign Affairs ⓦwww.mft.govt.nz.
US Department of State Bureau of Consular Affairs ⓦtravel.state.gov.

The Gambia

ASSET ⓦwww.asset-gambia.com. Site of the Gambia's Association of Small Scale Enterprises in Tourism, with information about its members including hotels and tour companies.
Columbia University Libraries African Studies Internet Resources ⓦwww.columbia.edu/cu /lweb/indiv/africa/cuvl/Gambia.html. Comprehensive academic resource compiled by the New York university.

Gambia Daily ⓦ www.gambiadaily.com. West African news from the World News network and links to Gambian sites.
Gambia Gateway ⓦ gambiagateway.atspace.com. Gambian portal with links to small business sites and a photo gallery.
Gambia Resource Page ⓦ resourcepage.gambia .dk. A mixed bag of general information on the country.
Gambia Tourist Support ⓦ www .gambiatouristsupport.com. Excellent and informative general interest site from a highly committed charitable organization.
Nijii ⓦ www.gambia.dk. Personal pages created by a Gambian enthusiast with general information about the country.
Office of the Gambian President ⓦ www .statehouse.gm. Official news and reports.

Africa

Africa Daily ⓦ www.africadaily.com. News portal.
The Africa Guide ⓦ www.africaguide.com. Informative general-interest site covering the whole African continent.
Africa on Roots World ⓦ www.rootsworld.com /africa. Features about the African music scene and audio clips.
Afrol ⓦ www.afrol.com. News and links.
AllAfrica ⓦ www.allafrica.com. Excellent searchable database of news from the African press, covering the whole continent; it also publishes extracts and articles from Gambian newspapers.
BBC Africa ⓦ www.news.bbc.co.uk/1/hi/world /africa. Daily news from Africa and audio bulletins.
Contemporary Africa Database ⓦ www .africaexpert.org. Information about prominent Africans.

Magazines

Africa Week ⓦ www.africaweekmagazine.com. News magazine from the team behind the long-running but now defunct *West Africa* magazine.
BBC Focus on Africa ⓦ www.bbcworldservice .com/focus. Hard-hitting but accessible news quarterly.
New African ⓦ www.africasia.com. Well-established monthly with wide-ranging news features.
Travel Africa ⓦ www.travelafricamag.com. Glossy travel quarterly with excellent features; strong on wildlife and safaris.

Disabled travellers

Attitudes to disabled people in The Gambia are generally good. You'll have no problems recruiting helpers and can expect overwhelming consideration. However, government provision for disabled needs is almost completely absent and, while most hotels are single-storey or have ground-floor rooms, dedicated facilities for wheelchair or frame-users are practically non-existent.

Getting around in a wheelchair on unpaved footpaths or soft sandy streets is extremely hard work, and visits to historical and archeological sites often require some climbing of steps or hiking through a bit of bush. Most of The Gambia's national parks are awkward to reach and hard to get around. No forms of public transport are wheelchair-adapted and guided tours in safari vehicles with good springs are rare.

Despite the difficulties, the effort is worthwhile if you count yourself a very outgoing individual, and are prepared to be carried repeatedly. The Gambia is sufficiently low-key, accessible and accustomed to visitors to make the hassles bearable.
Gambian Physical Disability Sports Association ⓦ www.freeweb.com/gpdsa.

Electricity

When there is some, it is 220V AC, and sockets may be either European-style 2-pin, or UK-style 3-pin type. Only some resort hotels have shaver points or outlets in the rooms. Resort hotels have back-up generators to cover power cuts; elsewhere it's wise to be prepared with candles, a torch and, if you'll be depending on your mobile phone, a spare battery.

Emergencies

Ambulance ☏ 16
Police ☏ 17
Fire ☏ 18

Entry requirements

All visitors to The Gambia require a full ten-year **passport**, valid for at least six months beyond the end of the trip. Citizens of the UK, Belgium, Denmark, Finland, Germany, Iceland, Ireland, Italy, Luxembourg, The Netherlands, Norway, Sweden, Spain, the Commonwealth and the Economic Community of West African States (ECOWAS) do not require a visa to enter The Gambia on a trip not exceeding 90 days.

On arrival in The Gambia, your passport will normally be stamped with a **tourist visitor's pass** that allows you to stay in the country for

15 or 21 days, unless you request a longer stay – the maximum allowed on entry is 28 days. This can be easily extended by a month at a time for up to three months (D250 per month) at the Immigration Office in Banjul.

French, Swiss, US and Japanese pass-port-holders are among those that need a **visa**, available for around £20/€29/$37 (single entry) or £40/€58/$74 (multiple entry) from any of The Gambia's embassies and consulates; enquire at a British consulate if there's no Gambian representative in your home country. Visas are normally issued for thirty days and can be extended like tourist visitor's passes. If applying by post rather than in person, you should allow at least two weeks, plus transit time, for processing. A **commercial visa service** may sometimes be able to speed up this process.

Only under special circumstances can you organize your visa at Banjul International Airport **on arrival** (assuming your airline allows you to fly without a required visa); you're likely to be issued with a temporary stamp giving you 48 hours to get a visa from the Immigration Office.

If you're entering The Gambia from an area classified by the World Health Organization as infected with yellow fever, you'll require a **yellow fever vaccination certificate**. Possession of a **cholera vaccination certi-ficate** is not an entry requirement for The Gambia, but there have been rare cases of border officials demanding to see one.

Gambian diplomatic missions abroad

Gambian embassies and consulates gener-ally open from Monday to Friday, and usually close on Gambian national holidays.

UK Gambia High Commission, 57 Kensington Court, London W8 5DG, UK ℡44-20/7937 6316.

USA Embassy of The Gambia, 1115 15th St NW, Washington DC 20005, USA ℡1-202/785-1399; 11718 Barrington Court 130, Los Angeles CA 90077, USA ℡1-310/274-5084.

France Ambassade de Gambie, 117 rue Saint-Lazare, 75008 Paris, France ℡33-1/42.94.09.30.

Japan Consul General of The Gambia, Hyana Building 504, 3-14, 1-Chome Hiroo, Shibuya-Ku, Tokyo, Japan ℡81-3/444 7806.

West Africa Gambia High Commission: 11 rue de Thiong, Dakar, Senegal ℡221/821 1440; 6 Wilberforce St, Freetown, Sierra Leone ℡232-22/5191; 162 Awolowo Rd, Ikoyi, Lagos, Nigeria ℡234-1/682192.

Insurance

It's essential to take out an **insurance policy** before travelling to cover against theft, loss, illness or injury. Before paying for a new policy, however, it's worth checking whether you are already covered: some all-risks home insurance policies may cover your posses-sions when overseas, and many private medical schemes include cover when abroad. Students will often find that their student health coverage extends during the vacations and for one term beyond the date of last enrolment.

A typical travel insurance policy usually provides cover for cancellation or curtail-ment of your journey, emergency medical treatment and/or repatriation and the loss of documents, baggage and cash up to specified limits. If you need to make a **claim**, you should keep receipts for medicines and medical treatment, and in the event you have anything stolen, you must obtain an official statement from the police.

Internet access

Internet cafés are opening in every Gambian town, and proliferate in the main urban and

Rough Guides travel insurance

Rough Guides has teamed up with Columbus Direct to offer **travel insurance** that can be tailored to suit your needs. Products include a low-cost **backpacker** option for long stays; a **short break** option; a typical **holiday package** option and others. There are also annual **multi-trip** policies for those who travel regularly. Different sports and activities can be usually be covered if required.

See our website (℗www.roughguidesinsurance.com) for eligibility and purchasing options, or call one of the following numbers: UK ℡0870/033-9988; USA ℡1-800/749-4922; Australia ℡1-300/669 999; other nationalities ℡+44 870/890 2843.

resort areas. Charges are reasonable but vary a great deal from place to place, as does the quality of the hardware and the speed and reliability of the service. Gamtel offices often have the lowest rates (less than £1/$1.90 per hour), and the highest rates are up-country, where computers are much rarer and everything – mains power supplies, generator fuel supplies, and phone connections – less reliable. For now, there's internet access in the rooms of only a few hotels – primarily those catering for business guests, such as the *Atlantic* in Banjul and the *Kairaba* in Kololi.

Laundry

All Gambian hotels can arrange to wash, iron and return your **laundry** at a speed determined by the weather – on rainy or humid days it will take a little longer than on a hot day in the dry season. Elsewhere, you won't find public laundries, but there are plenty of people willing to do the job. Hand-washing is the most common method; in rural areas, this may be done in a stream.

It's considered bad form to give your underwear to somebody else to be washed, but it's easy to find small quantities of cheap washing powder in *bitikos* (small shops). Ideally, dry your clothes indoors, and avoid spreading them on the ground – they may become infested by tumbu fly which lays its eggs on wet clothes. Ironing kills the eggs.

Living and working in The Gambia

While the Gambian government is keen to encourage foreigners to **invest** in The Gambia – the Gambia Investment Promotion and Free Zones Agency, GIPFZA (Ⓦwww .gipfza.gm) can provide details of opportunities and incentives – in general it's not easy for non-Gambians to find **paid work** in the country. Under-employment is a serious problem and work permit regulations make it near-impossible to land a job without pulling strings. Ideally you should have skills that can't be matched by a Gambian candidate and be prepared to work for a local salary.

Volunteering is more feasible, if you have appropriate expertise, and sufficient time to devote to a project. The sizeable expatriate volunteer community is cosmopolitan, active

and committed. As well as the programmes run by the organizations below, opportunities arise on local health, education, conservation, research and development projects from time to time. These are often advertised by word-of-mouth; a direct, personal approach to the appropriate ministry might open some doors.

Teachers, medical personnel, agriculturalists and engineers have the best chances of finding openings, paid or unpaid. The Gambia is going through a period of rapid structural and agricultural development and appropriate skills are in demand; the health service is badly under-resourced. English language tuition is of particular value to Gambian schools, especially up-country where there is an acute shortage of qualified teachers. Even children whose parents are fluent in English may have insufficient language practice at home, where everybody chats in Mandinka, Wolof, Fula, or whatever, rather than English. The Gambian education system rules that all lessons be conducted in English, rather than in African languages, so students' progress in other subjects such as maths or science can be severely hampered if their command of English isn't up to scratch.

Voluntary work and study programmes

Some universities which run courses in African studies offer study-abroad programmes to The Gambia. The following are independent organizations that run **volunteer programmes**.

Gambia Tourist Support Kololi ☎00220-462476, Ⓦwww.gambiatouristsupport.com. Imaginative and committed Anglo-Gambian organization which raises funds to support Gambian children through school, and can find work placements and study placements in The Gambia for gap year students and other self-funded volunteers.

Mondo Challenge UK ☎01604/858225, Ⓦwww .mondochallenge.org. Organizes placements for a small number of self-funded volunteers with the National Beekeepers Association of The Gambia, which aims to alleviate rural poverty and to encourage careful husbandry of the natural environment by providing Gambian villagers with the training and equipment they need to start beekeeping businesses. Also places volunteers in rural teaching posts.

Peace Corps USA ☎1-800/424-8580, Ⓦwww .peacecorps.gov. Accepts applications from US citizens over 18 for voluntary field work in developing countries, including The Gambia. They recruit people with knowledge of agriculture, education, engineering or health care; to be sent to a specific country, you must have skills required by that country.

VSO (Voluntary Service Overseas) UK ☎020/8780 7200, ⊛www.vso.org.uk. Respected charity that sends professionals qualified in key fields to spend two years or more working for local wages on projects beneficial to developing countries. The Gambian division is very well-established and efficiently run. Applicants can state their preferred country, but the organization's prime concern is to find the right people for the posts available.

Worldwide Veterinary Service UK ☎01725/519527, ⊛www.wvs.org.uk. Places qualified vets on clinical and educational programmes, such as working with the Gambia Horse and Donkey Trust.

Mail

Gambian **post offices** are called the GPO (General Post Office), a remnant of British colonial days. They usually have separate counters for different services; the Banjul GPO has a philately desk, where you can buy collectors' sets of the country's attractive stamps.

To post a letter costs D15 (around £0.30/€0.44) to UK/Europe and D18 (around £0.36/€0.52) to North America. As well as stamps, the GPO sells postage-paid **aerograms** for D15. International mail should arrive seven to ten days after posting; if your letter is **urgent**, the best post office to use is the one at the airport which may send it out on the next flight. If you have heavy or valuable items to send to the UK, Europe or North America, it's worth entrusting them to a friend or contact who's flying there (leave parcels unsealed for customs). A lot of ordinary mail is sent this way too – it's always quicker.

Poste restante

If you're staying at a reliable **hotel** in northern Kombo, you could have your mail sent there; otherwise, have it sent to a friend with a **PO Box**, or to the Banjul GPO **Poste Restante**. It can take some time for post to find its way up-country. Note, too, that some post offices only hold mail for a few weeks before returning it to the sender.

To **collect mail** from the poste restante desk at the Banjul GPO, write out your name as you'd expect it to appear on the letter, and bring your **passport**, without which

you'll rarely be allowed to collect mail. If in doubt, ask the assistant to check under both your first and second names. You'll be charged D15 (around £0.30/€0.44) per item.

Ask **senders** to put their own address on the back and to write your address in this form: GREGG Emma, Poste Restante, GPO, Russell Street, Banjul, THE GAMBIA. Mail posted from abroad is likely to be in transit for anything up to two weeks before you can collect it from Banjul.

Maps

There's presently a shortage of accurate, up-to-date **maps** of The Gambia. By far the most useful general interest map for touring the country is Macmillan's *The Gambia Traveller's Map* (1:400,000, 2005), which is clear and reasonably comprehensive, although The Gambia's ongoing road-building programme means that it's already out of date. This is available in Europe and from a few bookshops and souvenir shops in The Gambia.

For wider travels in **West Africa**, the single most useful item to take is the 1:4,000,000 Michelin map 741 *Africa North and West*. Freytag and Berndt publishes a 1:500,000 *Gambia and Senegal* Map.

Opening hours

Most Gambian **shops and offices** close on Friday and Saturday afternoons, and all day Sunday. Most tourist restaurants serve either from breakfast time or from late morning until around 10pm or whenever the last customers leave. Afra barbecues stay open much later. Bars and clubs keep going until the small hours of the morning.

Government offices open Mon–Thurs from 8am to 3pm or 4pm, and Fri–Sat 8am–12.30pm. Banks generally open Mon–Thurs, 8am–1pm & 4.30–6.30pm, Fri 8–11am. Telecentres and Gamtel offices generally open 8am–10pm daily. Post offices generally open Mon–Thurs 8.30am–12.15pm & 2–4pm, Fri 8.30am–12.15pm & 2.30–4pm, Sat 8.30am–noon. Shops and businesses open Mon–Thurs around 8am–5.30pm, sometimes later, and sometimes with a break for lunch, and Fri–Sat 8am–noon. Supermarkets have longer hours, which may include Sundays. Daily markets are generally open from 8am till dusk.

Photography

Insure your **camera**, and keep it in a dust-proof bag. Bring spare batteries, and all the film or memory cards you'll need – quality supplies are almost non-existent in The Gambia. Keep film cool by stuffing it inside a sleeping bag or roll of clothes. Local processing is hit and miss, so if you'll be away for some time, post your film home, or send it with someone flying back.

Early morning and late afternoon are the best times for photography: at midday, with the sun directly overhead, the light can be very flat. The green season brings particularly rewarding conditions, especially a few days after the first rains have broken. Months of dust are settled, the countryside has a lush, bold sheen and the sky is magnificent.

The contrast between light and shade in the tropics can be huge, so expose for the subject and not the general scene. A flash is useful to fill in shadows. Dark skin needs extra exposure: think of people as always back-lit. A half stop is normally enough. For photography etiquette, see p.34.

Telephones

To make a landline phone call in the Gambia, you can choose between using a **phonecard** (the cheapest option), using a commercial **telecentre**, or calling on a **hotel phone** account. Some hotels will charge a reasonable fixed rate for local calls, but those who allow you to call abroad direct mark up the cost considerably.

Gamtel offices (the state-run telecom company) and supermarkets sell several brands of phonecard, in various denominations, which give you an access code to make local or international phone calls from any landline. Special offers come and go, so ask which brand is currently the best bargain.

Without a card, you can call locally or abroad from booths in Gamtel offices or any of the private telecentres which are numerous in every town. You make the call and pay afterwards.

International phone calls from The Gambia sometimes take a while to connect, as do calls to mobile phones – you'll often get a message saying all lines are occupied. **Reverse charge** or **collect** calls are possible from landlines, but expensive; it's better to arrange in advance to receive a call at a certain time and number.

The cheapest way to **call The Gambia** from the UK is to use one of the discount call companies such as Telesavers (☎0844/566 7070 to call landlines or ☎0871/999 5454 to call mobiles, ⊛www .telesavers.co.uk) or Cheapest Calls (☎0844/566 1414 to call landlines or ☎0871/999 3838 to call mobiles, ⊛www .cheapestcalls.co.uk). The Gambia's **international dialling code** is +220.

Mobile phones

Mobile phones are now very common in The Gambia; many businesses and individuals use a mobile number as their principal means of contact and, despite their expense, phones have become essential urban accessories. The Gambia's two rival GSM networks, Gamcel and Africell, have agreements with many foreign mobile service providers, so your phone is likely to work in The Gambia. It's advisable to find out about charges before you leave home.

Network **coverage** is generally excellent in Gambian towns, with a few rare exceptions (Janjanbureh residents have been known to climb trees in search of a reliable signal). The signal drops off sharply to zero on the fringes of urban areas.

Calling abroad from The Gambia

Dial the following international **access codes** followed by the area code, omitting the initial zero if there is one, then the number.

Australia 0061
New Zealand 0064
Republic of Ireland 00353
Senegal 00221

South Africa 0027
UK 0044
US and Canada 001

What to pack

Binoculars are essential for bird-watching, small ones with good lenses are most practical.

A multipurpose **penknife** is useful, but avoid ones with blades longer than a palm-width which could be misconstrued, and remember not to carry knives or scissors in your hand luggage when flying.

A **torch – very useful for frequent electricity cuts**.

Plastic bags – carrier bags to keep dust off clothes, small sealable ones to protect cameras, film, tickets and documents.

If driving or hiking in remote areas, take a **compass** or a **GPS** gadget.

A lightweight **mosquito net**: although nets are cheap to buy locally, these are often bulky.

Disposable razors (available only at import supermarkets), or preferably an old-fashioned razor blade holder.

Condoms are best brought from home.

Tampons are expensive and only sold in supermarkets and shops in northern Kombo (they're extremely scarce up-country).

The best material for **clothes** is cotton; for dusty up-country roads, dark colours are best. For the resort areas you'll want beach wear and smartish light clothes; for clothing etiquette see p.34. Pack at least one warm jacket or sweater, and take the lightest, toughest, airiest footwear you can afford.

If you need to receive local calls during your stay, the most practical option is to buy a Gambian SIM card and pay-as-you-go **scratch cards** from either Gamcel or Africell in order to use your non-Gambian mobile (or a spare) on the local network. SIM cards cost around £5/€7; scratch cards come in various denominations. Calling internationally using a Gambian SIM is more expensive than using a Gambian phonecard or telecentre, but cheaper than using a hotel phone and much cheaper than making a roaming call with your SIM from home. With a Gambian SIM you'll also automatically have the benefit of **voicemail** retrievable from any Gambian landline – useful when you're out of mobile range.

If your phone is programmed to be used exclusively on your home mobile network it will need to be **unlocked** before you can use it with a Gambian SIM. Many Gambian mobile phone shops offer this service, but if your phone is a very new model, they may not have the necessary software, and you'll have to get it unlocked before you leave.

Time

Most of West Africa, including The Gambia, is on Greenwich Mean Time (GMT, often jokingly translated by easy-going locals as "Gambia Maybe Time"). The twelve-hour clock is generally used. Although The Gambia lies some distance north of the equator, it has roughly the equatorial twelve hours of daylight – a little more in summer, a little less in winter, with sunrise always between 6.30am and 7.30am, and sunset between 6.30pm and 7.30pm. The tropical dusk is very brief – worth remembering if it's late afternoon and you need to travel somewhere before dark.

Toilets

Except in tourist hotels and restaurants, where the facilities are generally good, paper is usually provided by the user rather than the owner; Gambians prefer to use water. In rural areas and less well-off urban compounds, the facilities are usually a hole in the ground, or a "**long-drop**" toilet built into a cubicle. A bucket or kettle of water for washing will be provided. The Gambia's more enlightened eco-lodges have begun to introduce composting toilets.

Guide

Guide

Kombo: Banjul and the north

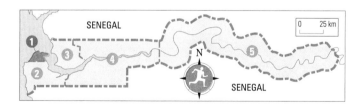

CHAPTER 1 # Highlights

* **Arch 22** Climb to the top-floor balconies of Banjul's monstrous-looking monument for fantastic views of the city. See p.107

* **Albert Market** One of the country's most accessible urban markets, brimming with colour, noise and pungent produce. See p.108

* **Microlighting** Get a whole new perspective on the Kombos from the back seat of a motorized kite. See p.112

* **Resort hotels** There's a great choice of accommodation along the Atlantic coast, offering swimming pools, entertainment and sumptuous buffets. See p.113

* **Beach bars** Sunshine, sand and sparkling sea, with fresh fish on the barbecue and cold beer in the icebox. See p.133

* **Nightlife** Forget the hotel discos and go where the in-the-know locals go – urban garden clubs playing rippling *mbalax* or high-energy *ndagga* music. See p.136

* **Abuko Nature Reserve** This small but fascinating forest park is home to birds, lizards, crocodiles and monkeys galore. See p.143

* **Tanbi Wetlands** Best explored by small boat, the mangrove creeks at the mouth of the River Gambia offer superb birdwatching and angling. See p.145

△ Atlantic Hotel, Banjul

Kombo: Banjul and the north

M ost visitors to The Gambia, and the vast majority of expatriate residents, spend most of their time in the northern corner of **Kombo district**. Kombo is a collection of sub-districts occupying a peninsula of around nine hundred square kilometres, edged by the mouth of the River Gambia to the northeast and 50km of tropical beaches to the west. Concentrated in the vicinity of the northernmost beaches are most of the hotels in the country, some of them in enclaves catering solely for foreign visitors.

Banjul, The Gambia's laidback, low-rise capital, lies on a small, flat island jutting into the mouth of the River Gambia at the district's northeastern tip. It's separated from the resorts and the more populous urban areas further inland by an expanse of saltwater wetlands. Hot and hemmed in by mangroves, river and sea, it's a small city, with a population that's actually decreasing. To a significant extent, it's a daytime centre only – at dusk, workers by the minibus-load pour back over Denton Bridge to the mainland and down the highway to their suburban homes.

Despite having a few noteworthy attractions such as the National Museum, an excellent market, and a rich architectural heritage, Banjul is not really geared towards tourists. Most visitors choose instead to enjoy the hotels, restaurants, bars and clubs of the **coastal resort areas**, where there are ample opportunites to chill out in the sun: the facilities here are unmatched anywhere else in the country. The main resorts of Bakau, Fajara, Kotu and Kololi each have their own distinctive character; some are upbeat holi-day centres, while others are swish residential neighbourhoods or large African villages that happen to be near the ocean. Its attractions as a **tropical sunshine** destination are considerable, with plenty of hotel guests content to relax and do nothing, pottering from pool to restaurant to bar. For the slightly more adventurous, tour companies offer excursions that showcase northern Kombo's most interesting features, such as Banjul's landmarks and the sacred crocodile pool in Bakau.

At the heart of the area, close to but very distinct from the tourist areas, is The Gambia's largest town, **Serrekunda**, which houses about fifteen percent of the total population and constitutes the country's commercial nerve centre. It's sometimes overlooked by beach-mad tourists, but it's a living, breathing, cacophanous West African town that's intriguing to explore.

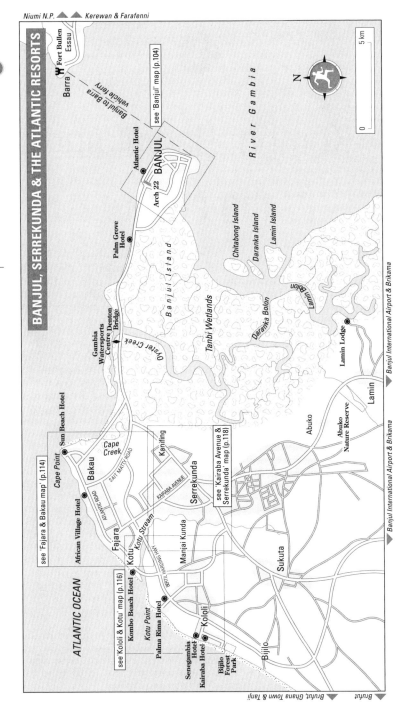

BANJUL, SERREKUNDA & THE ATLANTIC RESORTS

Independent travel in northern Kombo is straightforward once you get to know transport types, departure points, routes and prices. The hotel areas are served by taxis and some public transport routes, and none of the Atlantic beaches are more than a kilometre from the nearest surfaced road. The area is also a convenient starting-point for travels further afield, on foot, by bicycle, or by bush taxi or rented car.

For **naturalists**, especially ornithologists, the area offers opportunities to explore a rich variety of habitats, home to numerous species. If you're staying in one of the many hotels with a large garden, then spotting exotic species is as easy as stepping onto your veranda. Within walking distance of most accommodation options are bird-rich stretches of beach and countryside where you'll also see small colourful lizards sunning themselves on rocks, and possibly a few wild monkeys.

Barely half an hour from the resorts by road is one of The Gambia's finest protected areas, **Abuko Nature Reserve**, a well preserved small forest park in which birds and monkeys are habituated to visitors, so you stand a good chance of close-up encounters. East of here, and occupying the sixty square kilometres immediately south of Banjul, are the **Tanbi Wetlands**, a maze of mangrove-festooned creeks excellent for birdwatching and fishing. People also come here to enjoy leisurely cruises by traditional *pirogue*, and to visit **Lamin Lodge**, a wonderful rickety timber bar-restaurant built right over one of the broad and beautiful creeks.

Banjul International Airport

Before tourism took off in The Gambia, the international airport was no more than a shed next to an airstrip. Now there's an impressive terminal building with a modern, sculptural silhouette, and a runway registered with NASA as an emergency space shuttle landing site. The terminal, designed in 1997 by renowned Senegalese architect Pierre Goudiaby, has a bright, lofty interior, with soaring white pillars and subtle friezes depicting Gambian artisans, farmers and fishermen.

Arrival formalities are low-key and straightforward. At **passport control**, you're given an entry stamp (see p.84); you're then required to pay a **tourist tax** (a flat rate of D250/£5/$10/€10) at the Gambia Tourism Authority desk. Customs officials have been known to angle for bribes, so hold your ground if you suspect the rules are being bent, and ask the advice of a tour rep. Rates for **porters** are fixed at D10, £1 or $1, and there'll be a scramble for your stuff; luggage trolleys are free. For **currency**, the Trust Bank in the main hall (Mon–Fri 9am–5pm, Sat 9am–1pm) offers decent exchange rates but has no ATM. Also in the main hall are a small **tourist information office** (Mon–Fri 9am–4pm, Fri 9am–12.30pm) which can offer a few brochures and leaflets, a **post office** (Mon–Sat 8am–4pm or until after the last flight), a bar, an Internet café, public telephones and an outlet for mobile phone SIM cards and scratch cards. For details of flight arrivals and departures, the **information desk** (☏447 3000) is to the left as you exit the arrivals area.

Transport from the airport

Tour guests pre-booked into the package hotels are normally driven there from the airport by complimentary **coach**. Independent travellers without their own wheels can pick up a **rental car** from the Europcar desk in the main hall (☏777 3988, ⊛www .europcar.com). Fixed **tourist taxi** fares from the airport are posted on a board outside the arrivals area (D400–500 to Banjul or the resorts). You should be able to negotiate a lower price if you seek out a **yellow local taxi** – there may be a couple out in the car park. Otherwise, it's a three-kilometre walk to the main road, where, during the day, you can pick up a **bush taxi** to Brikama, or to Banjul via Serrekunda – change at Serrekunda for Kotu, Kololi, Fajara or Bakau.

Arrival

Most visitors to the area fly into **Banjul International Airport** near Yundum, south of Serrekunda, and 24km from Banjul city (it's actually closer to the coastal resorts than to the capital). A sleek, newly surfaced road leads from the airport north to Serrekunda and Banjul, and south to Brikama and the main south bank highway that runs up-country. A branch leading off the highway serves the resorts and connects to the Kombo coastal highway, which follows the southwestern coast south to Kartong. For information on arriving by road from Senegal, see p.30.

To get around Banjul and northern Kombo by **public transport**, you can choose between chartering a green **tourist taxi**, hiring a **yellow taxi** for a "town trip", or flagging down a **bush taxi**, which could be either a shared yellow taxi or a minibus, for a trip along a fixed route (see p.44). In the resorts, especially in high season, there's stiff competition among the tourist taxi drivers, and some may offer you better prices than the fixed rates displayed at the taxi ranks near the hotels. Note that tourist taxi drivers pay a premium to be allowed to work in the tourist areas such as the Senegambia, Kotu and Cape Point turnarounds, and confrontations between your driver and the police may result if you try to persuade a bush taxi to carry you to or from a tourist taxi zone.

Banjul

Sweltering, confined and at times seething with mosquitoes, the Gambia's capital **BANJUL** is not an obviously appealing town. Its tarmac streets seem to pump out heat in the dry season, and its alleys become a chaos of red mud and puddles during the rains. The dilapidated assemblage of corrugated iron and peeling paint, and, deep in the backstreets, open drainage channels with no slopes to drain them, complete a somewhat melancholy picture. With its population of less than 50,000, Banjul is too small to offer any of the ordinary facilities and diversions of a capital, and nightlife is all but nonexistent. Most city workers make an understandable exodus after business hours; few choose to live here.

To be won over by Banjul you need a little patience, or perhaps a specialist interest in West African history or architecture. More than any other Gambian town, the capital conveys a strong sense of the country's **colonial past**. Elements of this are being lost almost daily, as streets are renamed and new buildings replace old, but there are still interesting details and architectural juxtapositions to seek out. Banjul's architecture tells the story of its history and development, with visible remnants of a progression of building styles spanning nearly two hundred years, from early nineteenth-century *kirinting* houses (similar to wattle and daub) to late-twentieth-century banks and law courts. The city is ripe for regeneration – with some judicious preservation, improvement, and investment it could feel vibrant rather than drab, intimate rather than claustrophobic.

More immediately, Banjul has a few attractions which, by any standards, are worth a brief visit: the **National Museum** for its small but enlightening

△ Banjul (townscape from Arch 22)

collections relating to local and regional history and ethnography; the **Atlantic Hotel**, for its attractive swimming pool, beach and restaurants; **Albert Market**, for its colour, verve and range of commodities; and **Arch 22**, President Jammeh's vainglorious monument, for its inspiring rooftop views.

Though a capital, Banjul has an idiosyncratically relaxed **small-town atmosphere**. If you have business to get on with, whatever you need to accomplish here can usually be done in reasonable safety – and at less than three square kilometres, the town can easily be covered on foot. You may be warned by some Gambians that Banjul is unsafe after dark, but it's wrong to mistake the quietness of the place for any undue threat. The **security** presence is low-key:

when recently the local police were issued with bicycles, it was seen as a great innovation, as previously the only way they could get to a crime scene was to walk or take a taxi. Even so, it's a town with people constantly in transit, so take the same precautions as in any urban area at night.

Some history

The expansion and development of Banjul, known to the colonial British as **Bathurst**, was from the outset hampered by the serious drawbacks of its site. The British built Bathurst on St Mary's Island, a small, insect-infested landmass separated from the mainland by a band of creeks and swamps prone to flooding. Kankujeri Road (formerly Bund Road) forms a dyke that constrains the city on its present small patch, making further expansion impossible.

However, the early settlers were probably not thinking beyond their immedi-ate ambition of safeguarding British commercial interests in this corner of West Africa. St Mary's Island, which at the time seems to have had no permanent inhabitants, was acquired by Britain in 1816 to defend the River Gambia from **slavers** and to control trade with the interior. A detachment of the British Royal African Corps led by **Captain Alexander Grant** equipped the island with a battery of cannon to intimidate rogue traders from France, Spain and Portugal. The island itself was now secure enough to function as a trading base, and a number of British merchants moved their businesses from the Senegalese island of Gorée to the new town of Bathurst. The population then quickly grew, with an influx of Wolofs from Gorée and St Louis, and freed slaves from Freetown in Sierra Leone. Grant is generally credited with making a significant contribution to eliminating the slave trade on the River Gambia once and for all. One of his honours was to have a street named after him – most of the other streets of Bathurst were named after generals who served at the Battle of Waterloo, and prominent merchants.

Bathurst grew from a fort and **collection of villages** to a city in the space of a century. With a basin deep enough to dock ocean-going vessels, the port became one of the Senegambia region's principal trade gateways, with Wellington Street (now Liberation Street) the focus of commercial activity. In 1889, the city was declared capital of the newly-created British "Crown Colony and Protectorate of The Gambia", as present-day Gambia was first named, and the twentieth century saw a steady increase in trade as the coun-try's population expanded.

In 1973, eight years after independence, Bathurst was renamed **Banjul**. At this time, great optimism in the country's commercial future led to the expansion and modernization of the docks; however, the city itself had nowhere to grow, and Serrekunda took over as The Gambia's largest town. By the mid-1980s, an air of despondency and neglect had settled over the capital, its streets mostly unpaved, its colonial buildings crumbling, and its citywide network of drainage ditches choked with reeking refuse. Things went from bad to worse in 1986, when Albert Market was destroyed by fire. In the late 1980s, derelict buildings began to be replaced, and the change in government in 1994 brought with it a number of development initiatives, including improvements to the Royal Victoria Hospital, road surfacing and, more controversially, the construction of Arch 22. Later in the 1990s came the near-total eradication of the old British street names from the map of Banjul – even Grant Street and Clarkson Street, named after strident anti-slavery activists, were renamed after Africans – though in practice many locals stick doggedly with the old names. Today, **city renewal** appears to be gathering pace, with long-neglected buildings being torn down to make way for new. Unfortunately, historical structures are being lost in the process, and there's every chance that Banjul's cityscape will be barely recognisable within a few decades.

Arrival, orientation and transport

Banjul is not the first stop for most people flying into The Gambia – visitors staying in the resort hotels head straight for those instead (for information on arriving at Banjul International Airport, see p.97).

There are two approaches to Banjul. If you're coming **by road** from southern Gambia, Serrekunda or the Atlantic resorts, you take the Banjul-Serrekunda highway, driving past dense banks of mangroves on the way to Oyster Creek which separates the island from the mainland and is spanned by Denton Bridge. After the bridge, the highway follows the coast of Banjul Island, passing beach cemeteries on the way, until forking into Independence Drive, Marina Parade and Wallace Cole Road at Arch 22. No vehicles (apart from the president's) are allowed to pass under the arch, so you'll probably turn down Marina Parade, one of Banjul's more pleasant and shadier streets, fringed with somnolent government buildings and terminating, after the *Atlantic Hotel* and the Royal Victoria Hospital, at the guarded gates of State House. Independence Drive is graced with the impressive Court House and House of Representatives. The second approach to Banjul is from northern Gambia or northern Senegal; you make your way to the small port of Barra on the north bank of the River Gambia (see p.188) from which a regular **ferry service** (see p.102) brings you straight across to the terminal in Banjul town centre. Turn right outside the terminal to head towards Albert Market and the Atlantic Hotel; turn left and follow Kankujeri Road west to end up on the Banjul–Serrekunda highway.

Despite its compactness, Banjul's **layout** can initially be disorientating, as all the side streets look much the same; to add to the confusion, some addresses

Travelling between Banjul and Dakar

To travel **overland from Banjul to Dakar**, the capital of Senegal, you need to allow a day. First you take the ferry or *pirogue* to Barra (see p.94), and then take either a bus or a bush taxi. **Buses** tend not to run when relations with Senegal are strained, but in theory GPTC run two buses a day from Barra to Dakar, the first leaving around 8am and the second around 10am, or sooner if all the pre-booked passengers are on board. The buses wait just inside the Barra ferry terminal exit gate. Count on six to seven hours for the journey. It's possible to buy a ticket (D200) on board, but to be sure of a seat you need to book in advance at the GPTC depot in Kanifing near Serrekunda (☏439 4776).

By **bush taxi**, you travel to the Gambian border post of Amdallai by *gelleh-gelleh* van (D18) or shared Peugeot car (D30) from Barra's taxi garage adjoining the ferry terminal, a trip that currently takes up to an hour but should be must faster once the scheduled resurfacing of the road takes place. At Amdallai, you go through Gambian exit formalities, then either walk, sit on the back of a moped (D20), or join a shared Peugeot (D10) for the 2km of straight road to Karang, the Senegalese border post. Here you can find a vehicle going to Dakar via Kaolack; the best are Peugeot *"sept-places"* cars at CFA5000 (around £5/€8) per person which do the journey in around five hours.

Regular **flights**, one or two each day, (D4000/£85/€140 one-way) run from Banjul International Airport to Dakar.

Crossing the River Gambia from Banjul to Barra

The **Barra ferry** service is one of Banjul's lifelines, a crucial link in its line of communication to The Gambia's nearest neighbouring capital, Dakar. The service runs between Banjul's Liberation Avenue terminal and the wharf at Barra, on the opposite side of the mouth of the River Gambia. There are no bridges across the River Gambia, so the smooth operation of the ferry has a critical part to play in Banjul's activities as an import-export centre; unfortunately, the service is sometimes erratic.

There are presently three boats in operation – *Johe* and *Kanilai* are relatively new, and cross the river in as little as thirty minutes, while *Barra* is older and slower (45–60min). Each one can carry two large trucks, three or four smaller ones, or an equivalent number of cars, plus foot passengers (daily 7am–11pm, at least hourly on the hour in each direction; vehicles D145, foot passengers D5); contact the Port Authority ☏422 8205 for information on any delays.

Limited space on board means that vehicles sometimes have to queue for several hours, even when the ferries are running to timetable. **Delays** are fairly routine – sometimes for apparently trivial reasons – although often they are unavoidable, such as when unfavourable tides and strong currents stretch the journey to two hours. At the end of the dry season (May–June), dredging of the silted-up Gambia estuary can sometimes disrupt the service. Further delays can be expected in the few days before and after major festivals (see p.66), when the whole country seems to be on the move, and Liberation Avenue becomes one big ferry queue.

In order to buy a vehicle **ticket** at Banjul, you drive into the yard containing the slipway and report to the ticket office. From the north bank, however, you need to get a ticket before you can enter the terminal, from the Port Authority ferry office just south of Essau. On either side of the river, Port Authority security staff can assist you. If you're travelling as a **foot passenger**, in either direction, then having bought your ticket you make your way to the hot and crowded waiting room. If you're with a tour group, you're generally spared the waiting room and can board ahead of the melée.

It's worth remembering that it can be surprisingly cool and breezy on the river. Watch out for pickpockets on the ferry and in the jostling crowds in both terminals. There are plenty of hustlers, some of them fairly intimidating, touting transport on

still use the old British street names. The **Gamtel Tower** is a good landmark to navigate by, visible from many different angles and taller than all the surrounding buildings. You're likely to spend most of your time in the **commercial district** around July 22nd Square and Liberation Avenue down by the waterfront, where Albert Market, the post office and banks are all located.

Banjul has two **bush taxi turnarounds**: one opposite the National Museum, with minibuses serving Bakau (15–20min; D6), and the other on Mosque Road, serving Westfield Junction and Serrekunda (20min; D6) and Brikama (45min; D15). **Green tourist taxis** are found outside the *Palm Grove* and *Atlantic* hotels, and **yellow taxis** can be flagged down for short hops, or hired for town trips, all over town.

Accommodation

Despite its idiosyncratic appeal, The Gambia's capital city is not everybody's idea of the perfect base for a holiday. It has only two **tourist-class hotels**, the *Atlantic* and the *Palm Grove*. There's also a clutch of fairly down-at-heel **smaller**

the Barra side, particularly in the stampede for buses and bush taxis. The pedestrian gateways through which you leave either terminal on arrival are narrow and crowded, and can feel claustrophobic.

The crossing itself is an experience that's much more authentically Gambian than travelling by tourist transport. You'll see passengers crowd on board with all manner of stuff, from sheep on ropes and chickens held upside down by the ankles to wardrobes manhandled by two or three people. Some women carry huge headbundles, others may be chatting on their mobile phones. As well as transporting traders and trade goods, the ferry is a trading place in its own right, with hawkers peddling everything from natural remedies to plastic toys, and shoe menders busily cleaning and stitching up shoes whether invited to or not.

Early morning is a pleasant time to make the crossing, with a good chance of seeing dolphins plunging in the bow-wave. From midriver, there are good views of the Banjul skyline, and of Barra. The 7am ferry from Banjul is the slow one, and it sometimes holds up the 8am one outside Barra, but the 8am one can't overtake, so if you want to dash for onward transport then the first ferry gets you ahead.

An alternative way to cross the river is to take a passenger **pirogue**, but these are only worth considering on calm days, and not after dark, when the crossing is more dangerous and prices higher. They're faster than the ferry (20–30min) and more flexible, running not to timetable, but when full (bush taxi style), and so can be preferable to a long wait if the ferry's delayed. The fare is normally the same as the foot passenger fare on the ferry. The pirogues have been tightly regulated since a fatal accident in early 2002 when an overloaded boat tipped over midriver, drowning around sixty of its passengers and crew. Now everybody has to wear a lifejacket, and there are strict load limits of 20–40 people, depending on the size of boat. Deep decking means there's little chance of falling out, but the boats can be rather leaky and boys with buckets bale out from time to time. You're always close to the water, so if you sit on the ocean side you'll get mildly drenched – it's drier on the riverward side, and driest in the middle. You'll also get wet if you have to wade to get on and off the boat, particularly at the Barra end. If you'd like a burly Gambian to fireman's lift you onboard, that's extra.

hotels and **guesthouses** in the town centre, catering mainly for travelling Africans. The best of these are a little shabby, while the worst rent out rooms by the hour – but even some of these are worth investigating for a low-cost experience of Banjul.

Apollo Hotel Tafsou Ebou Samba St ☎ 422 8184. Stuck in a 1970s timewarp, this is a characterless place, but a reasonable choice if you're looking for something vaguely resembling an international-style self-contained room, on a budget. ❷

Atlantic Hotel Marina Parade ☎ 422 8601, ⓦ www.corinthiahotels.com. Comfortable and well-maintained hotel geared towards wealthy business travellers and the high-end tourist market, situated right on a pleasant stretch of beach, within walking distance of the centre of Banjul. The grandly proportioned bar and restaurant areas are popular with local movers and shakers. The two hundred-plus rooms are a little small and unimaginative, but well equipped. Most have views of the pool, the ocean, the flower gardens, or a jungly bird garden that attracts over 150 bird species and has a viewing platform. ❼

Banjul Ferry Guest House 28 Liberation Ave ☎ 422 2028. The best choice in this price range, located right in the thick of things near the Barra Ferry terminal, with a communal balcony great for watching the incessant activity in the street below. It looks unpromising from the outside – you enter through a dingy yard and climb some back stairs to the first floor – but the fifteen rooms are well-kept and a good size; some are self-contained with a/c, and a few on the higher floors have private balconies. ❶–❷

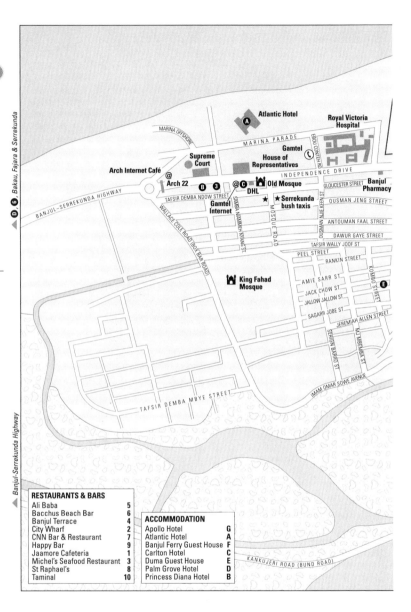

MARINA OFFSHORE

Atlantic Hotel Ⓐ

Royal Victoria Hospital

MARINA PARADE

EBOU CONTEH RD

Supreme Court

Gamtel Ⓒ

House of Representatives

Arch Internet Café @

INDEPENDENCE DRIVE

Arch 22 Ⓑ Ⓑ Ⓑ @ Ⓒ 🏨 **Old Mosque**

GLOUCESTER STREET

Banjul Pharmacy

TAFSIR DEMBA NDOW STREET

DHL

Gamtel Internet

SAMBA MAXIMEH NYANG ST

★ ★ **Serrekunda bush taxis**

EBOU JENG NI JYRIE RD

OUSMAN JENG STREET

BANJUL–SERREKUNDA HIGHWAY

WALLACE COLE ROAD (BOX BAR ROAD)

MOSQUE ROAD

ANTOUMAN FAAL STREET

DAWUR GAYE STREET

TAFSIR WALLY JOOF ST

PEEL STREET

RANKIN STREET

🏨 **King Fahad Mosque**

AMIE SARR ST

JACK CHOW ST

KOMBO STREET

Ⓔ

JALLOW JALLOW ST

SAGARR JOBE ST

JEREMIAH ALLEN STREET

SEIGON BAYHO ST

MJ MBENBA ST

IMAM OMAR SOWE AVENUE

TAFSIR DEMBA MBYE STREET

KANKUJERI ROAD (BUND ROAD)

RESTAURANTS & BARS	
Ali Baba	5
Bacchus Beach Bar	6
Banjul Terrace	4
City Wharf	2
CNN Bar & Restaurant	7
Happy Bar	9
Jaamore Cafeteria	1
Michel's Seafood Restaurant	3
St Raphael's	8
Taminal	10

ACCOMMODATION	
Apollo Hotel	G
Atlantic Hotel	A
Banjul Ferry Guest House	F
Carlton Hotel	C
Duma Guest House	E
Palm Grove Hotel	D
Princess Diana Hotel	B

Carlton Hotel 25 Independence Drive ☎ 422 8670. Old-fashioned four-floor, forty-room hotel with a slightly formal atmosphere. The rooms are self-contained and decently furnished; some have a/c, and some just about have views of Arch 22. At street level the outdoor terrace is leafy and cool. ②

Denton's Beach Resort Denton Bridge ☎ 777 3777. Recently opened at the mouth of Oyster Creek, with easy access by boat both to the Tanbi Wetlands and the open Atlantic, this British-run place is the perfect base for fishing and boating enthusiasts: sharing the spacious site are the Gambia Watersports Centre and Gambia

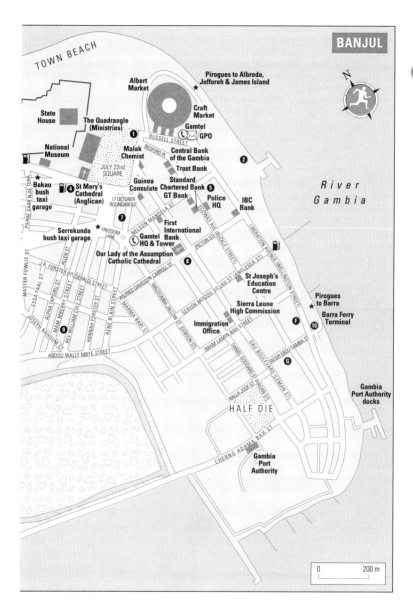

BANJUL

TOWN BEACH

Albert Market

Pirogues to Albreda, Juffureh & James Island

Craft Market

State House

The Quadrangle (Ministries)

Gamtel

GPO

RUSSELL STREET

National Museum

BEDFORD PL.

Malak Chemist

Central Bank of the Gambia

JULY 22nd SQUARE

Trust Bank

Bakau bush taxi garage

St Mary's Cathedral (Anglican)

Guinea Consulate

17 OCTOBER ROUNDABOUT

Standard Chartered Bank

GT Bank

Police HQ

IBC Bank

River Gambia

Serrekunda bush taxi garage

FREEDOM LANE

Gamtel HQ & Tower

First International Bank

PICTON ST.

ECOWAS AVE (BUCKLE STREET)

NELSON MANDELA ST.

LIBERATION AVENUE (WELLINGTON STREET)

PIERRE SARR NJIE TERR.

Our Lady of the Assumption Catholic Cathedral

MASTER FOWLIS ST.

J.R. FORSTER (FITZGERALD) STREET

ALLEN ST.

ESSA FAAL ST.

ALPHA JAPSIRU ST.

MAM MBERRY STREET

REV WILLIAM COLE STREET

HANNAH FORSTER ST.

JOSEPH BAHOUM ST.

MACOUMBA JALLOW ST.

WILFRED DAVIDSON CARROLL ST.

SERIGN MODOU SILLAH ST (ANGLESEA ST.)

St Joseph's Education Centre

MARINA BAH ST.

Sierra Leone High Commission

IMAM LAMIN BAH STREET

DANIEL GODDARD ST (DOBSON ST.)

Immigration Office

Pirogues to Barra

Barra Ferry Terminal

CAUL BOULEVARD (LEMAN ST.)

TAFSIR EBOU SAMBA ST.

ABDOU WALLY MBYE STREET

RENE BLAIN STREET

MAM MBERRY STREET

BALLA JOOE ST (HAGAN ST.)

HALF DIE

Gambia Port Authority docks

CHERNO ADAMA BAH ST.

Gambia Port Authority

N

0   200 m

Sports Fishing. The accommodation, in houses with high ceilings, is bright, airy and cool, and the many facilities include a small pool and a mini cinema. **4**

Duma Guest House 1 Jallow Jallow St ☎422 8381. Friendly guesthouse deep in a residential quarter, but not the easiest to find – look for a three-storey yellow and white building with a brown gate. Unfortunately the building is crumbling and the decor has definitely seen better days. Four of the thirteen rooms are self-contained. **1**

Palm Grove Hotel Mile 2, Banjul–Serrekunda Highway ☎420 1620, ⓦwww.palmgrovehotel -gambia.com. Tourist hotel with a pleasant loca- tion next to a lagoon and a quiet stretch of beach. Unfortunately, it's way outside the town centre, and guests mostly have to rely on costly green tourist taxis to get around – it's difficult to flag down bush taxis hurtling along the busy highway outside the hotel. It's an attractive enough place to spend time,

though; the 120 self-contained rooms are stylish, with optional a/c, and the decor includes works by local artists. ⑤

Princess Diana Hotel 30 Independence Drive ☎422 8715. Twelve-room hotel with plain self-contained rooms with fans or a/c. It's clean and adequate, but a little soulless, with narrow corridors. ①

The Town

Banjul's commercial bustle, centred around its **docks** at the city's eastern limit, makes an immediate, vivid impression on most visitors. Small though the port is, it's an important gateway for imports and exports, and the streets around the harbour are regularly clogged with fume-belching lorries waiting to pick up new consignments as fabric, tea and rice are disgorged from ocean-going vessels by the container-load – some commodities are destined for the shops and stalls of Liberation Avenue and Albert Market, others get moved on up-country and to other West African states.

The area just inland from the docks is Banjul's **shopping district**. The town can be a diverting place to shop, but don't expect to find any department stores, supermarkets or even boutiques with window displays – trading is done on a very informal basis on the street corners, in the market, or in the shops that are little more than market stalls with walls and doors, crammed together along the colonnaded shopping streets. Banjul's trading community is dominated by Gambian Lebanese, but you'll also find Mauritanians here, hazel-skinned and instantly recognisable in their long blue robes. You'll see Gambian and Guinean tailors, too, at work on the pavements, their treadle-powered machines whirring away. An ever-present element of Banjul street life are the travelling traders, many of them Senegalese, hawking trays of fake designer sunglasses, cartoon-character toothbrushes, or bootleg CDs.

Among the law courts, parliament buildings and ministries on the north side of town is the venerable old **Royal Victoria Hospital**, the only teaching hospital in the country. Like all The Gambia's health facilities, it's under-funded and reliant on the support of foreign benefactors to a consid- erable degree; visitors can join a two-hour tour (☎422 6152, Mon–Thurs 10am & 2pm, free) to find out more. Banjul also has an interesting collection of **mosques**, the principal of which is the King Fahad Mosque, built in 1988 and named in tribute to the Saudi Arabian monarch, and huge enough to be visible for miles around; if you fly over Banjul, the mosque's enormous sandy praying area is one of the easiest landmarks to spot. The nineteenth- century Independence Drive Mosque on the corner of Mosque Road and Independence Drive was Banjul's first; it stands right on the street, so when the gate-like doors and windows are open you can glimpse the elegant arches inside. On Freedom Lane, right in the middle of town, is a miniature mosque with jaunty green minarets. At prayer times worshippers spread their mats on the tarmac outside, and the blaring loudspeakers manage to drown out the car horns. Non-Muslim visitors can enter the mosques if they're suitably attired (see p.74).

The most pleasant time to explore Banjul on foot is in the golden light of late afternoon or at weekends, when the commercial and residential quarters in the west and southwest of town take on their most relaxed and appealing character. Once the frenetic crowds of wheelers and dealers have packed up and moved on, there's time to stop and look at the **architecture** with less danger of being bumped by an orange-seller's barrow or butted by a goat-seller's goat. Good areas to wander include Rene Blain, Hannah Forster and Rev William Cole streets where, side by side, you'll see examples of *kirinting* houses, with bamboo-weave walls sometimes daubed with plaster, and timber houses, faced with planks. The *kirinting* houses, quick and cheap to construct, are among Banjul's oldest buildings, originally home to the less-well-off African settlers on the island in the early nineteeth century. The next architectural wave – the timber houses – dates from the 1840s, built and owned by more affluent Aku settlers. Later in the nineteenth century, when Bathurst was a thriving trading post, the Portuguese, British and French merchants built the commercial houses that still line Russell Street, Liberation Street and ECOWAS Avenue, with arched colonnades at street level and roofed-in verandas on the first floor. While each year sees more of the oldest buildings being replaced and redeveloped, plenty of glimpses of the city's architectural history still remain.

Arch 22

Arch 22 (daily 8am–4pm; D50), a massive, cream-coloured free-standing monument spanning Independence Drive, was built to commemorate the coup of July 22, 1994 and to herald a new era in Gambian history. Completed in 1996, it's something of a monstrosity, and totally at odds with the rest of Banjul.

The best reason to visit Arch 22 is the unobstructed **view** from the top-floor balconies – rare in a country as flat as The Gambia, with so few tall buildings. From these you get a good sense of Banjul as an island city, ringed by river, ocean and mangrove. You might also be struck by the relative grandeur of the buildings that serve as reminders that this small town is the nation's capital: the circular Supreme Court, the House of Representatives, and the huge mosque. Even from the halfway level, the noise and clamour of the commercial district is diminished, and the over-riding impression – far less obvious on the ground – is of a maze of family compounds, palms, and baobabs, the elements of any Gambian village. The **terrace** at the half-way level is an excellent vantage point from which to watch the official celebrations and events sometimes held at this end of Independence Drive, with the Arch as a dramatic backdrop.

The **top floor** of the Arch houses a small department of the National Museum. The displays of ethnographic material (traditional tools, weapons, and textiles, including gorgeous ceremonial costumes) are good, though rather thin on explanation. The first exhibit you come to is easy to miss since it's so incongruous: the small, very ordinary stool on which Jammeh sat when he announced the AFPRC had taken over The Gambia.

The architect responsible for the Arch is Senegalese **Pierre Goudiaby**, whose work has become closely associated with the Jammeh regime (other commissions have included Banjul International Airport and the Farafenni and Bwiam hospitals). At a cost of US$1.15 million – an astronomical sum in local terms – Arch 22 is not Goudiaby's finest achievement, despite Jammeh's desire for a massive structure that would inspire patriotic pride. The Arch's formula of decorated pediment upon Doric columns (eight of them, big enough to house staircases and lifts) has nothing to do with modern Gambia. Goudiaby is noted for capturing the spirit of traditional Africa in his modern buildings, but here his only nod towards ethnic idiom seems to be the viewing balconies, which African architecture buffs describe as "curved like calabashes". Technically, it's a bit of a disappointment, too – soon after it opened, one of the lift shafts became unuseable due to the twisting of the structure as it settled into the soft ground. As a symbol of progress within the capital, its message rings a little hollow for many Banjul residents.

At the foot of the Arch is a gilded **statue** of a soldier holding an infant, supposedly representing the rescue of the nation by the military coup, although critics have remarked that the soldier looks more like a kidnapper than a rescuer. On the opposite side, the area where ceremonies are sometimes held is adorned by equally tacky statues of traditional musicians and elders, the work of Goudi-aby's brother, Tony.

National Museum of The Gambia

The **National Museum** on Independence Drive (Mon–Thurs 8am–4pm, Fri & Sat 8am–1pm; D50), though small, poky and badly lit, contains some gems – you just have to be patient to find them. Some visitors don't make it beyond the ground floor, where the worthwhile twentieth-century displays include a collection of **Oku marabout** oddments (including *jigida* waist beads, a *shukoo* bridal basket, like a big colourful laundry basket, and an *igba* engagement calabash, which would have contained the bride's dowry, engagement ring, kola nuts and spices). There's also **colonial ephemera**, including a first-class ticket for a passage from Bathurst to the UK "on or about 30 August 1959" aboard the MV *Apapa*, a banana boat which, pitching and rolling, would have taken about a week to make it to Liverpool.

If you take time to peer into some of the darker corners, you'll find, among the mouldering ethnographia, some interesting **old photos** of *jalis* playing the *kora* at ceremonies and gatherings, a few prehistoric artefacts, some illuminating maps, documents and generally informative stuff about the wars and migrations of the Senegambia region, and a good display on **Islam** in The Gambia.

However, kids used to interactive displays will be yawning within minutes at the yellowing notices against the exhibits; they might pause at the **traditional musical instrument** collection downstairs, but just for long enough to discover that you're not allowed to touch anything.

The building that presently houses the Museum used to be the **Bathurst Club**, a Europeans-only establishment, and it still has an appropriately quirky, old-fashioned atmosphere. Its garden, which has a drinks stall, is a green oasis which contains Banjul's last remaining well; the others were all abandoned in the 1930s, when piped water was introduced to the city.

Albert Market and the commercial district

Albert Market (daily 8am–7pm), a laid-back and unusually tidy version of the everything-under-the-sun kind of market found all over West Africa, is one of Banjul's big draws. It's quite a maze, but the stalls are reasonably well separated by paved paths. The produce stalls sell common West African culinary ingredients such as sticky brown tamarind, lurid scarlet chillies, lumpy tomatoes stacked in neat pyramids, lentil-like locust bean seeds, mounds of groundnut paste and baskets of pungent dried fish, plus all sorts of basic groceries sold in a vast range of quantities, from rice by the sackful to oil by the polythene-bagful or macaroni by the spoonful. Barrowloads of **fruit** are sold in season, especially mangoes in the rainy season, watermelon after the rains, and oranges and pineapples in the dry season.

Beyond the produce there are stalls selling **beauty products** such as shea butter (a natural moisturiser), handmade soap, and hair extensions, and household goods of every description. There are some great bargains in **clothing**: Chinese-made clothes are especially cheap, as import duty in The Gambia is very low. You may also come across **fetish stalls**, selling cowrie shells, bits of animal horn, bones, kola nuts, small pipes, trade beads and old rusty bangles. The *bantaba* area within the market is a treasure trove of fabric, and one of the best places in the country to buy the latest cottons, including wax prints and embellished damask in a riot of fabulous colours.

Deep inside the general market, among fig-draped trees, is the highly enjoyable **tourist market**. There's a good choice of batik clothing here, plus musical instruments (drums, *balafons*, *koras*, and all sorts of percussion), beads and handmade leather goods. There are also a couple of stalls selling African antiquities including masks from all over West Africa. Many stalls sell cheap and cheerful souvenirs – necklaces, bracelets, bangles and the ubiquitous carvings; be prepared to bargain.

Albert Market overspills into **Liberation Avenue** and the nearby roads, where shops and stalls sell more cheap, trashy shoes and clothing, plus household oddments and bootleg cassettes. Fabric wholesalers in this area are open to the public, and offer good selections of imported cloth in African designs.

You'll also find handmade clothes, tablecloths, and items of knitting, crochet and patchwork in the shop a block back from Liberation Street at **St Joseph's Adult Education and Skill Centre** (ECOWAS Avenue, ☎ 422 8836; Mon–Thurs 8.30am–3pm, Fri 8.30am–noon, closed for two weeks over Christmas and Easter and late-July–mid-Sept). The goods are all produced by the centre's talented students, young women aged 16–25, some from underprivileged backgrounds. They're usually happy to give you a tour of the centre so you can watch traditional craft techniques; staff encourage this, as it's a good opportunity for them to practise their English. The classrooms are bright and inviting, and there's an inspiring atmosphere of purposefulness to the whole place.

Eating, drinking and nightlife

Banjul suffers from a serious shortage of **restaurants**, particularly in the evenings, but there is first-class simple food to be had from local eateries and fast-food joints in the daytime. For rice and sauce, there's plenty of choice among the stalls in the Albert Market, where all the traders eat, and you'll find itinerant traders everywhere – especially around July 22nd Square – with fruit, fritters, frozen juices and peanut brittle.

There's not much **nightlife**, either, in the conventional sense. At the time of writing, the last club in town had closed, and the only option was the rather plush air-conditioned disco at the *Atlantic Hotel* (nightly till 3am). Banjul is the kind of place where people prefer to hang out with their mates in the streets, playing table football or checkers, or brewing *attaya* – after dark, the pavements are dotted with glowing charcoal braziers topped with little teapots.

Ali Baba Nelson Mandela St ☎ 422 4055. Popular Lebanese place that's highly recommended, even though it's not much to look at, with white plastic tables and a fair few flies. Decent snacks, sandwiches and main meals, including first-class *falafel*, delicately spiced *kafta*, and juicy burgers, plus mango and guava juice and fresh fruit smoothies. Subtitles itself *"The King of Chawarma"*, but is not to be confused with the less appealing *King of Chawarma Restaurant* a couple of doors down the street. Mon–Sat 9am–5pm.

Birdwatching around Banjul

Kankujeri Road, formerly known as Bund Road, passes through a variety of bird-rich habitats, and a few sessions spent here can easily yield sightings of over a hundred species. On the west side of the road are mangroves and the tidal mudflats of the estuary, with the rusting hulks of wrecked ships sunk into the mud, the roosts of pelicans and cormorants. At low tide, the mudflats are well populated with gulls, terns, herons and waders. To the east is reclaimed land, some of it cultivated, some of it wild and dotted with tamarisk and mangrove. Here you are likely to see little grebe, Senegal thick-knee and black-headed plover. The roadside itself is to a varying extent a vehicle scrap-yard, so you have to make your way carefully, and it's also preferable to pick a time when there aren't too many lorries thundering past, so weekends are best. The best choice of accommodation in the capital for birdwatchers is the *Atlantic Hotel*, which has plenty of bird-friendly foliage in its grounds.

Bacchus Beach Bar & Restaurant Mile 2, Banjul–Serrekunda Highway ☎ 422 7948. Situated on the lagoon behind what used to be the Wadner Beach Hotel (now derelict), this slightly overpriced bar/restaurant is aimed at tourists, with standards like steak and barracuda; it's too out-of-the-way to attract much passing trade, but popular with the guests at the nearby *Palm Grove Hotel*. It's on the beach but indoors, with mosquito screens, and there's a pool table.

Banjul Terrace 72 Gloucester St ☎ 422 7826. With a grand-looking streetside terrace, this place is smarter than most of the city's eateries, but still unexceptional. There's a mixed menu of seafood and grills. Daily till 8pm.

City Wharf Restaurant On the beach, off Liberation Ave, reached by the turning near the IBC bank. Friendly spot with a few waterside tables and chairs with sunshades, where you can enjoy a drink while watching the *pirogues* and other river traffic.

CNN Bar & Restaurant Rene Blain St. Serving *chawarmas*, chicken and chips and cold drinks, this extremely grimy bar can be near-deserted by day, but is often busy late at night.

Happy Bar Rev William Cole St. A tiny hole-in-the-wall drinking place with a very local atmosphere, in a quiet street where kids play table football on the corner.

Jaamore Cafeteria On the corner of July 22nd Square, near Albert Market. Pleasant outdoor café, with a few shaded tables in a fenced-off corner of the square, giving a new lease of life to a lovingly preserved 1930s drinking fountain. Visited mostly by tourists, but not touristy, this is a great place to relax over a drink and people-watch; you can also order simple meals, if you have time to wait while somebody fetches ingredients from the market. Daily till 8pm.

Michel's Seafood Restaurant 29 Independence Drive, opposite the Court House ☎ 422 3108. One of the very few relatively formal restaurants in Banjul outside the hotels, and the only one open late, this an old-fashioned place, functional rather than romantic. It serves a good choice of fish and a different West African dish every day at reasonable prices. Specialities include tiger prawns, lobster and fresh local juices. Daily 8am–late.

St Raphael's Wilfred Davidson Carroll St, opposite the Catholic cathedral. Low-key place that feels rather like a Catholic family drawing room, serving good-value *benechin*, *domodah*, and other West African dishes such as *chew-kong* (catfish) and *foofoo* with soup, plus wine and spirits.

Taminal Liberation Ave, by the Barra ferry terminal. Basic African-style fry-ups for travellers waiting for the ferry.

The Atlantic resorts and Serrekunda

The Gambia's principal **tourist strip**, which accommodates virtually all the country's package holidaymakers, covers just over ten kilometres of the Atlantic coast west of Banjul. This area is an appealing place to unwind, with its easy-going restaurants, low-key nightspots, and clusters of clifftop and beachside hotels. It provides many tourists with all the distractions they need, and it's common for visitors to return again and again without venturing further up-country.

There are four main **resort** areas, strung along the coast. **Bakau**, the most significant coastal community after Banjul itself, is long-established, and it has a large enough population to assert an identity of its own that's far from swamped by the presence of visitors. The sandy beaches at its northern limit, Cape Point, are among the most attractive in the area. Bakau's "old town", east of Sait Matty Road, is a swarming village of dirt streets and noisy compounds and home to many of the hotel staff, while the "new town", west of Sait Matty Road, has more villas and lawns. **Fajara**, adjoining Bakau on the coast, is one of The Gambia's most desirable neighbourhoods, with bougainvillea draping decoratively over walls enclosing large private houses. To the south-west, Fajara merges into **Kotu**, where a high concentration of tourists pack into a clutch of established hotels, at the debouchment of the small Kotu stream. Finally, further south, **Kololi** and its neighbouring villages of Manjai Kunda, Kerr Serign and Bijilo are a very mixed area where some of the most upmarket hotels, the most bohemian guesthouses and the trashiest tourist traps in The Gambia are found. At the hub of the resort area, and indeed of the whole country, but scarcely registered by many of the sunworshippers, is **Serrekunda**, The Gambia's largest town, a seething, cacophonous commercial centre that's on the go 24 hours a day.

The Gambia's holiday industry is extremely localized in this corner of Kombo, giving the area an atmosphere and relative affluence that's quite unlike anywhere else in the country. There are more newly surfaced roads in the resort area than in the rest of country put together, and far more vehicles cruising them, many of them taxis, Land Rovers and coaches exclusive to foreign visitors. There are also

Moving on from Serrekunda

Serrekunda is The Gambia's main terminus for public transport services. **Bush taxis** running along the main south bank highway to Basse, or covering the routes to and from Banjul, the resorts, the southern coast and the Senegalese border, plus most other villages in Kombo district, operate out of Serrekunda's several bush taxi garages and stops. To get from Serrekunda to Brikama (30min; D10), minibuses leave from the stop on Kombo Sillah Drive at Westfield Junction, and for points along the south bank highway beyond Brikama, such as Soma (5hr 30min–6hr 30min; D90), Sankulay Kunda and Bansang (8–10hr 30min; D180) or Basse (10–14hrs; D200), gelleh-gelleh vans leave from the garage near Bundung police station, further south.

The Gambia by microlight

The Gambia is more or less flat, so elevated views of the countryside are rare. By **microlight** you get a unique perspective on the Gambian landscape, covering large distances in a matter of minutes. There's also the physical thrill of being airborne at five hundred metres in a small craft, with no fuselage separating you and the breeze. Plus, if you're up for it, your pilot can take you through some stunt manoeuvres that will really get your pulse racing; you feel very exposed, so the experience is not for the faint-hearted, but microlights have an excellent safety record.

The Gambia has one microlight base, Madox Airsports (☎779 2119 or 702 1167, ⓦwww.madoxairsports.co.uk), in the grounds of Banjul International Airport. It's primarily a small-scale training centre with a CAA-authorized examiner – you can become an internationally qualified microlight or light aircraft pilot here. The Gambia is a good part of the world for clocking up flying time, since weather conditions are very favourable most days throughout the dry season. The instructors will also take visitors out on tours, for an hourly fee (you can arrange to be collected from one of the resort hotels for no extra charge). In this case, you'll be the passenger in a two-seater microlight, with a communication link from your helmet to the instructor's so you can talk during the flight. After taking off from the airport's main runway, within minutes you can be soaring over Makasutu or Serrekunda, or cruising from bay to bay along the Atlantic coast. The snaking mangrove creeks of the Tanbi Wetlands, in particular, are extremely beautiful when viewed from the air.

---

better (though far from perfect) supplies of water and electricity – not that any hotelier would consider operating without private generators and water tanks.

Some hamlets in the resort area are practically tourist ghettoes, populated entirely by visitors, tourism workers and bumsters. The towns and villages where Gambians actually live have expanded hugely since the first plane-loads of winter sunseekers arrived from Sweden in the 1960s, while up-country villages have been emptied of whole generations of school-leavers (and school dropouts) as youngsters get swept up in the coastward drift. Meanwhile, the coastal region's old rural economy of planting, fishing and palm-wine-tapping is fading fast.

Since tourism has had such a strong foothold in this area for so long, it's an accepted element of contemporary life for the Gambians living in northern Kombo. Most residents, remarkably, have retained an equable regard for visitors. Inevitably, where locals and tourists interact, the question of patronage sometimes creeps in, and even wise village elders here believe that a major benefit of tourism is the opportunity for Gambian youngsters to make their families' fortunes by marrying foreigners. Nonetheless, it's still possible to strike up lasting friendships with northern Kombo residents that have no hidden agenda.

Arrival, orientation and transport

A new tarmac road covers the 10km between the airport (see p.97) and the resort areas, and most visitors enter the area by this quick and easy route. The **Kombo coastal highway** connects the resorts and continues all the way down to Kartong, near The Gambia's southwestern limit. The stretch which runs between Kololi, Kotu and Fajara is known as **Bertil Harding Highway**.

Serrekunda, 12km from Banjul and 13km from the airport, is connected to Fajara and Bakau by **Kairaba Avenue**, The Gambia's four-kilometre commercial artery. At its southern end, Kairaba Avenue meets the Serrekunda–Banjul dual carriageway at the landmark Westfield Junction. Towards its northern end is the Bertil Harding Highway junction, marked by a Shell garage and what was until recently the only set of **traffic lights** in The Gambia.

Bush taxi (or "local taxi") rides around Banjul, Serrekunda and the main resort areas are all short hops of 10–20min (D5–6). Serrekunda is the hub. Banjul–Serrekunda minibuses run from Banjul's Mosque Road, along the Banjul–Serrekunda Highway to Westfield Junction. Banjul–Bakau minibuses run from opposite the National Museum, along the Banjul-Serrekunda Highway, then along either Sait Matty Road or Old Cape Road to Bakau's main turnaround on Atlantic Road near the market. Westfield–Bakau and Serrekunda–Bakau minibuses and cars run from the Banjul–Serrekunda Highway near Westfield Junction along Kairaba Avenue, Garba Jahumpa Road and Sait Matty Road to Atlantic Road. Cars sometimes run along Atlantic Road between Bakau and Fajara. Serrekunda–Kololi and Serrekunda–Kotu cars run from London Corner on Sayerr Jobe Avenue in Serrekunda to either the Badala Park or the Palma Rima junctions, then on to the Senegambia area (Kololi) or the *Bungalow Beach* area (Kotu). Ask for "Senegambia" or "*BB*". Town trips by yellow taxi start from D50, and tourist taxis and car rental are also available (see p.149).

Bicycles can be rented from stands outside most major hotels, giving you the freedom to explore the back-country near the resorts, the best beaches further south, or the bush tracks on the north bank of the River Gambia (accessible by ferry, see p.102).

Accommodation

With the exception of the pricier places, most of the **tourist hotels** along the coastal strip are quite basic by international standards, but they all have a swimming pool, restaurant and bar, and most have a pleasant garden. Nearly all the most popular places are very close to the beach (surprisingly enough, though, rooms with sea views are rather rare). Most guests arrive on flight-plus-hotel packages, rather than booking direct; by shopping around among the tour operators you're likely to come across some generous discounts.

Independent travellers looking for somewhere reasonably cheap to relax for a few days will find several friendly, **small independent hotels** and **guesthouses**, a few of which have pools and restaurants, a short distance away from the coast in Bakau, Fajara, Kololi or Serrekunda. **Self-catering accommodation** is taking off in a big way – there are enough produce markets, supermarkets and restaurants in the resort area to make catering straightforward. Finally, if you are interested in staying as a house guest in **a Gambian compound** (something which many in Bakau and Serrekunda are happy to offer, as they can charge, daily, the equivalent of a week's wages), then just ask around and take pot luck; you should expect to be asked anything from D300 to D500 per person per day, with meals included, depending on the season. It's easiest to find this kind of arrangement if you already have a base, even just a cheap hotel, so you won't feel under pressure to rush into any deals you're uncertain about.

While the **villages** in the resort area are all within easy travelling distance of each other, each has a distinctive character, so if you plan to stay here for more than a couple of days it's worth choosing your base carefully. The busiest and most touristy beach resorts are the Senegambia area and Kotu. The Palma Rima area, Bakau and Cape Point are considerably quieter; Bijilo and Fajara even more so. For a more 'local' experience away from the beach hotels, try Kololi Village, Bakau or Serrekunda.

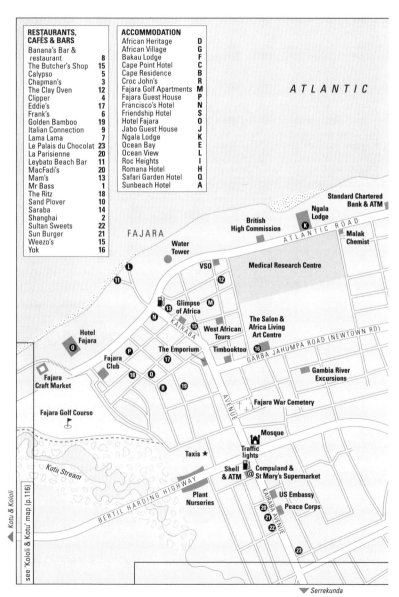

RESTAURANTS, CAFÉS & BARS

Banana's Bar & restaurant	8
The Butcher's Shop	15
Calypso	5
Chapman's	3
The Clay Oven	12
Clipper	4
Eddie's	17
Frank's	6
Golden Bamboo	19
Italian Connection	9
Lama Lama	7
Le Palais du Chocolat	23
La Parisienne	20
Leybato Beach Bar	11
MacFadi's	20
Mam's	13
Mr Bass	1
The Ritz	18
Sand Plover	10
Saraba	14
Shanghai	2
Sultan Sweets	22
Sun Burger	21
Weezo's	15
Yok	16

ACCOMMODATION

African Heritage	D
African Village	G
Bakau Lodge	F
Cape Point Hotel	C
Cape Residence	B
Croc John's	R
Fajara Golf Apartments	M
Fajara Guest House	P
Francisco's Hotel	N
Friendship Hotel	S
Hotel Fajara	O
Jabo Guest House	J
Ngala Lodge	K
Ocean Bay	E
Ocean View	L
Roc Heights	I
Romana Hotel	H
Safari Garden Hotel	Q
Sunbeach Hotel	A

Bakau and Cape Point

Bakau is a good choice of neighbourhood if you'd like the sense of staying in an African community, but don't want to be too far from the beaches and tourist facilities. The hotels and guesthouses here are refreshingly down-to-earth, and the village is a good place to start asking around if you're keen to stay in a family compound. The **Cape Point** hotels are tucked away in a quiet and

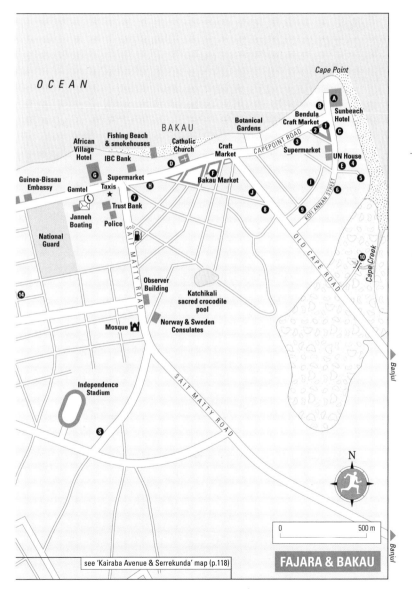

OCEAN

Cape Point

BAKAU

Botanical Gardens

Bendula Craft Market

Sunbeach Hotel

CAPEPOINT ROAD

Fishing Beach & smokehouses

Catholic Church

Craft Market

Supermarket

UN House

African Village Hotel

IBC Bank

Supermarket

Bakau Market

KOFI ANNAN STREET

Guinea-Bissau Embassy

Gamtel

Taxis

Trust Bank

Janneh Boating

Police

OLD CAPE ROAD

Cape Creek

National Guard

SAIT MATTY ROAD

Observer Building

Katchikali sacred crocodile pool

Mosque

Norway & Sweden Consulates

Independence Stadium

SAIT MATTY ROAD

N

0   500 m

see 'Kairaba Avenue & Serrekunda' map (p.118)

FAJARA & BAKAU

Banjul

KOLOLI & KOTU

0   500 m

N

Kotu Point

8

ATLANTIC OCEAN

Palma-Rima Beach

10

PALMA RIMA ROAD

11
12 → **i**

Palma Rima Hotel

13
14

PALMA RIMA AREA

K

15

M **L**

16

18

Kololi Point

K O L O L I

BERILL HARDING HIGHWAY

20
21

Brussels **N** **O**
SN Airlines

Lamtoro Clinic

Senegambia Hotel

Gambia Experience office

Q

S **23**

SENEGAMBIA ROAD

Standard Chartered Bank

Taxis ★

25
26 Gamtel

U **V** **W**

22 Village Gallery

KOLOLI VILLAGE

Y
a

Z

28

29

SENEGAMBIA JUNCTION

★ Taxis

30

31

Senegambia Craft Market

Kairaba Hotel

SENEGAMBIA AREA

b

33 **32**

34

35

36 **37**

c

40

41 **38**

d

39

Bijilo Forest Park

Brufut, Tanji & Airport

e Coconut Residence

42

KERR SERIGN

KOTU
Kotu Bengdula
Craft Market

Kotu Strand

Hotel Fajara
FAJARA

Fajara
Golf Club

Fajara Craft
Market

Barrier

Kombo Beach Hotel
Gamtel

Taxis

Fajara Golf Course

Kotu Stream

Badala
Park Hotel

Kotu Ponds

Pond

KOTU STREAM ROAD

Fajara & Bakau

BERTIL HARDING HIGHWAY
Plant Nurseries

Kotu
Police
Station

MANJAI
KUNDA

KOTU & PALMA RIMA AREA

ACCOMMODATION		RESTAURANTS & BARS	
Badala Park	H	"40 Foot"	16
Bakadaji	M	Ali Baba	9
Bakotu	D	Boss Lady	6
Bakotu Apartments	F	Calabash	14
Dutch Whale	J	Churchill's	13
Bungalow Beach	B	Destiny's	3
Bunkoyo	L	Domino	4
Fajara	A	Jazziz	14
Kombo Beach	C	Kotu Point Beach Bar	8
Luigi's Apartments	I	Kunta Kinteh Beach Bar	7
Palm Beach	G	Luigi's	12
Palma Rima	K	Paradise Beach Bar	1
Sunset Beach	E	Sailor Beach Bar	2
		Shiraz	15
		Solomon's	10
		Teranga Beach Club	11
		The Captain's Table	5
		Tiger Tiger	6

KOLOLI & SENEGAMBIA AREA

ACCOMMODATION		RESTAURANTS & BARS			
Balmoral Apartments	U	African Queen		The Kora	38
Bananaville	T	Al Basha/Paparazzi	25	La Valbonne/Kololi Casino	34
Baobab Beach Resort	h	Ali Baba's	28	Mama's	24
Bijilo Beach	g	Amber's Nest	31	Paradiso	29
Coconut Residence	e	Amsterdam Dolphin	17	Queen's Head	27
Coco Ocean Resort	j	Aquarius		Relax	19
Golden Beach Hotel	i	Avocado	42	Scala	36
Holiday Beach Club	b	Baobab	20	Seaview Beach Bar	21
Holiday Suites	P	Bodega Casa Fernando	23	Shikra	23
Kaira Du La	d	Coco Beach	35	Tao	33
Kairaba	S	Forest Beach	39	Taste of India	32
Keneba	V	Gaya Café	30	Village Gallery	22
Kololi Beach Club	c	GTS	41	Waaw/Wow	29
Kololi Tavern	X	Jade	40	Yasmina	26
Mango Club	f	Kololi Fast Food	18		
Mannjai Lodge	R				
Melrose Place	W				
Orchard Guest House	Y				
Paradise Suites	N				
Sarge's	Z				
Seaview Gardens	O				
Senegambia	Q				
Soto Bar Koto	a				

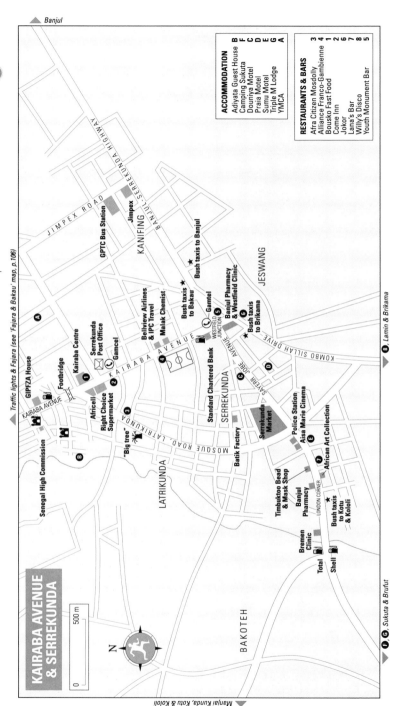

KAIRABA AVENUE & SERREKUNDA

0 — 500 m

N

ACCOMMODATION
Adiyata Guest House	B
Camping Sukuta	F
Douniya Motel	C
Praia Motel	D
Sumu Motel	E
Triple M Lodge	G
YMCA	A

RESTAURANTS & BARS
Afra Citizen Mosdolly	3
Alliance Franco-Gambienne	4
Bousko Fast Food	1
Come Inn	2
Jokor	6
Lana's Bar	7
Willy's Disco	8
Youth Monument Bar	5

Banjul

Traffic lights and Fajara (see 'Fajara & Bakau' map, p.106)

JIMPEX ROAD

KANIFING

BANJUL-SERREKUNDA HIGHWAY

JESWANG

GPTC Bus Station

Jimpex

Bush taxis to Banjul

Bellview Airlines & IPC Travel

Malak Chemist

Bush taxis to Bakau

Gamtel

WESTFIELD JUNCTION

Banjul Pharmacy & Westfield Clinic

Bush taxis to Brikama

KOMBO SILLAH DRIVE

GIPZA House

Footbridge

Kairaba Centre

Serrekunda Post Office

Gamcel

KAIRABA AVENUE

Africell

Right Choice Supermarket

"Big tree"

Senegal High Commission

KAIRABA AVENUE

MOSQUE ROAD, LATRIKUNDA

LATRIKUNDA

Batik Factory

SAYERR JOSE AVENUE

Standard Chartered Bank

SERREKUNDA

Serrekunda Market

Police Station

Aisa Marie Cinema

African Art Collection

Timbuktoo Bead & Mask Shop

Banjul Pharmacy

LONDON CORNER

Bush taxis to Kotu & Kololi

Bremen Clinic

Total

Shell

BAKOTEH

Manjai Kunda, Kotu & Kololi

Sukuta & Brufut

Lamin & Brikama

pleasant tourist enclave with beaches that, though unsafe for swimming, are very attractive. See map on pp.114–115.

African Heritage 114 Atlantic Road, Bakau ☎449 6778. Two excellent self-contained upstairs rooms, one overlooking Bakau market, the other overlooking the busy fishing beach, give you a real sense of involvement in your surroundings at this guesthouse, restaurant and gallery shop. Both rooms have the use of a fridge, TV, and a small but lovely garden. Four smaller rooms in an annexe provide down-to-earth budget accommodation. ❷–❸

African Village 98 Atlantic Road, Bakau ☎449 5384, 🖰www.africanvillagehotel.gm. Conveniently located in the heart of Bakau, this budget-class tourist hotel perched on Bakau's low cliffs is a little scruffy but recommended for its warm atmosphere. There's a brilliant pool bar, a very reasonable restaurant with great Atlantic views and a man-made terraced beach. Accommodation with fans or a/c is in roundhouses, crammed tightly into a leafy compound, and blocks, some with sea views. ❹

Bakau Lodge Off Atlantic Rd, Bakau ☎449 6103 or 990 1610. This urban guesthouse has simple but bright and generously sized rooms around a courtyard with a small pool. Great value and a good choice if you'd like to stay in the heart of a small African town. ❷

Cape Point Hotel Kofi Annan St, Cape Point ☎449 5005, 🖂capepointhotel@qanet.gm. Pleasantly old-fashioned, this compact tourist hotel is close to Cape Point's good beaches; there's also a tiny pool. Rooms vary in size; some have a/c and all are spotless. ❺

Cape Residence Kofi Annan St, Cape Point ☎449 4215, 🖂caperesidence@gamtel.gm. Not on the beach, and with a very small pool, this would nonetheless be a good choice if you need a self-catering apartment with space to spread out – the accommodation is huge and airy, with smart modern furnishings. ❼

Friendship Hotel Off Stadium Rd, Bakau ☎449 5833. Good-value choice, designed for sports teams, students and conference delegates, the four-storey blocks here have an institutional feel. It's definitely not a tourist hotel, and lies some distance from the sea and from Bakau and Fajara's bars and restaurants. However, the self-contained rooms are comfortable and clean, with hot water and TV; there's also a good-sized swimming pool plus a dining hall. ❶

Jabo Guest House 9 Old Cape Rd, Bakau ☎449 4906. A down-to-earth, reasonably priced place which feels more like a Gambian compound than a guesthouse, with six simple, self-contained rooms with fridge, and the use of a well-equipped kitchen. Young locals sometimes gather here to jam on their *djembés*. The beach at Cape Point is within walking distance. ❷

Ocean Bay Hotel and Resort Kofi Annan St, Cape Point ☎449 4265, 🖰www.oceanbayhotel.com. An impressive new addition to The Gambia's growing selection of resort hotels, this place is spacious and attractive, with groomed, palm-shaded lawns and comfortable, though conservatively decorated, rooms; opt for one on the first floor, if possible, as they're airier than those below. With plenty of variety on offer in the restaurant, some guests don't leave the site until it's time to check out. ❼

Roc Heights Sambu Breku Road, Cape Point ☎449 4528 or 991 8727, 🖰www.rocheightslodge.com. Upmarket but untouristy (visitors to the nearby UN building stay here), this tucked-away hotel is elegantly decorated with interesting African art and artefacts. All of its suites and mini-apartments are large and comfortably equipped, with a/c. There's a leafy garden; a pool is planned. ❺–❼.

Romana Hotel Atlantic Rd, Bakau ☎449 5127. Unpromising exterior, but inside this is a decent, basic, small urban hotel in a "high street" location. The eleven rooms have fans, and the easy-going bar and restaurant are very reasonable. ❷

Sunbeach Hotel and Resort Kofi Annan St, Cape Point ☎449 7190, 🖰www.sunbeachhotel.com. One of the better tourist hotels, brightly decorated and a good choice for young families, offering an excellent pool and play area, with sack races, treasure hunts and other games. For bigger kids there's table tennis, beach volleyball, swimming pool games, and nightly discos and live music. The restaurant serves safe European choices; the rooms, though not huge, are comfortably furnished, with a/c and satellite TV. It's a large hotel, with nearly two hundred rooms, but the whole site blends with its surroundings – it's on one of the best beaches in the resort area, a picturesque curve of fine white sand with thatched umbrella shades. ❼

Fajara and upper Kairaba Avenue

Fajara is a quiet, relatively affluent residential neighbourhood at the north end of **Kairaba Avenue**. Many of The Gambia's best restaurants are found here, and the accommodation options are often excellent value, with a measure of character and style that's all too often lacking in the other resorts. See map on pp.114–115.

Croc John's Off Atlantic Rd ☎ 449 6068. Clean, good-sized self-catering apartments in a compound that feels homely, secure and un-touristy: popular with volunteers and long-term visitors as well as independent travellers who don't need the facilities of a tourist hotel. Located in a quiet residential district, there's no restaurant or pool, but there's a charming courtyard garden with plenty of places to relax, and you can use the nearby *Safari Garden Hotel* pool if you eat there. ❺

Fajara Golf Apartments Off Kairaba Ave, Fajara ☎ 449 5800. In a pair of compounds made bright and colourful by the work of a local artist, these eight self-catering apartments are spotless, spacious and thoughtfully equipped, with useful extras like CD and cassette players and free mountain-bike hire. Not the closest accommodation to the golf course, and not just for golfers, but caddies and/or tuition can be organized. Recommended. ❸

Fajara Guest House Signposted off Kairaba Ave, near the Fajara Club ☎ 449 6122. A peaceful haven with 15 small, simple, clean rooms with fans and mosquito screens, around a bright white-pillared courtyard that looks faintly Greek. Good value, but no pool. ❷

Francisco's Atlantic Rd ☎ 449 5332. A clutch of eleven slightly tatty but clean rooms with fan, a/c, fridge and TV, in a small but very leafy tropical garden dotted with a pleasant restaurant. There's no pool, but Fajara beach at *Leybato* is five minutes' walk away. ❷

Hotel Fajara Atlantic Road ☎ 449 4576, ⓦ www.gambiaexpresstours.co.uk. Designed on a grand scale, but showing signs of neglect, this tourist hotel fails to capitalize on its spectacular oceanside location. The pool, surrounded by concrete, has a view of the sea through wire fences beyond dusty tennis courts. Some rooms

have a/c and self-catering facilities, but most need redecorating and the whole place lacks atmosphere. ❺

Leybato Guest House Off Atlantic Rd ☎ 449 7186, ⓔ leybato@hotmail.com. Known and loved for its beach bar and hammocks, *Leybato* has a few basic guest rooms – good if you want to be on the beach, but there are better-value places elsewhere. ❸

Ngala Lodge 64 Atlantic Rd ☎ 449 4045 or 449 7429, ⓦ www.ngalalodge.com. A former ambassador's residence in a tranquil garden with towering palms, converted into a hotel with 17 luxurious suites. Each is individually decorated with original paintings, textiles and quirky pieces of scrap-yard art. There's a small swimming pool, a jacuzzi, a superb restaurant and access to a tiny beach. Likely to appeal to anyone with a sense of the unusual, looking for somewhere secluded and serene, this is expensive but worth it. Bookings through The Gambia Experience (see p.29). ❼

Ocean View Off Atlantic Road ☎ 449 4725. Upmarket block of self-catering apartments, superbly located with gorgeous ocean views and a small pool. ❼

Safari Garden Hotel Off Atlantic Rd, near the *Fajara Club* ☎ 449 5887, ⓦ www.safarigarden .com. Good-value and thoroughly recommended small independent hotel with a dozen simple rooms around a colourful garden courtyard, a small but excellent pool, a good restaurant, and extremely friendly staff. Pleasantly situated in a quiet neighbourhood of sandy residential streets, the warm and genuine atmosphere attracts discerning independent travellers, volunteers and other expats. The beach, and some of Fajara's best restaurants, are within walking distance. The owners are committed to sustainable tourism, and are the owners of the new *Sandale Eco-Retreat* in Kartong (see p.159). ❺

Kotu

In high season, everything about **Kotu** feels crowded – the hotels, the craft market and supermarkets are often swarming with customers. However, it's a fun place to be if you're into the gregarious package-holiday scene, and there are some very good birdwatching sites within walking distance. The accommodation options are all medium or large tourist hotels owned or backed by major tour operators, either on, or very close to, Kotu Strand, a decent stretch of beach. While most have a low-rent feel, they're not particularly cheap. See map on p.116–117.

Badala Park Hotel Kotu Stream Rd ☎ 446 0400, ⓦ www.badalaparkhotel.gm. Popular with young independent travellers and birdwatchers, this is one

of the cheapest hotels offered by the package tour companies. Many customers are Gambian, so the atmosphere is distinctively African. Set in gardens so dense with trees and shrubs that insects can be a nuisance. Some of the two hundred rooms are shabbily furnished and noisy – the ones furthest from reception are quieter. A pleasant beach is a short walk away. ❸

Bakotu Hotel Kotu Stream Rd ☎ 446 5555. An attractive but rather cramped tourist hotel, a couple of minutes from the beach. The main compound has a small swimming pool and 88 characterful rooms with fans in blocks or octagonal buildings; the best are upstairs, away from the road and with a balcony. The hotel also has eight small self-catering apartments – they're a little tired, but have private balconies with fabulous views over Kotu Stream: excellent for bird- and monkey-watching. Rooms ❺, apartments ❻

Bungalow Beach Hotel Kotu Stream Rd ☎ 446 5288, ⓦ www.bbhotel.gm. Self-catering tourist hotel with friendly staff and a loyal clientele, mostly of retired Europeans and young families. The 110 mini-apartments in white-painted blocks are well-equipped, with optional a/c, but they're a little small; better-value options exist elsewhere. The pool is nothing special, but the site is right on a reasonable beach. There's a restaurant and plenty of other facilities, including a hair salon and Internet café. ❼

Kombo Beach Hotel Kotu Stream Rd ☎ 446 5466, ⓦ www.kombobeachhotel.gm. Popular with young European package tourists, this is a lively hotel with plenty of activities, set on a reasonable stretch of beach. The atmosphere is mass-market, with block after block of rooms – 250 in all – designed to a familiar international formula; huge crowds congregate in the bar to watch football on satellite TV. ❻

Palm Beach Hotel Kotu Stream Rd ☎ 446 2111. Sister hotel to the *Badala Park*, and with a similar atmosphere (much more Gambian than the other places in Kotu) but more upmarket. The accommodation – 120 rooms with TV and a/c – is in two-storey villas in jungly gardens. The pool area feels very tropical, and is close to a pleasant, palm-shaded beach. ❺

Sunset Beach Hotel Kotu Stream Rd ☎ 446 6397 or 446 3876, ⓦ www.sunsetbeachhotel.gm. Tidy tourist hotel in a good location on a well-kept stretch of beach, relatively secluded for Kotu. There's a good pool and two restaurants, one with a rooftop terrace; the food is excellent. Most of the 108 rooms are in rather airless and utilitarian bungalows in regimented rows, but the place is clean and well-furnished. ❼

Kololi: Palma Rima area

The huge *Palma Rima* resort complex dominates this area. Since the other accommodation options are limited, the attractive stretch of beach here is rarely over-crowded. There's also a handful of appealingly low-key places to eat, drink, shop or dance the night away. See map on pp.116–117.

Bakadaji Hotel Bertil Harding Highway ☎ 446 2307. Basic but pleasant and tranquil Gambian-owned place, with simple self-contained rooms with fans in large scruffy gardens that tend to attract mosquitoes, a few minutes' walk from the beach. ❸

Dutch Whale Guest House Palma Rima Road ☎ 778 9704 or 994 2361. One of the very few budget options close to the beach, this laid-back Dutch-run place offers accommodation in a few small and simple huts in a compound with a bar and restaurant. ❷

🏃 **Luigi's Apartments** Palma Rima Rd ☎ 446 0280, ⓔ luigis@gambianet.gm. A handful of well-furnished rooms, and apartments with self-catering facilities, with access to a pretty garden with an open-air jacuzzi, 50m from the beach. ❹

Palma Rima Hotel Bertil Harding Highway ☎ 446 3380, ⓔ palmarima@qanet.gm. A mega-touristy resort hotel, famous for its huge swimming pool, but not on the beach. This is one of the few places still to offer an all-inclusive option. The 152 rooms include bungalows in grounds shaded with palms. The packed entertainment programme includes karaoke, water polo, aerobics and show nights. There's also a choice of restaurants and bars (some guests never venture out, preferring to get rowdy here) and the *Moon Light Disco*, a tame but busy club cranking out Europop every night. Although there's a more than a whiff of holiday camp about the Palma Rima and the public areas are rather dreary, the largely British clientele seem mostly happy with it. ❼

Kololi: Senegambia area

With more than a hint of Benidorm and Blackpool, but with a rather ramshackle Gambian accent, the **Senegambia area** is the country's busiest tourist strip. It's a mixed bag: once you've made it through the crowds of hustlers and hedonists you'll find yourself at two of the country's best-established and most dignified tourist hotels, the *Kairaba* and the *Senegambia*. The beach here has been reconstructed to correct the serious tidal erosion of a few years back, but most tourists stick to the hotel pools. See map on pp.116–117.

Holiday Beach Club ⚟446 0419, Ⓔamatagaye @hotmail.com. Gambian-owned place on the beach. It's rather cramped and poorly maintained, and it's not highly regarded for its food, but it has a decent pool and reasonable rates for its simple rooms with fans. ❸

Kairaba Hotel ⚟446 2940, ⓌWWW .kairabahotel.com. Sleek and attentive but a little self-important, this top hotel has wide-ranging facilities including a very attractive pool and a choice of good restaurants. Loyal customers return again and again. Pleasant rooms, 150 in all, with direct-dial phones, excellent bathrooms, safes, TV – the lot – though those on the landward side have no views. An unusual feature is the astronomical observatory, which can be opened for a fee on cloudless nights. ❽

Kololi Beach Club ⚟446 4897, ⓌWWW.kololi .com. Started life as a timeshare, but now operates as an expensive hotel, with accommodation in self-catering villas in well-tended grounds, including a small golf course, and a pleasant pool edged by low palms. ❻

Paradise Suites Hotel ⚟446 3429. North of the main Senegambia area, and set in small but well-planted gardens a 10-minute walk from the beach, this accommodation is reasonably comfortable and well-furnished, with a variety of options from rooms to small self-catering apartments and large villas. ❺–❼

Sarge's Hotel ⚟446 0510, ⓌWWW.sargeshotel .gm. Formerly the *Tafbel*, this is an unpretentious three-storey, courtyard-style, tourist hotel, with a modest pool and indirect access to the beach. There are worse choices, but the 98 rooms with safe box and TV (and optional a/c) are a little shabby, with uncomfortable beds. ❺

Senegambia Beach Hotel ⚟446 2717, ⓌWWW.senegambiahotel.com. Gigantic tourist hotel, adjoining the *Kairaba*, but much more casual and a good deal cheaper. Recommended for its generally good service and impressive tropical gardens – great for birdwatching, although rather dusty between February and the rains. Some of the 360 rooms are rather small and tired, but all are clean and cool (with either a/c or fans). The standard rooms in the garden blocks are quieter than the deluxe rooms in the main building. ❼

Kololi Village and Manjai Kunda

Despite being part of the resort area, **Kololi Village** really does feel like a village, and it's a good place for budget accommodation if you don't mind forgoing a few creature comforts. Neighbouring **Manjai Kunda** is a gritty but generally relaxed suburb of Serrekunda with a couple of mid-range hotels that have a more African atmosphere than most beach hotels. All the options here are 1–2km from the beach. See map on pp.116–117.

Balmoral Apartments Kololi Village ⚟446 1079 ⓌWWW.balmoral-apartments.com. Apartment block with a small garden shaded by mature trees, and a pool, a short walk from the Senegambia area. Good standard rooms, with adequately equipped kitchen diners, popular with long-stay guests. ❹

Bananaville Kololi Village ⚟444 3716. Seven very pleasant apartments set along a shady, elongated garden courtyard. Fresh, new and excellent value. ❷

Holiday Suites Manjai Kunda ⚟446 1075. Adequate a/c suites with kitchenettes, satellite TV, and direct-dial phones. Although it's light, clean and reasonably furnished, it's overpriced and geared to local business people rather than tourists. ❹

Kaira-Du-La Lodge Kololi Village ⚟446 0529, Ⓔkaira.du.la@qanet.gm. Studio and family rooms in roundhouses set in a small, well-kept garden; each has a living room and a small patio and the family apartments have two bathrooms and a kitchen. Good value. ❸–❺

Keneba Hotel Kololi Village, no phone. Very basic budget rooms in a small village compound; one of the cheapest places in the resort area. ❶

Kololi Tavern Kololi Village ⚟446 3410. Budget option that's shabby round the edges but still a good place to unwind in cool, African surroundings. ❷

Mannjai Lodge Manjai Kunda ☎446 3414, ✉manlodge@gamtel.gm. Extremely basic tourist-class hotel about 1.5km from Kotu beach, with 53 plainly-furnished rooms arranged around a courtyard with a thatched bar area and small, unappealing pool. Sometimes hosts live music sessions at weekends, attracting crowds of locals. ❸

Melrose Place Kololi Village ☎446 0479. Formerly *Europa Apartments*, eight self-catering apartments in a compound with a small swimming pool and bar. ❸

Orchard Guest House Kololi Village ☎773 7541 (ask for Alex) or ☎902649. A few very basic rooms with self-catering facilities in a quiet and friendly leafy village compound. ❶

Soto Baa Koto Kololi Village ☎446 0399. Budget accommodation in shabby but appealing thatched roundhouses with a shared cooking area. ❸

Bijilo and Kerr Serign

On Kololi's southern fringes, the **Bijilo** coastal strip and the inland neighbourhood of **Kerr Serign** still have something of a frontier feel; the accommodation options here are peaceful and thinly spaced. It's a major growth area, though, and the gaps between Bijilo Beach and the new *Sheraton* further south are likely to fill rapidly over the next few years. New structures are popping up all the time, most of them aiming for the high-spending end of the market. See map on pp.116–117.

Baobab Beach Resort Badala Highway ☎446 5341 ⓦwww.baobab.gm. Recently renovated, this well-managed place on the landward side of the highway caters mostly for locals. Most of its rooms are self-catering, large and clean, with a/c and cable TV. Facilities include an Internet café and a restaurant specializing in grills. Good value. ❹

Bijilo Beach Hotel Bertil Harding Highway, Bijilo ☎446 2701, ⓦwww.bijilobeachhotel.com. A modest tourist hotel with ten mini-apartments and ten double rooms with optional a/c, all small but bright and finished to a high standard, European-style. The roof terrace of the restaurant block has fabulous views over gardens sloping down to the Atlantic. The pool is open to non-resident customers of the restaurant and bar. ❺

Coco Ocean Resort and Spa Bertil Harding Highway, Kerr Serign, information from *Coconut Residence* ☎446 3377. Close to completion at the time of writing, this is The Gambia's first major luxury spa complex, promising Turkish baths, steam baths and an impressive menu of massage treatments in a large, splendidly designed garden compound right on the beach. ❽

Coconut Residence Bertil Harding Highway, Kerr Serign ☎446 3377, ⓦwww.coconutresidence.com. A truly luxurious hotel, with 36 handsomely decorated suites: some have four-poster beds, all have huge bathrooms. There are two swimming pools in the main part of the hotel, surrounded by a lush garden shaded by mature trees. For total seclusion two villas with private pools, tucked away in gardens behind the main buildings, are also available. The reception areas, a mishmash of African and Asian colonial styles, are suave and the restaurant is one of the best in the country. Hardly the "real" Gambia, but a very appealing place to indulge. ❽

Golden Beach Hotel Badala Highway, 200m south of Bijilo Beach Hotel ☎446 5111, ⓦwww.goldenbeachhotel.gm. This European-style 24-room hotel, with modest pool, has good-sized, well-equipped rooms but is rather overpriced. ❼

Mango Club Kerr Serign ☎446 4153. Boutique hotel, with well-furnished mini-apartments, a good pool and bar in a small attractive courtyard, and a gourmet restaurant. ❺

Serrekunda and Sukuta

Serrekunda's budget accommodation options feel as close to real-life urban Africa as you can get in this corner of the country. The more central places are noisy day and night, but there are also a few appealingly simple options a little way out of the thick of things in Kanifing and Latrikunda, residential neighbourhoods that see few tourists. Like Bakau, the quieter areas of town are good places to look for lodgings with Gambian families. The spread-out suburb

△ Hotel pool, Bijilo

Birdwatching in hotel gardens

It's not unusual for tourists to come to the Gambia for a beach holiday and go away with a brand new interest in birds, just through watching jewel-bright little creatures hopping around outside their hotel window. If you choose a hotel with a large, leafy garden you could spot a couple of dozen different species within an hour of arrival.

Just about every well-planted hotel garden is visited by gems like the tiny red and brown firefinch, and its frequent companion the red-cheeked cordon-bleu, which looks much the same but with a different paint job – this time sky-blue with a jaunty scarlet spot on each cheek. Dipping into the hibiscus flowers will be sunbirds, West Africa's answer to the humming bird, tiny with delicate curved beaks and beautiful plumage. Hanging from tall bamboo stands or palm fronds may be the knot-like nests of weaver birds, scruffy, gregarious black and yellow birds of which The Gambia has several species. Then there are the raucous gaggles of long-tailed glossy starlings, which look a bit like common starlings dressed up for a night out, with fabulous iridescent blue-green wings and show-off tails. Senegal coucals, common bulbuls and yellow-crowned gonoleks are also frequent garden visitors.

Good tourist hotels for birdwatching in the resort area include the *Kairaba*, the *Senegambia* and the *Bakotu* self-catering apartments.

of **Sukuta** merges with Serrekunda's southern fringes and has The Gambia's only commercial campsite. See map on p.118.

Adiyata Guest House Well-signposted off Kairaba Ave, Latrikunda ☎ 439 5510, mobile ☎ 992 5537. A good choice if you want to experience a villagey Serrekunda neighbourhood, away from the bustle of Kairaba Avenue. Simple rooms with large beds, nets and fans in six mellow roundhouses around a small courtyard planted with trees and shrubs; there's also a very reasonably priced outdoor restaurant/bar. ❷

Camping Sukuta Bijilo Road, Sukuta ☎ 991 7786, ⓦ wwwcampingsukuta.de. Well signposted from Bertil Harding Highway and from Serrekunda, this campsite and travellers' lodge is very popular with European overlanders – and extremely good value. There's plenty of shade to park and camp, accommodation in simple huts and chalets, and spotless kitchen and washing facilities. The much-travelled owners are a great source of overland and travel information, and if you've crossed the Sahara by vehicle and are thinking of selling up, or want to ship your car or bike home, this is a good place to be. ❶

Douniya Motel Serrekunda ☎ 437 0741 A large, barrack-like boarding house with around twenty simple and clean but rather dingy rooms in an urban compound. Some have a/c but you'll need your own mosquito net. ❷

Praia Motel 3 Mam Youth St, Serrekunda ☎ 439 4887 or 990 0902. A somewhat rundown but adequate Gambian-owned place in a quiet back-street of Serrekunda with secure parking. There are twelve self-contained rooms with TV and either fans or a/c, and a bar and restaurant. ❷

Suma Motel Sayerr Jobe Ave, Serrekunda ☎ 439 4015. Formerly the *Green Line*, right in the heart of town, opposite the cinema. You enter through a grimy restaurant into a dim reception area, but upstairs the motel is surprisingly bright, clean and decent-looking, given that the rooms (self-contained, with nets and fans) can be rented by the hour. ❷

Triple M Lodge Sukuta ☎ 990 5826, ⓦ www .gambiafun.nl. Dutch-run place on the outskirts of Sukuta, with reliable water and electricity, clean, secure rooms with netted beds, and decent facili-ties. Ought to be good but the atmosphere lacks warmth. ❷

YMCA Off Kairaba Ave, Kanifing ☎ 439 2647, ⓦ www.ymca.gm. Adequate hostel accommodation; 34 single and double rooms with fans and shared bathrooms. There's an inexpensive restaurant (daily 9am–midnight), plus a computer centre next door. Decent value if you're counting every dalasi. ❶

Bakau and Fajara

Brimming with life, its population doubling every decade or so, **BAKAU** is an overgrown village that's part shanty town, part desirable suburb, and part coastal resort. Spread over Kombo's northernmost point, twelve kilometres from Banjul, Bakau includes busy, noisy Bakau Old Town, the salubrious Cape Point area, the less affluent Bakau New Town, and the elegant oceanside properties of Atlantic Road, which continues into **FAJARA**, home to politicians and prominent businessmen, plus diplomats and other well-off expatriates.

This is a part of the resort area where you can stay in comfort in either a package tourist hotel or a small independent hotel, but feel part of a vibrant mixed local community at the same time. You could also stay in a simple urban guesthouse or a family compound, and possibly take some West African music lessons. Although some visitors to Bakau and Fajara look no further than the craft stalls, restaurants and supermarkets, the residents are well used to tourists, and the residential streets are conducive to pottering about on foot or bicycle. While Fajara is generally pretty dignified, Bakau is livelier and you'll encounter some persistent bumsters; however, the general hassle is mild compared with the nearby resorts of Kotu and Kololi.

Bakau Old Town

For visitors, **Bakau Old Town**'s focal points are the areas around the junction of **Atlantic Road and Sait Matty Road**, with its banks, post and telephone offices, supermarkets and *bitikos*, and the tourist-oriented *bengdula*, or **craft market**, of Atlantic Road. Take a step or two off the main road here and you're immediately in urban Africa. Near the batik stalls and drum-makers of the *bengdula*, and almost directly behind the stalls selling well-scrubbed imported fruit and vegetables to tourists and expats, is Bakau's **village market**, where flies buzz between rickety stalls stacked with pyramids of knobbly local tomatoes and chillies, hung with bags of rice, couscous and powdered spices, and piled with whatever fruit is in season. Butchers chop up steaks and offal with cleavers in a blur of flies, and fishermen's wives sell buckets of greasy-yellow *bonga* fish, fresh from Bakau's busy fishing beach.

The **residential quarter** is a tight jumble of sandy lanes, urban compounds and small neighbourhood mosques just inland from the moorings and smokehouses of the fishing beach. It was originally settled by ocean-going fishermen and their familes; more recently, as tourism has taken over from fishing, there's been an influx of hotel and restaurant workers, guides and drivers. The neighbourhood, with its cement block houses, battered corrugated iron fences and reeking drainage ditches, is desperately overcrowded; however, there's little enough traffic here to make it far easier to explore on foot than similar areas in Serrekunda. Bakau Old Town's backstreets also have a few good local chop houses, simple places serving the big plates of Gambian food that are hard to find in some of the resort areas.

For **shopping** in Bakau Old Town, the Atlantic Road *bengdula* is a good one, where you can watch craftsmen at work under the trees by the roadside. Also along Atlantic Road, there are a number of tourist-oriented clothing shops selling West African-style dresses, trousers and skirts, and stalls selling batik hangings. Opposite the market in Atlantic Road, the highly recommended African Heritage Gallery has crafts and curios from all over West Africa, including ritual masks, small bronzes once used as weights for measuring commodities, and traditional wooden stools.

Katchikali Crocodile Pool

You'd be forgiven for doing a double-take when Bakau's bumsters ask you if you're "looking for Charlie". Charlie is, in fact, a wild but placid crocodile, and something of a local celebrity, generally found playing host to an adoring public at the **sacred crocodile pool** of Katchikali (also spelt Katchikally) on the south side of the Old Town. The pool is a low-key, innocuous tourist trap, often featuring on group guided tours of the Banjul area.

On foot, you can get to the pool in ten minutes from either Atlantic Road or from Sait Matty Road. The most direct route is the path leading almost straight to it from the junction of Atlantic Road and Old Cape Road, near the craft market; alternatively take the road leading off Sait Matty Road at the Norway and Sweden Consulates and turn right at the large tree after about 300m. Once you're away from the main roads it's easy to get lost in Bakau's maze of alleyways, so if you don't already have a guide, ask one of the local kids to show you the way to the crocodiles (*bambo* in Mandinka). On arrival at the site, visitors are asked for a standard donation of D30: the Bojang family, the pool guardians, are forbidden by family lore from exploiting the place for financial gain, lest it lose its sacredness, but feel justified in asking for money for "expenses". As

Sacred crocodile pools

The **crocodile** is a recurring image in traditional Gambian iconography. A single grinning crocodile features on the one-dalasi coin; the watermark on all Gambian banknotes is a crocodile's head, and stylized crocodiles are worked into the designs of textiles and jewellery. Believed by some to have supernatural powers, crocodiles appear in many Gambian folk tales, including Mandinka stories of the crocodile in the moon – the Gambian counterpart to the Western man in the moon. Gambian tradition reveres the crocodile as an intermediary between the living and the dead, communicating with human ancestral spirits; for example, the Bojang family of Katchikali claim that whenever Charlie the crocodile leaves the Katchikali pool and makes his way to their family compound, he has a message from their forebears.

Crocodiles are particularly associated with **fertility**, and the sacred crocodile pools at Katchikali near Bakau (see above), Berending (see p.192), and Follonko near Kartong (see p.170) are places of pilgrimage and prayer for childless women from The Gambia and Senegal. The pilgrims bring offerings of kola nuts, cloth and cash; half the kola nuts are thrown into the pool as a ritual sacrifice to the crocodiles, and everything else is shared among the elders of the families that guard the pools. Pilgrims undergo a ritual bathing in sacred water brought to them by the women of the pool-keepers' clan. They are then counselled in piety and fidelity by the elders, and given more water to take away and apply to their bodies morning and night. Fertility rituals are open to foreign visitors with a genuine wish to take part. The crocodile pools are also visited by those with other special requests, such as wrestlers hoping to win a championship, or businessmen trying to secure a new contract, and even leading Gambian politicians during election times.

Charlie and his co-residents at Katchikali are **Nile crocodiles**, The Gambia's commonest crocodile species. Preferring fresh water to salt, these reptiles are fairly widespread along the River Gambia, and in freshwater pools, where they breed. They are also sometimes found in the saltwater *bolons* and on the coast. Nile crocodiles have been known to live for over a century, and can in theory grow to a length of 7m, but in practice Gambian crocodiles have little chance of making it to such a grand size. Although they're protected under international law, they can be culled if they appear to pose a threat to human life, and it's rare to encounter one more than 2m long.

Birdwatching around Bakau

While Bakau's gardens, cliffs and beaches play host to a great variety of bird species, the most interesting areas for birdwatchers are around Cape Creek, which is crossed by Old Cape Road southeast of town, and Sting Corner, at the junction of Sait Matty Road and the Banjul–Serrekunda highway. Old Cape Road is a pleasant walk at any time of day, passing a lightly wooded area of oil palms, rhun palms, baobabs and tamarisk. Cape Creek is flanked by mudflats and mangroves; this area yields sightings of red-cheeked bee-eaters, various rollers, starlings, swallows and parakeets, plus, on the mudflats, plovers and thick-knees. In the creek you may see fish-eating birds such as pied kingfishers, reef herons, long-tailed shags and ospreys. On the way from Bakau to Sting Corner along Sait Matty Road you pass the vegetable plots worked by Bakau's women's co-operatives, and, particularly in the rice season, this is a good area to see lily-trotters, squacco herons, and cattle egrets.

well as buying fish for the crocs, they use the money to maintain a small ethnographic museum which details the history of the area.

The pool at Katchikali, like The Gambia's other sacred crocodile pools (see box below), is traditionally considered a magical place, where bathing in the water can cure infertility and generally bestow good fortune. Sacred **rituals** are still occasionally held here; if your visit coincides with one, the atmosphere will be highly charged, with accompanying drumming and dancing. Most of the time, however, the only visitors are tourists.

Past the site entrance, you approach the pool itself by way of a path flanked by mature trees frequented by birds and monkeys. You're unlikely to see much of the sacred water, choked as it is by a dense covering of water lettuce (a type of floating arum lily), but you'll almost certainly see at least a dozen of the hundred or so crocodiles said to inhabit the area. None of them are particularly big – all but the most mature are under two metres long – and they look singularly docile, either lurking in the water or lounging on the bank. No one fears these crocs unduly – you can approach quite close even when they're out of the water, but the only one you should get within striking range of is Charlie. There have been a few Charlies over the years; the current incumbent is a laid-back character who seems unperturbed by visitors patting his back and having their photo taken with him.

Despite being so close to the coast and the salt wetlands of Cape Creek, the water in the pool is fresh, with a healthy population of frogs, snacked on by the crocodiles between meals of *bonga* fish, Bakau's speciality, provided by the Bojangs. The water level is low, however, and, every few seasons, the Bojangs call a working party together to dig the pool a little deeper, and sometimes to introduce new crocodiles. The croc population is highest in the rainy season, when they breed here.

Cape Point and the Botanical Garden

North of the Old Town is **Cape Point**, and this area, also known as Cape St Mary, is a secluded part of town with a quiet, cul-de-sac atmosphere, home to diplomats, businessmen and United Nations employees. At its heart is a tourist village, with a supermarket, a couple of restaurants, a recently refurbished *bengdula* and a row of fruit stalls with identical stock. This is one of the tidiest of the resort areas, and the beach here is clean and pleasant, too. Cape Point marks the southwestern limit of the River Gambia where it meets the Atlantic, and the pale sands on the river side are caught by peculiar cross-currents, with waves lapping diagonally against the timber groynes. Round the point on the Atlantic side is the start of Bakau's softly crumbling russet laterite cliffs: the beach here is only accessible at low tide, and is swept clean by the ocean every high tide.

Between Atlantic Road and Cape Point is Bakau's **Botanical Garden** (Mon–Sat, D50), a small and rather beautiful hideaway just off the main road, near the clifftop. It's naturally greenest and most impressive after the rains – by the middle of the dry season everything is rather dusty. Particularly noteworthy are the fairy-tale teak tree and the prehistoric cycads. Few of the trees and shrubs are local and some need serious attention, so don't come here with high expectations. Even so, it's a pleasant place to relax, and you will see plenty of garden birds, such as bulbuls, red-cheeked cordon bleu, bronze mannikins, and Senegal firefinches.

Bakau New Town

Bakau New Town is a residential area shaded by mature trees that burst gloriously into flower in the rainy season. Its main thoroughfare, Garba Jahumpa Road (still sometimes known by its old name, New Town Road) runs between Kairaba Avenue and Sait Matty Road and has a few shops, offices and workshops, plus some vicious speed bumps. Bakau New Town is overshadowed by the **Independence Stadium**, The Gambia's principal sports venue, a large open arena surrounded by steeply banked seating. The whole district reverberates whenever there's a major sporting fixture or a live music event – big names from the Senegambian music scene sometimes play here to sell-out crowds.

Fajara

There are no formal boundaries between **FAJARA** and Bakau, along the coast to the northeast. Even so, Fajara has a distinctive atmosphere, with quiet sandy streets of elegant villas, semi-hidden behind high fences and flower-draped walls. It's first and foremost a residential district, with just a few shops, hotels and restaurants, but among these are some of the finest places in the country.

The **Fajara War Cemetery**, on Kairaba Avenue northwest of the traffic lights, is immaculately kept by the Commonwealth War Graves Commission. During the Second World War, The Gambia, like other British colonies in West Africa, was used as a military base and a staging post for aircraft heading towards the Middle East and the North African front, and ships bound for India and the near and far east via South Africa. Over two hundred casualties of the war, mostly West African, but also British, Canadian and others, are buried here, their graves laid out in neat rows under flame trees and frangipani. There's also a monument to 33 Gambians buried elsewhere.

Also in Fajara is the **Fajara Club** (☎ 449 5456, daily 8am–8pm), an old sports club that's seen better days, well-known for its eighteen-hole golf-course that has more dustbowls than grass in the dry season. With its main rooms a cross between an English church hall and a rundown country club, it's not an appealing prospect at first glance. But there's quite a range of facilities here: squash courts, tennis courts (lit after dark), a hall for badminton and table tennis, plus a programme of keep-fit with aerobics and yoga classes. The local Hash House Harriers have their notice board in the clubhouse (meetings on Mondays, ☎ 449 5054). Drinks and simple meals are cheap from the clubhouse bar, and the clean pool at the back has sunbeds and is popular with children. There's also a small lending library of dog-eared paperback fiction.

Birdwatching around Kotu

The Kotu tourist hotels are within easy reach of a variety of habitats, making this an excellent base for birders. The Fajara golf course is a good place to start – here you're practically guaranteed sightings of black-headed plovers, bee-eaters, blue-bellied rollers, glossy starlings, doves and wood hoopoes. The wetlands and rice fields around Kotu Stream are frequented by many species including egrets, herons, kingfishers, waders, and palm-nut vultures. Another rewarding area to explore (unappetizing though it may sound) are Kotu's sewage ponds, reached by a path on the opposite side of the road from the *Badala Park Hotel*. The rich pond life here attracts many bird species; you may see common greenshanks, black-winged stilts, white-faced whistling ducks, rose-ringed parakeets and various sandpipers, or even rarities like white-winged black terns, tufted ducks and red-necked phalaropes. The beaches are visited by shore birds; you will have to visit in the quiet early hours to see them in large numbers.

The **African Living Art Centre** on Garba Jahumpa Road, Bakau (T 449 5131) is unique in The Gambia, a lofty, light-drenched concrete-and-glass gallery space that's a work of art in itself, hung with textiles and crammed with a vibrant, eclectic collection of exhibits and merchandise: beads, statues, antiques, and some of the most original and creative clothing to be found anywhere in the country. There are also paintings by the owner Suelle, some featuring his trademark *kanaga* symbol, sacred to the Dogon people of Mali. The shop is also part-library and part-café/bar, and is a great place to enjoy Lebanese coffee, pastries, or a cocktail.

For other **shopping** in Fajara, Timbooktoo on Garba Jahumpa Road near the junction with Kairaba Avenue is worth a special trip; it's The Gambia's only good bookshop, with an excellent selection of fiction and non-fiction, including good material on and from Africa, plus local newspapers and magazines. There's a plan to open an information centre here too, where you can find out about local tours and guest houses. On the northern stretch of Kairaba Ave is Glimpse of Africa, which sells ethnic-inspired gifts and homewares including African masks and carvings, and rustic ceramics decorated with cowries. The restaurant at *Ngala Lodge*, Atlantic Rd, doubles as a gallery space, with good-quality interesting and original contemporary art for sale. Fajara's *bengdula* on the beach, close to Kotu Strand, sells the usual assortment of batiks, wood carvings, musical instruments and jewellery. To reach it from Fajara, follow the footpath which leads from the end of Atlantic Road past the golf course and down towards the beach; the only vehicle access is from Kotu.

Kotu and Kololi

The neighbouring coastal communities of **Kotu** and **Kololi** constitute the epicentre of The Gambia's extremely localized tourist industry. Most of the package tourists, and a good number of independent travellers, choose accommodation here, and if you fly over the area on your way in to Banjul International Airport you'll see a generous scattering of hotel swimming pools dotted among the palm trees, rice fields and sandy paths. You won't, however, see many Gambian family compounds, except inland in the oldest quarter of Kololi village – tourist facilities predominate. During the four months of the off-season, when many of the hotels, bars and restaurants are closed, both Kotu and Kololi are sleepy and directionless, only stirring into life in early October when the hoteliers and restaurateurs set about their annual programme of repainting and repairs after the rains. As soon as the first peak-season visitors arrive in November, they're transformed into busy, brash resorts once again.

Kotu

KOTU is a tourist village on the beach, with the Fajara golf course and the Kotu Stream wetland area just behind. It's an area busy with tourist taxis, bumsters and itinerant traders. Supermarkets, telecentres, Internet cafés and a *bengdula* are all within very easy walking distance of each other, and the hub of the action is pretty much right on the beach.

The tourist-trap atmosphere in Kotu may be too intense for some, but there are some excellent **bush walks** and **cycle rides** close by. The track that runs from Kotu Stream road, past the access road to the *Palm Beach Hotel*, and on towards Kololi, is a pleasant 2.5km walk. The Kotu Stream area is particularly beautiful during the rice-growing season (Aug–Nov), when the fields are emerald green. By the end of the dry season, the stream is almost dry, but at any time of year there are birds and beautiful mature palm trees to admire, and sometimes monkeys. You'll often see plastic bottles clustered round the tops of the oil palms, and palm wine tappers shinning up to collect the fermenting sap. You may also be invited to sample some (there's a palm-wine "ghetto" near the Fajara golf course), but watch out for con-merchants who try to overcharge.

Kololi

Once an inconsequential coastal village, set back from the sea, **KOLOLI** has been transformed by tourism, expanding considerably and spreading right down to the beach at what are now known as the **Senegambia** and **Palma Rima** resort areas, where many major tourist hotels are found. The original settlement, Kololi Village, now houses as many tourism workers and affluent professionals as rice farmers and palm-tappers; it's also a popular hangout for young independent travellers.

The **Palma Rima area** is a small collection of hotels (the massive *Palma Rima* and a couple of others), restaurants and clubs between the coastal highway and the sea, about 1km southwest of Kotu Stream. Though inescapably touristy, it's low-key compared to the Senegambia area, 1.5km further southwest.

The **Senegambia area** – Kololi's main beach resort, named after The Gambia's largest hotel – is the hub of the country's tourist activity, with a busy, fairly tacky strip of restaurants, bars and clubs and an assortment of tourist hotels. Nobody actually lives here; the area exists solely for tourists. Businesses come and go, partly because it's one of the most bumster-infested areas in The Gambia; only when the military police are around do the chancers make themselves scarce, lending the place an odd ghost-town feel. Development in the area is proceeding at an energetic pace for The Gambia, and the results are not particularly attractive; there are a few architectural oddities, such as the plastic-looking pagoda that houses an Asian restaurant. There's also a bank, some exchange bureaux, a Gamtel office, The Gambia Experience resort office, and a few supermarkets. The range of facilities makes it a convenient place to stay, but you have to escape the area to discover the country's real charm.

One of the Senegambia area's greatest assets is its newly constructed, up-beat **craft market**, with a good range of local crafts including quality batik clothing,

Northern Kombo beaches

At low tide, it's possible to walk between the major resorts at the water's edge; it's around 10km from Cape Point to Bijilo. While none of the beaches here come close to the sun-kissed ideal of spotless sand and sparkling turquoise sea, there are some impressive spots. There's considerable variation in the landscape, with laterite cliffs giving way to flat sandy areas. Some of the beaches are continually changing shape, though, as powerful Atlantic currents tug away at the shore (see below).

Probably the most pleasant beaches in the resort area are at **Cape Point**. Clean, quiet, and with soft white palm-shaded sand, this area is reasonably unspoilt, with all the development set well back from the water's edge. The *Sunbeach Hotel and Resort* (see p.119) has landscaped its part of the beach attractively with loungers and thatched umbrellas under the palms. Unfortunately, however, cross-cutting tidal and river currents make the water here unsafe for swimming.

It's possible to swim at **Bakau**, round the point to the southwest, but this is principally a working beach. Fishing *pirogues* land at the jetty near the local marketplace to haul out the catch (mostly *bonga*), some of which is sold fresh, while some is taken straight to the smokehouses on the shore. It's a colourful and absorbing scene if you can cope with the combined smell of woodsmoke and drying *bonga*.

Fajara's beaches, down the coast from Bakau, are dramatically located at the foot of russet-coloured laterite cliffs, strewn with tide-washed rocks. The view of the broad sweep of the Atlantic ocean from the cliffs is spectacular, making this one of the best places in the country to enjoy the sunset, or the rainy season's dramatic electrical storms; *Ngala Lodge* is perfect for this. Most of the other clifftop plots are privately owned, so access to the beach here is limited; in any case, it's not recommended near high tide, when the few chunks of sand that are not swallowed by the sea may be cut off. The currents and undertow here are treacherous at certain times of year, and the rocky area near *Leybato*, at the Kotu end of the Fajara beaches, is one of the more dangerous places to swim. Every year several swimmers drown in the Fajara and Kotu area, and it's wise to pay heed to the lifeguards' warning flags.

Southwest of Fajara, the landscape flattens out and the beach becomes an open curve backed by Kotu, Kololi and Bijilo's tourist strip, plus some endangered scraps of coastal forest. You can reach **Kotu Strand** either from Kotu's main drag (Kotu Stream Road), or from the path which leads from the end of Atlantic Road in Fajara to the beach below. This area is hugely popular with young Gambians who arrive in droves at the end of the afternoon and at weekends for picnics, impromptu football matches, and drumming sessions. It's definitely the grubbiest and most touristy of all the beaches, with hotels backing onto the sands and plenty of **beach bars**, **fruit stalls** and **juice-pressers' stands**. The fruit stalls are all regulated and were introduced to replace the vendors who used to wander the beaches with trays of fruit on their heads. Instead of hawking from one sun lounger to the next, the fruit-sellers now heckle for custom from their stalls, and customers are faced with a row of vendors all selling identical stuff. The juice-pressers are similarly regulated; they too heckle persistently. They provide a useful service in a country where very few conventional bars serve fresh juice, but you should watch out for how much sugar and water the presser adds to your glass. Most of the Kotu beach hotels and beach bars offer free sun loungers, and some hire out watersports equipment such as bodyboards and windsurfers.

jewellery and beads, handmade leather shoes (which can be made to order) and bags, and fresh produce such as honey and cakes from local women's co-operatives. The traders share an agreed code of conduct, which precludes hassling tourists for business. Nevertheless, you need to go in a relaxed mood, mindful of the frustration of many stallholders who would probably much prefer to be out

The beach at **Kololi** seems particularly vulnerable to erosion but for now, at least, it's impressively wide thanks an engineering programme to replace the sand and keep it in place. Beyond here, **Bijilo** beach, presently on the very fringe of the resort area, has yet to recover from the decimation of its palm trees and from sandmining crews raiding the beach to supply the construction industry. Further south, the beaches are emptier and more attractive, with fishing centres punctuating the broad empty stretches of sand (see box on p.154). It's possible to walk or cycle along the beach all the way from Bijilo to Kartong in the far south of the country, a glorious way to appreciate the ocean scenery. The further south you go, the quieter it is and the fewer bumsters you'll encounter (see p.48).

Beach bars

Beach bars are a colourful part of the Gambian beach scene, and some visitors spend their whole stay moving happily from one to the next, or choosing just one and spending nearly every waking hour there. They cultivate a laid-back alternative to the inland tourist restaurants and bars, with reggae on the sound system and local live music from time to time; many serve excellent **fresh food**, notably prawns, grills, and fish baked in foil. Gambian beaches are simply too hot to lie out on for long periods, so beach bars provide a shady haven, with grass-thatched umbrellas and canopies woven from palm fronds. You have to allow time to enjoy the experience, as food tends to be prepared to order (sometimes even the shopping is done to order). Opening times can be unpredictable, although some stay open at night and during the rainy season.

The Kombo beach bar scene has gone through some **major changes** over the last decade. Like the fruit stalls and juice-pressers' stands, they're subject to checks from the Gambia Tourism Authority as part of their campaign to keep the beaches safe and free from bumsters, drugs and sleaze.

Coastal erosion

Coastal erosion, a natural phenomenon which affects the entire West African coast, ravaged the Kombo beaches during the 1990s, washing away great swathes of sand. Thanks to a costly and ambitious programme of remedial engineering work, most of the worst-affected beaches have now been rebuilt, but the problem remains and will soon have to be tackled again. Its **causes** are complex and little understood: cyclical changes in tidal patterns and ocean currents seem to play a part, but the cutting down of palm trees and the industrial-scale mining of sand from Bijilo and Kartong beaches (now outlawed) has exacerbated the situation. It's ironic that massive construction projects like Banjul International Airport, built in the late-1990s and intended to raise The Gambia's profile in West Africa and reinforce its standing as a world-class tourist destination, contributed to the near-destruction of some of the country's greatest tourist assets.

The visible consequences of erosion amount to an unfortunate character change in the beaches – broad gold or silver sands become narrow, grubby grey-beige ones, with chunks of the soft laterite cliffs behind the sands simply tumbling into the ocean.

In Kombo district, the beaches which seem to suffer least, such as those near Sanyang, Gunjur and Kartong, are south of the main tourist area and little-developed at present.

on the street, catching passing trade. Round the corner from the craft market is *Gaya*, an excellent craft and homeware shop with a pleasant café.

Kololi Village, on the opposite side of the Bertil Harding Highway from the Senegambia area, is a quiet residential area of family compounds and sandy streets that is distinctively African, in marked contrast to the tourist area close by. Among the residences of middle-class Gambians and expats who can't afford Fajara – or don't appreciate its relative rarification – there's a scattering of cheap local-style guesthouses, and one or two places to study music and dance. Kololi has its own gallery, the *Village Gallery* (☎446 3646, daily 10am–late; free), which displays paintings, photography and sculpture by West African artists. In a country where it's difficult to track down local art, this is a good exhibition space; displays change on a regular basis, and everything is for sale. There's also a restaurant and bar. Another interesting spot in the area is Daru Salaam Arts Creation, an open-air workshop and side-of-the-road "gallery" by the highway, about 400m south of the Coconut Residence hotel, where a supremely laid-back sculptor, Pa Peace, displays his unusual wares.

Bijilo Forest Park

Bijilo Forest Park and Nature Trail (daily 8am–6pm; other times by arrangement; D30, under-12s free), sometimes known locally as the Monkey Park, is a half-square-kilometre woodland reserve near the beach at the south end of the Senegambia area, near the entrance to the *Kololi Beach Club*. The reserve contains one of the country's last remaining stands of striking **rhun palms**. The Gambian coastline was once bristling with these trees, but they have been ravaged by builders and developers – beams and poles cut from palm trunks are a commonly used building material in The Gambia.

There are good chances of seeing red colobus and vervet **monkeys**, squirrels, large monitor lizards and a galaxy of **birds**. Trails are clearly marked, with a choice between long and short circuits of the park. Weekly tickets are available, a good idea if you're a birdwatcher lodging nearby and plan to come and go at different times of day. Unscrupulous guides encourage tourists to feed the monkeys in the park; as a result, they are extremely tame, affording great photo opportunities. It's worth being aware of some of the negative consequences of feeding wild animals, though – the tamer they become, the more damage they do to local crops, and the more likely they are to be exterminated by Gambian farmers.

Serrekunda

SERREKUNDA, the largest town in the country, lies just 3km inland from the resorts. Spending a little time here is an excellent way to get close to the heart of Gambian life; the centre of town gives you a strong flavour of modern, urban West Africa – a choking racket of diesel engines, with music blaring from hundreds of cassette players and radios, and streets lined with half-collapsed wooden trolleys and bricolaged stalls selling a riot of dust-covered imports. The focus of all this is the town's central market – in fact central Serrekunda is effectively just one big market. It's a lot of fun to wander round here, and not unsafe, as long as you keep any valuables out of sight.

If you stay in Serrekunda, you can take a taxi to the nearest beaches in ten minutes, or cycle there in twenty, and get the best of both worlds: the beach bars and restaurants on the coast, and the chop houses and local dives in Serrekunda. Staying in town doesn't necessarily mean suffering the noise and fumes of the centre – there are a few simple places in the residential quarters that will give you a real feel for daily life in this large town.

The thoroughfare that links Fajara and Serrekunda is **Kairaba Avenue**, the former Pipeline Road that, until a couple of decades ago, was a rutted track running through fields and orchards. Today, Kairaba's three-kilometre length is lined with shops, bars, restaurants and offices, and commands the highest rents in the country. It meets the Banjul–Brikama highway at Westfield Junction, The Gambia's answer to Piccadilly Circus or Times Square but without the lights. The Gambia has yet to have any shopping malls, but one or two large stores down Kairaba just about fulfil the role. The **Kairaba Centre** is the biggest of them – this is the place to come for that rowing machine or widescreen TV. Towards the southern end of Kairaba Avenue is the area's principal cultural centre, the **Alliance Franco-Gambienne** (or Alliance Française, ☎437 5418). It's a hive of activity, with a small outdoor amphitheatre-style performance space, where theatre and live music shows and English and French film nights are staged. The centre also offers French language classes, puts on art exhibitions, and has a library and recording studio.

If you turn down Mosque Road from Kairaba Avenue, look out for the **Big Tree** – a venerable and truly immense silk cotton on the west side. The whole of Mosque Road is pleasantly shady with trees and a great street to wander down. The commercial hubbub becomes increasingly frenetic as you walk south.

Serrekunda has few monuments or noteworthy landmarks, and one of the main reasons to spend time here, apart from just enjoying the energy of the place, is to shop. Near the **covered market** at the corner of Mosque Road and Sayerr Jobe Avenue, every inch of streetside space tends to be occupied by traders and pedestrians, and every bit of road is choked with vehicles, bikes, barrows, and more pedestrians. A maze of stalls, workshops and eating places occupies the market building and the large area behind. Inside, the stalls are separated by narrow alleys that all look very similar; it's a good idea to visit with a local friend or guide who can also advise you on prices. This is the kind of crammed-to-the-rafters place where you can find almost anything, from bicycle locks to flowery foam mattresses to babies' waist beads. There's also a large outdoor produce section, where women sell seasonal vegetables from stalls or enamel bowls and heaps laid out on the ground, while the market building's street side balconies are great for people-watching.

Beyond the market, the busy **commercial streets** make for interesting browsing, with a huge range of commodities on offer. You'll pass barber shops with hand-painted signs showing examples of the latest styles, furniture workshops where craftsmen make elaborately decorated bridal beds, and ironmongery shops, with strings of ladles and stacks of gleaming cooking pots, roughly cast from moulds made from hollowed-out sand. There are also shops selling brightly painted trunks made from recycled oil drums.

Close together on Sayerr Jobe Avenue are two excellent **craft** shops – Timbuktoo Bead & Mask Shop and Art Collections – which sell antique and contemporary masks, carvings, bronzes, beads, musical instruments and textiles from all over West Africa including *bogolan* mudcloth from Mali. Art Collections has some fascinating pieces, including oldish "colon" figures (painted colonial figures carved in wood), while Timbuktoo is very good for beads.

For **batik** and tie-dyed fabrics, Serrekunda has a famous "batik factory", Musu Kebba Drammeh's place in Dippa Kunda, signposted off Mosque Road. Musu Kebba died in 2003 and it's now run by her daughter. You can't normally watch craftspeople at work here, but there are plenty of textiles for sale, including garments and hangings, plus stalls selling drums and carvings. It's generally a good place to buy stuff without too much painful pressure.

Well worth seeking out is The Gambia's **Paper Recycling Skills Project** (☎779 3358, Sun–Wed 8.30am–4.30pm, Thurs 8.30am–12.30pm). At the time of writing it's located in Fajikunda, near Latrikunda, but it's hoping to move across town to a new 'craft village' which will be shared by a number of local artists and craft workers; you're advised to enlist the help of an experienced guide or driver to find it. Set up by an English artist to create training and employment opportunities, support educational projects and encourage a recycling culture in The Gambia, the project produces beautiful handmade paper, cards, albums and lampshades from discarded materials.

Serrekunda is a good place to get a taste of local – as opposed to tourist – **nightlife**, and it's home to The Gambia's most celebrated club, *Jokor* (see p.142). Serrekunda by night might seem an intimidating place to the uninitiated; like most Gambian towns, it's poorly lit, and unlike the resort areas, it makes no special concessions to tourists. In reality, however, there's little to fear, particularly if you're with local friends.

Eating, drinking and nightlife

As tourism in northern Kombo has expanded in recent years, so has the choice of **restaurants**, with a huge range of styles on offer, from modern European to Lebanese, from simple barbecues to elaborate Asian banquets. Unfortunately, however, too many restaurants in The Gambia favour quantity over quality – with enormously long menus of mediocre food. The resort area has the greatest concentration of international-style restaurants in the country – in fact, it's not all that easy to find traditional Gambian food in any of the tourist restaurants. For the real thing, you need to head for the low-key places the locals frequent in the urban centres of Bakau and Serrekunda, where you can eat your fill for next to nothing.

Go to restaurants in a relaxed mood, because you're likely to find that the service is slow, even at the so-called fast-food places. Most of the tourist places have a terrace so you can dine in the sun by day or under the stars by night, but local places may just be a few wooden benches and oilcloth-topped tables inside a hot room that doubles as the kitchen.

The **bar and club scene** here is similarly divided into two camps – tourist places and local places – although there's often a healthy overlap of clientele between the two. Many tourists get their first taste of the resort nightlife on a "Gambia by Night" tour organized by their hotel reps – a coach-driven bar crawl for a flat fee of around £15/€25, where you are driven from bar to bar, sampling a free glass of something at each, and dancing to whatever sounds they've slapped on to celebrate your arrival. For live music, the local radio, guides and taxi drivers can be good sources of information about forthcoming events – many of which aren't widely advertised. If you're planning a full-on night out, remember that nothing really gets going before midnight here.

Bakau and Cape Point

While **Bakau** has no truly excellent restaurants, it has some great mid-range options with loads of African atmosphere, and a few friendly, intimate bars with a good crossover between tourists and locals. The **Cape Point** area is more tourist-oriented; it's relaxed and a good choice for families. See map on pp.114–115.

 African Heritage 114 Atlantic Road, Bakau. With a terrace up on the cliff above Bakau's | fishing beach, the breezes here can be pungent, but it's still a quiet, pleasant place to stop, and there's a great gallery shop to browse. The café-restaurant serves an eclectic menu of good-value light meals, including African and Danish specialities and freshly squeezed lime juice. Mon–Sat 10am–6pm.

African Village Atlantic Road, Bakau. The hotel restaurant, perched on a low cliff, has a terrace with great ocean views – a good choice for lunch-time omelettes, sandwiches, kebabs, or sunset cocktails. In the evening there's a varied à la carte menu with tarragon chicken or yellowfin tuna in caper sauce. Prices are reasonable.

Bananas Bar & Restaurant Old Cape Rd, Bakau. A laid-back, cosy place on the edge of Bakau with a European-inspired menu. The only banana-themed option is grilled ladyfish with banana and lime; otherwise the choices are standard tourist restaurant fare, including fish, grills, and Gambian dishes, at average prices.

Calypso Beach Bar Off Kofi Annan St, Cape Point. Well-established place with a castaway feel, on a tide-bitten beach. The main restaurant is a brick and thatch *bantaba*; there are also private, romantic mini *bantabas* almost at the water's edge. Although the food is nothing special it's a relaxing spot. Daily 10am–late.

Chapmans Cape Point Rd, Cape Point ☎778 0999. Large, cheap and cheerful tourist-friendly courtyard bar-restaurant with masses of choice, from slap-up breakfasts to steaks, and a long list of cocktails. Not the cheapest place to drink, but big on atmosphere, with occasional live music and dancing.

Frank's Kofi Annan St, Cape Point ☎449 7362. Hungarian-run place that's good for goulash, Hungarian wine and cheap draught JulBrew. Daily except Sun, 3pm–late.

Italian Connection 1 Kofi Annan St, Cape Point ☎982 8695. This cheerful Italian-owned place serves up some of the most

authentic-tasting pizza and pasta to be found in The Gambia. Daily from 4pm.

Lama Lama Bar and Restaurant Off Atlantic Rd, Bakau. There's live music nightly, usually reggae or drum bands, at this bar with a busy local vibe. Daily 8.30am–12.30am.

Mr Bass Kofi Annan St, Cape Point. Street corner bar, on the edge of the craft market, selling beers and soft drinks at well below hotel prices.

Ocean Clipper *Ocean Bay Hotel*, Kofi Annan St, Cape Point ☎449 4265. Airy and elegant, and in a great location right on the beach, this upmarket Asian/European restaurant has attentive service and is the best place in The Gambia for Thai specialities.

Sand Plover off Old Cape Road, Cape Point ☎449 4559 or 990 0231. Like a miniature version of *Lamin Lodge* (see p.148), this rickety timber-built creekside beach bar has bags of character. Lunches are simple, the food is simple, generous and good – local oysters and shrimps are a speciality – but you have to be happy to wait a while for it to appear.

Saraba Off Newtown Road, Bakau. Don't be put off by the unlikely exterior (it sometimes looks closed): this low-key place, tucked away in a quiet neigh-bourhood, seves top-notch *afra* to in-the-know locals. There are a few tables in the garden at the back where you can enjoy spicy beef and onions in sauce or grilled chicken with mouthwateringly fresh *tapal-apa* from the next-door bakery. Nightly 7pm–3am.

Shanghai Chinese Restaurant Cape Point Rd, Cape Point. A small, cheerful place with plenty of Chinese standards and a few more unusual choices, such as squid with spicy sauce, shrimps with pineapple, plus Gambian and international dishes. Nothing special, but decent and reasonably priced. Daily noon–midnight.

Fajara and upper Kairaba Avenue

Fajara is the classiest neighbourhood in The Gambia, with some of its most up-market places to eat and drink. It's also possible to eat well here on a budget at some of The Gambia's most imaginative "boutique" restaurants. See map on pp.114–115.

Art Café African Living Art Centre, 9 Garba Jahumpa Rd ☎449 5131 or 779 1791. A tiny, elegant gallery café serving tea and impec-cably presented patisserie in serene surroundings. Daily 11am–6pm.

The Butcher's Shop 130 Kairaba Ave, ☎449 5069. Fajara's superb butchery, organic greengrocer, delicatessen, bakery and wine shop has an equally fine restaurant on the deck at the front: chic by day and romantic by night,

with particularly flamboyant salads and fresh fruit juices. For civilised nibbling, there's a long list of tapas, some Mediterranean, some Asian. Daily 8.30am–late. Prices are above average, but offer excellent value.

The Clay Oven Near VSO and MRC, signposted off Atlantic Rd ☎449 6000. The Gambia's best Indian restaurant takes itself extremely seriously, and has a loyal local following. The starters can be disappointing, but the main menu includes subtle and inspired variations on familiar South Asian dishes. At the "sizzler night" on Tuesdays you can sample a whole range of specialities. Daily noon–3pm and 7pm–late.

Eddie's Off Kairaba Ave. In a residential street in Fajara, this very small, informal grill fills the neighbourhood with smoke when there's bushpig on the barbecue. It's also good for chicken and chips.

Flavours Restaurant *Safari Garden Hotel*, Fajara ☎449 5887. A charming poolside restaurant, with an inspired menu that gives a creative twist to contemporary dishes by including Gambian ingredients wherever possible. Global influences include Thailand (booking is recommended for the highly popular Thai buffet evenings) and England (with bangers and mash and traditional fish and chips sometimes appearing among the choices). Look out for superb special culinary events. Daily 7am–11pm.

Francisco's Atlantic Rd, corner of Kairaba Ave ☎449 5332. In a leafy tropical garden setting dotted with large West African wood sculptures, this restaurant has a friendly, neighbourhood feel. The menu is standard fare – grilled meat, fish, omelettes – at slightly higher than average prices.

Golden Bamboo Chinese Restaurant Off Kairaba Ave, Fajara. In a country that has no good Chinese restaurants, this is a reasonable one with a long menu of standards.

Leybato Beach Bar Off Atlantic Rd, Fajara. Long-established beach bar, with hammocks strung over the sand. It's a great place to catch the sunset, or sample home-style African cooking. There's also a long menu of omelettes, fish, and grills, including excellent seafood kebabs. Not a place to choose if you're in a hurry.

MacFadi's Kairaba Ave. This Gambian version of an American fast-food joint serves fried food – but not fast. Chicken, chips, and burgers available.

Mama's Kairaba Ave (near Atlantic Rd) ☎449 7640. A reasonable mid-range choice, popular with expats for its *rosti* and its buffet nights, with occasional karaoke. Daily except Mon, 9am–late.

Ngala Lodge Restaurant 64 Atlantic Boulevard ☎449 7672. One of the finest places to eat in The Gambia. The evening ambience at this hotel restaurant is particularly seductive, with subtle live music and the sound of the ocean not far away. There's a mouthwatering modern European menu and a

good wine list – high prices, but worth it. Daily until late.

Le Palais du Chocolat Kairaba Ave. A good attempt at a French-style café, serving probably the best coffee in The Gambia; the hot snacks – *croque-monsieur* and hot dogs – and service are disappointing, but the pastries are good, while the gorgeously calorific cakes are well worth a splurge. Tues–Sat 8am–9pm, Sun 8am–1pm & 5–9pm.

La Parisienne Kairaba Ave. French-style pastries, ice cream, drinks and sponge cakes frosted in lurid colours; a relaxed place, but outclassed by *Le Palais du Chocolat*.

The Ritz Near *Safari Garden Hotel*, off Atlantic Rd, Fajara ☎992 4205. A friendly, casual place in a small courtyard, catering for tourists wanting a change from more formal hotel restaurants. Best-known for its steaks, with over a dozen different options at very reasonable prices. Daily except Fri, 10am–late.

Sultan Sweets and Restaurant Kairaba Ave ☎439 0151. Popular with young mobile-toting locals, this restaurant and café is good for Lebanese-style kebabs, mezze and baklava-style pastries. The best bargain is the spit-roasted chicken. Daily, 24 hours.

Sun Burger Kairaba Ave ☎437 4453. This bright place serves decent paninis and plates of Lebanese specialities at very reasonable prices, plus unusual specialities such as date bread. It's much visited by American volunteers from the nearby Peace Corps HQ.

Weezo's Kairaba Ave ☎449 6918. Casual but upmarket, well-to-do Fajara's most stylish restaurant has a mixed personality. At lunchtimes it's sleek, with a contemporary European menu, featuring imaginative salads and other light options. In the evenings it's part cocktail bar, with lounge jazz subtle in the background, part-Mexican restaurant (the really one in The Gambia, and outstanding), and part-gourmet à la carte. There's another total mood change when party animals drop in to dance to corny Europop in the bar, on "Gambia-by-night" tours organized by tour operators. Restaurant open Tues–Sun 11.30am–3pm & 7–11pm; bar open till late. Higher than average prices.

Yok African Living Art Centre, 9 Garba Jahumpa Rd ☎449 5131 or 779 1791. Asian-fusion cooking, including imaginative dim sum and stir-fries, in one of the most intimate and atmospheric restaurants in The Gambia. Part botanical garden, part bohemian palace, it's lush by day and glittering by night.

Kotu

Kotu's cheerful holiday-resort image is borne out by its concentration of touristy places to eat and drink. There are also plenty of beach bars, juice bars and fruit stalls in this area and a showy three-storey nightclub complex. See map on pp.116–117.

Al Baba Kotu Stream Rd, near the junction with Bertil Harding Highway. Impressive eastern-Mediterranean restaurant with a slick, urban feel, professional service and well-prepared, inexpensive food.

Boss Lady Kotu Stream Rd. Loads of fun, this is one of the few tourist restaurants which specializes in Gambian food such as Wolof rice and chicken *domodah*, washed down with palm wine or local juices such as baobab or *wonjo*. Daily 3pm–11pm.

The Captain's Table *Bakotu Hotel*, 2 Kotu Stream Rd ☎ 446 6111. Popular with both residents and non-residents of the hotel, this is a semi-open air restaurant with a look that's part-African, part-Mediterranean. While the cooking isn't as excellent as the prices suggest, it's better than average: the fish is pretty good, the bread well-chosen and the *bouillabaiss* particularly famous.

Destiny's Kotu Strand. Conceived as The Gambia's swankiest nightclub, this white elephant of a place is nothing if not lavishly decorated, with masses of showy Malaysian furniture and glitzy fabrics. Its hiphop and jazz nights are popular with tourists but locals tend to stay away, convinced that all three storeys could tumble into the sea at any moment. Fri–Sun 10pm–4am.

Domino Bar and Restaurant Kombo Beach. West African music, roots and reggae booms out of huge speakers from this beach terrace bar/restaurant, a friendly, down-to-earth haunt of *djembé* players and beach-lizards, serving good-value, decent food including sandwiches, burgers, noodles, omelettes, chicken, fish and African dishes. Open 24 hours.

Kunta Kinteh Beach Bar Kotu Beach. Upbeat, well-established and very popular, this place serves good-value, no-nonsense food, with a beach barbecue on Wednesdays and Sundays.

Paradise Beach Bar & Restaurant Kotu Beach. Right on the sand and a firm favourite with package tourists staying in the Kotu and Fajara areas, some of whom practically live here during their stay, this informal restaurant serves all-day English breakfasts, sizeable sandwiches, and generous platefuls of burgers, omelettes, salads and Gambian dishes at reasonable prices. Service is slow, but this is no hardship for the sun-worshippers who choose to be served at their sunbed. Daily 9am–late; happy hour Mon–Sat 5–7pm; barbecues with live music at weekends.

Sailor Beach Bar and Restaurant Kotu Beach, next to Fajara Craft Market. One of the better beachside restaurants, but not expensive. It's particularly good for seafood such as calamari in lime and garlic, or peppered barracuda steak. The menu also includes sandwiches, pizza, omelettes and pasta, plus freshly squeezed juice. Daily 10am–11.30pm; live music every evening except Thurs.

Tiger Tiger Kotu Stream Rd. Tiny but rather cool, this relaxed streetside bar is a good place to enjoy beers and cocktails into the early hours.

Kololi: Palma Rima area

The **Palma Rima** area is a real mixed bag, with a couple of good restaurants and clubs, a few beach bars, and a down-to-earth English pub. See map on pp.116–117.

40 Foot Food & Drink Bertil Harding Highway. In a converted shipping container at the side of the highway, this experimental place run by a German-Gambian couple is surprisingly appealing, serving locally-priced hot food and cold drinks.

Calabash Palma Rima Rd ☎ 446 8893. Styling itself as a night club for grown ups, with nightly DJ sets, *Calabash* also occasionally lets its hair down for special events such as "Mr Muscle" and "Miss Waistbeads" beauty pageants. Close to the *Palma Rima*, the crowd is a good mixture of Gambians and tourists. Thu–Sun 7pm–late.

Churchills Palma Rima Rd ☎ 446 0830. Archetypal holiday-resort-style British pub, with draught beer, juicy steaks and other familiar favourites. Football fans pile in here when there's a match on TV and karaoke nights attract a good crowd.

Jazziz Palma Rima Rd ☎ 446 2175. Bar/restaurant and live music venue, with jazz, blues, afrobeat and hi-life on Fridays, and salsa and reggae on Saturdays. Recommended.

Kotu Point Beach Bar and Restaurant Kotu Point, signposted from the back of the *Palma Rima*. One of the most attractive beach bars in the resort area, and one of the simplest, on a quiet stretch of good sand with a few sunbeds and thatched shades. The restaurant has a terrace with wicker chairs where you can tuck into fresh fish. Beer, soft drinks and palm wine are good value. Daily 9am–late, happy hour Sun 5–7pm followed by a barbecue with live drumming.

Luigi's Palma Rima Rd ☎446 0280. Busy, established Italian restaurant, popular with families. The food – pizza, pasta, risotto and jacket potatoes – is mixed, but there's plenty of choice, and big portions. The largest pizzas are gargantuan; the staff will wrap anything you can't manage. There's also a long list of aperitifs, liqueurs, speciality coffees and cocktails. Daily noon–4pm and 6–11.30pm.

Shiraz Palma Rima Rd ☎991 0990. One of The Gambia's finest eastern-Mediterranean-style restaurants, with mezze that are so good they could have been home-made, plus an interesting bar list including Lebanese wines.

Solomon's On the beach at the end of Palma Rima Rd ☎446 0716. Good-value beachside restaurant, serving simple meals like chicken *yassa* and fish baked in foil.

Teranga Beach Club This open-air nightspot, in a walled compound right on the beach, hosts highly popular DJ and live music nights at weekends, pulling in enthusiastic crowds of locals; the sound quality is often pretty dire but that doesn't seem to dampen the atmosphere.

Kololi: Senegambia area

The Gambia's brashest tourist strip has plenty of **restaurants**, **bars** and **clubs** in an area so small you can walk right round it in minutes – many tourists staying in the area don't bother to venture further afield. There are one or two gems among the trashier venues, with popularity swinging swiftly from place to place. See map on pp.116–117.

African Queen Near the Senegambia Craft Market. Scratch *djembé* bands play on the terrace at this informal, inexpensive restaurant and bar, one of the most popular on the strip, usually heaving with tourists and guides, bumsters and girls.

Al Basha Senegambia Rd ☎446 3300. Excellent Lebanese mezze in an air-conditioned, stylish atmosphere. Good value if you have an appetite.

Ali Baba's Senegambia Rd. Lebanese-run street corner terrace bar and restaurant, a perennially tourist popular hangout that's packed in the high season despite its mediocre cooking. The garden restaurant behind (also *Ali Baba's*, entrance round the corner) is a much better option – leafy and quirkily decorated, with a good house band every night. Daily till 1am; band 9pm–11.30pm.

Amber's Nest Bertil Harding Highway ☎446 4181. Gambian-owned Anglo-Mediterranean restaurant, with vegetarian options, a pub-style bar and Saturday night buffets. Mid-priced and very popular with local professionals.

Aquarius Near the casino ☎446 0247. A cocktail bar and disco with an international style far removed from traditional Africa. Just about big enough to dance; popular with tourists and smart young Gambian-Lebanese. Daily till 3am.

Baobab Bar and Restaurant Kololi beach. Friendly, informal beach bar a short stroll from the Senegambia strip, serving simple fish dishes at bargain prices.

Bodega Casa Fernando *Kairaba Hotel* ☎446 2940. The Kairaba's least formal restaurant has

a Mediterranean and Middle Eastern influenced menu, including pizza from a wood-fired oven, tapas, charcoal grills, fresh fish and seafood. Daily 4pm–midnight.

Coco Beach Restaurant *Kololi Beach Club*. A cut above most beach restaurants, elegantly decorated and prettily situated on a tranquil stretch of beach (despite its proximity to a busy tourist area). Lunch includes excellent quiches and salads; the evening menu has more elaborate and expensive choices, such as spare ribs in honey and black pepper marinade, or *châteaubriand* with *béarnaise* sauce. Recommended.

Forest Beach Bar & Restaurant Kololi Beach, by Bijilo Forest. The southernmost beach bar in the Senegambia area. Happy hour 5-7pm, Friday night reggae. Snacks menu includes English breakfast and fish & chips.

Gaya Art Café Bertil Harding Highway ☎446 4022, www.gayaartcafe.com. Interesting gallery shop, with a stylish though rather pricey café-bar serving organic snacks, tapas and coffee. Mon to Sat, noon–11.30pm.

GTS Restaurant Beyond the casino. On the edge of the Senegambia action, but definitely worth seeking out, this welcoming and characterful restaurant is run by Gambia Tourist Support (see p.33). Relaxed atmosphere and good simple African and European food, including tasty options for vegetarians and for kids, at extremely reasonable prices. Regular live music sessions in the evenings.

Jade Chinese Restaurant Near the casino ☎446 2638. Friendly staff serve largely Cantonese dishes, including hot pots, sizzlers, and several interesting dishes like fried crab with ginger and spring onion and chicken wings with spiced salt. Reasonable and recommended.

La Scala opposite the casino ☎446 0813. Rather formal, Franco-Italian style place with higher than average prices.

La Valbonne at Kololi Casino ☎446 0226. Serves mostly Italian food in a refined atmosphere. Expensive.

The Kora Senegambia Rd ☎446 2727. One of the better and more expensive restaurants in the tourist strip, with an international *à la carte* menu.

Paparazzi Jazz Bar Senegambia Rd. Popular with young tourists and well-dressed locals, this bar has a pre-club feel, with loud music and banter, and is often the last to close. Daily 9.30pm–late.

Paradiso Senegambia Rd. This ordinary-looking place on the tourist strip serves the best pizzas in The Gambia; there's also a good choice of salads and the usual standards at keen prices: steak, chicken, seafood, pasta. They do take-aways – perfect for pizza on the beach.

SeaView Beach Bar & Restaurant On the beach near *Senegambia Beach Hotel*, signposted from Bertil Harding Highway ☎446 3502. Busy late on Fridays when the house salsa band struts its stuff. A good place for a drink, but eat somewhere else first, as the restaurant is disappointing and over-priced. Daily 9am–late.

Shikra *Kairaba Hotel* ☎446 2940. The *Kairaba*'s most expensive restaurant, popular with honey-mooners, with an international menu. Mon–Sat 7pm–midnight.

Tao opposite the casino ☎446 1191. Gambia's only Thai restaurant, with pan-Asian influences, in a building like a theme park version of a pagoda. Popular but disappointing. Daily 7.30–10.30pm.

Waaw Senegambia Rd ☎446 0668. A small upstairs club that's something of a pick-up joint, playing soul, funk, ragga, hiphop and old-fashioned disco nightly to a mixed crowd of Gambians and tourists. Open nightly till late, entrance fee at weekends.

Yasmina Bar & Restaurant Senegambia Rd ☎446 5245. Breezy corner location, good for watching the passing scene, serving reasonably priced eastern Mediterranean salads, pittas and grills.

Kololi Village

Kololi Village has an eclectic mix of restaurants and clubs, appealing to independent travellers and anyone wanting a break from the mass-tourism atmosphere of Kololi's mainstream places. See map on pp.116–117.

Amsterdam Dolphin Palma Rima Rd, on the way into Kololi village ☎446 0590. Caters for a tourist and expat crowd, with draught JulBrew and inter-national food at decent prices, including *bratwurst*, goulash, and a good selection of shrimp dishes. Middle-of-the-road music on the stereo; the large TV comes on for sports and British soaps.

Kololi Fast Food Palma Rima Rd, on the way into Kololi village. Decent fast-food outlet with good prices.

Mama's Kololi Village, on the bush taxi route between Kotu/Kololi and Serrekunda ☎992 9951. An excellent local restaurant (not to be confused with *Mama's* in Fajara) with a cheer-ful, shaded roadside terrace, serving simple food at low prices, such as omelettes, spaghetti, steak with peppers, and *chicken yassa*. Particularly good break-fasts. The owner makes you feel like one of the family.

Mannjai Lodge Manjai Kunda ☎446 3414. The courtyard bar at this hotel is occasionally the venue for live music sessions featuring big names from the Gambian and Senegalese scene. The sound system isn't great, but there's a mellow, apprecia-tive atmosphere to the place.

Queen's Head Kololi Village, on the bush taxi route between Kotu/Kololi and Serrekunda. British-style pub that attracts a male-dominated crowd of local expats with beer, pool, karaoke and more beer. Light meals are available, and there's a happy hour 5–7pm daily.

Relax Palma Rima Rd, on the way into Kololi village. Traditional West African food such as *plasas*, *domodah* and *benachin*, at low prices.

Village Gallery Kololi Village ☎446 3646. The garden courtyard outside this interesting art gallery is a restaurant, serving simple, cheap but good daily specials such as grilled chicken or fish.

South Kololi: Bijilo and Kerr Serign

Choices are limited in **South Kololi** for now, but this is the next expansion hotspot – new restaurants and bars are sure to spring up along the main highway and on the beach. See map on pp.116–117.

Avocado Restaurant *Coconut Residence*, Bertil Harding Highway ☎ 446 3377. One of The Gambia's finest restaurants, and an excellent choice for a special occasion –

President Jammeh sometimes entertains here. Imaginative menus with inspiration from all over the world, with careful attention to detail, and impeccable service.

Serrekunda and lower Kairaba Avenue

While **Serrekunda** has no tourist restaurants, it has some great down-to-earth local eating places, especially around the market, and The Gambia's best and most famous club, the legendary *Jokor*. Serrekunda's nightlife is as gritty and energetic as the daytime commercial activity. The action doesn't really get underway much before midnight, then carries on until 4 or 5am, when revellers head off in search of *afra*. As well as *Jokor*, there are a number of local bars in town which come alive at night; many of these see few foreign visitors, but you'll almost certainly be made welcome. See map on p.118.

Afra Citizen Mosdolly Mosque Rd. Cave-like *afra* shop run by Mauritanians; it may look medieval but their barbecued lamb is as good as it gets. Choose a chunk of meat from one of the joints hanging from hooks over the chopping block, and see it cut up in front of you, seasoned, and tossed into the furnace to grill. When it's done, it's wrapped in brown paper with mustard and salt. Daily, eves only, till late.

Alliance Franco-Gambienne Kairaba Avenue ☎ 437 5418. This French cultural exchange centre has a good-value garden bar/restaurant which sometimes has French and Senegalese dishes on the menu.

Busoku Fast Food Kairaba Ave. Sunny by day, strip-lit by night, and with the radio always turned up loud, this place serves cheap and decent fish or chicken sandwiches, chicken or beef *chawarma*, and meat pies. Daily 9am–7pm, or later if busy.

Come Inn 17 Kairaba Ave ☎ 439 1464. Popular with a mixed crowd of Gambian, German, British and Dutch regulars, this *biergarten* with an African twist is a good place to mingle with locals and expats over a drink or a meal – they do steaks, fish, pizza and German fare. The German owner claims to serve the best draught JulBrew in the country, and it's cheaper here than at most of the resort bars and restaurants. Great value.

Jokor Westfield Junction ☎ 992 2555. The best club in the country, primarily a hangout for fast-living Gambians, but with a friendly and relaxed atmosphere; visitors rarely

feel out of place. The mood is different every night, depending on whether they're playing African, Caribbean, or European music, but it's the West African sounds that really get the crowd moving. You dance under the stars in a garden with trees laced with fairy lights, and bands – even big West African stars – play on the tiny stage. Sunday night can be steamy – the house band of *sabar* drummers do their stuff to electrifying effect, and Gambian and Senegalese women take the floor for an *mbalax* dance competition in which practically anything goes. Thu–Mon, nightly till late.

Lana's Bar London Corner. A place to sit and enjoy a cheap beer or soft drink while you watch the busy Serrekunda street life. Open till late, closed Sun.

Willy's Disco Near Yundum police station, Lamin, just outside Serrekunda. A fun, relaxed local dive with an interior like a circus tent lit with traffic lights. Young Gambians in baseball caps and baggy shirts come here to dance to reggae and ragga; there aren't many females about, but anybody's welcome. Opens irregularly, weekends only.

Youth Monument Bar and Restaurant Westfield Junction. A park that's essentially a traffic island in the middle of one of The Gambia's busiest road junctions may seem an unlikely venue for a restaurant, but this casual, low-key place is surprisingly good as a place to grab a beer, a simple cheap meal – good kebabs and grills – or a coffee. Open all day, but especially busy as a pre-club venue for *Jokor*.

Abuko Nature Reserve and the Tanbi Wetlands

The area around the village of Lamin, about 8km southwest of Serrekunda, draws large numbers of birdwatchers, wildlife enthusiasts and other day-trippers, not for the village itself, which is nothing special, but for **Abuko Nature Reserve** and the **Tanbi Wetlands**. A walk along Abuko's shady paths can yield excellent sightings of birds, monkeys, chameleons and colourful lizards, many of them inquisitive and apparently tame. Exploring the Tanbi Wetlands, the network of mangrove creeks just inside the mouth of the River Gambia, can be equally rewarding for birdwatchers and anglers. A perfect way to end an excursion into the creeks is to relax at *Lamin Lodge*, a charming restaurant and bar built on the banks of the calm and majestic Lamin Bolon.

Abuko Nature Reserve

Abuko Nature Reserve (daily 8am–6.30pm; D31.50) was The Gambia's first protected area, gazetted as a reserve in the 1960s. Rich in flora and fauna, the reserve is justly popular, and at under two square kilometres it's compact enough to explore on foot in a couple of hours. Though suffering from a shortage of water, it still preserves one of the last surviving examples of **gallery forest** (mature tropical riverine forest) in the country; the variety of healthy trees and shrubs here is excellent, and there are three-hundred-odd bird species and dozens of varieties of small mammals and reptiles. One of the reserve's best locations for birdwatching and crocodile-spotting is close to the entrance: the **Bambo pool**, a densely-fringed freshwater pond. Exploring the deeper reaches of the forest can be illuminating too – the only real disappointments at Abuko are the Animal Orphanage, essentially a small zoo of bored-looking caged animals, and the tatty craft market at the exit gate.

The founder of the reserve, conservation expert Eddie Brewer, first recognised the unique significance of **Lamin stream** (the tip of Lamin Bolon) and its stunning necklace of forest in 1967, and Abuko was fenced the following year. Apart from pond-dredging, path-clearing and hide-building, the reserve is left more or less as it was found. Particularly impressive are the magnificent gallery forest trees, spiralling up from the webbed fingers of their buttress roots through a canopy of trailing creepers and epiphytes to create dark cathedrals of evergreen vegetation. The reserve also encloses more thinly wooded Guinea savannah.

Abuko is a narrow rectangular shape, with a single 2.5-kilometre **marked trail**, a crooked path leading up the southeast side towards the Animal Orphanage, then back down the northeast side to the craft market and exit. The whole walk around the marked trail takes a couple of hours, but it could easily turn into half a day or more depending on your interest in the various bird species – more often heard than seen – and your curiosity about the monkeys and the more bizarre life-forms on the forest floor, such as crazy-coloured beetles and seething columns of soldier ants. The one path that branches off the main route is a shortcut to the exit, which reduces the circuit by about three-quarters.

Birdwatching in Abuko

Abuko is the closest patch of tropical forest to Europe, and each winter it attracts thousands of birdwatchers, as well as a host of palearctic migrants (willow warblers, chiff-chaffs, black caps and melodious warblers) to swell the numbers of its native species. Most obvious are the water birds – a couple of photo hides overlooking the stream and pools are usually occupied by birders murmuring in raptures over them. Look out for kingfishers (blue-breasted, Senegal, malachite and pied), the "umbrella fishing" black heron, and two great birdwatcher's sights: the painted snipe (the male incubates the eggs) and the stunning red-bellied paradise flycatcher, with its thirty-centimetre tail feathers. You can generally see hammerkops around the pool at the start of the trail; in flight, their swept-back crest of feathers and pointed beaks make them look like miniature pterodactyls, and their huge nests, courtship displays and trumpet calls are remarkable. In the clearings, wait to see fanti rough-winged swallows and the occasional shikra darting through the light and, above the forest canopy, hooded vultures, black kites, swooping bee-eaters and rollers and maybe palm nut vultures.

You've a very good chance of seeing all The Gambia's species of **monkey** here – patas, callithrix (sometimes called vervet monkeys) and the particularly attractive western red colobus. There are also plenty of **monitor lizards** which you might spot darting across the paths and clawing their way through the undergrowth. Most monitors here are small, but they can grow as long as two metres. With patience, it's normally also possible to spot **crocodiles** at the Bambo pool from the large lookout veranda at the Education Centre, particularly on cool mornings when they emerge from the water to sun themselves on the banks. Watch for two distinct species: the larger, pale Nile crocodile, and the small, darker, nocturnal dwarf crocodile, critically endangered and very rarely seen. You may also see a **bushbuck** grazing on the banks of the pool. **Snakes** are sometimes seen at Abuko, including green mambas, puff adders, royal and African rock pythons, forest and spitting cobras – but snake phobics should note that there has never been a case of snake-bite involving a visitor or member of the reserve staff.

The **Darwin Field Station** (ⓦ www.darwingambia.gm) near the Bambo pool is a biodiversity research, education and training centre incorporating the headquarters of the Makaustu Wildlife Trust (see p.177). On show in the main timber building are some displays relating to local wildlife and wider conservation issues. Allow plenty of time at the upstairs veranda lookout, which has great views over the Bambo pool; there are plenty of kingfishers, herons, egrets, francolins, sandpipers and turacos in the vicinity. It's a gorgeous spot, ringed with fine mature palms and candelabra trees; by the second half of the dry season (March–June) the pool is the only fresh water in the area, so it's a wildlife magnet. There are a couple of **hides** nearby, which allow you to get very close to smaller pools of fresh water frequented by birds.

At the top of the standard circuit is the **Animal Orphanage**, a rehabilitation centre set up by the Department of Parks and Wildlife Management in 1997. Despite its good intentions, it's a forlorn place. Monkeys and parrots comprise the vast majority of animals taken in, and those unsuitable for release remain here alongside the orphanage's other permanent residents, including hyenas, which swagger round their enclosures or just sprawl despondently in the dust. There are, at least, well-written explanations outside the enclosures.

All the biggest gallery forest trees are in the first quarter of the walk; the rest of the circuit is mostly through more open Guinea woodland savannah, green with foliage all year round. From time to time you have to duck under arches of vines; frustratingly often you will hear scuttling noises in the bush ahead of you, indicating that an animal has disappeared from view just before you've seen it; but equally often you'll be rewarded with very good sightings, particularly of monkeys, who happily outstare visitors from the trees.

Practicalities

To get the most out of your visit, avoid the **Abuko excursions** organized by tour operators (around £15/€22 per person for a morning or afternoon, including return transport from your hotel). These groups tend to visit in the late morning and early afternoon, which are not the best times for wildlife-spotting – shouting guides and chattering crowds of up to thirty people shatter the tranquillity, and you'll see far more of your fellow visitors' backs than you will of birds and monkeys.

It's almost as straightforward, and usually more rewarding, to visit the reserve **independently**, either alone or in a small group. The entrance to Abuko is on the main Serrekunda–Brikama road, a busy bush-taxi route. You can get here from the resorts by making your way to Kombo Sillah Drive, near Westfield Junction, Serrekunda, where you can take a minibus **bush taxi** heading for Lamin or Brikama (D7); you get off at the reserve entrance immediately after the weighbridge on the main road. Travelling in this direction, you first pass the exit, conspicuous because of its near-derelict craft market; the entrance is 500m further south. Alternatively, you could hire a taxi to take you there and possibly wait for the return trip (typically D500 by tourist taxi, less for a yellow taxi).

While it's hard to get lost at Abuko, **guides** are often very knowledgeable and know exactly where to find certain species. Jobbing guides tend to hang out around the Darwin Field Station looking for custom. Park rules forbid them from charging for their services, but they naturally expect a "gift" of some kind – D100 for an hour or two is standard. As elsewhere in The Gambia, early morning and late afternoon tend to yield the most wildlife sightings, and there are spectacular movements of flocks of fruit bats at sunset. Keen naturalists may like to arrange a visit outside normal hours, by paying the gatekeeper direct if you arrive before the ticket booth opens, or letting them know as you go in if you want to stay on late.

It's worth bringing **food** and **drink** with you if you intend to stay a while. Bring mosquito repellent, too, especially during the rains.

The Tanbi Wetlands

Immediately southwest of Banjul, and easily accessible from the main beach resorts, the **Tanbi Wetlands** are a wilderness of mangroves, saltwater *bolons* (creeks) and mudflats just inside the mouth of the River Gambia. They occupy a total area of about sixty square kilometres, making them one of the largest wetland areas in the country; they're also home to some rare mammals including the marsh mongoose and the West African manatee. A popular area for boat-trips, the wetlands are particularly beautiful at the beginning and end of the day, when the waters are calmest, the air coolest, and the spectacular and prolific birdlife most active. Sunset is a magical time, when you can see pelicans settling down to roost in the baobabs.

The tranquil creeks are best explored by small boat – the smaller the better, to enjoy the narrowest, shallowest creeks to the full. Since every creek is bordered by **mangroves**, with nothing but sky and the occasional baobab on the horizon, and no sounds but the noise of the boat, the cracking and plopping sounds from the mangroves, the occasional bird-call, and perhaps the distant pounding of drums, the sense of remoteness is complete, close though you are to the major urban areas. The mangroves are beautiful, eerie and surprisingly tall – up to 20m. Fiddler **crabs** beckon manically on every mudbank, seemingly gathering in silent, jostling droves as boats approach; the quicksilver, dun-coloured hopping things are **mud-skippers** – fish seemingly intent on becoming terrestrial – which always seem to have gone just before you get a good look at them. Occasional inhabitants of the mangroves are **monkeys**, bounding through the foliage, presumably taking refuge from persecutors on the farm plots inland. Sadly, over-hunting in the past means hippos are never seen this far downstream.

The northern limit of the wetlands is in Banjul: **Kankujeri Road** (sometimes still known as Bund Road) runs along the edge of it, and the wetlands hug **Oyster Creek**, the channel separating the capital from the mainland. The southern limit is near **Mandinari**, a village southeast of Lamin and about 8km from the main highway. The fields between Mandinari and Lamin are a popular place for bird-walks, particularly during the rice-growing season – from August to October the fields and nearby foliage are lush, with so many birds they make the creeks look dead in comparison. Ornithologists also come here between November and January specifically to observe Temminck's coursers, which appear while the watermelon and groundnut fields are being cleared.

The whole wetland complex is a network of tidal channels where oyster-collectors and fishermen make their living, while trying to ward off poachers

Gambian oysters

Gambian oysters are a delicacy, though not a rarity, and when shelled they look and taste rather like juicy mussels. Harvesting them in the mangrove creeks is considered women's work; however, the women who do this, often Jola, have a reputation for being particularly tough and masculine – they even wear trousers, otherwise unheard-of in traditional Gambian society. They work at mid- to low tide, paddling their dugout canoes close to the mangroves where oysters cling to the roots near the water line, cutting them away with a cutlass.

The oysters are later boiled or smoked in a barrel, making it easy to separate the flesh from the shell. The **shells** are kept for a year, then burnt and ground to produce a form of lime used to strengthen clay or made into whitewash to paint huts. The shells are also mixed with tar and used like gravel in road surfacing – many Gambian roads, including major ones, have a shell-and-tar surface. Sometimes the shells are simply abandoned in general middens, old examples of which are of great interest to archaeologists. By measuring the rate of growth of shell mounds started in the time of the Gambian Stone Circles, and analysing their contents, researchers have been able to piece together data about prehistoric societies.

Boat trips from Denton Bridge

The mainland side of **Denton Bridge**, which carries the Banjul–Serrekunda highway across Oyster Creek, is a base for boat-trip operators covering the Tanbi Wetlands and the River Gambia beyond. Bush taxis travelling along the highway between Bakau or Serrekunda and Banjul will stop at the turning to the Denton Bridge landing area on request. On the Atlantic side of the bridge is a site shared by two highly professional outfits, Gambia Watersports Centre (℡777 3777) and Gambia Sport Fishing (℡777 4777), which charter boats for cruising or sport fishing from £45 per person.

On the creek side of the bridge is an informal jumble of timber huts, bamboo shacks and shipping containers that's the closest The Gambia gets to a marina; here you'll find boat owners willing to discuss tailor-made fishing, birding, or sightseeing trips, or just share stories about their adventures.

All approximate rates quoted here are per person. A two-hour local **creek trip** by small boat is likely to cost around D1000; a half-day to *Lamin Lodge* typically costs D1000 return. **Sport fishing** costs D2000 per day: you've a good chance of hooking red snapper, tapandar, captain fish, or angelfish in the environs of Denton Bridge, and metre-long barracuda are a common enough catch. You could also arrange a longer-distance trip, taking you beyond the wetlands, such as **dolphin-spotting** in the Gambia estuary for D1500 per half-day, a full day to **James Island** and back for D2500, Kemoto for D4000, or Tendaba for D5000. The *Harbour Café* and *The Bridge*, near the shore, serve drinks in the shade and are usually busy with yarn-spinning sport fishermen.

---

who over-fish the waters with drag nets, even in the breeding season; illegal sand-miners have been also working clandestinely in the area. Although it's been identified as a site of international importance by the Ramsar Wetlands Convention, the Tanbi Wetlands are not yet officially gazetted as a protected area.

Practicalities

Many visitors to the Tanbi Wetlands get there by **organized tour**. The wetlands can be explored on a number of excursions (see p.48), starting from the resort hotels, then setting off into the waterways by large *pirogue* from Denton Bridge outside Banjul, the waterfront in Banjul, or *Lamin Lodge*. These include creek fishing trips, the well-known "Champagne and Caviar" trip and the classic "Birds and Breakfast" and "Sunset Cruise" trips that end up at *Lamin Lodge* for food, drink and entertainment. It's sometimes possible to combine a boat trip in the creeks and a walk round Abuko as part of the same excursion. Enjoyable though these tours often are, they're not recommended for serious wildlife enthusiasts – there'll probably be too many people making too much noise, most of them far more interested in the breakfast or fruit punch than the birds.

It's also straightforward enough to make **independent arrangements**, a good plan if you'd like to travel in a very small group or target a particular location or time of day. You can arrange private **boat hire** with one of the small-scale boat-trip operators at Denton Bridge (see box above), or informally with fishermen on the shore north of the Barra ferry terminal in Banjul. Hiring a boat at *Lamin Lodge* costs from around D225 per hour. Take plenty of water and food, binoculars, and sun protection. If you're in a motorboat, ask the captain to cut the engine from time to time to enjoy the surroundings at their tranquil best.

Birdwatching in the Tanbi Wetlands

You'll almost certainly see several heron species in the creeks, including goliath herons standing sentinel on the muddy banks; you might also see ospreys, pied and malachite kingfishers, white- and pink-backed pelicans, yellow-billed storks and sacred ibis. African darters with their curiously sinuous necks perch on low mangrove branches, while on the topmost branches you're likely to see bee-eaters in candy-bright colours. The dawn chorus is particularly impressive in this environment, as well as the hour before sunset when birds are heading for their island roosts. In the middle of the day, many birds retreat from the heat of the sun, and the glare on the water makes viewing conditions uncomfortable.

Lamin Lodge

A popular destination for creek trips is 🏛 **Lamin Lodge** (☎449 7603, ⓦ www.gambiariver.com), situated on the snaking Lamin Bolon, one of the River Gambia's many saltwater tributaries. It's a large, triple-storey bar-restaurant built on the bank at the creek head, 3km from the village of Lamin, roughly halfway between Serrekunda and the airport, and a couple of hours' lazy cruise from Denton Bridge or Banjul. Everything is made of rustic timber, and there are plenty of seemingly rickety walkways to negotiate and staircases to climb. It's well worth investigating the upper levels, which afford breathtaking views over this grand sweep of water, mangrove, and fields, a special treat in a country where tall buildings are so rare that you hardly ever get to see anything from above. *Lamin Lodge* is also well known as a **birdwatching** base, and it's possible to hire expert birding guides here, in particular members of the recommended Habitat Africa (see p.49) group of guides, who will tailor-make tours on request.

The **food** here is moderately priced and very good, but if you arrive unexpectedly it may take some time to prepare. Specialities include fresh fish and oysters, of course, grilled or lightly fried with limes; they also provide elaborate Gambian-style buffets with all the usual dishes such as *domodah*, chicken *yassa* and *benechin*. Watch out for the bold-as-brass monkeys that operate well-orchestrated raiding parties whenever a group of tourists shows up.

While most people arrive by boat, *Lamin Lodge* is a fine place to come to by road, too, especially early in the morning. Bush taxis running along the main highway between Westfield Junction in Serrekunda and Lamin or Brikama can drop you in Lamin at one of the two access roads for the lodge, one of which is marked by an unmissable sign. From here, it's a pleasant three-kilometre walk along bumpy roads; you wind your way out of Lamin, then continue through more scenic farmland to the lodge. A tourist taxi to *Lamin Lodge* from the resorts costs around D600 return; a town trip by yellow taxi is around D250. It's close enough to the airport (15–20min by taxi or private vehicle) to be an excellent stop for one last drink in The Gambia before you leave: you could check in your luggage way ahead of the queues then head over here to relax for an hour or so before going back to catch the plane.

Listings

Air freight and shipping DHL, Independence Drive, Banjul ☎ 422 8414; Saga Express (Fedex agent), Kanifing ☎ 447 2405; UPS, 42 Antouman Faal Street, Banjul ☎ 422 4422. *Camping Sukuta* (☎ 991 7786) can organize vehicle shipping (approx €500 for motorbikes and €2000 for cars).

Airline offices Air Guinée, 17 OAU Boulevard, Banjul ☎ 422 7585, ☜ www.mirinet.com/AirGuinee; Air Sénégal International, ECOWAS Ave, corner of Mandela St, Banjul ☎ 420 2117, ☜ www.air-senegal-international.com; Bellview Airlines, 16 Kairaba Ave ☎ 437 0594, ☜ www.flybellviewair.com; Gambia International Airlines: Satellite House, Banjul ☎ 422 3702, Midway Centre, Kairaba Avenue ☎ 437 4100, ☜ www.gia.gm; Sierra National Airlines, ☎ 439 7551, ☜ www.sierranationalair.com; SN Brussels Airlines, Bertil Harding Highway, Kololi ☎ 446 6880, ☜ www.flysn.com. The Gambia Experience (see Travel agents, p.29) acts as agent for Astraeus and for charter flights from Banjul to London.

American Express agent Gamtours, Kanifing Industrial Estate, Serrekunda ☎ 439 2259.

Banks and foreign exchange Standard Chartered: 8 ECOWAS Ave, Banjul ☎ 422 8681, ☜ www.standardchartered.com; Senegambia area, Kololi ☎ 446 3277; Kairaba Ave, Serrekunda ☎ 439 7475; Atlantic Rd, Bakau ☎ 439 5046; IBC Bank: Liberation Ave, Banjul ☎ 422 8145; Atlantic Rd, Bakau ☎ 449 5120; Sayerr Jobe Ave, Serrekunda ☎ 439 2572; Trust Bank: 3–4 ECOWAS Ave, Banjul ☎ 422 5777; Sait Matty Rd, Bakau ☎ 449 5486; Banjul International Airport ☎ 447 2915; Sayerr Jobe Ave, Serrekunda ☎ 439 8038. Most are open Mon–Thu 8.30am–3pm, Fri–Sat, 8.30–11am. Standard Chartered branches have ATMs and will cash British cheques if presented with a cheque guarantee card. IBC and Trust Bank are Western Union Agents. Bayba Express, for instant currency transfers, has offices in Banjul (☎ 422 2344) and Serrekunda (☎ 439 4505). There are exchange bureaux in all the main resort areas.

Bicycle rental You can rent bikes from the stands outside many major hotels for around D200 per day or D150 for half-day.

Books Timbooktu on Garba Jahumpa Rd is the most useful general bookshop in The Gambia. There are small selections of books for sale at supermarkets and hotel shops, and the *Fajara Club* has a small library of paperbacks.

Car and motorbike rental AB Rent a Car (☎ 446 0926, ☜ www.ab.gm), a reputable local independent agency, has an office near the *Senegambia Hotel*. Europcar has a desk at the airport and a branch on Kairaba Avenue (☎ 777 3988). West African Tours (☎ 449 5258, ☜ www.westafricantours.com) hires out Land Rovers with drivers and guides: a good option for trips off the beaten track. *Camping Sukuta* (☎ 991 7786) offers cars for local self-drive (25km max radius) at good rates. D 'n' D Bikes and Buggy Safaris, Senegambia area (☎ 771 9756 or 982 2486, ☜ www.bikesnbuggies.co.uk) hires out motorbikes and beach buggies. M & M, Senegambia area (☎ 703 4563 or 702 3700, ☜ www.m-m-scooterforrent.com) hires out mopeds.

Cinema Alliance Franco-Gambienne, Kairaba Ave, Serrekunda is the best place to watch films, though they only have showings twice a week, at 8.30pm on Mondays (mainstream English language films) and Thursdays (French language films). Aisa Marie, Serrekunda is a sweltering concrete box showing football from satellite TV or cheap imported action movies.

Dentist Swedent, signposted off Bertil Harding Highway on the opposite side from *Palma Rima Hotel* ☎ 446 1212.

Doctors The Lamtoro Clinic (☎ 446 0934), near the *Senegambia Beach Hotel*, is highly rated but pricey; the Royal Victoria Hospital, Banjul (☎ 422 3756) has out-patient facilities. Westfield Clinic, Westfield Rd, Serrekunda (☎ 439 2213) is recommended for malaria treatment. Alternatively, try the Momodou Musa Memorial Clinic (Banjul ☎ 422 4320, Serrekunda ☎ 437 1683); The Medical Research Council, Fajara (☎ 449 5442) has a British nurse on duty, while Sheelagh Fowler, the British High Commission nurse, also runs a clinic (☎ 449 5133, mobile ☎ 999 4785). The call-out fee for a private doctor is typically around £25-30.

Embassies and diplomatic missions Austria, 3A Russell St, Banjul ☎ 422 7436; Belgium, c/o *Kairaba Hotel*, Kololi ☎ 446 1179; Denmark, 1A Cotton St, Banjul ☎ 422 7432; France, Ecole Française, Atlantic Rd, Kairaba Ave end ☎ 449 5487; Germany, Independence Drive, Banjul ☎ 422 7783; Ghana, 18 Mosque Rd, Latrikunda ☎ 439 1599; Guinea, 78 Daniel Goddard St, Banjul ☎ 422 6862; Guinea-Bissau, Atlantic Rd, Bakau ☎ 449 4854; Lebanon, 26 ECOWAS Ave, Banjul ☎ 422 8419; Netherlands, c/o Shell Company, Macoumba Jallow St, Banjul ☎ 422 7437; Norway, Kanifing ☎ 439 2505; Nigeria, 52 Garba Jahumpa Rd, Bakau ☎ 449 5803; Senegal, Off Kairaba Ave, Fajara ☎ 437 3752; Sierra Leone, OAU Blvd, Banjul ☎ 422 8206; Sweden, Mamakotu

Rd, Bakau ☎ 449 6869; UK, 48 Atlantic Rd, Fajara ☎ 449 5133; USA, Kairaba Ave, Fajara ☎ 439 2856.

Emergencies Ambulance ☎ 16; Fire service ☎ 18; Police ☎ 17; Royal Victoria Hospital ☎ 422 8223; Banjul police station ☎ 422 3146; Bakau police station ☎ 449 5739; Kotu police station ☎ 446 3351.

Golf The Fajara Club (☎ 449 5456) has an 18-hole course, with nine par 4s, seven par 3s and two par 5s. Early morning weekdays are the best times; green fees are D500 per player per day, plus membership fees and clubs and caddies if required. Tidy attire essential. The Kololi Beach Club (☎ 446 4897) has a nine-hole course; fees are £7 per round or £35 per week.

Hairdressing and beauty treatments The best place in the Gambia is The Salon, under the African Living Art Centre, 9 Garba Jahumpa Road, Bakau ☎ 449 5131 (afternoons only, from 3pm). They also do manicure, pedicure, reflexology, body-scrub and massage. Many tourist hotels have hair salons, and some have aromatherapy and massage parlours. Recommended hotel hair and beauty salons include those at the *Senegambia* and the *Palma Rima*. Hair braiders work on the beach at Kotu Strand, hotel salons or Gambian salons in towns.

Horse riding Sololo (☎ 770 3204) and Lama Barry (☎ 777 6689) arranges horse riding along the northern Kombo beaches (D500/hr).

Immigration 21 OAU Boulevard, Banjul ☎ 422 8611 (Mon–Thu 8am–4pm, Fri 8am–12.30pm), for visa extensions (D250 per month).

Internet access There are plenty of Internet cafés in the resort area, with new ones springing up all the time. Gamtel tends to have the lowest rates, and QuantumNet is reliable; look out for special offers.

Official Tourist Guides The guides' main station in the resort area is outside the *Senegambia Hotel*. Rates are fixed at D400 per day or D250 per half-day.

Pharmacy Banjul Pharmacy: Independence Drive, Banjul ☎ 422 7470; Liberation Ave, Banjul ☎ 422 7648; Sayerr Jobe Rd, London Corner, Serrekunda ☎ 439 1053; Kairaba Ave ☎ 439 0189; Malak Chemist: Atlantic Road ☎ 449 6661; Stop Step: Kairaba Ave ☎ 437 1344; Senegambia ☎ 446 5298; Westfield ☎ 439 8437.

Post office The GPO, Russell St, Banjul (Mon–Thu 8.30am–12.15pm & 2–4pm, Fri 8.30am–12.15pm & 2.30–4.30pm, Sat 8.30am–noon) is the country's main GPO, and the best place to have mail sent to you poste restante. There are other post offices on Atlantic Rd, Bakau, and off Kairaba Ave, Serrekunda.

Quad bikes Quest Quad Trekking, Palma Rima Road, between Abi's and Churchill's (☎ 446 4146),

offers one- two- or three-hours self-drive or bush and beach safaris with a qualified instructor on 125cc Yamaha Breezes.

Sports facilities Fajara Club ☎ 449 5456. Club-house open daily 8am–8pm; bar/restaurant 9am–8pm; swimming pool 9am–7pm; golf course 7am–7.30pm. Temporary membership of D200/day, D800/week gives access to clubhouse, swimming pool, table tennis, badminton, tennis, squash, aerobics and yoga.

Supermarkets The resort area has a multitude of supermarkets, mostly of the standard of a small town supermarket in Europe or the US, selling imported food, toiletries, wine and spirits, household goods, and newspapers. Most are along Kairaba Ave; there are a few in Cape Point, Bakau, Kotu and Kololi. Most open Mon–Sat 8.30am–7.30pm, Sun 10am–2pm; some close later. Each hotel zone has its complement of minimarkets which generally open until late. Many petrol stations also have minimarkets. Banjul has no supermarkets as such, just a couple of small grocery stores.

Telephones The Gamtel offices in Russell St, Banjul; Atlantic Rd, Bakau (opposite the *African Village Hotel*); at the bottom of Kairaba Ave, Serrekunda; and near the *Senegambia Hotel* are all open daily 8am–midnight. Various private telecentres are widely scattered around the urban area, sometimes offering cheaper call rates.

Tourist taxi ranks (for green taxis) are found near the *Atlantic* and *Palm Grove* hotels (Banjul); at Cape Point (Bakau); near the *African Village Hotel* (Bakau); near the *Hotel Fajara* (Fajara); near the *Kombo Beach Hotel* (Kotu); near the *Palma Rima Hotel* (Kololi), in the Senegambia area (Kololi) and at Banjul International Airport. Typical prices for a return trip, including a couple of hours' waiting time, include: Banjul to Fajara D800, Banjul to Pirang or Marakissa D1400, Senegambia to Tanji D700. Typical one-way fares include: Airport to Senegambia D400, Fajara to Bakau D200, Fajara to Senegambia D300.

Travel agents The Gambia Experience, *Senegambia Hotel*, Kololi ☎ 446 3867 (Mon–Fri 9am–5pm, Sat 9am–1pm), acts as agent for charter flights to the UK from Banjul to London. For other flight bookings and general flight information, try Banjul Travel Agency, ECOWAS Ave, Banjul ☎ 422 8813; IPC Travel, 16 Kairaba Ave ☎ 437 5677, @ ipctravel@qanet.gm; or Continental Travels, 70B Daniel Goddard St, Banjul ☎ 422 4058.

Watersports Gambia Watersports Centre, *Denton's Beach Resort*, Denton Bridge, Banjul (☎ 777 3777) offers catamaran and jetski hire, waterskiing, wakeboarding, windsurfing, banana boat rides and power boat trips.

Travel details

This is a brief summary of journey durations and frequencies; more thorough details are given throughout the chapter.

Ferry

Banjul to: Barra (daily, at least hourly on the hour; 30min–1hr).

Bush taxis

Banjul to: Bakau (15–20min); Brikama (45min); Serrekunda (20min).

Serrekunda to: Abuko (15min); Banjul (20min); Bansang (9hr 30min–11hr 30min); Basse (10–14hr); Brikama (30min); Lamin (20min); Soma (3hr 30min–4hr); Sankulay Kunda for Janjanbureh (8hr 30min–10hr 30min); plus all villages in Kombo district.

2

Kombo: Brikama and the south

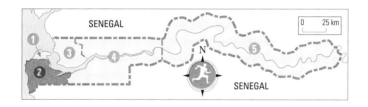

CHAPTER 2 # Highlights

* **Southwestern beaches** The best beaches in The Gambia, broad and fringed with palms, are found between Brufut and Kartong. See p.162

* **Tanji** This coastal village has a lively fishing centre, a great little museum of Gambian culture, a camel safari centre and the country's only officially protected bird reserve. See p.167

* **Traditional music lessons** Many of the country's greatest *kora* players come from Brikama, making this bustling town an excellent place to get some expert tuition. See p.171

* **Makasutu Culture Forest** The Gambia's most celebrated ecotourism project, and the site of a beautiful and luxurious lodge. See p.175

* **Pirang Forest Park** A superb little pocket of gallery forest surrounded by farmland, great for birdwatching and strolling. See p.179

* **Tumani Tenda** A picturesque rural retreat, where visitors can learn about up-country life as guests in a traditional Jola village. See p.180

△ Cows on the beach

Kombo: Brikama and the south

You don't have to travel far from The Gambia's busy resorts and urban areas to find quiet villages, intriguing up-country towns, unspoilt stretches of wilderness and glorious empty beaches. **Southern Kombo** – the clutch of districts to the south of the Kombo peninsula, bounded to the west by the Atlantic, and to the south by the border with Senegal – is so accessible that the region can easily be visited on day-trips from the resorts, particularly if you hire your own transport or join organized excursions. If you'd like stay deep in the countryside, or if the resorts aren't really your style but you're still keen to spend time near the ocean, it's worth finding accommodation in southern Kombo for a few days or more – especially if you have an interest in wildlife or traditional music.

To the southwest of the region lie the country's broadest and emptiest **beaches**, and its busiest ones too: those used by local fishermen to moor their brightly painted boats and haul in the catch. The local fishing communities have their village centres a short distance inland. The most visited is **Tanji**, partly because it's close to the **Tanji River Karinti Bird Reserve** – an obligatory stop on all birdwatching tours of the region – and partly because it has a unique museum of Gambian culture and natural history; it's also the only place in The Gambia where you can ride camels along the beach. Further inland, dozens of small, back-country villages set in an appealing, random patchwork of forest, savannah and farmland are accessible on foot, by bicycle or by bush taxi or rented car.

At the hub of the region is the district capital of **Brikama**, a staunchly religious town with a vibrant musical tradition. East of here lies the **Makasutu Culture Forest**, The Gambia's best-known ecotourism site, a private nature park with woodland and waterways to explore by guided tour and a new luxury lodge. Further east again is the bird-rich **Pirang Forest Park** and, close to the river, **Tumani Tenda**, a successful experiment in community-managed cultural tourism, where you can experience rural culture from the inside by spending time as a guest in a traditional Jola village. South of Brikama, in the area around **Marakissa** near the Senegalese border, you'll find some of southwest Gambia's most beautiful untamed bush, with mature woodland and savannah that remains lush well into the dry season, perfect for exploring by 4WD vehicle and excellent for birdwatching.

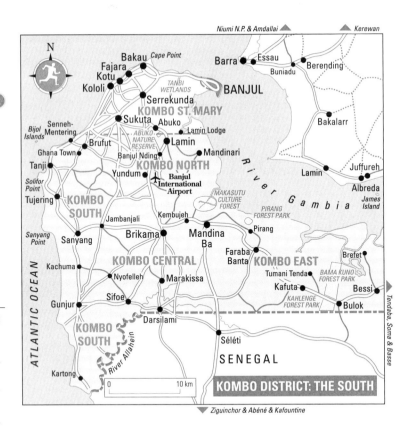

N

Bakau *Cape Point*
Fajara
Kotu
Kololi
TANBI WETLANDS
Serrekunda
KOMBO ST. MARY
Sukuta Abuko
Senneh- *ABUKO NATURE RESERVE*
Bijol Islands Mentering
Brufut Lamin
Ghana Town
Banjul Nding
Tanji
KOMBO NORTH
Solifor Point
Yundum
Tujering KOMBO SOUTH
Banjul International Airport
Jambanjali Kembujeh
MAKASUTU CULTURE FOREST
PIRANG FOREST PARK
Sanyang Point
Brikama Mandina Ba
Sanyang
KOMBO CENTRAL
Kachuma
Nyofelleh Marakissa
Faraba Banta KOMBO EAST
Sifoe
Gunjur
Darsilami
KOMBO SOUTH
Kartong
River Allahein

Barra Essau Berending
Buniadu
BANJUL
Bakalarr
Lamin Lodge
Lamin
Mandinari
River Gambia
Lamin Juffureh
Albreda
James Island
Pirang
Tumani Tenda
BAMA KUNO FOREST PARK
Kafuta Bessi
KAHLENGE FOREST PARK Bulok
Brefet
Séléti
SENEGAL

0 10 km

KOMBO DISTRICT: THE SOUTH

ATLANTIC OCEAN

The southwest coast

The Gambia's **southwest coast** still feels wild and undiscovered, with miles of
sandy beach where you can walk for hours without seeing another soul. The
only busy spots along this breezy stretch of Atlantic shore are its traditional fishing centres, working beaches where local fishermen drag their heavy *pirogues* up
the sand in a flurry of seabirds, then sort through the catch and spread out their
nets to dry in the sun. Behind the beaches are dunes, palms and a hinterland of
thinly populated bush and beautiful tropical woodland that becomes progres-
sively lusher the closer you get to Senegal.

Right on the doorstep of the main resorts, this is an excellent area to relax,
swim or fish in the ocean, or to sample something of the "real" Gambia of
thatched huts and winding country tracks. It's particularly well-suited to the
ecologically aware: hidden in the bush just inland from the ocean are a growing
number of imaginative, low-impact **eco-retreats** which pride themselves on
keeping water consumption to a minimum and making good use of renewable

energy and locally grown produce. The coast itself is thinly scattered with simple **beach bars** and **lodges** – laid-back, low-key hideaways which appeal to travellers who don't mind forgoing a few basic comforts. For those who prefer their comforts laid on thick, there's an impressive new **luxury beach hotel** in the north of the region.

The coastal area is dotted with **villages**, most of which lie several kilometres back from the beaches which bear their names. It's unusual for Gambians to choose to live within sight of the ocean – even the fishermen prefer to base themselves some distance from the shore, in small fishing communities which are effectively satellites of the farming settlements even further inland. Villagers in this part of the country live traditional rural lifestyles; many have to get along without mains electricity and water or private vehicles, but most are self-sufficient and have no reason to go anywhere near the tourist areas further north from one year to the next. The villages you're most likely to visit, or at least pass through, are the ones strung out along the Kombo Coastal Highway, which is the southern extension of Bertil Harding Highway: **Ghana Town** and **Brufut**, just 8km from Kololi; **Tanji**, with its bird reserve and busy fishing centre; **Tujering**, **Sanyang** and **Gunjur**, all farming and fishing communities; and **Kartong**, 45km from Kololi, and the last coastal village in The Gambia, with a sacred crocodile pool. In the beautiful forested countryside further inland are numerous tiny hamlets which see very few visitors, despite their relative proximity to the resorts.

Until recently, much of southwest Gambia was isolated by poor roads and a shortage of transport, but the region is much more accessible now that good tarmac connects once-remote villages with Serrekunda and Brikama. With further improvements to the local infrastructure in the pipeline, tourist development, which has so far been proceeding at a gentle pace, is likely to accelerate. The Gambian authorities seem to be fully aware of the fragility of the marine environment, but they're also wise to the commercial potential of the area – if you like the idea of escaping to an unspoilt coastal wilderness, you'd better move fast.

For now, however, getting around by public transport is still surprisingly slow. To reach the villages by **bush taxi**, you have to start by travelling to Brikama or Serrekunda, where you can pick up a southwest-bound minibus or *gelleh-gelleh* van. For example, to get from the northern resorts to Kartong by bush taxi, you first go to Serrekunda, then from Serrekunda to Brikama, then Brikama to Gunjur, and finally Gunjur to Kartong – and after this you may still have quite a walk to the stretch of beach you'd like to visit. The same journey by privately hired green **tourist taxi**, straight down the Kombo coastal road, would be much quicker, though costs up to twenty times as much. Driving straight from Kololi to Sanyang takes about fifteen minutes, and from Kololi to Kartong, about thirty minutes.

Most of the **lodges** are located outside the villages, existing in their own micro-environment either on the beach or in the bush, so, unless you're content just to chill out in one place, you may feel isolated without transport. With your own wheels, the whole area is easy to get around no matter where you're staying, and most visitors therefore choose their lodge for its unique atmosphere, rather than for its proximity to specific attractions. This is a rewarding area to explore by mountain bike, or by hired 4WD vehicle, allowing you to leave the tarmac road and head off down bush tracks. Don't leave the tracks, however: vehicles carving up the beaches or tearing through virgin bush are beginning to damage the environment and disturb wildlife, such as breeding turtles, crabs and nesting birds.

Some exploration of the southern coastal area is built into standard **group excursions**, notably the all-day adventures called "Bush and Beach" or "4WD

Adventure", which combine village visits, bush–driving, and lunch on one of the beaches. These can be great fun, as well as a good introduction to the region. You can also join half-day group excursions to Tanji to go camel riding, with a beach barbecue thrown in.

Accommodation

If you like the idea of drifting off to sleep to the sound of the ocean and maybe beachcombing at dawn along the empty sands, it's well worth treating yourself to a few nights at a **beach hotel or lodge**, even if you already have a northern Kombo resort hotel booked for your entire stay in The Gambia. Facilities vary a great deal – from the reasonably priced but verging-on-shabby to the downright luxurious – but, in all cases, the sense of tranquillity is worth a fortune. At the simplest places you can stay in a basic room, pitch your own tent in the grounds, or even just rig up a mosquito net over a beach mattress to enjoy the night sky to the full.

It's also possible to use one of the beach lodges as a base if you're just visiting the southwest coast for the day. Like the beach bars (see p.164), all can provide cold drinks and a shady retreat from the blazing sun. Most also offer freshly cooked food, though you may have to wait a while – life moves at a relaxed pace here, even for The Gambia.

The **inland lodges**, secluded in lush bush on the fringes of the villages, are an excellent choice for birdwatchers. As a rule of thumb, the further south you go, the more unspoilt the atmosphere.

Beach hotels and lodges

Boboi Beach Lodge Two kilometres north of Kartong ☎ 777 6736 or 771 2136, ⓦ www.gambia-adventure.com. Right on a glorious stretch of empty beach, this successful lodge consists of a few simple but brightly equipped thatched roundhouses (each sleeping 2–3) in a small compound shaded by palm trees; there's also room to camp if you have your own tent. The lodge aims to be ecologically sound – the facilities are basic, the kitchen uses local organic produce, and there's no mains electricity, just solar power. Transport can be arranged from the airport or the resort area, and the staff can arrange bird walks and boat trips around the River Allahein. ❷

Gunjur Beach Lodge South of Gunjur fishing centre ☎ 448 6065 or 701 1383, ⓦ www.gunjurbeach.com. Under new management and much improved, this guesthouse has a great coastal location and an upbeat, welcoming atmosphere. The rooms are spacious, pleasant and good value. They don't have a sea view – they're separated from the very pretty beach by the restaurant, the kitchens, and the garden – but if you'd like to fall asleep to the sound of the waves you can pitch a tent in the grounds. ❸

Jungle Beach Bar and Resort Just south of Sanyang fishing centre. Nearing completion at the

time of writing, the simple guest rooms at this upbeat spot will be practically on the beach itself, and within stumbling distance of the bar (see p.165), making them the perfect place to crash after one of *Jungle*'s late-night weekend reggae sessions. ❷

Kobokoto Tourist Camp Northwest of Sanyang ☎ 772 7238. On a stark and isolated stretch of beach just round the point north of Sanyang's fishing beach, reached by a track signposted off the main coastal highway, this laid-back beach bar has basic guest accommodation in a few rooms with private showers supplied by solar power and a solar water pump. There's also a simple restaurant (see p.165). ❶

Nyanya Safari Lodge Kombo Coastal Highway, Tanji ☎ 779 7251 or 983 2934. A beautifully located, homely place, with a breezy restaurant overlooking the mouth of the River Tanji and guest roundhouses scattered over sand dunes planted with trees, right on the beach a short walk from Tanji fishing centre and village. The rooms are small and basic but freshly decorated. Huge platefuls of Gambian stews with rice are served all day. ❷

Osprey-Paradise Beach Bar and Restaurant On the beach north of Sanyang fishing centre

☏992 4010 or 777 5174. A new addition to "Paradise Beach" is the very low-key guesthouse attached to this popular beach bar (see p.165). In a quiet, sandy location that's good for swimming and safe for kids, it should prove to be a great little retreat. ❷

Rainbow Beach Bar Just south of Sanyang fishing beach ☏982 7790 or 993 2090. This upbeat and welcoming bar-restaurant offers space for visitors to camp and, at the time of writing, was building guest rooms, too. ❷

Rasta Kunda Near Gunjur, ⊛www.rastakunda .com. On the wonderful beach between Gunjur fishing centre and Kartong, signposted off the coastal highway, this camp is a laid-back place, its large beachside bar playing nonstop reggae. There are twelve rough-and-ready twin rooms in huts in the big, leafy garden. Come well-prepared for mosquitoes. ❶

🏃 **Sandale Eco-Retreat** North of Kartong Pre-opening enquiries c/o *Safari Garden Hotel*, Fajara ☏449 5887, ⊛www.safarigarden .com. Not yet open at the time of writing, this promises to be an outstanding place to stay, offering luxurious accommodation on a remote and supremely peaceful stretch of coast. Unique in The Gambia, its beautiful, Indian-inspired design incorporates a wealth of ecologically sound features – the bricks and tiles were made on site and use of timber and cement is minimal. Developed and run in close harmony with the local community, who will receive a significant percentage of profits, the retreat will

incorporate a learning centre hosting yoga sessions, spiritual retreats and courses in ethical business practice and sustainable development. ❽

🏃 **Sankule Beach** North of Gunjur fishing centre ☏448 6098. The new guest rooms in the leafy garden of this eccentric but attractive British-run place are a generous size, colourful and stylish; the owner plans to decorate them with contemporary ethnic art. It's also possible, on request, to camp in the grounds; you'll sometimes have the chance to jam with, or listen to, visiting musicians in the beach bar (see p.165). ❸

🏃 **Sheraton Gambia Beach Resort** Near Brufut, ⊛www.starwoodhotels.com. Close to completion at the time of writing, this vast new five-star resort hotel and conference centre is set to be one of The Gambia's leading upmarket accommodation options. Dramatically situated in a grove of ancient baobab trees on the sandstone cliffs overlooking Brufut beach, it has the look and feel of a large, luxury safari lodge with well-groomed thatched roofs, impressive public areas and African-inspired decor. The rooms are spacious, comfortable and contemporary, and the facilities include a spa. ❽

Tesito Kartong, ☏441 9025. This friendly lodge, with accommodation in simple huts, is a community-run initiative set up by young villagers with UNDP support. The *bantaba* bar serves local food, if ordered in advance, and the staff can organize nature walks in the locality. ❷

Inland lodges

Balaba Nature Camp North of Kartong ☏991 9012. Deep in the leafy wilderness on the inland side of the Kombo Coastal Highway, roughly halfway between Gunjur and Kartong, this lodge is rustic in the extreme, with palm-thatched huts in a shady garden compound. Village visits and music sessions are on offer but the place may feel too quiet and isolated for some. ❷

🏃 **Footsteps** Near Gunjur village ☏779 4855 or 998 0212, UK bookings ☏020/8517 1507, ⊛www.natureswaygambia.com. This appealingly down-to-earth British-run bush lodge has set new standards for responsible tourism in The Gambia. Ecologically sound measures include alternative energy generation, permaculture gardening, recycling and composting, and guests enjoy a comfortable and relaxed place to stay. The lodge, with ten thatched roundhouses set in a leafy compound surrounded by coastal woodland, is simple but attractive, with a small (chemical-free) pool, and space for camping.

There's also a friendly and informal restaurant open to residents and non-residents; prices are above-average for an up-country place, but the menu is very good with imaginative cross-cultural dishes from the lodge's own organic orchards and vegetable plots. ❻

Hallahin Bar and Restaurant Off the Kombo Coastal Highway, north of Kartong, ☏993 3193, 709 5705 or 778 7224. An unassuming place, with airy but unremarkable rooms in simple rondavels set in a large compound a short walk from the beach. The best reason to stay here is the chef's superb local-style cooking, including first-class fish *yassa* and chips (see p.164). ❷

🏃 **Hibiscus House Brufut** ☏995 8774 or 778 4552, ⊛www.hibiscushousegambia. com. Attractive and imaginative new British-owned guest house in the village of Brufut, well away from the tourist scene but five minutes' drive from Brufut beach. On site is a Holistic Treatments Centre, open to residents and non-residents,

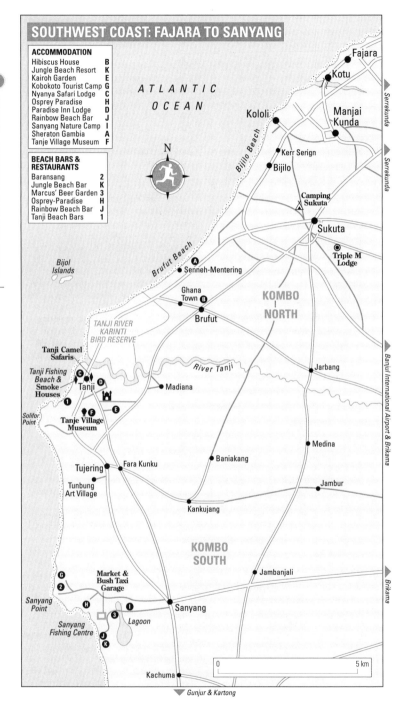

SOUTHWEST COAST: FAJARA TO SANYANG

ACCOMMODATION
Hibiscus House	**B**
Jungle Beach Resort	**K**
Kairoh Garden	**E**
Kobokoto Tourist Camp	**G**
Nyanya Safari Lodge	**C**
Osprey Paradise	**H**
Paradise Inn Lodge	**D**
Rainbow Beach Bar	**J**
Sanyang Nature Camp	**I**
Sheraton Gambia	**A**
Tanje Village Museum	**F**

BEACH BARS & RESTAURANTS
Baransang	**2**
Jungle Beach Bar	**K**
Marcus' Beer Garden	**3**
Osprey-Paradise	**H**
Rainbow Beach Bar	**J**
Tanji Beach Bars	**1**

ATLANTIC OCEAN

Fajara
Kotu
Kololi
Manjai Kunda
Bijilo Beach
Kerr Serign
Bijilo
Camping Sukuta
Sukuta
Triple M Lodge

Serrekunda
Serrekunda
Banjul International Airport & Brikama
Brikama

N

Bijol Islands

Brufut Beach
Senneh-Mentering
Ghana Town
Brufut

KOMBO NORTH

TANJI RIVER KARINTI BIRD RESERVE

Tanji Camel Safaris
Tanji Fishing Beach & Smoke Houses
Tanji
River Tanji
Jarbang
Madiana

Solifor Point

Tanje Village Museum
Medina

Tujering   Fara Kunku
Baniakang
Jambur

Tunbung Art Village

Kankujang

KOMBO SOUTH

Jambanjali

Market & Bush Taxi Garage
Sanyang Point
Sanyang
Lagoon
Sanyang Fishing Centre

Kachuma

0	5 km

Gunjur & Kartong

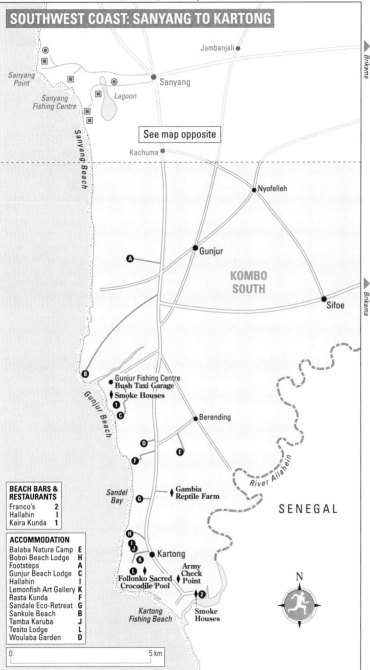

Kololi, Serrekunda, Sukuta & Tanji

SOUTHWEST COAST: SANYANG TO KARTONG

Brikama

2

KOMBO: BRIKAMA AND THE SOUTH

Jambanjali

Sanyang Point

Sanyang

Sanyang Fishing Centre

Lagoon

See map opposite

Kachuma

Nyofelleh

Sanyang Beach

Gunjur

KOMBO SOUTH

Brikama

Sifoe

Gunjur Beach

Gunjur Fishing Centre
Bush Taxi Garage
Smoke Houses

Berending

River Allahein

BEACH BARS & RESTAURANTS
Franco's 2
Hallahin I
Kaira Kunda 1

Sandel Bay

Gambia Reptile Farm

SENEGAL

ACCOMMODATION
Balaba Nature Camp E
Boboi Beach Lodge H
Footsteps A
Gunjur Beach Lodge C
Hallahin I
Lemonfish Art Gallery K
Rasta Kunda F
Sandale Eco-Retreat G
Sankule Beach B
Tamba Karuba J
Tesito Lodge L
Woulaba Garden D

Kartong

Army Check Point

N

Follonko Sacred Crocodile Pool

Kartong Fishing Beach

Smoke Houses

0   5 km

specialising in reflexology, Reiki therapy and Indian head massage. **7**

Kairoh Garden Guest House Tanji village ☎ 990 3526, ⓦ www.kairohgarden.com. This peaceful retreat, signposted from the coastal highway, is deep in the backstreets of Tanji village, about 5km from the beach. The compound, planted with fruit trees and flowering shrubs, is huge, but the dozen simple rooms (some self-contained) are all squashed together in thin-walled blocks. They're clean, though, and appealing simple, with African-style beds. There's also plenty of room to camp, and a sleepy bar/restaurant which can provide Gambian and European meals (and cappuccino) on request. **3**

🏃 **Lemonfish Art Gallery** Near Kartong, overlooking the sand dunes ☎ 439 4586 or 992 2884, ⓦ www.lemonfish.gm. This brightly decorated contemporary art gallery with a lovely tranquil garden terrace occasionally operates as a guesthouse. The pretty rooms have spotless shared bathroom facilities. Both the village and a wild, empty stretch of beach are a short, pleasant walk away. **2**

Paradise Inn Lodge Tanji village ☎ 880 0209, ⓦ www.paradiseinngarden.com. This lodge is very popular with groups of birdwatchers – and not just because all twenty rooms are named after local bird species. It is set in woodland which rings with birdsong by day and resonates with owl calls by night, right on the banks of the River Tanji which, at this point, is as narrow as a creek. The rooms are in attractive Fula-style roundhouses; some are a little small but all have mosquito nets and fans, and there's power from a generator in the early mornings and evenings. In peak season the Sunday evening buffets include freshly barbecued fish under the lodge's huge spreading mango tree. **3**

Sanyang Nature Camp near Sanyang ☎ 994 5730. Signposted off the main coastal highway, and situated in bushland about 2km inland from Sanyang's fishing beach, this quiet lodge was expanding at the time of writing. Aimed principally at groups on educational or volunteer programmes, it will provide 32 simple rooms and a meeting centre in a huge dusty garden compound. **2**

Tamba Karuba North of Kartong ☎ 702 0620. Very simple place in a large sandy compound shaded by gingerbread plum trees, a short walk from the beach. Set up as a lodge and campground for drivers participating in the Amsterdam–Dakar rally, it's open to all. The rooms (in rondavels or a block) are basic but reasonably well kept. A percentage of the proceeds funds a community clinic in Kartong. **2**

Tanje Village Museum Tanji village ☎ 437 1007 or 992 6618. This gem of a museum (see p.168) has visitor accommodation in a dozen simple huts at the far end of the garden compound. In keeping with the mission to demonstrate what traditional village life is all about, the huts are sparse, with simple furnishings and shared washing facilities. Guests have the run of the museum and the opportunity to learn about traditional weaving or metalwork from the museum's resident craftsmen. There's also a restaurant on the site. **2**

Woulaba Garden Medina, near Gunjur ☎ 994 7183, ⓦ www.woulabagarden.com. There's a warm welcome at this new, simple bush lodge, thoughtfully managed and prettily located in a lush garden. The rooms are basic but appealing, music sessions and local meals can be arranged, and the beach is a 15min stroll away along pleasant bush tracks. **1**

The southwestern beaches

The Gambia's southwestern coast is a continuous strip of shallow bays harbouring sandy **beaches**, about 50km as the crab crawls, or 35km by road. The landscape varies along the way: some of the bays are much broader than others, some are fringed with mature palms and others are backed by low sandstone cliffs or by scrubby dunes bound by beach convolvulus. Some are totally empty, while some are busy fishing centres. Some rarely see tourists, while others have rustic beach bars or lodges where you can enjoy a meal or even stay for a few nights, enjoying barbecues under the stars and informal music sessions by campfire. While tidal erosion has claimed sand, trees and buildings elsewhere on the Gambian coast, the southwestern beaches have so far escaped the worst ravages. The contrasts sometimes come as a surprise to tourists who, before visiting this part of the coast, have just stuck to the beach nearest their northern Kombos hotel, perhaps imagining that there can't be too much variation in such a short stretch of Atlantic shoreline – a tiny bite in the side of the African continent.

At low tide, tackling the journey in manageable chunks, it's possible to cover the entire length of The Gambia's southwestern coastline **on foot** or **by bicycle** without leaving the water's edge. If you do take the time to trek along the sand you should make sure you're well protected against the sun and have plenty of water with you, as some of the beaches are more than five kilometres from the coastal highway, with gasp-inducing gaps between eating and drinking places.

Heading southwest from the tourist resorts of the northern Kombos, the beach first begins to change character south of Bijilo, near **Ghana Town**, where you're likely to see fishing *pirogues* bobbing just off shore, strung with flags and painted white with bold geometric designs in dazzling primary colours. Here and at neighbouring **Brufut beach** you may also see boats waiting on the sand for the tide to turn, the fishermen mending nets and the women sorting out the latest catch. The fishing areas are very localized – away from these, the beaches are normally practically empty, bar a few kids larking about, young men jogging or working out, or villagers walking from one fishing centre to the next.

On the cliffs above Brufut beach, accessible by a steep path, or from a track leading off the coastal highway just south of the new Sheraton resort hotel, is the holy site of **Senneh–Mentering**, a marvellously meditative spot around a craggy old baobab tree, the air wafting with incense burned by the incumbent marabout. Local people come here for cures, consultations and peace, and it's a good place to visit at sundown.

Tanji beach, about 3km southwest of Senneh-Mentering, is one of the biggest fishing centres. Tourists arrive here on organized excursions which give an overview of the whole region, to watch the flurry of birds, boats and people as the fishing boats come in, and sample the eye-wateringly pungent smoky aromas inside the large shed-like smoke houses where blackening *bonga* fish, neatly laid out in rows, are preserved for local consumption or export. South of here is **Tujering beach**, a long empty stretch, where, with supplies, you could pitch a tent under the stars in almost complete isolation, apart from the cattle often seen strolling freely – the herders take them down to the beach to lick salt from the rocks.

Sanyang beach, just round the point at the southern limit of Tujering beach, is called "Paradise Beach" by the tour companies – it's one of The Gambia's most appealing strands, a broad arc of pale sand backed by coconut palms, that seems to have escaped the recent tidal erosion vitually unscathed. There are a few good beach bars here, and a busy fishing centre, all of which make for a lively scene, but there's plenty of space if you're after isolation and tranquillity – especially if you wander round the point, either north or south, to the next bays. Just behind the beach is a fish market where you can see the latest ocean haul laid out on slabs of ice; there's also a lagoon much frequented by wading birds.

More empty sand and a pretty track passing wonderful baobabs connects Sanyang beach with **Gunjur beach**, 10km further south, where the fishing centre is the biggest focus of Kombo South District – a messy, active seafront where fish are more important than tourists and you'll probably be ignored. Here, parked on the shore, you'll see smart, brightly painted Senegalese fishing *pirogues* and rather shabbier Gambian ones.

South of Gunjur fishing beach are some of The Gambia's wildest, emptiest and most beautiful bays, where the sand seems softer than anywhere else and the water is shallow and clean. The last working beach before the Senegalese border is **Kartong beach**, a long, lonely spit of sand where fishermen from Gunjur, Ghana and Senegal haul in squid, *bonga*, "lobsters" and small sharks for the traders to sell from the shack that constitutes the fish market in this isolated spot.

Southern fishing centres

Southwest Gambia's **coastal fishing centres** are always buzzing with activity, and are absorbing places to spend an hour or so. The Gambian Atlantic is fished by communities of Gambians, Ghanaians and Senegalese, all of whom use heavy wooden *pirogues* with outboard engines and pointed prows, brightly painted in traditional designs. The boats sail out with the tide and back with the tide, hauled in and out of the water on logs, or (in the case of the largest ones) left a few metres out to sea at anchor. The biggest boats take a crew of a dozen, the smaller ones just three or four. Whatever the size of boat, fishing trips can be perilous and lives are lost in storms from time to time.

The **local catch** includes ladyfish, catfish, small sharks, and seasnails; *bonga* fish are caught by night. Once the fish have been distributed among the crew and to waiting traders, the nets are spread out to dry beside the beached boats. Just behind the fishing beaches are small fish markets; practically all the fish served in the resort restaurants originates here. Meanwhile, jobbing fish salesmen make a living by pedalling round the remotest villages with the latest catch in handwoven baskets lashed to their bicycle handlebars.

Bonga, span-length, yellowish-white fish that are one of the commonest catches, are either sold fresh, or preserved by smoking over smouldering wood, typically by Ghanaians, Guineans or Malians resident in The Gambia. The **smokehouses** are long, low huts where racks of fish cure for two to five days in clouds of pungent smoke, the light slanting dramatically through gaps in the roof. The finished product, like kippers, and bony but good, can be seen all over The Gambia, packed in crates or baskets for export, or for sale to locals in the up-country markets. Unfortunately, the practice has contributed to rampant deforestation in the Kombos, although it may in time be superseded by freezing. Ice plant development is well underway at Sanyang and Gunjur's fishing centres, but the modernization process has been slowed by a serious slump in the local fishing market, caused by illegal trawler fishing.

Beach bars and restaurants

As you'd expect, the beach bars which are dotted along the southwestern coast specialize in **fish** and **seafood**. This is probably the best area in the whole country to try local fish at its freshest, hauled out of the ocean a few hours before, and prices are way below the northern Kombos restaurants. Most places have lobster on the menu, which are in fact large crayfish; they're relatively expensive, and not always available. Once caught, the fishermen corral them, alive, in buoy-marked baskets just off the beach, then bring them in to order. Other standards include giant prawns in garlic, and grilled barracuda, ladyfish, or butterfish, plus African stews and sauces. Some places stay open in the evening, lighting a campfire on the beach for a mellow session of drumming and dancing under the stars, and a growing number are beginning to offer informal accommodation, too.

Baransang Beach Bar & Restaurant Near Sanyang, on the bay north of Sanyang fishing beach. Barely a shack, this modest little beach bar serves fish, curry, omelettes or salad at low prices.

Franco's South of Kartong, near the smokehouses on the north bank of the River Allahein. Strictly speaking a riverside bar, rather than a beach bar, this simple place has a supremely tranquil watery outlook. The Italian owner serves cold drinks and first-rate pizza and pasta, and can organize boat trips by *pirogue*.

Hallahin Bar and Restaurant Off the Kombo Coastal Highway, north of Kartong, ☎993 3193, 709 5705 or 778 7224. Easy to get to, as it's close to the main road, this place is a short walk from the beach. The chef is brilliant, serving up extremely good local food such as fish *yassa* or *domodah* and chips. Call in advance to place an order (unless you're happy to wait a while).

Jungle Beach Bar and Resort Just south of Sanyang fishing centre. With an energetic manager and an unbeatable location, this is a promising new enterprise, serving cold beer, spirits and local juices all day and throwing "Reggae on the Beach" parties and live *ndagga* events after dark at weekends. At the time of writing, guest accommodation was being built here (see p.158).

🏃 **Kaira Kunda Bar and Restaurant** Just south of Gunjur fishing centre ☎ 998 5819. Cool, relaxed, friendly shack-type beach bar, a place to play drums or just hang out over cheap drinks, couscous or barbecued fish.

Kobokoto Tourist Camp Near Sanyang beach ☎ 772 7238. This friendly but rather isolated beach bar on a skinny stretch of sand serves good breakfasts, fish dishes and tourist standards at reasonable prices. The thatched beach seating area is good for lounging; people come here to fish and hang out, or to stay overnight (see p.158).

Marcus' Beer Garden Near Sanyang fishing centre. Not on the beach, but with a beach-bar feel and within easy striking distance of the waves, this extremely friendly rasta hangout, open till late, offers cold drinks and a hammock slung up in the shade.

🏃 **Osprey-Paradise Beach Bar and Restaurant** On the beach north of Sanyang fishing centre ☎ 992 4010 or 777 5174. Improved by a new management team, this place serves big portions of the usual selection of grills at keen prices. Tour groups are sometimes brought en masse to this part of "Paradise Beach", so you may find bumsters too, but it's an attractive spot that's great for swimming, with pale powdery sand that's beautifully kept, as if groomed daily – a very pleasant change after the scruffier beaches in the busiest resort areas. It's now possible to stay here, too (see p.158).

🏃 **Rainbow Beach Bar** Just south of Sanyang fishing centre ☎ 982 7790 or 993 2090. Bright, upbeat bar and restaurant, serving

well-prepared food (including the best fish on the beach) under a thatched shelter like a beach marquee. Competition between the Sanyang beach bars is stiff, so the food and drinks are keenly priced, and groups should book in advance. This isn't the best part of the beach for swimming – it's a little too close to the fishing centre for comfort – but there's empty beach a couple of minutes' stroll away. Happy hour is at 4.30pm, and on special occasions there are sunset buffets and campfire nights. It's possible to camp out here (there are freshwater showers for daytime and overnight guests), and visitor accommodation is being built, too (see p.159).

🏃 **Sankule Beach** North of Gunjur fishing centre ☎ 448 6098. In a gorgeous, remote setting, reached by an unmarked bush track from the highway or via Gunjur beach, this appealingly eccentric place functions as a restaurant (if you give them notice of your arrival) and a relaxing bar. Colourful and beautifully designed, it has a lovely beachside garden, shaded with trees. The British owner is a drumming and *kora* aficionado, and Sankule Beach is often the scene of impromptu jamming sessions – a great reason to stay overnight (see p.159).

Tanji beach bars Near Tanji. The beach leading to Solifor Point is, in complete contrast to the frantically busy fishing centre to the north, very quiet. This stretch is undeveloped, but for a string of rough and ready beach bars with fairly random opening hours, minimal facilities, and a cheerfully laid-back atmosphere. You reach them by walking down the sand from the fishing centre or by following the main highway south and then taking the signposted track to the *Whale* beach bar. The best of the bunch is *Ali Baba*, where you can relax over a glass of fresh juice or a plate of Fula-style food such as *toura* (cassava and baobab sauce) in a pretty garden decorated with shells. *Merel and El's* is good for reasonably cold drinks.

The southwestern villages and reserves

The **villages** which lie between the northern Kombo beach resorts and the southern border are small, traditional rural communities, typically home to half a dozen or so families representing all The Gambia's major ethnic groups (see p.276). There are also small communities of animist Manjagos on the village fringes, living from harvesting palm nuts and palm-wine tapping. In contrast, rural villages further up-country tend to be dominated by members of a single tribe. The southwestern villages are built around their mosque, and the marketplace, where women trade fruit and vegetables grown in the village vegetable plots, and fish, fresh and smoked, from the nearby fishing centres. With the

Birdwatching in the Tanji River Karinti Bird Reserve and Bijol Islands

The Tanji River Karinti Bird Reserve is particularly good for sightings of both **coastal and woodland species**. Many gulls, terns and waders feed and roost around the lagoons near the mouth of the River Tanji, including Caspian, royal and lesser crested terns, and white-fronted plovers. Inland you're likely to find four-banded sandgrouse, whistling cisticolas, Bruce's green pigeons, yellow-fronted tinkerbirds, yellow-crowned gonoleks, northern crombecs and western palearctic migrants such as melodious, olivaceous and subalpine warblers, and rufous nightingales. The area supports plenty of fish, small mammals and amphibians which make tempting prey for over thirty species of raptor, including the African hobby. From March to September, royal terns, Caspian terns, western reef herons, kelp gulls and grey-headed gulls all nest and breed on the Bijol Islands – there are no other known breeding sites for these species in the country – and access to the islands is prohibited at this time. At other times, it's an excellent location to watch seabirds.

exception of **Tanji**, which is close to The Gambia's only bird reserve and a unique museum of traditional culture, these villages have little in the way of conventional tourist attractions, but they're relaxed and enjoyable places to experience traditional village life. You'll nearly always find simple local places serving rice and sauce near the market or bush taxi garage.

The rich green forested and palm-planted countryside in this area is a great wilderness to explore on foot, mountain bike or by 4WD vehicle, where birds are easy to spot, particularly in the rainy season and the early dry season, and you may see several species of monkey – keeping them away from crops is a nightmare for farmers.

Brufut and Ghana Town

BRUFUT and **GHANA TOWN** are adjacent coastal villages lying between the ocean and the forest about 7km south of Kololi. Both are farming and fishing communities that don't see many visitors, although the stretch of coastal highway which passes them is increasingly busy thanks to a vast new development consisting of modern housing, a conference centre and a luxury resort hotel.

Brufut is a long-established village of old-fashioned brick compounds with corrugated iron roofs, home to Mand-inka farmers and vegetable gardeners, while Ghana Town is a community of Ghanaian fish-driers and smokers. There's an unusually strong Christian community in Ghana Town, as well as Muslims. The village is also well known for its natural healer, Dr Alhaji Al-Hassan. Compared to Brufut, Ghana Town is a down-at-heel place, with half-built cement block walls and unkempt compounds.

Apart from the beach, the main reason to visit the Brufut area is to go birdwatching in **Brufut Woods**, a large area of community forest on Brufut's eastern edge, accessed via bumpy back-roads; there's a sign near the mosque. It's locally managed as a conservation area (D50), and there's one hide. Species you may see in the savannah woodland and gallery forest here include Verreaux's eagle owls (which breed here), Senegal batis, Klaas' cuckoos, lesser honeyguides, pin-tailed whydahs (particularly impressive in the breeding season when the males' tail feathers grow to three times the length of their bodies) and various sunbirds, bee-eaters and raptors; you may also spot rarities such as cisticolas and yellowbills.

Tanji River Karinti Bird Reserve and Bijol Islands

The **Tanji River Karinti Bird Reserve** (daily 8am–dusk; D31.50), established in 1993, was the first bird reserve to be gazetted in the Gambia, due largely to the efforts of a group of passionately committed British bird enthusiasts. A narrow strip of land on the north side of Tanji village, encompassing the River Tanji, its estuary and the Bijol Islands, it contains in just over six square kilometres a wide variety of bird habitats, including mangrove, salt flats, lily pools, dry woodland, coastal dune scrub woodland and lagoons. Small though it is, over three hundred species of bird have been recorded here. Unfortunately, the wildlife has been disturbed by wood-gatherers and by the growing volume of traffic through the area, so it's rather elusive. Little has been done to make the reserve visitor-friendly, either – there are no trails officially mapped or hides built – so to get the best out of a visit you should go with an experienced bird guide.

The **Bijol Islands**, or Kajonyi Islands, are the only offshore islands in The Gambia, situated in the Atlantic 1.5km from Brufut and Tanji. They form part of the Tanji River Karinti Bird Reserve, and they have important breeding populations of sea birds and green turtles, and visiting populations of sea turtles, the very rare Mediterranean monk seals, minke whales, Atlantic humpback dolphins and bottle-nose dolphins. Unauthorized access to the islands is prohibited to protect the wildlife, but small groups with a research interest can arrange to visit the islands by boat with a representative of the Department of Parks and Wildlife Management. You leave from the beach at Brufut or Tanji, and may glimpse turtles and dolphins during the crossing. For further information, contact the Department HQ at Abuko (☎437 5888) or the TRKBR warden (☎991 9219 or 991 0398).

Tanji village

Around 12km southwest of Kololi, straight down the coastal highway and within easy cycling or driving distance of the resorts, is the coastal village of **TANJI** (also spelt Tanje). One of the few Kombo South villages very close to the beach, it's the most-visited village in this area, featuring on "Bush and Beach" tours (see p.51). Unfortunately, its popularity with tourists means you often get "*toubabed*" mercilessly by local kids; even so, it's a friendly and accessible place which offers a good opportunity to see the hectic, noisy, colourful scene of a Gambian fishing community at work. The beach here is not the best for swimming – it's a working beach, strewn with fishing nets and, inevitably, fish – but there are bathing places a short stroll or bike ride away. Tanji's main street leads inland from the coastal highway, which itself passes close to the ocean just south of the narrow, mangrove-lined River Tanji. The village is regularly served by direct *gelleh-gelleh* van bush taxis from Serrekunda.

Just south of the bridge over the River Tanji, opposite *Nyanya Safari Lodge* (see p.158), Tanji Camel Safaris (☎779 2023 or 446 1083), a long-established operation, offers camel rides along the beach for D275 per person (30min) or D550 per person (1hr).

Tanje Village Museum

Right on the main coastal highway on the southern edge of Tanji village is the **Tanje Village Museum** (T992 6618, daily 9am–5pm; D100), a small but well-thought-out private museum of nature and traditional culture. It's an education centre that's all about participation – there are musical instruments to play, craftsmen and *kora* players to chat to, a traditional compound to nose around, and a nature trail to follow. Tour companies often build a stop here into their tours of the area.

Inside the gate is a small exhibition hall with information about Gambian **wildlife** and a roomful of **musical instruments** – visitors are free to find out what sounds they all make – the instruments, though traditional, are not irreplaceable. Much of the museum's interest is outside in the large garden, where the craftsmen, compound, and nature trail are found. Part of the museum's policy is to promote traditional **crafts**, and you can usually watch weavers creating strips of cotton cloth on hand-looms, and blacksmiths making jewellery using hand-pumped bellows. Weaving is a traditional craft passed from father to son, and senior weavers present traditional ebony shuttles to their students in recognition of good progress. Weaving by hand is a painstaking process – rethreading a loom can take a whole day. Blacksmithing, too, is a traditional occupation in Gambian society; smiths also make tools and knives, and have a further role in the village, circumcising boys at initiation rites.

A major part of the museum garden consists of a **family compound** arranged and furnished in traditional Mandinka style, with explanations of which family members would sleep in which huts and how their roles fit together. Much of the rest of the garden is taken up by a **nature trail**, planted with numerous indigenous trees, herbs and shrubs – a leaflet identifies and describes them all, explaining their uses, whether as food, medicine, or building materials. Look out for the wild coffee plant – its roasted beans can be used as a coffee substitute, but when raw they're used as rat poison. You'll also see the locust bean tree, whose seeds cure all sorts of ailments and are known as the "Gambian Viagra". The trail is best appreciated at the very beginning of the dry season when it's lush; in winter, it's rather bare and forlorn-looking.

The museum has a *bantaba* bar where there's often a *kora* player ready to entertain visitors, and a gift shop with some interesting goods not often seen elsewhere, such as *warri* boards (see p.282), hand-woven textiles made by the weavers, stools made from tree-stumps, and dried herbs such as *kinkiliba* and *wonjo*, used to make infusions. There's also a restaurant which serves good, simple meals; above this is a breezy roof terrace with views of the coastal strip. At the back of the plot are meeting rooms and some simple visitor accommodation (see p.162), a good choice for anyone wanting to learn more about traditional Gambian crafts in quiet surroundings.

Tujering, Sanyang, and Gunjur

About 7km south of Tanji on the Kombo coastal highway, and 4km inland from the beach, is **Tujering**, a pleasant old Kombo South village that owes nothing of its character to tourism or colonialism. Here, you'll find whitewashed mudstone houses and a central crossroads with meeting place, mosque and market. Tucked away in the bush just beyond the village is the fascinating Tunbung Art Village (see box, opposite).

South of here, the highway bends inland to **Sanyang**, 8km from Tujering, and, another 10km on, **Gunjur**, both tranquil mango-shaded settlements of sandy streets and cement-block compounds, around 6km inland and little-visited by

Kora, drumming and dance

Music and dance colour every corner of daily life in The Gambia. Live performances, which often continue late into the night, are an unmissable introduction to Gambian social life at its most exuberant. But traditional music is far more than just entertainment; it's the most valued and celebrated of the arts, used to spread news, tell stories, cement relationships and express religious beliefs. As such, it has a crucial role in cultural rituals.

▲ Jola dancers at *futampaf* celebrations in Kanilai

Kora music

The gentle acoustic *kora* music of the *jalis*, the traditional musicians of the Mandinka tribe, is Gambian music at its most melodic and contemplative. The **kora**, a distinctive West African harp-lute, is usually played solo to accompany lilting songs which relate folk tales or praise the *jalis'* benefactors and guests. Skilled players can pick out a melody and a bass line at the same time, adding a rhythmic accompaniment by drumming their fingers against the body of the instrument.

You'll often come across *kora* players busking in The Gambia's resort hotels and restaurants, but traditionally the *jalis'* main responsibilities include custodianship of their tribe's oral history and providing musical accompaniment to official meetings and ceremonies. Theirs is a role that's passed from father to son.

The *jalis* are related to the Manding or Mandé *jelis* of Mali and Guinea, who in turn trace their ancestry back to the thirteenth-century empire of ancient Mali. They are craftsmen, making their own instruments from a large half-gourd covered with cured cowhide, with a hardwood neck and between 21 and 25 nylon strings secured with leather thongs.

▲ Kora master Jaliba Kuyateh in concert

In recent years, some contemporary *kora* masters like Jaliba Kuyateh and Tata Dindin have given the ancient instrument a new twist by amplifying the sound and playing against explosive backing groups of drummers and *balafon* (traditional xylophone) players, with acrobatic dancers completing the high-energy line-up.

International Roots Festival

Planning a visit to The Gambia around musical performances can be a challenge, as advance information is hard to track down; locally, events tend to be promoted by word of mouth. Time your visit to coincide with the country's biennial **Roots Festival**, though, and you are guaranteed a high-octane introduction to the best of Gambian music.

Taking place over seven to ten days in June, the festival includes a range of events celebrating Gambian and West African culture. At the heart of the proceedings are a pilgrimage to the up-river heritage sites of Juffureh, Albreda and James Island, and a ceremony based on traditional Jola initiation rites in which visitors of West African ancestry are invited to reconnect with the homeland of their forefathers. Each event is accompanied by high-spirited music-making – drumming, percussion and carefully choreographed dancing

▶ Drum and dance troupe playing in Kololi

at the pageants and parades, praise-singing from *kora* musicians at the formal events, and dance music at the late-night parties. The troupes taking part usually include not only Gambians but also performers from Senegal, Guinea, Guinea-Bissau and beyond, with headlining acts that may include megastars such as Youssou N'Dour.

Music and dance lessons

A great way to immerse yourself in The Gambia's musical traditions and get under the skin of local culture is to sign up for a series of **lessons** with a professional musician or dancer. A number of *kora*, *djembé*, *sabar* and *balafon* players are happy to offer interested visitors an introduction to the basics

▲ Learning to play the kora in Brikama

of their instrument; the musicians who play at the resort hotels can sometimes make useful introductions or offer themselves as a tutor. A lesson could be a simple jamming session on the beach, or a more intense session of detailed technical instruction.

Your tutor may be able to arrange simple accommodation, too, in their own compound or with relatives. Since music-making is a community activity, staying with a family adds greatly to the experience, and you will certainly be invited to participate in any family celebrations which may take place during your visit, from naming ceremonies to weddings, all of which call for good music, and plenty of it. Brikama (see p.171) is a particularly good place to make enquiries, as several musical clans hail from here.

Mbalax

Mbalax – the brash musical style which sets dance floors alight all over The Gambia and Senegal – was invented in Dakar in the 1970s. At the time, the Senegalese were engaged in a steamy love affair with Latin music. Having grown up swaying to Cuban sounds mixed with Congolese rumba, the new generation of young Wolof musicians, among them Youssou N'Dour, started mixing up Latin rhythms, electric guitar riffs, snappy *sabar* and *tama* drumming and jazzy horn playing. One of the ingredients of the new style was *ndagga*, pioneered in The Gambia by the Super Eagles.

Fast-paced, rowdy and often rather raunchy, *mbalax* inspires its fans to flirt and show off with their most suggestive and acrobatic dance moves. Thirty years on, it's still the music of choice at The Gambia's most popular nightclubs.

▶ Sabar drummer

Five Senegambian greats

Gambian musical tastes are hugely influenced by those of its nearest neighbour, Senegal, a cultural powerhouse which has produced a number of international stars. Traditional Senegambian music is as diverse as the mosaic of cultures which make up the region; as well as Mandinka *kora* music, the dominant sounds include the plaintive melodies of the Fula and the irresistibly energetic strains of Wolof *mbalax* (see overleaf).

1. Youssou N'Dour

Dakar's legendary champion of *mbalax* has done more than any other performer to raise the international profile of Senegambian music, issuing numerous albums, working with stars including Peter Gabriel and Paul Simon and taking centre stage at the Live 8 Africa Calling concerts. At home, he's a hero; the Gambians embrace him as a brother.

2. Baaba Maal

Brilliant and articulate, Baaba Maal is not only a highly gifted singer and band leader, he's also a dynamic political force and a respected spokesman for African rights. A Fula from Senegal who was not born into a family of musicians, he has embraced his calling with a passion and has become the region's second greatest musical export after Youssou N'Dour. His dance music blends reggae, rap and *mbalax*.

▲ Youssou N'Dour and his band the Super Etoile de Dakar

3. Jaliba Kuyateh

The Gambia's most popular contemporary *kora* master is a tireless performer; he often tours overseas but also plays to ecstatic home crowds on a regular basis. Recently, his work has taken on a more political tone and he's been an active campaigner for HIV/AIDS awareness.

4. Cheikh Lo

The songs of this free-spirited, dreadlocked Senegalese singer and percussionist are suffused with references to Baye Fall, the Islamic brotherhood of which he is an ardent member. A recent creative collaboration with Brazilian musicians has inspired him to lace his distinctively multi-layered sound with spicy South American rhythms.

5. Tata Dindin

A leading member of one of The Gambia's greatest musical dynasties, the Jobarteh clan, Brikama-born Tata Dindin is an innovative *kora* artist, best known for his upbeat, contemporary interpretations of traditional songs which have been handed down through the centuries.

Kombo South art galleries

Traditional Gambian society sets great store by the oral arts of singing and storytelling and pays relatively little attention to the visual arts. It's largely thanks to these cultural preferences that the standard wares you'll see on display in all the *bengdulas* – locally produced sculptures, carvings, batiks, pottery and woven objects – tend to be formulaic, following well-worn "tourist-friendly" themes. The country's genuine artists are, on the whole, rather elusive, but Kombo South district has a few places where you can find work of true originality and talent. **Tunbung Art Village**, signposted off the Kombo Coastal Highway just south of Tujering (Ⓣ998 2102, Ⓔetundow@yahoo.com), is unique in The Gambia, and well worth a stop.

This is the open-air studio of Bakau-born painter Baboucarr Ndow, known as Etu, who attaches found objects and materials to his canvases and adds dazzlingly vibrant colours to produce richly textured, flamboyant mixed-media paintings full of abstract symbology. His "village" is an installation – it's a collection of thatched huts arranged under beautiful, spreading trees, decorated and adapted by the artist on an ongoing basis. This is a working studio, but visitors are welcome, and Etu, a gentle and charismatic character, sometimes runs creative workshops.

In Kartong, the **Lemonfish Art Gallery** (Ⓣ439 4586 or 992 2884, Ⓦwww.lemonfish.gm, Tues–Sun 9am–6pm) has been stimulating fresh interest in art from The Gambia and elsewhere in West Africa by staging shows of paintings, batik and one-off clothing in airy, peaceful surroundings. Names to look out for here include Malick Ceesay, whose colourful canvases incorporate stylized African figures, and Toyimbu, a master batik artist. In Tanji, the museum shop at the **Tanje Village Museum** (see p.168) sometimes has a few original artefacts, including weaving made on the site.

tourists. In this area, the action tends to be concentrated on the beaches to which the villages lend their names: busy and attractive, these boast fine sand, hectic fishing centres and excellent beach bars.

The coastal woodland savannah between the villages and the sea is lush with palms and cashew trees. Rich in bird species, particularly raptors, this is an excellent area for bush walks. Further inland, the patches of woodland just north of Gunjur also offer great birdwatching; they're frequented by species rarely seen outside southern Senegal. All three village centres are served by *gelleh-gelleh* **bush taxis** from Serrekunda and Brikama, and are good places to find simple Gambian food in local eateries.

Kartong and around

One of the oldest villages in The Gambia, **Kartong** (also spelt Kartung) lies close to the coast, near the mouth of the saltwater **River Allahein** (San Pedro), where The Gambia finishes and French-speaking Senegal takes over. The new coastal highway ends here, so it's a bit of a cul-de-sac, with an atmosphere distinctly different from the other villages of the southern Kombos. It's a remote and utterly relaxing place to enjoy the coastal landscape and its wildlife, and there's also a sacred crocodile pool and a reptile farm.

Kartong has a population of around 3500, mostly Mandinka plus some Jola and other minority ethnic groups; the sense of community is extremely strong. There's an old-fashioned atmosphere of courtesy, order and calm about the village which makes it an appealing place. The sealed road is still something of a novelty here, and Kartonka children watch wide-eyed when vehicles drive into the village. The villagers recently decided to encourage tourists to visit their community, in a controlled, sustainable and eco-friendly way. As part of this drive they have established the Kartong Association for Responsible Tourism (KART), with an **information office** in the middle of the village where visitors can hire bikes or local guides; visitors are also made very welcome at the annual cultural festival (Ⓦ www.kartongfestival.com) which takes place in the village in March.

The village is surrounded by sea, bush, sand dunes, and the eerily empty salt flats and mangrove swamps which border the river. The sand mining that scarred the dunes between the village and the sea was outlawed several years ago; the new pools created where sand was removed now attract a stunning variety of **birds**, including migrants from northern Europe. Species commonly found here include African jacana, African crake, purple swamphen, green sandpiper, wood sandpiper, and various plovers.

Gambian Reptile Farm

Signposted off the main south coast highway north of Kartong, the **Gambian Reptile Farm** (daily 8am–6pm; D50), is home to a fine collection of snakes, lizards, geckos, chameleons and turtles. The place is set up not as a zoo, but as a research and education centre. There has recently been a high-profile campaign in The Gambia attempting to raise awareness of the need to protect the wild snake population, since snakes have a crucial role to play in the natural ecosystem and can be very beneficial to humans (for example, they eat rodents that would otherwise damage grain stores). The Reptile Farm encourages people to get rather closer to snakes than they might normally choose. Among the healthy-looking collection here are slender, green common bush snakes, and African beauty snakes. There are a couple of puff adders, a species which kills more people than any other African snake – its sluggish nature makes it easy to step on, and an adult specimen carries enough venom to kill eight elephants. The puff adders are kept at a safe distance, but you can have a more friendly two-metre royal python draped around your shoulders.

Follonko crocodile pool

On the seaward edge of Kartong, near the dunes, is the **Follonko crocodile pool**, a murky green, lily-choked swamp in a deep, shady grove; local kids or representatives of Kartong's Association for Responsible Tourism (KART) will guide you to the place. Home to a fair number of crocs, it's an atmospheric and sacred place, similar to the Katchikali pool at Bakau, but far less visited by tourists and more regularly used as a place of pilgrimage and prayer. Female elders from two of Kartong's communities, Muslim Mandinka and Christian Karoninka (Karoninka is a Mandinka dialect), visit to pray and ask favours on Monday and Friday mornings. They also preside over the pilgrims, who come here bringing money, salt, kola nuts, candles or other offerings. For more on crocodile pools, see the box on p.127).

The River Allahein

If you have your own transport, you'll be able to leave the centre of Kartong and drive south, through open countryside planted with gingerbread plums, big banana plants and palms, to the last extremity of Gambian territory, a military checkpoint near the mouth of the River Allahein. A short drive from here, you can turn right towards the ocean fishing centre (see p.164). Alternatively, turn left towards the **river fishing base** on the River Allahein, where sharkfin and shark steaks are salted and laid out on tables to dry in the sun. Most of the shark caught here is sold to exporters with customers in Ghana and Asia (sharkfin destined for Hong Kong fetches well over £30/$55 a kilo). Some fishermen specialize in only hunting shark for this market, in small *pirogues* which you can see moored in the river. There are also *bonga* smoke houses on the shore.

From here it's possible to cross the river by *pirogue* and continue to **Abéné** and **Kafountine** in Casamance, Senegal. However, this is not the best place to cross the border, unless you're planning on coming straight back by the same route – the military officials at the Gambian post may check your stuff, but they won't necessarily stamp your passport with an exit stamp, resulting in questions and hassle in Senegal.

Brikama

Heading inland from Serrekunda and the resorts, the first substantial town you reach is **BRIKAMA**, a regional capital which is the gateway to the up-country provinces. The town centre lies to the south of the main south bank highway, right in the middle of the Kombo peninsula, about 35km southwest of Banjul.

While its population has long outstripped that of Banjul, Brikama is still much smaller and more easy-going than The Gambia's largest urban centres, Serrekunda and Bakau. It's not really geared up for tourism – its woodcarvers' and craft markets are its only conventional attractions, and there's very little in the way of visitor accommodation – but its busy but relaxed and unintimidating commercial scene and quiet sandy streets shaded by spreading mango trees make it an appealing provincial town.

Brikama is most famous for its rich **musical heritage**. Many Gambian traditional musicians hail from here and the town is home, or has been home, to much of The Gambia's musical "royalty", including Dembo Konte, Foday Musa Suso, Malamini Jobarteh and Tata Dindin. With such an abundance of homegrown talent, you'd expect the town's live music scene to be astounding. In reality, however, if you're not on the inside track, it may seem a little hit-and-miss. The town has just one major venue, *Jokor*, like its sister club in Serrekunda it sometimes hosts visiting stars, including Senegambian greats, but its programme is rather limited.

Taking the time to forge personal connections is the best plan if you'd like to tap into Brikama's musical heritage in a meaningful way. The locals are generally very warm and welcoming, making Brikama a good place to experience life in a **Gambian compound**, and by seeking out an invitation to stay you may be lucky enough to witness the kind of private occasion at which the local *jalis* play. Brikama's social scene is very family-oriented, with naming ceremonies and other celebrations turning into big events which can go on late into the night. To get actively involved, you could try contacting one of the town's eminent musical families; some are prepared to host students on an ad hoc basis, offering them first-rate tuition in *kora*-playing, drumming, *balafon* and dance (see p.71).

The local community is known for being traditional, conservative, and deeply religious, and the imams here are particularly powerful; they strongly opposed the opening of *Jokor*, concerned that this would attract sex workers and drug dealers and hasten the town's moral decline. It's a town with plenty of character and a good degree of apparent prosperity. Unlike most Gambian towns, the main road is lit by streetlights, all the major access roads are newly surfaced, and

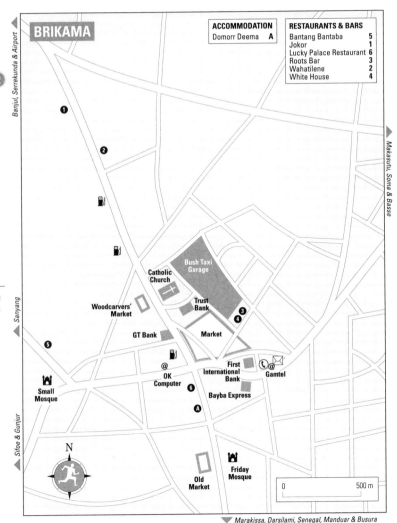

BRIKAMA

ACCOMMODATION	
Domorr Deema	A

RESTAURANTS & BARS	
Bantang Bantaba	5
Jokor	1
Lucky Palace Restaurant	6
Roots Bar	3
Wahatilene	2
White House	4

Banjul, Serrekunda & Airport

Makasutu, Soma & Basse

Sanyang

Sifoe & Gunjur

Bush Taxi Garage

Catholic Church

Woodcarvers' Market

Trust Bank

GT Bank

Market

First International Bank

Gamtel

OK Computer

Bayba Express

Small Mosque

N

Old Market

Friday Mosque

0   500 m

Marakissa, Darsilami, Senegal, Manduar & Busura

new housing has been built on the western outskirts. There's also a plan to build The Gambia's first large shopping mall not far out of Brikama, at Nyambai, on the road to Serrekunda. However, despite this relative affluence, the town shares up-country Gambia's occasional **power and water shortages**. If you decide to spend some time in Brikama and are invited to stay in a family compound you may end up helping carry water from a shared tap, a few streets away.

Arrival, orientation, accommodation and transport

Brikama is a busy transport hub. Buses no longer serve the town but minibus bush taxis from all over the Kombo area and beyond arrive at the **taxi garage** in the middle of town. Travelling independently from Banjul or Serrekunda to the north, or from the up-country districts to the east, you have to make a deliberate diversion off the main south bank highway to reach the town centre. Approaching from the north, you turn right into Brikama, passing *Jokor* and the woodcarvers' market on your right before you reach the market and shops, all on your left, in the centre of town. Approaching from the east, you turn left off the highway onto the road taking you into the east side of town; once you're in the centre, the market is on your right. The main roads from the Kombo South villages of Sanyang, due west of Brikama, or Gunjur to the southwest, lead straight into the centre.

Brikama's **post office** is open Mon–Fri, 8am–4pm and Sat, 8am–1pm. The Gamtel offices next door are open daily 8am–9pm for **phone** and **Internet** services. There's also Internet access at OK Computer just west of the centre on the Gunjur road (daily 8am–10pm). The town has three **banks**: Trust Bank, First International and GT Bank (Mon–Fri 8am–noon & 4–6.30pm, Sat 9am–1pm); all will exchange foreign cash and travellers' cheques but none has an ATM (the closest is at Westfield Junction in Kanifing near Serrekunda). There's also a Bayba Express office (Mon–Fri 9am–5pm, Sat 9am–noon) for currency transfers. The main **fuel stations** are in the middle of town.

Currently, the only **accommodation** option in Brikama, unless you're invited to stay in a family compound, is the *Domorr Deema Mini Hotel* on Mosque Road (℡990 3302; ➊). This simple place with a very local feel is reasonably clean, but can be noisy. It has four very small rooms with fans and shared shower. There's also a restaurant – you can sit at the streetside table and eat omelettes, chicken, steak, or rice and sauce at low prices.

The town is small enough to explore on foot, but should you wish to venture further afield, there are always plenty of yellow **local taxis** waiting on the town's exit roads.

The Town

Brikama's famous **woodcarvers' market** (daily 8am–dusk), on the main road leading southeast from the south bank highway towards the town centre, is much bigger than its rather tatty street entrance suggests. There's a large area of gift stalls inside the entrance, and behind this, the "factory" where craftsmen cut up newly arrived timber into rough forms for the carvers manning the stalls to

Moving on from Brikama

Plenty of **minibus bush taxis** run throughout the day from Brikama's main garage to Lamin (D5, 20min), Serrekunda (D10, 30min), Westfield Junction in Kanifing (D10, 30min) and Banjul (D15, 45min). There are also a few minibuses and *gelleh-gellehs* covering the routes to Sanyang, Sifoe and Gunjur in the southwest, with occasional departures for Kartong. If you're heading up-country, look for the *gelleh-gellehs* heading for Bulok (D15, up to 1hr), Soma (D80, 4–6hr), Sankulay Kunda and Bansang (D150, up to 10hr) and Basse (D190, up to 11hr). Journey times on this route will remain unpredictable until the road is repaired. The road to Zigunichor in Senegal via Mandina Ba and Séléti is also due to be repaired; a good number of bush taxis ply this route. The alternative route via Marakissa and Darsilami (both D8, 30–40min) is less-travelled and is impassable during the rains.

If you're based in the resorts and are visiting Brikama for a night out, the best way to be sure of getting back in the small hours is to come with your own cab and pay him to wait; the alternative is to hope to find a late-night minibus bound for Serrekunda, or to pay a premium to hire a local taxi.

finish with adze, sandpaper and wax polish. As you wander about you'll hear a constant background noise of tapping and rubbing over the usual racket of radios and cassette players. The market vendors can be very persistent, but they have to abide by a code of conduct which means you shouldn't be chased from stall to stall by touts. You'll need to hone your bargaining skills, and it's wise to visit at a quiet time, rather than with a big mob of tourists.

Most of the **carvings** here are formulaic – you'll see plenty of lions, hippos, giraffes, elongated Africans, and abstract forms, plus ashtrays, dolls and masks, just like the ones for sale at tourist-trap craft stalls all over the Gambian coastal resort area – but with careful sifting, you might come across something original with real style and character. The wood most commonly used is teak; mahogany is rarer, and ebony extremely rare. Some "ebony" carvings are in fact teak rubbed with black shoe polish, and some carvings have been distressed to make them look antique. You won't find genuine fetish objects here, whatever the vendors claim, but some stalls sell beautiful masks and statues made to traditional ritual designs.

Brikama's **main market** is also worth a visit. The produce on sale is like that found at any other large Gambian market – there's still the same amazing jumble of ripe and over-ripe fruit and vegetables, malodorous fish, garish plastic household goods, richly coloured bolts of fabric and cheap imported clothing – but the atmosphere is comfortable, without the cramped areas of covered stalls that can be oppressive in markets elsewhere. There's also a new **craft market**, with textile workshops as well as the usual jumble of stalls selling batiks, jewellery, carvings and clothing.

The southwest edge of town is a Manjago area, easily identified by the presence of hairy pigs scuttling around under the palms and mango trees. Some residents work as palm-tappers; you can sample their hooch at the local palm wine "ghetto". On the outskirts of Brikama is the **Santangba** at Kotokali, a sacred grove of trees that's frequented by small animals and numerous birds, and which marks the site of the first settlement in this area of the thirteenth-century Mandinka migrants who travelled from Mali in the time of Sundiata Keita. The grove is said to be occupied by ancestral spirits, so the locals are forbidden from hunting and fruit-gathering here, and prior to circumcision ceremonies it becomes "bush school", where initiates are brought for their instruction in tribal lore. To visit the site, first ask for directions to the compound of the *alkalo* of Brikama, and then ask there for a guide.

Eating, drinking and nightlife

Brikama's entertainment scene only really sparks into life when there's a gala music event at *Jokor*, drawing visitors from the northern urban areas and all over the Kombo peninsula. Tour groups sometimes visit the *Bantang Bantaba* for a drink; all the other options in town are low-key, with a very local atmosphere.

Bantang Bantaba Methodist Mission, Sanyang Rd. The Brikama Methodists serve low-priced drinks including *wonjo*, sandwiches and snacks from their small kitchen adjoining an open-sided café area, but the place doesn't have much atmosphere. In the grounds there's a short forest walk and an orchard where fruit is grown for the mission's jam-making enterprise. Tour groups sometimes stop here, so local kids sometimes hassle visitors. Mon–Fri 10am–3pm.

Jokor On the main road into town from Serrekunda, Brikama's coolest club has a mellow atmosphere and is aimed at the slick young Gambian middle class; it's open to all, but not many tourists come here, partly due to Brikama's shortage of accommodation. Big name Senegambian artists sometimes perform – listen out for radio ads, or ask taxi drivers and guides – and local DJs play international and West African dance tracks. The main space, a crazy-tiled garden in which the trees are wound with coloured rope lights and the walls hung with local contemporary art, has three bars. Over-21s only, no trainers. Open for special events, till 4am (D25–150).

Lucky Palace Restaurant Mosque Rd. Guinean-run local restaurant, not to be confused with the slot-machine joint opposite. It looks shabby, but everything – from omelettes, chicken, and rice with *tapalapa* bread to excellent coffee, Gambian-style – is very fresh and tasty.

Roots Bar Opposite the Area Council offices, near the market. This scruffy joint serves basic West African fare such as *foofoo* and pepper soup, and sometimes hosts local bands. Its unmarked near-neighbour, known locally as the *White House*, also holds informal music sessions from time to time.

Wahatilene Restaurant and Garden On the main road into town from Serrekunda. A simple but upbeat place to stop for a drink or a plate of *domo-dah*, with a couple of roadside tables at the front and a garden of sorts at the back.

Around Brikama

Within easy reach of Brikama are a few pockets of well-preserved wilderness, perfect for relaxed hiking. The best-known is **Makasutu Culture Forest**, a beautiful private reserve that's home to a high-profile ecotourism project offering guided tours of Makasutu's woodland paths and mangrove creeks – popular with day-trippers from the coastal resorts – and luxury accommodation deep in the bush at the exclusive and attractive **Mandina Lodge**. Further east are a couple of lower-key, locally run eco-ventures: an embryonic conservation project at **Pirang Forest Park**, and a village camp at the Jola hamlet of **Tumani Tenda**. South of Brikama, around the villages of **Marakissa** and **Darsilami**, is a little-visited area of woodland and savannah particularly good for bird-watching. Much of this area is earmarked to become part of an ambitious new conservation and ecotourism initiative, the **Ballabu Conservation Area**, extending all the way north to Banjul.

Makasutu Culture Forest

Makasutu Culture Forest (daytime visits daily 8am–4.30pm; D700/500 per day/half-day; early morning and evening visits by arrangement) was The Gambia's first high-profile ecotourism project, and has been open to the public since 1999. It has since become one of the most popular day-trip destinations from the coastal resorts. It lies about 5km east of Brikama, situated on a lovely bend in the Mandina Bolon, a glassy-smooth mangrove creek. The forest here is inspiring and varied, with clearings and areas of dense foliage, termite mounds, and some truly beautiful glades, mature trees and saplings – young trees are still growing to replace those lost to loggers. Visitors to the park are introduced to the natural environment on a guided walk through the forest, and a cruise, by hand-paddled dugout, along the creek. There's also a chance to enjoy some high-energy local drumming, and join in the dancing. For those who would like to spend more than a day in the area, there is **luxury accommodation** at Makasutu's *Mandina Lodge*, a stunning creekside bush lodge that sets high standards of quality and service for hotels in The Gambia, and is colossally expensive in local terms – but worth it.

Most tourists visit Makasutu by organized one-day excursion, including return transport from the resorts and the park entry fee, for about £35/€51. The park entry fee covers the standard full-day **guided tour**, including lunch and entertainment. This is highly enjoyable, but not really recommended for ardent

△ Dancing at Makasutu

wildlife watchers, as you'll be touring in a group of up to 25 people, and you won't be there at the best times of day to see birds or mammals. Wildlife-watchers are advised to join a more specialist trip, such as the early morning "Bushtrackers' Breakfast" promoted by a few tour operators. It's possible to visit independently, too. If you're staying at *Mandina Lodge* (see p.179) you can wander round the forest whenever you choose; if you're just visiting the park, you have to pay either the half-day or full-day entry fee when you arrive, and join a guided tour, making it expensive compared to Abuko Nature Reserve. However, Makasutu offers more than Abuko – the site is larger and includes more habitats, and the guided walk, creek cruise, lunch and entertainment are all excellent. Visitor numbers are normally limited to a total of around fifty per day to minimize the

Makasutu is a testament to the remarkable vision of two unstoppably energetic British business partners, engineer **James English** and architect **Lawrence Williams**. The pair came across the forest in 1992, during a lengthy search for a site for a new travellers' lodge. At the time, Makasutu (meaning "ancient and sacred deep forest" in Mandinka) was uninhabited – local legend maintained it was haunted by djinns and giants plus a *ninkinanka*, or dragon-devil, and the area was therefore used mainly for tribal rituals. Undaunted, the Brits secured four acres of land here, and left the country to earn enough capital to start construction. Unfortunately, in their absence, with the myth of the forest blown, locals set about cutting down trees, and hundreds of mature specimens were lost before English and Williams were able to buy the remaining four square kilometres of the forest and fence it, creating a woodland habitat conservation project which has gone on to win several prestigious international awards.

English and Williams have succeeded in making the forest environment accessible to visitors, partly through building sympathetic and imaginative structures to a standard never before seen in The Gambia, using local craftsmen – only their design is non-Gambian. In the process, they have guaranteed the survival of this beautiful habitat and opened the eyes of many visitors not only to The Gambia's natural biodiversity, but also to elements of village culture and tradition. They have also shown great commitment to the local community, and have provided employment for a large, and growing, number of villagers.

Makasutu hosts a registered wildlife conservation charity, **Makasutu Wildlife Trust** (T 778 2633, W www.darwingambia.gm/mwt, E drumohq@qanet.gm), which operates a membership scheme, open to all. It aims to involve local communities in active preservation of wildlife and habitats threatened by urbanization, hunting, and farming, and to encourage greater awareness of The Gambia's biodiversity. Its activities include educational programmes for schools and community groups; training sessions in wildlife-guiding, biodiversity and conservation for various organizations; publishing conservation information; and running an animal clinic for injured and orphaned wild animals. The trust sometimes organizes guided wildlife walks and talks for tourists and locals, with all proceeds going to its education, conservation and research projects. Membership is open to individuals, families and groups.

daily impact on the forest environment. You find the site by heading east beyond Brikama along the main south bank highway, looking out for the roadside sign for Kinderdorf Bottropp, then turning north along an unmade track marked by a carved signpost and a totem pole.

Guided tours of Makasutu

Visiting Makasutu on an organized day trip, you start by making your way towards the tour meeting place through a woodland area distinguished by an enormous **termite mound** (see box on p.178) and dotted with **treestump sculptures**, the work of a local artist. Representing highly kinetic running, leaping and flying creatures, they're like frozen animal spirits, breathing new life into the remains of trees cut down before the forest could be protected. There is then a welcoming talk at the *Baobab Bar and Restaurant*, a spectacular space like an open-sided cathedral of timber and cane, hung with carvings, with a soaring thatched canopy where bats sometimes sleep.

The order of the day's programme of guided walk and creek cruise depends on the tides. Along the route through the forest, which is an easy walk along shady paths, you're likely to pass the hideout of a **traditional herbalist**, who makes remedies and infusions from plants found in the forest, and sells

Termite mounds

Termite mounds, found all over the Gambian countryside, are commonly well over two metres tall, and look rather like fairytale castles, with turrets and towers. Colonies of termites build these mini-kingdoms by binding the soil with half-digested cellulose, the by-product of their diet of wood and straw, fetched by the worker termites. Inside the mound, the queen termite spends her life breeding. When the queen dies the colony migrates elsewhere, and squirrels, snakes and lizards move in to the abandoned mound.

Active termite mounds are used by female **monitor lizards** as incubators for their eggs. The lizard digs into a mound and, depending on the species, lays between eight and sixty eggs inside. The termites then industriously repair the damage, effectively sealing the eggs inside in a protected and temperature-controlled environment. It can take many months for the eggs to hatch, normally in the rainy season when the mound is soft enough for the young monitors to dig their way out.

Termites are generally seen as a **pest**, wreaking havoc anywhere wood and thatch are used as building materials. However, they do have a use in **water divining**: the presence of termites indicates a high water table, so villagers planning to dig a new well start by looking for a termite mound. In addition, the fine clay from mounds makes extremely good water jars, as it's an effective insulator.

animist amulets made from knotted rhun palm fronds. There'll also be a stop to admire the athleticism of a local Manjago **palm-tapper**, who shins up a palm tree in typical style, with the help of a loop sling encircling his body and the tree trunk.

Your guide will point out some of the different species, such as the camel foot tree, whose bark is used to make *kankurang* costumes (see p.288); young mahogany trees, one of The Gambia's protected species; ironwood trees, named because their timber is so solid; and strangler figs, common in this area, wound around host trees. You probably won't see many birds or animals on the way, though, because of the size of your group and the time of day. The Makasutu monkeys are much more elusive than those in the woods at Abuko or Bijilo, but your guide may well spot one in the distance for you; the rainy season, when fruit is ripening on the trees, is the most likely time of year.

The tour of the *bolon* in a traditional **dugout**, hollowed from a single mahogany log, is one of the highlights of the day. The water is glossy and utterly peaceful, with no noise but people's voices, the dip of the paddle, and occasional bird-calls. You may see thick-knees and herons watching from the mudbanks under the shade of the mangroves. Lunch is an excellent **buffet** of Gambian food served in the Baobab area. It's here that you might notice that Makasutu is right beneath the flight path into Banjul International Airport – aircraft occasionally shatter the peace.

There's more noise of a much more melodious sort after lunch when a troupe of Jola **drummers** and **dancers** from the neighbouring village of Kembujeh, many of whom work at the forest full-time in other roles, start performing on the natural platform under the big baobab tree. Everybody is encouraged to join in – the women pass around strings of beads as an invitation to dance – and it's a lot of fun.

There's even more entertainment on offer – much of it highly energetic – if you visit Makasutu's Base Camp for the **Evening Extravaganza** which takes place once a week. Jugglers, acrobats, drummers and dancers all strut their stuff as you enjoy a feast of a barbecue by firelight, deep in the bush.

Mandina Lodge

The opening of ⚐ **Mandina Lodge** (Ⓦ www.makasutu.com; book through The Gambia Experience, Ⓦ www.gambia.co.uk; ❸) was a new departure in Gambian tourism. It was the country's first truly luxurious bush lodge, and the first upmarket accommodation to be designed with ecologically sound principles in mind; its success in providing environmentally aware guests with excellent food and service in gorgeous surroundings has inspired other businesses in The Gambia to aim just as high.

The accommodation, which houses a maximum of sixteen guests in total, is attractively situated in the wilderness on the northern edge of Makasutu Forest, beside a peaceful stretch of the Mandina Bolon. The most luxurious lodge stands over the water on stilts, four others float like anchored house-boats in the *bolon*, and there are three new pavilion-like rooms in the garden. The lodge on stilts is reached by way of a timber walkway crossing a mangrove thicket, with water and mud below and tangled roots to left and right. Guests staying here have the use of a deck with hammocks and, above this, a timber tower with a day bed, for sleeping or catnapping in the open air. Each of the floating lodges has a private **jetty** where the occupants' personal guide can pull up his dugout *pirogue*, ready for a trip around the creeks. The garden (or "jungle") lodges are like mini North African palaces, their windows studded with coloured glass and their spacious roof terraces offering great views over the mangroves. Inside the lodges, everything is exquisitely detailed, with a four-poster bed decorated with *bogolan* mudcloth under a lofty ceiling, and huge windows overlooking the *bolon* or the garden.

The shared areas of the lodge have stunning vistas and more lovely detailing – cowries, carvings, old drums and pounding pestles are all worked into the design, and the swimming pool must be the most beautiful in The Gambia, its curves inspired by the positions of the trees bounding the natural clearing chosen for the site. The lodge's eco-friendly credentials aren't impeccable – the pool uses a lot of water, there's a diesel generator, and mahogany features heavily in the construction – but there are, at least, solar-powered lights, and the waterside rooms have composting toilets, designed to avoid polluting the *bolon*.

A little further downstream, *Joyea Lodge*, a low-cost alternative to *Mandina*, is currently being renovated. This creekside lodge has timber cabin rooms, plenty of space to camp, and a large garden; it will have a huge new *à la carte* restaurant with the same kind of swagger as the gorgeous timber constructions at Makasutu, and also a swimming pool.

Pirang Forest Park

East of Brikama, between the main south bank highway and the River Gambia, the well-watered landscape is broken into an attractive and varied patchwork of salt flats, rice fields, vegetable gardens and woodland, bordered by mangroves. For birdwatchers and walkers, the area's finest asset is **PIRANG FOREST PARK**, a 64-hectare pocket of beautiful riverine gallery forest 11km from Brikama, immediately northwest of the village of Pirang. It's accessible in well under an hour from the resorts (2km before Pirang, a track leading off the highway, marked by an Irrigation Project signboard, takes you there) and is perfect for gentle strolling –its proximity to a wide variety of habitats makes it particularly rich in bird species.

A community-run conservation group, the Pirang-Bonto Ecotourism Project (☎ 448 7071 or 983 9186), plans to protect the forest, charging a small entrance fee and possibly building visitor facilities including hides and an eco-lodge; for now visitors can wander freely, with or without a local guide, along winding forest tracks made by palm-wine tappers and cattle. Pirang's mighty trees and abundance

Birdwatching around Pirang

Cool, shady and rich in vegetation, Pirang Forest Park is home to an impressive list of **forest species** including green crombecs, white-spotted flufftails, western bluebills, green hylias, various turacos, greenbuls, sparrowhawks, noisy African pied hornbills and all three of The Gambia's more common species of honeyguide. The paths which skirt the forest offer the clearest view of the birds. Carry on beyond the forest towards the mangroves and the disused shrimp pools and you're likely to see eagles, black-headed herons and, possibly, black-crowned cranes – rare in this part of the country. Parakeets and brown-necked parrots sometimes roost in the lofty palms.

of birds (more easily heard than seen among the dark, dense foliage) offer a glimpse of the way Abuko used to be before its wildlife began to thin out through water shortages and human disturbance. As well as birds, you may come across dragonflies, clouds of rare butterflies (particularly abundant late in the year), and bold, gregarious families of mongoose, skittering across the tracks.

Tumani Tenda

TUMANI TENDA is a hamlet in a picturesque location deep in the Gambian countryside, on the banks of the Kafuta Bolon, about 3km north of the main south bank highway, around 25km east of Brikama. It's home to a Jola community of seven extended families, and in many ways it's a typical rural village – but unlike many similar small communities it has the special distinctions of being economically self-sufficient, and of being the site of a community-run ecotourism project. Visitors are able to spend a day or longer at Tumani Tenda, learning about traditional rural culture and enjoying the peaceful environment.

In 1997, the villagers were awarded a £2000 prize for outstanding community forest husbandry, with the proviso that the money be spent on a community project. The result was ⚒ *Kachokorr Camp* (☎990 3662 or 984 5823, ⓦwww.tumanitenda .co.uk, ❷), established as a base for visitors, 500m from the village itself, in thin woodland right on the edge of the creek.

To **get to Tumani Tenda**, you can phone the camp manager to arrange a pick-up, travel all the way by private taxi, or take a bush taxi from Serrekunda or Brikama heading for Bulok or Bwiam, and get off at the signposted track between Sotokoi and Bulok. You may have to walk the final 2.5km stretch into the village and to the camp beyond. The camp has accommodation for around thirty people in very simple rooms in thatched huts with little more than a bed, window and mosquito net. There's a separate washing block, and everything is spotless. It's rarely busy, as the villagers have made it a policy not to invite tour groups in order to minimize the impact of visitors on community life. Near the creekside is an attractive *bantaba* with a bar, a kitchen, hammocks, and a huge dining table.

Some visitors come here just to enjoy the complete peace – the camp has no electricity or phone and vehicles seldom come anywhere near here. Others come to experience something of village life, and there are plenty of activities to choose from, including guided tours of the village, the school, plantations, and vegetable gardens, on foot or by cart; walking in the rice fields and community forest, where medicinal plants are gathered; exploring the mangrove creeks by dugout canoe;

fishing for tilapia and ladyfish; salt-making, oyster-gathering, batik-making and tie-dying. There's a flat fee of €7 per group for each activity. In the evening, the villagers can arrange a night of traditional Jola drumming and dancing, including the re-enactment of tribal ceremonies (€17). Meals are provided using local ingredients including fish from the *bolon* and fruit and vegetables from the orchards and gardens.

All the money raised from visitors goes to community projects such as running the nursery school, fencing the vegetable gardens, planting trees in the forest, and buying new dugout canoes for the fishermen and oyster-collectors. The camp is entirely owned and managed by the villagers themselves, and is very much a shared enterprise.

△ Kachokorr camp, Tumani Tenda

Village children are taught to view visitors neither as aliens nor as patrons – you won't hear any yells of "*toubab!*" here.

The *Kachokorr Camp* **guides** speak good English and are friendly without being pushy. The only slight disappointment is that the camp is distinctly separate from the village, so if you'd like a true sense of integration as a guest you have to make sure your guide knows this: there's nothing to stop you spending a day with the villagers as they work in the rice fields or clear land to plant new cassava, or you could just hang out under one of the village *bantabas* with some of the kids. You could also plan an excursion to the Bama Kuno and Kahlenge forests, a couple of kilometres to the west, both of which are excellent for birdwatching. The best way to get the most out of a stay at Tumani Tenda is to come with a clear objective in mind – the guides are not very proactive in "entertaining" guests, but respond well to suggestions and requests for particular activities.

Marakissa

South of Brikama are the villages of Marakissa and Darsilami, reached by way of attractive stretches of savannah, palm stands and woodland. It's a quiet rural area that's popular with birdwatchers and other wildlife enthusiasts, especially since the recently constructed Allahein dam has kept the area well-watered. The road from Brikama is unmade, and the red dust becomes boggy and impassable during the rainy season, but in the dry season bush taxis ply the route several times a day.

MARAKISSA is a quiet rural village of around five thousand inhabitants, 6km south of Brikama. A little under 3km south of the village, on the road to Darsilami, is *Marakissa River Camp* (☎777 9487, Netherlands ☎31-613/646974, ✉marakissa@planet.nl; ❸). This lodge, owned and managed by a Dutch/

Birdwatching around Marakissa

The area around Marakissa is particularly good for kingfishers (including the African pygmy kingfisher), raptors, rollers, and parties of **migrating waders** and other birds. Black crake are seen regularly around the pond by the bridge over the River Allahein, between the village and *Marakissa River Camp*, and African green pigeons are sometimes seen in the village. The grassland around the lodge is also good birdwatching territory, with Verreaux's eagle owls, various species of snipe, yellow-throated leaf-loves and hammerkops all seen in the vicinity. North of the lodge, the Marakissa Community Bird Sanctuary (D50) is a good place to spot white-breasted cuckoo shrikes and spotted honeyguides.

Gambian partnership, is a little run down but beautifully located: it's in a palm grove on a lovely meander in the River Allahein, close to the Senegalese border. There are five rooms in small huts which are cool even in the heat of the day; all have mosquito nets, screened windows, and fresh, northern European-style decor. Solar panels power the water pump and a few lights; apart from that, you have to rely on candles and lanterns. The restaurant, which serves basic meals at reasonable prices, is open to non-residents (groups should call ahead); above it is a sun trap of a roof terrace, with a great vantage point overlooking the river. It's a quiet spot and keen birdwatchers will typically clock up sightings of more than one hundred species in a morning here, including hornbills, plantain eaters, kingfishers, pelicans, African spoonbills and grey-headed bush shrikes. It's also a good place just to relax and watch the sun dip behind the palms in the late afternoon. There have been no recent sightings of crocodiles in the river, so people do swim there, but you should be very cautious and never swim alone.

The Senegalese border post, 4km south of Marakissa at the unremarkable village of **Darsilami**, is lax enough to be used by smugglers from time to time. This makes it an awkward border crossing for tourists, as you may get a Gambian exit stamp but no Senegalese entry stamp, creating problems later on. If you're going to Kafountine on the Casamance coast from Serrekunda or Brikama, it's much easier to take the main road south towards Ziguinchor and go through the border formalities at Séléti.

Travel details

This is a brief summary of journey durations and frequencies; more thorough details are given throughout the chapter.

Bush taxis

Brikama to: Bansang (9–11hr); Basse (10–12hr); Sankulay Kunda for Janjanbureh (8–10hr); Serrekunda (30min); Soma (4–6hr); plus to Séléti, Senegal, for other towns and villages in Casamance.

The north bank:
Niumi district

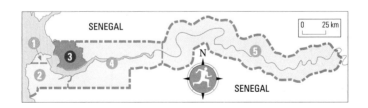

CHAPTER 3 # Highlights

❋ **Dolphin-watching** Between November and January, bottle-nose dolphins are regularly seen cruising in schools along the Atlantic coast or leaping in the bow waves of boats in the mouth of the River Gambia. See p.189

❋ **Juffureh** This north bank village, made famous by Alex Haley's novel *Roots*, is home to a small but thought-provoking slave trade museum. See p.193

❋ **James Island** Squabbled over for decades by the Portuguese, British and French, this tiny midriver island's fort is now a crumbling ruin, but remains a tangible reminder of slave trading days. See p.197

❋ **Jinack Island** An appealing back-to-basics retreat for nature-lovers, with remote beaches, woodland savannah, mangrove creeks and traditional villages to explore on foot or by *pirogue*. See p.201

△ James Island

The north bank: Niumi district

S eparated from the Kombo peninsula by the wide brown mouth of the River Gambia, **NIUMI DISTRICT** is worlds apart in pace and style from the tourist and residential development mushrooming to the south. It's a district that's rich in historical sites and areas of natural interest, but the shortage of hotels, lodges or camps this side of the river means that, for now, few visitors end up staying here overnight. Most choose instead to dip in and out for a day on a *Roots* tour to **Juffureh, Albreda** and **James Island**, or a road-and-river trip to **Jinack Island**, part of **Niumi National Park** on the Atlantic coast. Others only see Niumi fleetingly, through a car window: long-distance travellers heading from Banjul to Dakar and elsewhere in northern Senegal tend to rush straight across the district via the overlanders' corridor that connects Niumi's small district capital of **Barra** with the border post at **Amdallai**. For some visitors, however, the limitations of Niumi's tourist infrastructure are a positive attribute: Niumi is largely unspoilt, and can be a supremely relaxing region to spend a few days.

Much of Niumi District is very accessible by public or private transport. The ferry from Banjul can churn across the estuary to Barra in under thirty minutes on a good day, and while few visitors would choose to spend long in Barra itself, both Juffureh and Jinack Island are less than an hour away overland by private transport (a little longer with bush taxis). The road from Barra to Kerewan, 52km to the east in Baddibu district, is in excellent condition and opens up much of inland Niumi, including the village of **Berending**, famous in the surrounding area for its sacred crocodile pool.

Meanwhile, for those keen to spend time off the beaten track, there are rural backroads ideal for exploring on two wheels or four. The region is scattered with traditional **Fula and Mandinka villages**, mostly clutches of thatch-roofed huts surrounded by mango trees, rhun palms and baobabs, and you may find places to stay in family compounds. The backroads are no more than rough tracks, and the best time to explore them is the first few months of the dry season, when the going is firm but the vegetation is still spectacularly lush.

Upper Niumi is an essential stop for anyone interested in the history of the West African slave trade. Human beings were among the most valuable commodities bought and sold here between the seventeenth and nineteenth centuries, and the tiny but informative **National Museum of the North**

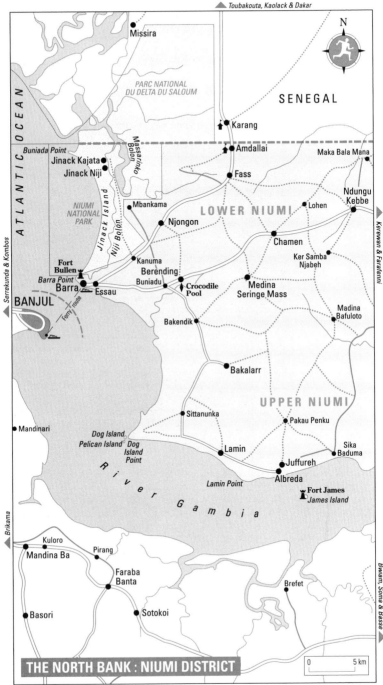

THE NORTH BANK : NIUMI DISTRICT

0   5 km

Bank in the village of **Juffureh** pulls no punches in documenting the grisly details. Juffureh itself was just another rural backwater when, in the 1960s, African-American author Alex Haley's genealogical researches first led him here. Believing (somewhat implausibly) that he had found his ancestral home, he went on to enshrine the village in his novel *Roots*, catapulting Juffureh, its inhabitants, and The Gambia itself into the international spotlight. It's still Niumi district's busiest destination – and up-country Gambia's most famous village – receiving large groups of visitors on peak days in the tourist season.

△ North bank villagers

While Juffureh's claim to fame as a historical site is rather arbitrary, there are less questionable remnants of The Gambia's pre-colonial past in the immediate vicinity. The badly ruined period buildings in the riverside village of **Albreda**, the bush-covered architectural remains of **San Domingo** and the crumbling fort on **James Island** were all once European trading stations. Together, Juffureh, Albreda, San Domingo and James Island comprise The Gambia's most cherished cultural heritage site, and the area figures prominently in the country's biennial **International Roots Festival** (see p.68).

Another attraction of Niumi district is its unusually rich **biodiversity**, mostly overlooked by the *Roots* pilgrims and Dakar-bound travellers who pass through at speed. Bounded by the Atlantic coast to the west and the last lazy sweep of the River Gambia to the south, and watered by snaking creeks and streams, the district is little-affected by the encroaching aridity of the Sahel, and during the rains the bush is gorgeously green. **Birdwatchers** visit in search of species rarely seen south of the river, and there are plenty of reptiles and mammals here, including the rare, extremely shy West African manatee and a leopard or two. The northwest coastal region forms part of **Niumi National Park**, a little-known protected area that neighbours Senegal's Saloum Delta. Glimpses of this wilderness of beaches, wetlands and woodland savannah feature on a few tour operators' itineraries. To do the park justice, however, it's worth staying for a few days on **Jinack Island**, a remote and peaceful corner of The Gambia that's becoming a favourite stopover for nature-lovers, its unspoilt coastal, wetland and savannah habitats harbouring a varied wildlife population.

Barra

The small town of **BARRA** is the kind of place you pass through rather than choose to visit for its own sake. Barra's defining feature is its **ferry**, which connects the north bank of the River Gambia with Banjul, around 5km away. For traffic and travellers heading north from Banjul and Kombo district, the terminal is the gateway to Niumi and Jokadu districts in northwest Gambia, and a pivotal point on the route to Kaolack and Dakar in Senegal. Heading south, those travelling from northwest Gambia or Senegal and aiming for southwest Gambia or Casamance converge on Barra, since the next point on the river with a regular public ferry service is over 60km up-country, just south of Farafenni, at Bambatenda. All this traffic gives the otherwise impoverished Barra a distinctive bustle; it's rare for the town not to be crowded with people either actively on the move or kicking their heels waiting for a ferry or vehicle to materialize.

If you find yourself with time to spare between transport connections, you could do worse than nose around the daily **market** which runs from the main market hall in the town centre right down to the pedestrian exit from the ferry terminal, selling seasonal produce and a jumble of shoes, clothing and household items. Those with an interest in military history should investigate the squat hulk of **Fort Bullen**, built by the British in the early nineteenth century. The fort is visible from the river crossing, on the grassy shore at Barra Point on the northwestern edge of town. The town's only other landmark is its groundnut-loading plant, looming over the wharf near the ferry and disused for most of the year, with Serer boatbuilders working on the shore close by.

Some history

In the nineteenth century, Barra had a significant role in Britain's armed crusade to stamp out the slave trade in this part of West Africa. Britain outlawed slave trading in all its territories in 1807; however, the French and Portuguese slavers based on the River Gambia defied the ban. As a result, in 1816, the British leased Banjul Island and set up the **Bathurst Six Gun Battery** on the shore to police the river mouth.

Since the Bathurst cannons lacked sufficient range to cover the whole breadth of the river, **Barra Point** was chosen as the site of a second battery. However, acquiring the land on which to establish this defensive position proved problematic. In the early nineteenth century, Barra Point was the southwestern limit of the Mandinka kingdom of **Niumi**, which had several capitals, one of which was at Essau, the village on the eastern edge of what is now Barra. The British traders at the new settlement of Bathurst had for some time been harassed and intimidated by the natives of Niumi, the Niuminka; the fortification of Barra Point was intended not only to restrict the movement of slave ships, but also to guard against the possibility of land-based attack. It was only in 1826, after a period of lengthy negotiations and, finally, naval pressure, that Mansa (king) Burungai Sonko of Niumi agreed to hand over the mile-wide strip of his people's shoreland where Barra now stands.

Over the next ten years, **Fort Bullen** (named after regional naval commander Commodore Charles Bullen) was built. Straightforward defence, however, was not the fort's sole purpose; as long as they could be said to be upholding the law, British naval vessels had free rein to harass their enemies the French under suspicion of illicit slave trading, and the fort provided artillery backup for this. The cannons proved a successful deterrent, and the fort was to see little active conflict. It was abandoned in 1870, but adapted for service by the British once again at the beginning of World War II, when Senegal, having sided with the Vichy government in France, posed a potential threat.

Practicalities

The Banjul to Barra vehicle and passenger **ferry service** and the less sluggish but more precarious passenger **pirogues** operate daily (see box on p.102). Most of the **road** traffic into Barra is heading from Senegal to the northeast, or from Kerewan and Farafenni in up-country Gambia.

If you arrive in Barra as a foot passenger on the ferry from Banjul, you'll find it difficult to avoid the **bush taxi garage**, close to the ferry terminal – the crowds and hustlers will all jostle you in that direction, and you'll be greeted by taxi touts as soon as you enter.

Dolphin-watching

The sight of **dolphins** plunging in the bow wave adds an unexpected touch of magic to the otherwise prosaic experience of crossing the mouth of the River Gambia by the Banjul–Barra ferry. Small schools of bottle-nose dolphins are regular visitors to the area around Barra, especially between November and January, and sometimes venture upstream: very occasionally, they're seen as far east as James Island. The Gambia's Atlantic coast north of Barra is sometimes patrolled by Atlantic hump-backed dolphins, endemic to this part of West Africa. Several tour operators (see p.48 & p.147) offer dolphin-watching trips that take you out by boat to the most likely parts of the Gambia estuary. Sightings are far from guaranteed, but the cruise is, nonetheless, enjoyable for its own sake.

Moving on from Barra

For details of **ferries** and **pirogues** from Barra to Banjul, see the box on p.102. **Bush taxis** from Barra run to Kerewan (D30 by van; 1hr) and Farafenni (D60 by van or D75 by car; 3hr) via Berending (15min) and Kuntair (45min); to Albreda and Juffureh (D20 by van; 1hr); to Jinack Kajata in Niumi National Park (D20 by Land Rover; 40min); and to Amdallai at the Senegalese border (D18 by van or D30 by car; 1hr), where travellers to Kaolack and Dakar will need to change vehicles. A slow and unreliable daily **bus** service runs from Barra to Dakar (see p.204); all other buses from Barra are suspended. The **road** from Barra to Fass and Amdallai is long overdue to be rebuilt; at the time of writing it was still pockmarked with potholes all the way. The 55km laterite road from Kerewan to Farafenni is also scheduled to be rebuilt: for now it's a bumpy and dusty two-hour drive. By contrast, the road from Essau just outside Barra to the bridge crossing the Jowara Bolong at Kerewan is a ribbon of perfect tarmac.

Barra has a couple of petrol stations, a Gamtel office and some telecentres, and a few moneychangers dealing in CFA, particularly around the areas of the market and bush taxi garage. There's only one **hotel**, the *Barra Hotel* (☎779 5134; ❶), close to the ferry dock – after leaving the terminal, follow the road towards Fort Bullen by bearing left. It's badly run down, with grubby and uncomfortable rooms, unreliable water and power, and questionable security, so is only worth considering if you're stranded on the way to or from Banjul.

Eating and drinking possibilities are as you'd expect in a town that is essentially a transport stop – you'll find plenty of very simple bars, eateries and street vendors around the market, ferry terminal, and bush taxi garage, all within easy walking distance of each other: a good choice is *Awa Jarra Jensuma*, a local restaurant near the terminal.

Fort Bullen

Proclaimed a national monument in the 1970s, **Fort Bullen** (Mon–Sat 8am–7pm; D50) was built over the course of a decade or so from 1826, and stands as a lasting reminder of the British campaign to eradicate slavery in West Africa. While earlier European-built forts like Fort James on James Island (see p.199) had been set up for the express purpose of exploiting West Africa's natural resources, slaves included, for profit, Fort Bullen is different: it postdates the British abolition of the slave trade, and the presence of its cannons helped enforce the ban. Today, its primary function is to house the navigation light that marks Barra Point. The Gambia's National Council for Arts and Culture had hoped a **restoration programme** would give Fort Bullen a new lease of life as a performance space. In reality, however, the fort is seldom visited, and the old officers' quarters within the courtyard, earmarked for a tiny museum, remain empty.

While the history of Fort Bullen is interesting, the building itself has little to detain you for long. The fort is essentially an open courtyard enclosed by a rectangle of low, sturdy walls of russet-coloured laterite stone, cemented with oystershell lime and patched up with concrete. There's a commanding view of the estuary and the northern shoreline from the circular bastions, one in each corner – with binoculars, you can pick out the massive perimeter wall of the State House in Banjul, behind which the Six Gun Battery, counterpart to Fort Bullen's cannons, is hidden. The southeast bastion still

Birdwatching around Barra

The Atlantic shoreline and the mouth of the Niji Bolon north of Barra, and the tidal mudflats near Essau to the east, are home to a unique combination of bird species, including some rarely seen on the south bank of the river. Among the species recorded here recently are African darter, lesser crested tern, black-headed heron, crested lark, white-billed buffalo weaver, African goshawk, blue-cheeked bee-eater, black-eared wheatear, village indigobird and white-rumped seedeater.

contains a World War II anti-aircraft gun emplacement – disarmed, stuck fast, and overgrown by a tree. In the opposite corner of the courtyard is a magazine uncovered during restoration work, but quickly refilled with rubble when a stash of live ammunition was discovered inside. Lying in the grass outside the fortifications are three cannons including one, trained across the river, which is said still to be loaded.

The elegant but decrepit timber house on stilts at Barra Point, near the fort, was once a government rest house, but is now defunct. At low tide it's possible to cross the Niji Bolon near the point onto Jinack Island (see p.201) and walk along the beach; it's an isolated stretch, with gulls and terns overhead and wading birds picking along the shoreline.

Around Barra

Barra's hinterland is dominated by its busy transport route – a high volume of Senegambian traffic thunders in and out of town and tears along the **road to Senegal**. As well as bush taxis and haulage vehicles, this region also sees tourist trucks on a pretty regular basis: some group day-trips to Jinack Island which take in the *bolons* of Niumi National Park (see p.201) drive northeast through **Fass**, **Amdallai** and **Karang** in order to approach the park's remarkable wetlands from the Senegalese side of the border.

Away from the road to Senegal, the countryside around Barra is peaceful, thinly scattered with villages where chickens scuttle across compounds fenced with palm fronds and women work in well-watered vegetable plots. The bush here is luxuriant in the rainy season and the first months of the dry season, with mango and cashew trees shading the villages and mature palm stands fringing the horizon.

South of Barra, the lower River Gambia curves gracefully into a bay, thickly bordered with mangroves, and fed by the Buniadu Bolon that flows down from **Berending**, a village easily accessible from Barra. Berending's sacred crocodile pool is lusher, quieter and more rural in feel than the much-visited Katchikali pool in Bakau, though the chances of actually seeing any crocodiles are slim. Marking the bay's southern point are the small rocky outcrops of **Dog Island** and **Pelican Island**.

The route to Senegal

Travelling along the main road from Barra towards Dakar or the Saloum Delta National Park in Senegal, the last Gambian town vehicles pass through before the border is the small but busy commercial settlement of **Fass**. Here, opportunistic traders pitch their stalls along the highway – even butchers, whose stock can't be improved by exposure to the fumes and dust stirred up by passing traffic. The only reason to stop is to pick up basic provisions if you're travelling long-distance independently. The shell-and-tar road that leads between Barra and the border is, at the time of writing, in desperate need of repair, the potholes deepened by the lorries that ply this route.

Travellers heading into Senegal are required to stop at the tiny border town of **Amdallai** to clear customs and have passports stamped by immigration. On passing through Amdallai, you are immediately in Senegal; at **Karang**, 2km north, there are Senegalese border formalities to complete. The change of atmosphere is immediate, not least because of the French signage everywhere, and the sudden improvement in the road surface. Both Amdallai and Karang have clutches of market stalls, itinerant hawkers and a few money-changers. If you're travelling between Gambia and Senegal by bush taxi, it's normally necessary to change vehicles a couple of times (see box on p.101). From Karang, it's a drive of around four hours to Dakar, or less than an hour to the attractive, though pricey, tourist lodges in Toubacouta and Missirah, both good jumping-off points for excursions into the rich wetland environment of the Saloum delta.

Berending

The small Mandinka village of **BERENDING** lies 8km east of Barra, on the smooth new Kerewan road that forks off the road to Senegal a couple of kilometres beyond Barra. The village is unremarkable except for its **crocodile pool** nearby. Like its more famous counterpart at Katchikali in Bakau (see p.127), the pool is a sacred place, and pilgrims come here to offer prayers to the ancestral spirits represented by the Nile crocodiles lurking, rarely seen, in its weed-clogged waters. Typically, the supplicants are women desperate to conceive, or farmers wishing for a bumper harvest. Visitors will be lucky to see any crocodiles, but it's a picturesque spot.

The crocodile pool is one of a series of small pools linked by stands of reeds and surrounded by rhun palms and luxuriant shrub foliage. Villagers bathe and wash their clothes in the water, apparently unperturbed by any potential threat, but if you ask them where the crocodiles are, they'll all point together in the same direction to one particular pool. Its custodians are the Sonko family, descendants of Burungai, the incalcitrant Mandinka king who caused

Dog Island

Dog Island, an uninhabited rocky outcrop barely 300m long and 150m wide, and its smaller neighbour **Pelican Island**, are passed on the river route from Banjul to Juffureh and Albreda (see *Roots* tours, pp.198–199). Both islands lie close to the north bank of the River Gambia at Dog Island Point. Dog Island was named by Portuguese explorers who heard loud barking as they approached; this turned out to be baboons, but the name stuck.

The island was briefly colonized by the British during the 1660s, who built a fort on it and named it Fort Charles after their monarch, Charles II, but found it impossible to defend as anybody could walk across the mud from the riverbank to the island at low tide. It's possible to make the same crossing today, in theory, though in practice access to this part of the bank is awkward and the scrap of wilderness that is the island is rarely visited. Nothing of the fort remains, partly because in the nineteenth century the island was used as a source of stone recycled as building material for the new city of Bathurst and its river defence at Fort Bullen.

so much trouble to the British settlers in Niumi in the early nineteenth century. If you have time, and an interpreter, you can learn the entire family history from the elder who is currently the senior guardian. If you'd like to visit the pool you should, in any case, make a polite visit to the *alkalo* of the village, and ask for a local guide.

Berending is easy to reach by public transport: **bush taxis** from Barra or Kerewan will stop here on request. The village is marked by a vast silk cotton tree close to the main road. To find the *alkalo*'s compound, take the sandy road that leads off the main road northwards opposite this tree into the main part of the village, and ask somebody to point it out. The pool itself is then reached by returning to the main road and taking the track that leads off southwards, just before the silk cotton tree if approaching from Barra.

Juffureh, Albreda and James Island

The area around the Mandinka villages of **JUFFUREH** and **ALBREDA**, which rub shoulders on the north bank of the River Gambia, is The Gambia's longest-established destination for heritage tourists. This corner of Upper Niumi would have had its place on the tourist circuit even if Alex Haley's novel *Roots* had never made Juffureh internationally famous: it includes **JAMES ISLAND** and **San Domingo**, two of the few sites in The Gambia in which ruins of buildings dating from the slave trading era still exist.

Most visitors are escorted around briefly on one-day **Roots tours** – an enjoyable excursion, though seriously over-rated as a meaningful experience. The district is rich in history, and deserves greater attention than a high-speed visit can afford. Juffureh itself has an interesting little **National Museum**, and is a good place to take the opportunity to stay in a simple village lodge. When there's a tour group around, the villages have a hectic, slightly artificial "show-time" atmosphere, and the hassle from locals can be persistent. However, after the tourist boats and vehicles have departed for the day, the villages become serene once more, with women chatting good-humouredly to their neighbours, men lounging under the *bantabas*, and children chasing home-made toys through the sandy streets.

Some history

From the fifteenth century onwards, the region that is now The Gambia was a crucial base for European traders. **San Domingo** was settled by the Portuguese in the early fifteenth century and, later, by the British, as a retreat and a source of fresh water for troops from the midriver trading station of Fort James, on James Island. It was at San Domingo that African middlemen of the **Luso** tribe acted as host brokers in trading slaves for commodities such as cloth and guns.

Albreda, too, was once a trading station, where not only slaves but also gold and vast quantitites of ivory changed hands. The station was controlled by the French from 1681 to 1857, and was one of Senegambia's four principal slave "factories". Two of the others, St Louis and Gorée Island, both in what is now Senegal, were also in French hands; the fact that the fourth, Fort James, not far offshore from Albreda, was more often than not occupied by the rival British, caused a near-permanent state of high tension in the region. It was largely thanks to their good relationship with the local Mandinka population that the British managed to cling onto another, smaller, trading base at **Juffureh**, which remained active until the early nineteenth century when the traders diverted their energies into developing the new commercial settlement of Bathurst (now Banjul).

Alex Haley and Roots

There's no doubt that The Gambia owes the African-American author **Alex Haley** a debt of gratitude. Before 1977, the year that Haley's bestseller **Roots** won the Pulitzer Prize and the television mini-series based on the novel broke all previous popularity records (over 130 million viewers tuned in to the first run in the US), few Americans, black or white, had heard of The Gambia, and even fewer could point to it on the map. Wittingly or otherwise, Haley blazed the trail for a new brand of West African tourism that's still thriving – the ancestral homecoming tour.

Roots is a rambling family saga that spans two centuries, describing the Juffureh boyhood of a young Mandinka named **Kunta Kinte**, his capture by white slavers in the 1760s, and the horrors of his lengthy Atlantic voyage, then following his fortunes and those of his family, generation by generation, as they struggle through life on the plantations in America's Deep South. Haley claimed that his celebrated novel was inspired by the experience of meeting the people of Juffureh, and sensing a deep spiritual connection with them that, he felt, confirmed a shared ancestry centuries old.

Haley first set foot in Juffureh in 1967. During his visit, his escorts assured him that Juffureh *griot* **Kebba Kanji Fofana** had a detailed knowledge of the history of the Kinte clan that stretched back many generations; Haley hoped that Fofana's histories might include reference to Kinte, from whom he was directly descended, and whose name had been preserved in the oral history of his American family. Sure enough, Fofana's tales included one about Kunta Kinte, which seemed to match the story that Haley had learned on his grandmother's front porch.

From the way that Haley describes his encounter with Fofana in the epilogue of *Roots*, it's evident that the *griot* had been primed prior to Haley's visit, and cynics have suggested that Fofana simply recited a story he knew Haley wanted to hear, passing it off as genuine history (possibly under pressure from Haley's escorts, who were anxious to satisfy their client, possibly with an eye on the potential rewards). What's certain is that Haley was profoundly moved by his encounter with the Juffureh villagers. He describes the bewildered shame he felt on comparing his own brown skin to the dark colour of the Mandinkas, as if he were "impure among the pure", and the paradox of feeling intimately connected to these people, yet isolated by his inability to understand their language. It was this encounter that led him to spend the next nine years of his life working on *Roots*.

Haley, already well known as a Black Power activist and as the author of *The Autobiography of Malcolm X*, which sold over six million copies, now found an eager audience in a generation of African-Americans who had allowed themselves to be persuaded that they were not so much Americans as victims of Americanization, and that they and their ancestors were a lost African people. Inspired by Haley's search, both academic and literal, for a corner of West Africa that he could claim as his ancestral home, others wanted to do the same. Those that had no way of pinpointing the geographical origin of any of their forbears chose to make a symbolic journey instead, by following in Haley's footsteps to Juffureh.

Inevitably, tour operators caught on to the **commercial potential** of excursions to Juffureh. When the *Roots* industry was at its peak, thousands of African-Americans made the pilgrimage to see the village they believed Haley had been describing in the opening chapters of his book. So convincing was the hype that the author himself embraced it completely – pictures of Haley with Binta Kinte, widow of *griot* Fofana, became part of the myth of modern Gambia, used to boost the small

When, in the late 1960s, **Alex Haley** embarked on a passionate quest for the place of origin of one of his African ancestors, he found an end-of-the-line of sorts in Juffureh, and the inspiration to write his bestselling novel. Haley, and

country's respectability on the world stage. But then the rumour came out that Haley had already written his Africa passages when he first came here, which explains why his descriptions of Juffureh don't quite fit with the location of today's village. The likelihood that Juffureh used to be 1km from its present site does little to iron out the inconsistencies. In Haley's account, Kunta Kinte is surprised by a party of slave-raiders – an implausible fate for anyone from Juffureh, whose inhabitants had been living more or less shoulder to shoulder with the traders at San Domingo, Albreda and Fort James all their lives. Kinte's captors were white Europeans, but it's extremely unlikely that the slave-raiders who supplied the buyers at the River Gambia trading stations were white.

Haley made a crucial mistake in presenting his novel as "fictionalized fact", taking creative reconstruction to an extreme. Research by investigative reporter Philip Nobile and others has shown that many of the key characters described in the book never existed. Even if we forgive Haley's feeling a stronger familial identification with Kunta Kinte than with any of his 63 other sixth-generation forbears, it's hard to understand why he seemed so determined to persuade his audience that the Kintes of present-day Juffureh were definitely his own people: Kinte is a common enough family name, and the story Fofana told, taken by Haley as proof of the connection, was a simple and familiar history. Doubts about Haley's motives exploded into a near-total debunking of the *Roots* story when, in 1979, writer Harold Courlander success-fully sued for **plagiarism** – significant chunks of *Roots* were proved to have been lifted almost verbatim from Courlander's 1967 novel *The African*. Haley's publishers coughed up the bulk of Courlander's $650,000 settlement, and all interested parties rallied to protect Haley from further discreditation.

Even after Haley's death from a heart attack in 1992, powerful forces continued to work to preserve the *Roots* myth and when, in 1997, the BBC produced a docu-mentary based on Nobile's damning investigations, US television networks refused to show it. Their argument was that any critical examination of what was by now a sacrosanct work of African-American literature could spark a race-related incident. In 2002, Haley's younger brother George, who served as US Ambassador to The Gambia from 1998 to 2000, unveiled a Kunta Kinte–Alex Haley memorial in Annapo-lis, Maryland, as if to cast the myth in stone. Today, the future of the *Roots* message is in the hands of a Florida investor, who bought all the literary rights and royalties for $10,000 after Myran Haley, the author's widow, filed for bankruptcy.

While *Roots* earned Haley several million dollars, there's little evidence that much of it ever found its way to Juffureh: Haley put up the cash for a new village mosque, and the Kinte compound seems more affluent than some, but most villagers still live very simply. Tourists on organized trips pay a tour operator to take them there; few spend much time, or money, in the village.

Haley himself claimed that his intention had always been to "give his people some myths to live by". In this he has been extremely successful, despite the controversy since his novel was published. Historical inaccuracies aside, *Roots* tells a story that's still well worth reading. The several millions of copies sold since 1976 have played a significant part in raising awareness about the transatlantic slave trade and its legacy, as well as stimulating debate about origin and identity within black communities of the diaspora. And the villagers of Juffureh are still proud of the fame that Haley's saga bestowed upon them; "Yes, the story is just a story," they'll tell you, "but the history behind it is true."

the myth-making machine that his novel engendered, turned this corner of the North Bank into a legend. The Gambia's tourist industry was quick to grasp the potential of the *Roots* connection, but slow to develop it in a sustainable fashion. For years, visitors to Juffureh, black or white, brought here by their curiosity as to whether or not their own ancestors had played a part in the story of the transatlantic slave trade, found themselves in a hot, dusty village, besieged by children, and with little to see but villagers carrying out traditional roles to order – pounding millet and tinkering with carvings. It was only in 1996 that Juffureh seemed to realize it was time to rethink what it was actually offering visitors. The creation of the small but well-thought-out **Exhibition of the Slave Trade**, now a national museum (see opposite), gave the village something new of genuine interest to tourists: it remains one of the area's best features. Further improvements within the village are made prior to the biennial **International Roots Festival**. The festival programme includes a one-day pilgrimage to Juffureh, with the opportunity to follow the Roots Heritage Trail to a living reconstruction of a traditional village compound as it might have looked in Haley's supposed ancestor's time.

The villages

To the many visitors to **JUFFUREH** and **ALBREDA** who have never visited an up-country village before, it's their simplicity that makes the biggest impression. Compared to more isolated areas up-river, this region is relatively prosperous: there's an impressive new health centre nearby, and far more litter than you'd find in a place where the locals have less spending power. But the villages themselves – scattered with corrugated-roofed cottages, shady *bantabas*, goat pens, dusty lanes, gigantic trees, and gaggles of scruffy kids squawking "*toubab!*" when any white visitor comes in range – remain unremarkable. What *is* remarkable is that their simplicity has endured through three decades of world attention.

Albreda, also known as Albadarr, lies right on the north bank of the river, around 30km upstream from Barra. Its inland neighbour, Juffureh, lies so close to Albreda that the two villages have merged into one community, home to Mandinka farmers and Serer fishermen. If you're visiting Juffureh and Albreda by boat, you moor at Albreda's lengthy jetty and make your way to the village's main riverside "square", an open space dominated by towering silk cotton trees. Here, an old cannon points fiercely out across the river under a reconstruction of Albreda's **Freedom Flagpole** – legend has it that any slave who managed to break loose, make a dash for the pole, and touch it, would be granted their freedom.

Down on the shore a hundred metres or so upstream is the shell of an old trading house, the **CFAO building**, which used to be described by fanciful would-be guides as a slave house. In reality, the building may never have been used by slave traders, as it was probably built in the early nineteenth century, after the British started enforcing abolition of the trade. Albreda's other monument is a roofless structure which is billed as the "oldest chapel in West Africa" but the iron cross that marks it is clearly not original and the building was probably just a store.

To visit ruins which have a definite, documented connection with the slave trade (as opposed to more recent commercial dealings in other commodities), the most rewarding plan is to cross from Albreda to **James Island** (see opposite), but there's also another, less dramatic, site on-shore, about 1km northeast of Albreda's jetty and 500m beyond the recommended **National Museum of** the **North Bank** (see below). It's marked by a sign beside the main laterite road that leads from Juffureh to Kuntair and Kerewan. The slave traders' sub-station of **San Domingo** once stood here; all that remains is a crumbling chunk of a laterite stone building, under a much-carved baobab tree.

Nearby, an archway marks the start of the **Roots Heritage Trail**, intended as a journey of reflection: it's a gentle thirty-minute walk through the kind of creekside landscape that Alex Haley's hero Kunta Kinte, and thousands of captured Africans like him, might have longed for bitterly on the harrowing Atlantic crossing.

National Museum of the North Bank

If doubts about Alex Haley's integrity leave you in need of some solid facts about what really happened in slave trading days, it's worth visiting Juffureh's tiny **National Museum of the North Bank** (Mon–Thurs & Sat 10am–5pm, Fri 10am–1pm; D50, or D100 including Fort James on James Island). The museum is roughly on the border between the neighbouring villages of Juffureh and Albreda, a short stroll inland from Albreda's jetty: it's about 500m from the village "square" on the right-hand side, just before you reach the laterite road which connects Juffureh with Barra and Kuntair.

The permanent **Exhibition of the Slave Trade** which takes up most of the space has plenty of well-written display boards, and you'll come away with a good insight into the origins, mechanics, and eventual abolition of slavery in this part of the world. Quotes from period sources throw the brutality of capture and transportation into vivid relief. One describes how the process of branding with a hot iron "caused little pain, the mark being usually well in four to five days, appearing very plain and white thereafter", and in another, a ship's captain claims with satisfaction that out of a consignment of seven hundred slaves he "delivered 372 to the company's factors in Barbados, alive". There are a few artefacts, too: shackles, beads, and small iron bars which the Europeans used as currency to buy slaves. A coffle-yoke – an iron neck-brace with a huge lock and a heavy chain – is displayed graphically on a lifesize cutout of an African slave, suggesting just how painfully it must have dug into the wearer's neck. There's also a dusty scale model of Fort James (see p.199) which will help you visualize the place more completely if you take the trip across to James Island to visit its ruins.

Inevitably, there are some nods towards the **Kunta Kinte legend**, such as a copy of the cutting from the *Maryland Gazette* unearthed by Haley in his researches. The snippet, dated October 1, 1767, is an announcement, in which "a cargo of choice healthy slaves" are advertised for sale. This particular batch of slaves had left The Gambia on July 5, 1767 aboard a British ship named the *Lord Ligonier*, and it's certainly possible that Kunta Kinte was among them.

The Manuel Freres Building which houses the museum was British-built in the 1840s, and has the feel of a Victorian village hall transplanted from England. Outside, you'll find a *bantaba* and a booth selling drinks.

James Island

A visit to **James Island** by cruiser or *pirogue* is highly recommended to anyone interested in the history of the transatlantic slave trade. It was on this bleak, rock-strewn outcrop – barely 200m in length, and vulnerable to erosion by the relentless drag of the River Gambia's tidal waters – that many slaves spent their last days on African soil, a fact that leaves few visitors unaffected.

Situated at a pivotal defensive position midriver, 30km upstream from the Atlantic coast, James Island was one of the first European settlements in West Africa and an obvious location for a trade fort. Discovered by Portuguese explorers in the mid-fifteenth century, the island was bought two centuries later by agents of the Duke of Courland (now Latvia and Lithuania), who in 1651 set about fortifying it in order to develop trade between Courland and the West Africans living near the River Gambia. Over the century to follow, the fort was subjected to occupations, routings, sackings, desertions and rebuildings – whoever controlled the fort had almost total control over the shipment of trade goods into and out of the area. In 1661 it was seized by the British, who bundled out the Baltic occupants and set themselves up under the Royal Patent of Charles II, buying gold, ivory, peppers, hides and slaves for the American colonies – Britain's first imperial exploit in Africa.

In one mercantile guise or another, the British and the French fought over the fort for more than a century. In the late eighteenth century, friction between the two rival powers reached a peak, as France continued to run their slave trading "factory" at Albreda on the nearby shore long after

Roots tours

One-day **Roots tours** from the resorts are among The Gambia's most popular organized excursions, although rather overrated. If you're interested in learning more about the machinations of the slave trade, examining tangible relics of the old trading stations, and trying to imagine what went through the minds of the African captives as they were bundled aboard ship, never to return, you may feel frustrated. Being herded around on a *Roots* trip is not conducive to quiet contemplation, and you're likely to miss out on much of your guide's (limited) explanations, and many of the exhibits in the museum, just because there are too many heads in the way. The most you can expect is either a relaxing river cruise or a less relaxing but more scenic road trip, followed by a brief glimpse of north bank village life, with enough of a taste of the place to enable you to decide whether you'd like to arrange to stay longer, or to return another time under your own steam.

The tour groups either travel to Juffureh from Banjul by boat (generally a cruiser with two decks, offering both sun and shade, and a bar) or, much less typically, by road from Barra, having crossed on the Banjul-Barra ferry. If you're familiar with Alex Haley's *Roots* then you're likely to find the road route more interesting, as it takes you through the open country that Haley describes so vividly in the opening chapters of his book. Coming by road, you'll miss out on James Island, however, unless, once at Albreda, you make your own arrangements to get there by "unofficial" (and uninsured) *pirogue*.

The **boat trip** from Banjul typically takes a couple of hours, and begins with great views of whatever action there might be that day at the port: containers being loaded or unloaded; ships hovering midstream as they await a vacant berth; the Barra ferry churning across the estuary; passenger *pirogues* coursing through the waves. While you might be lucky enough to see dolphins at the river mouth near Banjul, the rest of the journey is a lazy cruise with little to see. The river here is salty and broad – over 12km at its broadest – and the scenery pretty monotonous, with near-featureless water banked by dense mangroves. The boats don't usually take a central course, but shallow muddy water generally prevents them from sailing close enough to the north bank for you to spot much in the way of wildlife in the foliage. Meanwhile the opposite bank is an indistinct strip of greenish-grey sandwiched between the glare of the river and the glare of the sky.

the British had opted for a new role as anti-slavers. In 1779, French troops, under orders to stamp out all potential threats to their nation's trading interests, kicked the "meddlesome" British off the island for good, and destroyed the fort. By 1829, James Island had been completely abandoned, by which time British efforts to police the river had shifted downstream to Bathurst and Barra.

The remains of **Fort James**, founded in 1651, still haunt the island. The outcrop provided only just enough space for a simple fortified arrangement of apartments, courtyards, and strategy rooms, which must have been almost as claustrophobic for the occupying troops as for the slaves housed in shed-like buildings outside the walls. Since the mid-seventeenth century, the island has shrunk considerably, and preserving the fort against further decay has become a serious concern. Today, what little remains of the fort – some crumbling bastion walls, fragments of the central administrative quarters and a few strewn cannon – is dominated by a grove of large baobabs, skeletal and streaked with guano in the dry season. There's next to nothing left of the out-buildings where slaves were held, at the southern tip of the island, furthest from the landing stage.

While Albreda's concrete jetty and massive silk cotton trees are still dots in the distance, and James Island, midriver, a vague shape beyond, a welcome party may motor up to the boat in *pirogues*: locals waving Gambian flags and shouting "Welcome back!" Thus begins the part of the trip which black visitors making the trip as a pilgrimage may find most moving. The sense of completing a river journey that might have been made centuries ago by a distant ancestor, but in reverse, is a powerful one, and the shouts of welcome as the boat approaches the jetty, increased as the visitors set foot on dry land, are likely to heighten a bittersweet feeling of homecoming in anyone psyched up about the history and mystique of the place.

Once ashore, your visit will probably include a quick skirt round the colonial buildings and the museum. You should, for the sake of politeness, be invited to pay your respects to the **alkalo**, who at the time of writing, is one of The Gambia's small minority of female village chiefs, and you may be asked to sign a battered visitors' book, just as Alex Haley did on his visits. You will definitely be escorted to the **compound of the Kinte family**, or rather to the ugly corrugated-roofed and concrete-floored meeting area attached, in which you will meet some representatives of the Kinte clan. Proudly displayed are framed **photos** of Kebba Kanji Fofana, the *griot* who impressed Alex Haley so much; of Haley with Binta Kinte, Fofana's widow; and of one of the actors who played Kunta Kinte in *Roots*; cash donations are expected for any photos you take yourself. Somewhere along the line there will be some **traditional musicians** playing (and stopping abruptly once the group has moved on). There will also be an obligatory stop at the **tourist craft market**. Few groups make the extra walk to the Roots Heritage Trail and the San Domingo ruins.

Whistlestop tour over, it's back to the boat for lunch (generally good) and the short cruise to **James Island**, if the boat didn't take you there earlier. At some point in the proceedings you may be given a photocopied "**certificate of visitation**" stating that you've visited Kunta Kinte's ancestral home, and the "popular slave prison, James Island" – so now you know it's official. (For details of operators running *Roots* tours see p.49.)

Practicalities

While most visitors to Juffureh, Albreda and James Island arrive in a **tour** group (see p.51), it's perfectly possible (and sometimes speedier) to cross to the north bank by ferry from Banjul to Barra (see p.102) and then take either a **bush taxi** for D20 or a **private taxi** (price negotiable) from the Barra taxi garage (see p.101). To reach Juffureh and Albreda with your own vehicle from Barra, take the Kerewan road to Buniadu, where you leave the tarmac by turning right and follow the laterite and sand road south. The going can be rough, and you'll need 4WD after recent rain. Approaching from Kerewan, turn left off the tarmac at the village of Kuntair and again head south along dirt tracks. The road sometimes forks with no indication of which way to follow, so it's best to keep checking with passers-by. If you'd like to travel from Kombo district by river, but not by large tour boat, check out the operators based near Denton Bridge (see p.147) outside Banjul, who can organize day-trips by small boat; one operator can whisk you from Banjul to Albreda or James Island in forty minutes by powerboat.

If you're interested in sifting through the *Roots* hype in search of Juffureh and Albreda's genuine character, then your best chance of a satisfying experience is to stay here overnight, rather than limiting yourself to a standard day-trip (see box on pp.198–199). The villages' badged Official Tourist Guides (☎990 4625, 771 0276, 990 0728) can provide local **information** – you'll generally find them at their base (the Juffureh-Albreda Youth Society office on the road to the museum, just north of Albreda's "village square") or at the *Rising Sun* (see below).

Accommodation options are limited, however. West of the "square", *Kunta Kinte Roots Camp*, (☎991 4508; ❷), a newish lodge with views towards the river and plans for a pool, has simple but pleasant thatched roundhouses and can cater for large groups of heritage tourists, but is a little lifeless if there's no group booked in – you may have to make a special request for power from the generator. The alternative is the *Juffureh Rest House*, a little beyond the museum, on the main dirt road that leads west towards Barra and northeast towards Kuntair and Kerewan (☎995 5736 or 770 1715; ❶). Founded as a community project by the French-run Kounta Kinté Association, it's used as a regular venue for residential music classes and workshops, is open to participants and non-participants, and has a friendly atmosphere. The *Rest House* has small, basic rooms with mosquito nets – some in a block, some in thatched huts – and shared washing facilities that are just about acceptable. There's a generator here, but again, if only a few people are staying, you'll have to rely on candlelight. Simple meals can be prepared if ordered in advance.

The most obvious place to **eat and drink** is the *Rising Sun Restaurant*, on the "square" by the jetty. Although unashamedly touristy and overpriced for an up-country place, it's welcoming, with a canopy roof smothered in bougainvillea and a short menu of fried standards including chicken, omelettes and garlic shrimps.

A visit to James Island is automatically included in the *Roots* day-trips which cruise up-river from the coastal resorts (see p.198). The cruisers moor at a safe distance from the island and passengers are ferried to the rickety jetty in groups by *pirogue* or launch. If you're travelling independently, you should be able to hire a **pirogue** in Albreda to take you to James Island and back (ask around near Albreda's jetty or at the *Rising Sun*; the round-trip should cost no more than D500 in total for a boat taking six passengers).

Niumi National Park and Jinack Island

North of the River Gambia, all but half a kilometre or so of the Gambian coastline lies within one of the country's most intriguing wilderness regions, **Niumi National Park** (D31.50, included in the price of organized visits, or payable at the park office near Kanuma). This protected area was gazetted in 1987 and is as yet relatively unexplored; it's possible to visit as part of an organized excursion, or independently, but either way you'll encounter few other travellers during your visit. The park's 49 square kilometres contain a remarkable range of habitats – not just the Atlantic coast with its dunes, lagoons, and shallow waters, but also dry woodland savannah, grassland, cultivated land, and saltwater wetlands. Niumi adjoins the Parc National du Delta du Saloum in Senegal, and together the parks protect one of the last remaining untouched stands of mangroves in West Africa.

At the heart of the park is the **Massarinko Bolon**, a broad mangrove-flanked creek overlooked by laterite escarpments which provide commanding lookout points. Massarinko Bolon connects with a narrower creek, the **Niji Bolon**, which runs roughly north–south, and in places is so shallow at low tide that local fishermen leave their boats midstream and continue on foot, as if walking on water. The long curving kilometre-wide strip of land west of here, between the Niji Bolon and the sea, is known as **Jinack Island** (sometimes spelt Ginak or Ginack). Like many of the beaches further south, the 10km stretch of sand along Jinack's Atlantic coast is gradually narrowing, due to tidal erosion; at high tide, the waves lap against the beach convolvulus, but at low tide the sand is broad and firm. Inland, the savannah landscape, flat and thinly wooded with baobabs, tamarisk and twisted acacia trees, is rewarding to explore on foot, especially for birdwatchers.

Niumi National Park is rich in **bird species**, including an abundance of palearctic migrants who stop here during the European winter to build up their fat reserves before continuing south. Other wildlife includes the elusive West African manatee, once hunted for meat and now few in number and very rarely seen; the endangered clawless otter; and green turtles, which lay their eggs on the beach by night. Monitor lizards, snakes, and mammals such as bushbuck, spotted hyena and even leopard are also around, but keep a low profile, although the sharp-eyed will spot plenty of tracks. More conspicuous are the large schools of bottle-nose and Atlantic humpbacked dolphins that sometimes play offshore, but their visits are only occasional – December and January are the months you're most likely to see them.

Most of Jinack Island is Gambian, but the northernmost chunk is in Senegal. The ruler-straight border that has divided the countries since colonial times slices through the island just north of Buniadu Point, but it's unmarked, and is of no great conseqence to the small population, who pass freely between the Gambian villages of **Jinack Niji** and **Jinack Kajata**, and **Djinack Diakoto** on the Senegalese side. Conveniently enough for them, the island is wreathed in mystique and taboos powerful enough to keep officials well away – local legend holds that any government law-enforcer who tries to set foot on the island will be attacked by ancient spirits. Thus the islanders pursue whatever variety of cultivation and trade they choose, notably marijuana, while the law turns a blind eye. Despite the potential for mild anarchy, visitors have no need to feel vulnerable.

Some of the tour companies (see p.49) that bring groups to Jinack Island on **day-trips** market the place as "Treasure Island" or "Paradise Island", names which conjure images of a palm-fringed coral atoll lapped by a turquoise sea,

Birdwatching in Niumi National Park

The bird population on Jinack Island has been studied in detail by a group of British ornithologists who have recorded a few rarities including European Scops owl, bar-breasted firefinch and red-footed falcon, and a nesting population of white-fronted plover. Inland, the birdwatching opportunities are outstanding, with an abundance of woodland and grassland species and seventeen species of warbler, distinguished by subtle variations in plumage. Offshore, Jinack's shallow waters provide excellent feeding for gulls and other fish-eating birds, and pelicans are often seen in and around the lagoon near Buniadu Point, where a sandspit reaches far out into the Atlantic. Here, and in Niumi National Park's beautiful mangrove creeks, hunting ospreys soar overhead with eyes trained on the water, and terns zoom downwards like darts. Equally conspicuous on mangrove perches are numerous herons and kingfishers.

setting their clients up for disappointment. In fact, Jinack doesn't really have an island feel, as it's basically a long narrow chunk of mainland that happens to be cut off by a creek, and the beach landscape is stark rather than exotic, with baobabs, not palms, punctuating the skyline, and scrub tangling over low dunes. However, Jinack does have an attractive feeling of remoteness so complete that when, after dark, the line of lights across the bay confirms just how close Banjul is, it's something of a surprise. The Atlantic beach may not conform to the tropical ideal – thanks to coastal erosion the waves lap against the scrub when the tide is at its highest – but at low tide the broad grey-blond sands are perfect for long lonely walks, and heaven for inquisitive children, with animal and bird tracks to follow, crabs to chase into their holes, and shallow water that's safe for swimming – although watch out for sea-urchins.

Visiting Niumi National Park on a standard organized day-trip from Kombo district will give you a feel for the geography and atmosphere of the place. You're likely to cruise the Massarinko Bolon and the top of the Niji Bolon by rustic *pirogue*, pass through the village of Jinack Kajata, cross Jinack Island on foot or by local cart, and have lunch under a thatched shelter on the empty beach. For wildlife enthusiasts, however, these trips are pretty much a non-starter, as you'll be cruising the wetlands and crossing the bush in the middle of the day when birds are hard to spot, the presence of the group will make mammals and reptiles even shyer than usual, and your guide may not be as clued up about the local ecology as you might like – some tourists come away from "Treasure Island" excursions without even realizing they've spent most of the day in a national park.

Practicalities

Most visitors arrive on organized excursions from the resorts. To reach Niumi National Park by public transport, however, you can take one of the infrequent Jinack-bound **bush taxis** from Barra (D20), which set off up the road towards Fass and Senegal and turn left into the park at Kanuma, and can drop you just across the Niji Bolon from Jinack Kajata, the second of the two Gambian villages. This road through the park, bumpy but passable without 4WD in the dry season, runs roughly north-south, parallel to the Niji Bolon. A small **pirogue** will ferry you across to the island for a fee that's negotiable depending on the size of your party (D10–25 per person is typical for a small group) – although the *bolon* may look very shallow, the presence of crocodiles makes it inadvisable to wade across. The *pirogue* owners have mobile phones, and can call a taxi for your return journey to Barra. If you'd rather not wait for a bush taxi to get you into the park, it's easy enough to hire a **private taxi** at Barra to take you to whichever part you'd like to explore independently – but be aware that taxi drivers here have a reputation for trying to overcharge, as do the *pirogue* owners at Niji Bolon and some of the would-be guides from the villages. If you make an early start and are content with the briefest of visits, it's possible to get to the park and back from Kombo district in a day.

The best way to get to the ocean side of the island and *Madiyana Safari Lodge* (see below) is to make arrangements with the owners to take you there, usually by motorized *pirogue* from Banjul for £10–12.50 each way per person, depending on group size. The run across the estuary and up the Atlantic coast of Jinack Island takes around an hour, and you may be lucky enough to spot dolphins on the way. Alternatively, from Jinack Kajata, follow the path west across the island towards the sea. It's hard to get lost – even if you miss the back gate and end up on the beach, you should be able to spot the lodge's jetty – but the village has no shortage of youngsters willing to show visitors the way. If you'd rather not walk, ask around in the village for a horse and cart (it's twenty minutes or so along sandy paths, sometimes spiky with burrs, or waterlogged, depending on the season, so tough going if you're heavily laden).

Jinack Island has a few **accommodation** and **eating** options which fit the island's best-kept-secret atmosphere perfectly: they have a back-to-basics, castaway feel. 🏕 *Madiyana Safari Lodge* (book at least 24 hours in advance through Paradise Tours, ☎449 4088 or mobile ☎992 0201, ⓦwww .paradiseisland-gambia.com, Ⓔtrawallyfoday@hotmail.com; ❷), right on the beach on the seaward side of the island, not far from the Senegalese border, is a simple but relaxing hideaway. Visitors who stop by for lunch often decide to stay here overnight, won over by the peaceful character of the place and the excellent cooking. The sleeping arrangements are romantic – a few reed-walled huts with attractive brick floors and slatted windows that dapple the mudcloth bedspreads with sunlight. The washing arrangements, however, are basic, there's no generator and cows regularly wander through the sandy garden in search of anything edible. To get the most out of a stay here, you need to be ready to enjoy simple pleasures like pottering on the beach, stargazing (the owner has a telescope), drifting off to sleep to the sound of the ocean and waking to the dawn chorus.

There are also a few budget options near the villages. In Jinack Niji, *Camara Sambou Beach Bar* (mobile ☎778 9295; ❶) right on the shore of the Niji Bolon, has a couple of very simple huts with shared bucket showers. *Dalaba Lodge* (mobile ☎992 5052 or 990 7957; ❷), inland on the western edge of Jinack Kajata, has a few rooms in thatched huts in an open sandy compound, but is rather neglected. 🏕 *Coconut Lodge* (mobile ☎994 9067 or 995 4814; ❷), between the two villages, is a better bet. The rooms here have solar electricity, and have been made bright, clean and colourful by the resident English co-owner, who runs an alternative therapy clinic for the village. With hammocks slung under the gingerbread plum trees, and generously sized meals available to order, it's a laid-back spot.

Travel details

This is a brief summary of journey durations and frequencies; more thorough details are given throughout the chapter.

Buses

Barra to: Dakar (2 daily; 6–7hr).

Ferry

Barra to: Banjul (daily, hourly on the hr; 30min–1hr).

Bush taxis

Albreda & Juffureh to: Barra (1hr); Kuntair (1hr); Farafenni (3hr).

Barra to: Albreda & Juffureh (1hr); Amdallai (1hr); Berending (15min); Kerewan (1hr); Farafenni (3hr); Kuntair (45min); Jinack Kajata (40min).

Central Gambia

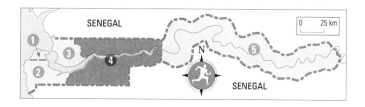

CHAPTER 4 # Highlights

* **Bintang** Pretty creekside village with a rustic lodge built over Bintang Bolon, a great place to relax for a day or two and watch life go by.
See p.211

* **Tendaba Camp** A perennially popular riverside lodge which makes an ideal base for short wildlife excursions and longer journeys up-river. See p.217

* **Kiang West National Park** A large, little-explored expanse of up-country woodland and bush, harbouring more of The Gambia's wildlife species than any other protected area in the country. See p.219

* **Farafenni** Up-country town famous for its Sunday *lumo*, a real Gambian country market, bustling with activity and bright with colourful produce and textiles. See p.224

* **Bao Bolon Wetland Reserve** One of The Gambia's most fascinating protected areas, excellent for birdwatching, with a maze of mangrove creeks to explore by boat.
See p.226

△ Festival crowd, Kanilai

Central Gambia

W ith the country's tourist industry firmly anchored in the coastal resorts, and its transport infrastructure in desperate need of improvement, even the briefest journey into central Gambia can feel like an adventure. Up-country road travel can be exhausting, so it's best not to rush your explorations. However, if you have time to spare there is plenty to discover a few hours outside the coastal areas, including accessible traditional villages, country markets and national parks.

The Gambia's two principal west–east highways, one along the south bank and one on the north, mimic the River Gambia's meanderings. The contrast between north and south is apparent as soon as you travel beyond the Kombos. On the **south bank**, the roads are dusty, potholed and tiring. Fringing the road are lofty palms, well-watered fields, and mango trees laden with fruit from May to September. Meanwhile, on the arid, impoverished but scenically inviting **north bank**, the main road has only recently been sealed for the first time, and life still moves at an unhurried pace. The central Gambian stretch of the north bank highway passes some outstanding areas of unspoilt wilderness, scattered with remote mudblock and thatch villages, where subsistence farmers sustain traditions that, in essence, have changed little for centuries.

Travelling east along the south bank highway from the Kombos, you first pass through **Foni district**, its creeks and palm groves once the haunt of European slavers who set up trading stations here, strategically located a short river crossing away from the larger outposts of Albreda and James Island. Today, by contrast, the shortage of river transport means that north–south commercial interaction of any sort is relatively rare. A major focus of development, deep in the Jola heartlands, is the village of **Kanilai**, President Jammeh's birthplace. There's an irrepressible new energy here, showing itself most plainly whenever a major festival is held.

Throughout central Gambia, there are side-tracks off the main road which quickly get you within sight of the river, broad and slow-moving even before its final yawning arc towards the Atlantic. Well-worn tracks lead to **Bintang**, on the creek of the same name, and **Tendaba**, a small village with a large, well-established riverside lodge. This is a favourite stopover on up-country safaris – it's adjacent to **Kiang West National Park**, home to the largest concentration of Gambian mammals and birds, and just across the river from Bao Bolon Wetland Reserve.

Senegal, never more than 25km away wherever you are in the region, has a noticeable commercial influence, creating a growing sense of cultural osmosis, despite resistance from the most staunchly nationalistic Gambians. This is most strongly felt in the east of the central region, where the river is barely one

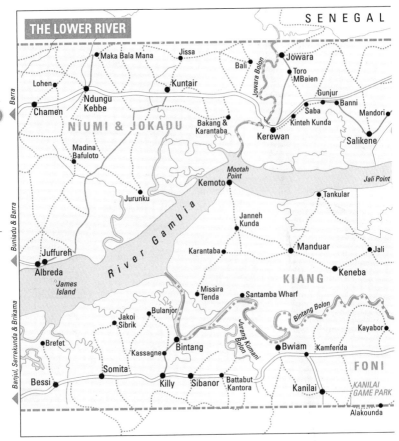

kilometre wide, and the international **Trans–Gambian highway** cuts right across The Gambia to connect Dakar with Casamance. **Soma** and **Farafenni**, the two Gambian towns on the highway, benefit from the interchange. While noisy Soma, on the south bank, is up-country Gambia's transport hub, Farafenni, a bustling yet relaxed rural centre, is the north bank's focal point, and a good starting place for visits into the beautiful and unspoilt **Bao Bolon Wetland Reserve**.

Foni District

Bounded to the north by the River Gambia and Bintang Bolon, the river's longest and most majestic tributary, and to the south by the northern reaches of Senegal's richly fertile Casamance region, **Foni district** is a well-watered slice of woods and farmland. If you're heading east into the interior of The Gambia from the Banjul area, Foni is the first up-country district you'll reach after leaving the Kombos.

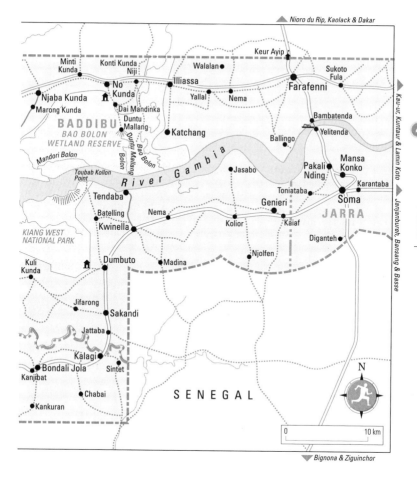

Keur Ayip

Minti Kunda   Konti Kunda   Walalan   Sukoto Fula
Niji   Farafenni
Illiassa
No Kunda   Yallal   Nema
Njaba Kunda
Marong Kunda   Dai Mandinka   Bambatenda
Duntu   Yelitenda
BADDIBU   Mallang   Katchang   Ballingo
BAO BOLON
WETLAND RESERVE
Mandori Bolon   Mansa Konko
Pakali Nding
Toubab Kollon   Jasabo   Karantaba
Point   River Gambia   Toniataba
Tendaba   Genieri   Soma
Batelling   Nema   JARRA
KIANG WEST   Kwinella   Kolior   Kaiaf
NATIONAL PARK   Diganteh
Kuli   Dumbuto   Madina   Njolfen
Kunda
Jifarong   Sakandi
Jattaba
Kalagi
Bondali Jola   Sintet
Kanjibat
Chabai   SENEGAL
Kankuran

N

0   10 km

Like Casamance, Foni district has a distinctively **tropical** flavour, punctuated by pockets of green where winding creeks descend to the river, creasing the otherwise flat terrain into a series of shallow valleys. Graced by tall palms, these little oases are a blaze of emerald in the rice-growing season between August and early December. As in Casamance, much of the population of Foni is **Jola**, and the district is the birthplace and home of the Jola people's most celebrated son, Yahya Jammeh.

European traders operated from bases here from the seventeenth to the nineteenth centuries, notably at what are now the small creekside villages of **Brefet** and **Bintang**. The river and its creeks were once the area's main thoroughfares, and a considerable volume of traffic, friendly and hostile, used to make the crossing over to the once-pivotal trading centres of Albreda and Fort James, a short paddle away by dugout *pirogue*. While there's practically nothing left to see of the traders' warehouses and slave "factories", the riverside villages along the south bank are sometimes visited by travellers tracing West African slave trade routes. Now that the usual means of travel around the country is by road, this sense of proximity between north and south bank settlements has been almost completely lost.

The district's largest village is **Bwiam**, where a brand new hospital stands as a visible sign of the present government's commitment to rural regeneration – and its predeliction for showy architectural projects. President Jammeh's partiality, and popularity, is conspicuous elsewhere in Foni, with dark green APRC flags fluttering outside family compounds and over village shops. The six-kilometre side-road that leads south off the main Banjul to Basse highway to the village of **Kanilai**, his birthplace and habitual residence, is currently the only well-surfaced road in the district.

The main **highway**, which passes almost due east through this section of the south bank from the Kombos to the bridge across Bintang Bolon at **Kalagi**, is mostly in an appalling state of repair. In the places where the road has been graded prior to resurfacing, everything by the roadside – animal, vegetable or mineral – is coated with a thick, sticky layer of russet dust. It can also be a dangerous route, especially at dusk, when all it takes is one speeding 4WD to overtake your vehicle for visibility to be near zero. Where the roadworks have yet to start, it's a matter of swerving to avoid the potholes, or driving with two wheels on the road and two on the verge. Bush taxi drivers know the route well and fly over the bumps; as a passenger, all you need to do is hang on and try not to inhale too much dust or worry about the state of your clothes. Driving your own vehicle, it's best to pace yourself: if you're heading on east towards Soma, the worst is yet to come.

Brefet

The creekside hamlet of **BREFET**, 6km north of the main south bank highway and very close both to the Kombos and the River Gambia, was once the site of a European trading station. The port was busy from the mid-sevententh to the early nineteenth centuries but today it's a quiet and unremarkable settlement. The remains of the colonial buildings, lying 1km west of the village, are all but obscured by vegetation for much of the year and there's practically nothing to see, but the remote wilderness of the Foni bush offers a feel for the conditions under which slaves were captured. A succession of British and French trading parties ran ruthless operations here, and violent incidents flared up on a regular basis, both between Europeans and Africans, and between rival traders.

Practicalities

Brefet is reached by turning north off the main south bank highway at the village of **Bessi**, 53km from Serrekunda and 30km from Brikama (**bush taxis** running along the Brikama to Bwiam, Kalagi and Soma route will stop at Bessi on request), then following the sandy, five-kilometre track more or less due north. If you're not driving, you can walk, or ask around in Bessi for a lift by local cart. (Incidentally, ignore the sign at the Brefet junction for "Sankaliba Lodge", long gone.)

Accommodation in Brefet is limited to the good-value *Jombombantang Cultural Camp* (☎880 2637; full-board with showers ❹), a fairly new community lodge situated in a grove of baobabs a couple of kilometres beyond the village. The small huts, named after sponsors, are built of mahogany planks, with corrugated-iron roofs, and they're pretty stuffy during the day. But the place has very friendly staff and should mellow soon enough, and there's 24-hour water and evening electricity from a generator. Drinks (and meals when people are staying) are served in the main *bantaba* restaurant, the *Boboli Sarr Restaurant*. The camp organizes **ox-cart excursions** and **boat trips** across the river to James Island.

Bintang

East of Brefet, another former colonial trading post is the traditional village of **BINTANG**, 6km off the south coast highway and about 73km east of Serrekunda. Bintang is a relaxed place with a tiny commercial district and an impressive modern mosque dating from the 1980s. A better reason to visit, rather than hunting for evidence of the area's trading past (the ruins here are no more visible than those at Brefet), is to spend time in the quiet creekside environment. Bintang lies on the south bank of **Bintang Bolon**, the River Gambia's longest and most beautiful tributary. The *bolon* snakes its way from its source in Senegal to meet the River Gambia at Bintang Point, 50km upstream from Banjul. This is Foni District's northern limit, densely forested with mangroves. Like all the River Gambia's mangrove creeks, the *bolon* is tidal, and at Bintang stretches of gunmetal-grey mud are exposed at low tide, inspected by crabs and wading birds. It's a great place to observe the life of the river – fishermen glide by in dugouts, women search for oysters and kingfishers dart onto their prey.

Practicalities

It's possible to get all the way through to Bintang direct from Brikama – two bush taxis leave Bintang in the early morning to take the day's fish and oysters to market, and return from Brikama (D30) in the afternoon. Ask at Brikama which taxi is going all the way to Bintang rather than just passing its junction, at Killy, which is 45km from Brikama, between Somita and Sibanor. If you don't have a vehicle and end up getting dropped at Killy, it's a hot but not unpleasant six-kilometre walk along the track to Bintang through perennially leafy riverine woodland. Heading from the direction of Soma by bush taxi, you may have to change vehicles at Sibanor, which has the nearest fuel and Gamtel office to Bintang. When you're ready to leave Bintang, it's best to take one of the early morning village taxis – if you walk to Killy, you may be in for a long wait at the junction as taxis zoom past full.

Bintang has had an off-on relationship with Gambian tourism through its pretty and unusual ⚓ *Bintang Bolon Lodge* (☎448 8035 or ☎992 9362; B&B with showers; ❸). For several years this was an enchanting place, but its maintenance fell behind and gradually the huts built on stilts sank into the creek. Now the owners seem serious about renovating it. The new rooms, which are fresh and simple, each have a veranda overlooking the *bolon*. The main attraction is the large *bantaba* restaurant, a peaceful, breezy spot, also built over the water. Given a little notice, the staff will prepare a meal from whatever's available locally – fish is abundant, of course. They can also make arrangements for you to explore Bintang Bolon by canoe.

Around 5km east of **Sibanor**, note that if you follow the sign on the north side of the road indicating "Karanai Village", where "A relaxing fishing and camping site awaits you, 1.5km" you'll be led along a winding, sandy, overgrown 3.5-kilometre track to the peaceful shore of Bintang Bolong. Here, a few dugouts of dubious seaworthiness await you and, save the remains of a hut, nothing else. It's a very pleasant spot if you're fully self-sufficient.

Bwiam

The small town of **BWIAM** is a progressive rural settlement, further east along the main south bank highway, about 18km from Bintang and 88km from Serrekunda. Conspicuous on the north side of the highway as you pass through town, the new **Sulayman Junkung Hospital** is Bwiam's most prominent landmark. This government-funded hospital plays a crucial role in improving basic healthcare south of the river, and it has received much-needed equipment, supplies and training from Europe and the US. The hospital was designed by Pierre Goudiaby, the Senegalese architect responsible for Arch 22 in Banjul – as you might guess from the oddly portentous, and slightly dangerous-looking arch over the main gate.

St Joseph's Family Farm, signposted off the main road close to the hospital, is a community development project where women who have been engaged in subsistence farming all their lives are being trained in sustainable agricultural practices, with a view to increasing their productivity while raising environmental awareness. Typical projects include helping women set up a cooperative to run an orchard, or just giving a young girl a bucket, a spade and a banana plant – one plant can generate enough income to pay for the owner's schooling. It's possible to visit the farm and watch whatever practical work is going on that day.

Bwiam also has a peculiar totem, the **kalero**, or iron pot, a knee-high lump of metal sunk into the ground on the east side of town north of the highway, just beyond the hospital. Legend has it that the *kalero* would spin round in times of conflict, indicating the direction of oncoming attackers. Locals claimed it was impossible to dig up – until a group of teenagers did just that. It appears to be part of an armoured vehicle or gun emplacement, and, with the mystery over, is not worth the visit.

Plans have been mooted to develop the expanse of waterfront land near Santamba, northwest of Bwiam, as a **wildlife park**. This area of woodland, enclosed on three sides by the natural boundaries of Bintang and Jurungkumani *bolons* and, to the south, by the proposed boundary of a massive electric fence, is planned to be the permanent home of the animals presently residing at the Kanilai Game Park (see p.214).

Bwiam is easily accessible by **bush taxi**. There are direct services from Serrekunda (2–3hr; D45), Brikama (2hr; D35) and Soma (2hr; D35), and any vehicle travelling between Soma and the Kombos will stop there on request.

Kanilai

The Jola village of **KANILAI**, close to the Senegalese border, about 6km from the south bank highway, is the birthplace of President Jammeh. It's hard to find on older maps of The Gambia, but, since Jammeh took control of the country in 1994, Kanilai's fortunes have changed radically. He spends so much time here that critics accuse him of wanting to shift the seat of government out of Banjul. This once-obscure up-country settlement now has a tarred access road, a luxury lodge, a large wrestling arena, a game park stocked with imported wildlife, good healthcare facilities, an electricity supply, a fire station with two gleaming fire engines, and a vast presidential palace.

From the first advertising hoardings at the junction to the colossal conference hall at the hotel, you know Kanilai is going to be different. And it turns out to be not just unusual, but uncomfortable, as you see the evidence all around you of Gambian public funds spent in one obscure corner of the country – almost a cliché of modern African nations where financial transparency is poor and democracy flawed. The Jammeh connection makes Kanilai unlike anywhere else in The Gambia, most startlingly at night when the palace generators run street lighting – a service that even the Senegambia area of Kololi still lacks.

Jammeh has bestowed many gifts on his people and they, in return, are fiercely loyal to him. As a visitor, you'll experience this if you're in Kanilai for a major event such as a wrestling championship or circumcision ceremony, when the presidential drummers, dancers, praise-singers and various camp-followers are out in exuberant force. Jammeh himself likes to party, and can be seen living it up with the best of them until the early hours.

Kanilai village is made up of a clutch of simple scattered compounds – simple apart from the unusual number of television aerials bristling from the roofs. Its natural focal point is the particularly impressive central *bantaba* area, a rough circle of immense silk cotton trees with deeply pleated trunks, where special events are sometimes held. In recent years, Kanilai has been the venue for what are the most exciting and extraordinary two days of the **International Roots**

△ Stilt dancer, Kanilai

Jola festivities

The Jola people have a special relish for loud, spectacular **cultural celebrations**, and Kanilai is a good place to witness them at their best. Occasions such as national holidays, wrestling tournaments, and community rites of passage are times of communal celebration, and strangers may well be invited to watch the proceedings, or even to join in.

Jolas are distinguished from many other Senegambian cultures by not having a caste of *griots* (traditional musicians and praise-singers whose role is hereditary, and who are the custodians of ancestral history); instead, Jolas are free to choose to be musicians, whatever their parentage. This might in some way explain their particular passion and enthusiasm as performers.

As all over West Africa, the **percussionists** set the tone of the occasion and get pulses racing. The Jola are famous for the warm-toned *boucarabou*, a threesome or foursome of drums of different pitches played simultaneously by one drummer, but they also play *soruba* and *sabar* drums, single goblet-shaped drums played with hand and stick. Women, with loops of beads crossing their torsoes from shoulder to hip, bang on iron or palm-stalk percussion blocks and sing strident choruses, then take it in turns to dance at high speed with stamping steps and flapping or whirring arm movements to a crescendo of drumming and whistle-blowing. Unnerving but compulsive to watch are the baggy-trousered **knife-dancers**, who strut fiercely, displaying elaborate *jujus*. Every few steps they knock back potions prepared by their marabouts to make them invincible. They then set about mutilating themselves (or, at least making a big show of attempting to do so) with cutlasses and razor blades – none of which leave as much a scratch, no matter how energetically they hack at their chests, limbs, and, particularly horribly, eyes and tongues. Even the sanest of Jolas believe implicitly that there is no trickery about the blades used or the force with which they're wielded.

Then there are the daring stunts performed by the **fire-eaters**, blowing plumes of flame over the crowd, and the **kumpo dancers**, who bounce around like animated haystacks under shaggy palm-frond costumes, suddenly up-ending themselves onto a wooden spike and spinning round in a blur. Meanwhile, a gang of **cannon-firers** may be playing sweet, flute music somewhere in the crowd, but don't be fooled by their gentleness – when it's time to spring into action, they ram iron pipes stuffed with gunpowder into the ground, light the fuses, and run like hell as the charges explode with ear-splitting force. Every drum beaten, chime struck, whistle blown, chant chanted, and cannon fired rings out simultaneously at top volume, and the sheer noise can be overwhelming.

Festival (see p.68), when visitors can undergo a ceremonial version of the *futampaf* (traditional Jola initiation rites). Part of the ceremony takes place under the silk cotton trees amidst a riot of colour and noise.

The area around Kanilai, close to the Senegalese border, is generally quiet and well-wooded, and the traditional occupations here are cereal farming, hunting and livestock rearing – Jammeh's parents tended cattle and sheep. The lodge can arrange **excursions** in this area with a vehicle, driver, and guide, including bird-watching trips (D300 per person for 2hr) and village visits, offering an insight into traditional Jola lifestyles and music (D250 per person for 2hr).

Kanilai Game Park

Behind the presidential palace, through whose extensive compound you enter, is **Kanilai Game Park** (daily 7–10am & 5–7pm; D250). Originally conceived as a holding area for animals to be moved to the planned new park at Santamba near Bwiam (see p.212), this is now, unless that project is completed, simply a rather underwhelming safari park. The park and its denizens, mostly imported from South Africa, are supposedly a presidential conservation project, but it's hard to see much evidence of that in this spurious menagerie – where the species count is very much a here-today-gone-tomorrow business. The park contains numbers of Burchell's zebra, impala and wildebeest, all of which you're quite likely to see, and two white rhinos – open-country animals presumably wretched in this dense bush – which keep well hidden. Over the years, various other species have been imported, including giraffes, which did not survive.

In the middle of the park is an extensive area of **crocodile-rearing ponds**, purpose unclear, containing hundreds of reptiles, some nearly three metres long. You can walk around the banks and take close-up photos, but there's no real security apart from the ranger accompanying you, and, as the crocs get bigger, there's an accident waiting to happen here.

Senegambian wrestling

Watching traditional **Senegambian wrestling**, which has its origins in the thirteenth century, is a favourite pastime of President Jammeh, and of Jolas in general. Wrestling teams comprise members of a single tribe, and the Jola are renowned for winning most of the time (for some years, the Gambian champion was a native of Kanilai) and for losing with good grace, a sure sign of a true sportsman in Gambian society. Wrestling is officially The Gambia's national sport, but it's been gradually fading over the last decade with the universal growth of football fever. Jammeh is keen to keep the sport alive, and the large arena at Kanilai is one of the few places where major tournaments are still held, albeit irregularly.

Visitors are welcome at wrestling matches, and there's a small entrance fee. The Kanilai arena is basically a square of sand surrounded by long thatched shaded areas for the audience to sit, between the *bantaba* area and the palace. Drumming and whistling teams (from various ethnic groups, each with their own distinctive drums and tunes) keep up steady competitive rhythms as the action builds slowly, the first few wrestlers pacing or dancing around the court, flexing their muscles and psyching themselves up, daring the others to challenge them to a bout. Stripped to the waist, they wear special trunks known as *dala*, made for them by female followers and decorated with coloured cloth strips and tassels. All but the most supremely self-confident wear an abundance of *jujus* or amulets. Superstition plays a large part in the wrestlers' preparation, and they may be required by their marabouts to blow dust at their opponents, or recite an incantation, or go through a special sequence of body movements in order to activate the most powerful charms.

The referee starts whistling the men into order and gradually the opponents pair off to start their bouts. Contestants are evenly matched, it being unusual for small wrestlers to take on bigger men, however much the crowd roars its approval. The object is to land your opponent on his back as quickly and cleanly as possible. With dust flying, bodies slicked with sweat and charmed potions to weaken the opponent's grip, this usually takes a few seconds. However, some bouts can last for several minutes, as contestants bluff and threaten, facing each other with backs bent and hands trailing in the dust to make a good grip. Dozens of bouts take place during a tournament, and judges keep track of results. The winner of each bout takes a triumphal turn around the edge of the arena, accompanied by his drum team, and collects a few dalasis in appreciation as he goes – you should take a pocketful of small notes.

Taking **photos** is quite accepted, but you'll need a telephoto lens and fast film to capture the excitement as the contest develops and the sun goes down. Events are sometimes organized or cancelled at short notice; for the latest information, listen for announcements on Radio Gambia (see p.66) or ask the staff at *Sindola Safari Lodge* (see p.216).

Close to the presidential villa are several ugly **pens**, one containing a large number of entertaining ostriches and several emus, one holding a pair of morose lions, and one with some truly disturbing captives – a pack of African **hunting dogs**. This is the continent's rarest predator, used to ranging across hundreds of square kilometres, confined here in squalor. These caged inmates are a disincentive to visit the place at all.

Entry to the park is by vehicle only, accompanied by a ranger. To arrange your visit, you should first call at *Sindola Safari Lodge* (see below); if you don't have your own vehicle (any kind will be fine, the park is flat and the tracks graded), the lodge can provide a car and driver (D150 per person for 2hr).

Practicalities

The turning for Kanilai leads southwards off the main south bank highway around 106km east of Serrekunda, at a junction marked by a rigorous police checkpoint and a sign for *Sindola Safari Lodge*. Most people visiting Kanilai do so as an **excursion** to *Sindola* arranged with the *Kairaba Hotel*, travelling from Kololi or direct from the airport in a pre-booked hotel vehicle, or by other private means. It's not easy to reach Kanilai by public transport, but if you're dropped at the highway junction you're likely to find a lift with a private vehicle for the last 6km.

Kanilai's only tourist **accommodation**, the upmarket ⚘ *Sindola Safari Lodge* (☎448 3415, Ⓔsindola@gamtel.gm, or c/o *Kairaba Hotel*, Kololi ☎446 2940, Ⓦwww.kairabahotel.com; B&B ❹; suite B&B ❺) lies on the edge of the village, not far from the presidential palace. A sister lodge to the *Kairaba* on the coast, in functional terms it's the best up-country lodge in The Gambia and a good place to relax or to use as a base for trips. The decor and furnishings are in taste-free motel tradition, but the forty rooms, in ten thatched roundhouses, are comfortable and well-kept, with AC, fan and fridge. The landscaped grounds go overboard slightly on maze-like casuarina hedges, but include a decent swimming pool, tennis courts and an organic vegetable plot supplying the *Sindola* and the *Kairaba*. The attractive **restaurant** opens onto the gardens, with a menu that includes good pizzas and sandwiches and a cosmopolitan assortment of main dishes, including Indonesian *nasi goreng*, grilled sirloin steak, and Gambian dishes, which offer the best value. Don't plump for the overpriced set menu.

Kalagi

Situated on the main south bank highway at Foni district's eastern tip, immediately south of Kiang West district, **KALAGI**, 120km east of Serrekunda, is the kind of village that travellers on the way to *Tendaba Camp* and Kiang West National Park would pass straight through if it weren't for the police checkpoint. However, just off the highway outside the village on the northeastern side is the *Jalaa Kolong Bar & Restaurant*, aka *Kalagi River Site*, an attractively situated **bar/restaurant** that serves basic drinks and snacks and makes an ideal stopover in a long journey over the potholes. Basic rooms here (B&B; ❶) are in simple roundhouses, with well water and long-drop toilets – somewhat overpriced for the facilities. It's a quiet, peaceful, wide open space, on the bank of Bintang Bolon, where the creek runs through a broad floodplain bristling in places with the eerie but beautiful skeletons of lofty mangrove trees, the victims of a shift in the salinity of the water here. Next to the bar is the bridge across the *bolon*, over which the main road continues in the direction of Dumbuto (for the Kiang West park HQ), Kwinella (for Tendaba) and Soma.

Tendaba and Kiang West District

One of The Gambia's longest-established up-country tourist destinations is **Tendaba Camp**, in the village of the same name. It lies on the river, 5km north of the south bank highway, just over 140km from Serrekunda by road and, by river, about 100km upstream from Banjul. This large riverside bush lodge is a good base for river trips and off-road explorations by 4WD or on foot – it's only a short boat trip away from **Bao Bolon Wetland Reserve** (see p.226), and lies right on the edge of the thinly populated **Kiang West district**. This expanse of forest, farmland and mangrove, sandwiched between the River Gambia, to the north, and Bintang Bolon to the south, includes **Kiang West National Park**, a wild and little-explored protected area easily visited from *Tendaba*.

Since *Tendaba Camp*'s early huntin' and fishin' days in the 1970s, a couple of alternative accommodation options in Kiang district have opened, but *Tendaba* remains the most accessible and most-visited: the four bumpy hours it takes to get here by road from the coastal resorts are about as much as you're likely to want if you're only coming for a short stay. The nearest sizeable village, on the junction at the main highway, is **Kwinella**, which is at its liveliest on market day (Thursdays). If you have to hang around in Kwinella for a while on the way to or from the lodge, it's worth seeking out the group of silk cotton trees in the village, the habitual roost and nesting site of hundreds of cacophonous pelicans – an extraordinary sight close up.

Tendaba

The village of **TENDABA**, huddled around the grounds of *Tendaba Camp*, has a down-at-heel, shanty-town atmosphere and isn't much visited by tourists staying at the lodge. Hassle from begging local children can make some new arrivals at *Tendaba* feel uncomfortable, though it's no worse than in any other touristy area of The Gambia.

Even though Tendaba ("Big Wharf" in Mandinka) is a considerable distance from the Atlantic, the river here is broad, salty and tidal, exposing acres of mud twice a day. Hazy in the distance is the grey-green fringe of tall mangroves that marks the opposite bank, the sense of space making for romantic sunsets and stunning nights lit by a dome of stars.

Practicalities

Most visitors arrive on organized two-day standard excursions (see pp.54–55) from the coastal resorts, or as part of a tailor-made itinerary with a specialist tour company or a privately hired driver and guide. In theory, small planes can land at Tendaba's airstrip, a forty-minute flight from Banjul, but there are no regular services. It's also possible to travel independently by public transport. Both the village and lodge are reached by taking one of the two signposted northbound turnings off the main south bank road at the village of Kwinella. **Bush taxis** running between Serrekunda or Brikama and Soma will drop you at Kwinella, and there's a telecentre here from which to call the lodge to pick you up, which will cost D100 per person, or can be included for large bookings or long stays. Otherwise, you could walk the five kilometres to the river from Kwinella, or ask around to arrange for a local donkey cart to take you.

⚓ *Tendaba Camp* (☎554 1024, ☎991 1088; PO Box Tendaba Camp, LRD; riverfront rooms with showers ❷; basic roundhouses ❶; accommodation is room only – they make their money on meals), by far the best-known **accommodation** option in Kiang West District, lies in a prime location on the

Birdwatching around Tendaba

Tendaba is a standard stop on Gambian birdwatching itineraries, since there's an abundance of species in the countryside lying within easy walking distance of *Tendaba Camp*. These include river eagle, African darter, sacred ibis, marabou and white-necked storks, wood ibis, plus herons, parrots, and the lumbering ground hornbill. At night you may hear scops owls, milky eagle owls and standard-winged nightjars, which have the perilous habit of resting on the warm road after dark; carry a torch if you want to see some. The rarely used airfield southeast of the lodge is visited by various raptors, and sandgrouse may fly up from under your feet in the adjoining savannah woodlands, behind the camp to the south. Other species to look out for include blue-breasted kingfisher and white-shouldered black tit and you can see finfoot in the creek that boat trips normally visit, on the north bank across from the lodge. Keen birders generally find enough to keep them interested in the Tendaba area for at least a couple of days.

riverbank side of the Tendaba village. The "VIP rooms", self-contained and complete with TV, all have views over the water, as does the restaurant, with its big, cone-shaped thatched roof, and the *Bambo Bar* by the jetty. The remaining accommodation (the lodge has 150 beds) is in thatched and whitewashed roundhouses, crammed together in a grove of neem trees as tightly as caravans in a holiday resort, and out of sight of the river. These rooms are very plain, with African-style cement-and-foam beds and shared washing facilities, but they have more a genuinely Gambian character than the pricier riverside rooms. All the rooms have mosquito nets and are sprayed every evening, with good reason. Although *Tendaba* is rarely fully booked, a place on this scale could never be described as intimate, and it has more of a mass-tourism feel than any of the other up-country bush lodges.

One of the lodge's greatest assets is its small but clean **swimming pool**, with decent showers, available to anyone visiting for the night or just for a meal – reason enough to make a diversion here if you're travelling on the highway. *Tendaba* started up as a hunting lodge, but tends to downplay this these days, since birdwatchers far outnumber hunters among the guests. There's a reminder of old times in its trademark: a strutting bushpig, or warthog, and it's still a regular feature of the **restaurant** menu, along with more standard fare, generally well-prepared and reasonably priced – buffet lunch or dinner D225, breakfast D95, snacks D50–100. After dinner, bands of villagers drum and dance on the terrace.

If you want to do things in strictly local style at Tendaba, then you can eat at *Bouywallo* restaurant on the waterfront just next to *Tendaba Camp*, which serves great *domoda*. Meals need to be ordered in advance and prices are negotiable. The owner can also arrange *pirogue* trips.

Standard **excursions** organized by the lodge include a three-hour trip by road to Kiang West National Park (see opposite) – these trips are fun but dusty, bumpy, and there's only a small chance of seeing any large wildlife – and a recommended creek trip either to Toubab Kollon Point or across the river and up the Duntu Mallang Bolon within Bao Bolon Wetland Reserve (see p.226).

All excursions cost D200–250 per person, subject to a minimum cost of D1000 per jeep or D800 per *pirogue*. If you'd rather explore independently, the eastern boundary of Kiang West is just about within walking distance of the lodge – about 7km, so make a very early start to avoid the heat. The jetty near the lodge is also the start/finishing point for Gambia River Excursions' three-day river trips between Tendaba and Janjanbureh (see p.52).

Kiang West National Park

Kiang West National Park (daily 8am–6.30pm; D31.50) is among the country's wildest, least-explored regions, a chunk of southern riverbank land west of Kwinella and north of Bintang Bolon, 145km from Banjul. The 115 square kilometres – mainly dry deciduous woodland and Guinea savannah, but also mangrove creeks and tidal flats – was designated a national park in 1987, and is one of the most important wildlife reserves in The Gambia. Most of the wildlife will elude the casual visitor, but, with patience, it's possible to see primates, antelopes and plenty of birds.

Bounded to the north by the Gambia River and dissected into three areas by the Jarin, Jali and Nganingkoi *bolons*, the park contains habitats rich in animal species. Every single wild mammal ever recorded in The Gambia has been found here at some time, and Kiang West presently harbours most of the remaining mammal species permanently resident in the country, including sitatunga (an unusual semi-aquatic antelope that thrives in salt marshes), bushbuck and duiker, clawless otter, warthog (bushpig) and spotted hyena. Humpbacked dolphins and West African manatees, which are very rare, are occasionally seen in Jarin Bolon. The area also possesses an impressive tally of over three hundred bird species, more than half the total recorded in the country (see box, p.220).

A good place for wildlife watching is **Tubabkollon Point**, close to a sandy beach on the river in the extreme northeast of the park, and reachable either by boat or on foot from *Tendaba Camp*, 7km along the river. There was once a Portuguese trading station here, hence "*toubab kollon*" ("white man's well"). There's a hide, with elevated views over a waterhole visited by warthogs, bushbucks and sitatunga; the surrounding area is patrolled by troops of guinea baboons and western red colobus monkeys. Also seen here are the world's fastest monkeys, the patas (see p.293). Night-time explorations may reveal nightjars, more often heard than seen, and Senegal bushbabies. Leopards, also nocturnal, are occasionally reported from here, but they are extremely elusive: a sighting in 2006 was at Jaanyaang-Faraa. Lynx-like caracals have also been seen at Kiang West, notably between Dumboto and Batelling.

Just west of Tubabkollon Point is a 25-metre **escarpment** which runs parallel to the river, giving an extra dimension to this otherwise flat region; there are beautiful views of the riverbank from the top.

Practicalities

Most visitors approach Kiang West from *Tendaba Camp* (see p.217), driving around by group 4WD excursion or privately hired vehicle. You can also **drive** straight into the park from the south bank highway via the Kiang West National Park headquarters near Dumbuto, which is on the highway, 12km north of Kalagi and 6km south of Kwinella. The park HQ is reached by a rough, overgrown one-kilometre track leading off the highway from the village towards the river. Alternatively you could travel to Dumbuto by public transport – **bush taxis** running along the highway from Serrekunda, Brikama, and the up-country south bank towns pass the village – and hire a vehicle having walked

Birdwatching in Kiang West National Park

Kiang West National Park is becoming well-known as a birdwatching destination, and a high proportion of The Gambia's native species can be found feeding and breeding here. The official symbol of the park is the bateleur, named for its aerial acrobatics (*bateleur* means "juggler" or "tumbler" in French). This striking short-tailed eagle is frequently seen here, hunting for pigeons and sandgrouse, especially between July and September. It's also possible to see the booming ground hornbill in Kiang West, and all ten Gambian species of kingfisher. Rarer species include the endangered brown-necked parrot, a chattering bird which breeds among the mangroves and, occasionally, magnificent crowned cranes and woolly-necked storks, both of which were present in 2006. During the dry season, the concentration and variety of raptors – 21 species, including vultures, harriers, eagles, hawks and falcons – is particularly high in the park.

to the park HQ (at around D750 per day or D400 per half-day for the whole vehicle, this is cheaper than at *Tendaba* if you're in a small group). Both *Tendaba* and the park HQ can recommend guides. Driving in the park is, of course, noisy and usually dusty, and you'll see more wildlife by boat from *Tendaba* or the *Kemoto Hotel* (see opposite), or on foot.

The park HQ offers guest **accommodation** for up to 24 people in plain, rather tired and dusty, self-contained bungalows (no phone on site; warden's mobile ☎986 0925, ✉mawjami@yahoo.com). The bungalows were originally intended for visiting natural-history students and researchers, but in practice they're open to all with prior arrangement (❶). The HQ is in an isolated spot, with minimal facilities, borehole water and intermittent electricity when there is fuel for the generator, but the bungalows are a reasonable option for intrepid wildlife enthusiasts interested in exploring Kiang West, especially if you're on foot or want to explore by night.

There's a plan underway to open a community-managed Kiang West lodge for ecotourists at **Batelling**, north of Dumbuto, signposted from Wurokang. Batelling itself has a rusting set of iron cannon barrels in the village centre, remnants of a colonial military installation from the time when Batelling was the capital of the whole Lower River Division.

If you're interested in flora, the best season is the end of the rains, usually between late August and October, when the trees are greenest and shrubs are in flower. August to January is the best time to see the widest variety of bird species, including winter migrants. By March – or May at the latest – much of the tall grass and other vegetation that can block views and clog paths has shrivelled and died or been burnt off by bush fires, making this a good time to look for mammals. In the dry season (Nov–June), as in many parts of The Gambia, particularly near the river, you can occasionally be pestered by biting flies, so it's best to use plenty of insect repellent.

Kemoto

The riverside hamlet of **KEMOTO**, 20km downstream from Kiang West National Park by river, is a long bumpy drive from the nearest sealed road. As the crow flies, it's less than 40km from Sankandi or Dumbuto on the south bank highway, but the journey along winding country tracks can take over two hours – and Sankandi is itself more than three hours from Serrekunda. It's worth the effort if you'd like to experience the peaceful countryside en route to this remote stretch of river, from which you can visit Kiang West by boat. On the riverbank at Mootah Point is the well-located, but sadly closed *Kemoto Hotel*. It's near some of the river's most interesting creeks and if you have time try ☎446 0252 to check if it's reopened. An alternative route to Kemoto is to start from Banjul, take the ferry to Barra, follow the road to Kerewan, and then, from the disused Jowara Bolon ferry wharf on the Kerewan side of the road bridge, take a *pirogue* across the river.

Soma and Farafenni

The area around **Soma** and **Farafenni** is The Gambia's off-centre fulcrum, a crossroads between Dakar and Ziguinchor in Senegal and between eastern Gambia and the Atlantic coast. The grand-sounding **Trans–Gambian highway**, heading from northern to southern Senegal, cuts through Farafenni to the Bambatenda–Yelitenda ferry across the River Gambia, then picks up again to continue through Soma and on to the Casamance district of southern Senegal.

Travelling between western and eastern Gambia, you'll pass through Soma on the up-country south bank road route from the Kombos to Janjanbureh or Basse. Farafenni, 18km north of Soma by road and ferry, is Soma's counterpart, an essential staging post in explorations of the north bank. While neither town has any tourist attractions in the conventional sense, they do have places to stay, and they offer visitors the chance to gain a real insight into what makes an up-country Gambian town tick.

Nowhere is The Gambia's north–south divide more evident than in the difference in atmosphere and affluence between the two. Soma's population is barely a third of Farafenni's, but it has a much grittier, faster-paced, urban atmosphere, and it's more affluent, if less immediately appealing. Farafenni, while it's The Gambia's fifth largest town, and expanding fast as farmers arrive seeking work and escape from poor groundnut harvests, feels, in contrast, like an overgrown

Toniataba

Just north off the highway, and 4km west of Soma, lies the unremarkable village of **Toniataba**. Unremarkable, that is, except for the enormous grass-thatched **roundhouse** in the compound of Fatikunda ("Fati's place"). Fatikunda is the home of the Fati, or Fatty, family: the family head, Boubakari Alhaji Fode Fatty, is one of the district's most senior religious leaders, or marabouts. First constructed in the nineteenth century by the Alhaji's grandfather Sheikh Othman, the house is the largest traditional home in The Gambia, at around sixty metres in circumference.

It's important to realize that the Alhaji's family home is not a tourist attraction, and unless you speak Mandinka you should not visit without a local guide to introduce you. First of all, you should find the Toniataba *alkalo*, or headman, and make enquiries of him. If you intend to visit Fatikunda, dress modestly, come armed with a gift – a modest cash donation will not offend – and take your shoes off if you're invited into the nearby guest reception room. The roundhouse itself, which wasn't fully occupied at last visit, is of an unusual design, its outer wall surrounding an interior house divided into separate rooms. In the middle is an inner sanctum, a private area traditionally reserved for family prayers.

village, animated but traditional and easy-going. The town has begun to benefit from rural development programmes such as the impressive new hospital. Farafenni's weekly country market, selling colourful produce from all over the region, is its greatest attraction for visitors. It is also a jumping-off point for explorations of **Bao Bolon Wetland Reserve**, The Gambia's largest protected area, west of the town.

In theory, this part of the country should benefit from excellent connections, but in fact its main **highways** are in desperate need of repair. Some residents of Banjul and the Kombos avoid travelling this far up-country from one year to the next simply because of the inevitable wear and tear on vehicles and drivers' nerves. A resurfacing plan is underway, but progress is slow. The Trans-Gambian highway is in a particularly deplorable state, with Gambians pinning the blame on overloaded Senegalese and Guinean trucks that grind along the route to and from Dakar. In truth, Gambians in the district benefit nicely from their role as hosts to traffic from other West African states, and the mechanics and street food vendors are kept constantly busy serving the passing trade.

Soma

The thinly spread town of **SOMA**, 180km from Serrekunda, sits at the junction of the Banjul–Basse and Dakar–Ziguinchor *trans-gambienne* highways. As such, it's effectively a gateway to eastern Gambia, up-country northern Senegal

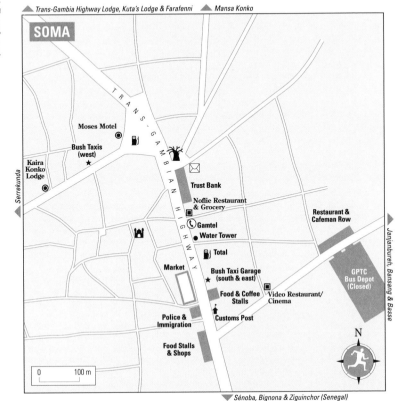

and the Casamance district. There are other routes to southern Senegal further upriver, but this is the easternmost point in The Gambia at which you can easily turn north towards Kaolack if you're heading towards Dakar overland.

Soma is little more than a bustling truck stop, a charmless string of petrol stations, cheap restaurants, bars and shops where you can get all sorts of Senegalese imports, including Gazelle beer and the latest cotton fabrics. There's a Gamtel office and a new branch of Trust Bank but, at the time of writing, still no public Internet access. Since the road deteriorated so badly, buses no longer come to Soma. Instead, bush taxis whirl up the dust, collecting passengers for the short ride to the ferry crossing for the north bank and Farafenni.

A couple of kilometres outside Soma to the northeast is Mansa Konko ("King's Hill"), prominently marked on maps because it's the capital of Lower River Division. However, all there is to see here is a collection of local government offices and schools that's quiet and uncommercial in inverse proportion to Soma's racket. If you're in the Soma area, but looking for somewhere quiet to stay, it's best to head for the little haven of calm that is **Pakali Nding**, a satellite village 3km north up the Trans-Gambian highway, on the way to the Yelitenda river ferry. It's basically a clutch of compounds with a telecentre, but it has a couple of accommodation options, including the best – and cheapest – lodge in the area.

Practicalities

Soma is the hub for **bush taxis** from all points on the south bank highway, and for points immediately north and south on the route from Senegal. Bush taxis from Serrekunda stop on the Serrekunda road, near the junction with the Trans-Gambia highway; most other bush taxis stop at Soma's main taxi garage in the middle of town. From eastern Gambia, there are services from Sankulay Kunda near Janjanbureh (D35), Bansang (D35), and Basse (D40). Local vehicles arrive here from Pakali Nding and the Yelitenda ferry (D4) north of town, and from the Gambia-Casamance border (D4). Long-distance Senegalese bush taxis from Dakar via Kaolack and Farafenni and from Ziguinchor via Bignona also pass through. The two GPTC **buses** a day that used to run in each direction between Serrekunda and Basse were not operating at the time of writing.

Accommodation

Unlikely though it may sound, the best **accommodation** in central Soma is at the local Scout Group headquarters, a place called *Kaira Konko Lodge* (☎553 1453 twins without showers very cheap; doubles with showers ❶), on the Serrekunda road. Decorated with bits of scouting memorabilia, the place has an old-fashioned, institutional feel but the rooms are secure and reasonably well-kept. Food can be provided, but there's only well water and no generator. The much less attractive option in town is *Moses Motel* (☎553 1462 or ☎991 9542; with showers ❶), on the Serrekunda/Trans-Gambian highway junction, a rundown Rasta place with a standby generator but no discernible appeal.

At **Pakali Nding**, 3km north towards the river, lies the recommended 🏕 *TransGambia Highway Lodge* (☎553 1402 or ☎993 9868, ✉bangakinte@hotmail .com; ❶) Although it's right beside the highway, past the centre of the village on the left if you're heading north, it's really quiet (until they fire up the generator in the evening), and a favourite of locally based NGOs. The large compound provides secure parking and accommodation for individuals and groups. The best rooms (self-contained, with fans) are in neatly painted thatched roundhouses, and simple but edible food (D50–60) can be provided on request. Internet access from a laptop is available, too. Another good option, its

Yelitenda–Bambatenda ferry

The Yelitenda–Bambatenda vehicle **ferry** that carries Trans-Gambia highway traffic across the River Gambia operates from 7am to 6.30pm (cars D65, foot passengers D3). The Yelitenda ramp is on the south bank, 10km north of Soma, and Bambatenda is on the north bank, 6km south of Farafenni. Travelling with a vehicle, you first need to buy a ticket from the Ports Authority: on each side of the river there's an office just off the highway, a few hundred metres before you reach the ferry dock. The river is less than 1km wide here, and the crossing takes only ten minutes; however, vehicles, particularly trucks, can get stuck in a queue for some time – even days – with plenty of hawkers working the captive clientele. Bush taxis and private vehicles can normally queue-jump the trucks.

self-catering accommodation aimed at passing businessmen, is *Kuta's Lodge* (☎5531572 or ☎5531558; rooms with and without showers; ❶), signposted off the Trans-Gambia highway in the centre of Pakali Nding, off the road to Mansa Konko. The AC rooms in the house are well-furnished, and include the use of a kitchen and a living room area with TV. There's also a generator.

Eating, drinking and entertainment

Central Soma has an abundance of informal **eating** options, including good street-food in the open-air canteen-like area of small benches, tables, coffee stands and braziers around the bush-taxi garage. Here slabs of meat are chopped up in front of you, seasoned, sizzled over charcoal and served in *tapalapa* bread while you wait. The **restaurants** in town are all simple local places where you can get omelettes, hot drinks and bread in the mornings, and chicken, fish or rice and sauce from lunchtime onwards. *Noflie Restaurant and Grocery*, on the main road near the Gamtel office, has good views of whatever's going on in the street, but there's better-quality food to be had in the smaller places. There are more local restaurants in the quiet spot just south of the police and immigration post. In the evening, check out the *Video Restaurant* on the Basse road, which has benches inside permanently set up for video nights. For a drink, *Roadside Bar* adjoins *Noflie* and does a busy trade in beer.

Farafenni

Less than 3km from the Senegalese border at Keur Ayip, **FARAFENNI** is, like Soma, a fairly cosmopolitan junction town, but situated as it is on the north bank, more isolated and with a more rural feel.

The highlight of every week is the energetic **lumo**, or country market (Sun 7am–6pm), held on the northern edge of town, beyond the stadium. Market day is by far the best day of the week to be in Farafenni, when the place is busy with horse and donkey carts, carrying buyers, sellers, and huge bundles of merchandise. If you don't have your own transport, the best way to get here is to join the locals in travelling by cart, which operate like bush taxis from the centre of town (D2). Visitors generally find the *lumo* much more relaxed than the crowded urban markets like those at Serrekunda and Banjul: the air here is fresher, and you have more room to wander and browse. The merchants are a mixture of Gambians, Senegalese, Guineans, and Mauritanians, and you'll hear plenty of Wolof and French spoken as well as Mandinka. From rickety stalls laid out in a sandy area shaded with tarpaulins and thatch, you'll see vendors selling vermilion palm oil, locust beans by the canful, and kola nuts from large sacks.

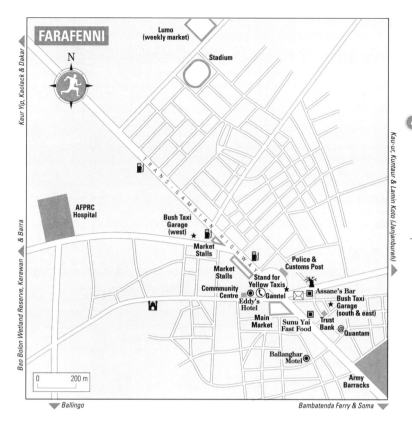

FARAFENNI

N

Keur Yip, Kaolack & Dakar

Bao Bolon Wetland Reserve, Kerewan & Barra

Lumo
(weekly market)

Stadium

TRANS-GAMBIA HIGHWAY

Kau-ur, Kuntaur & Lamin Koto (Janjanbureh)

AFPRC
Hospital

Bush Taxi
Garage
(west)

Market
Stalls

Market
Stalls

Commmunity
Centre

Gamtel

Eddy's
Hotel

Main
Market

Sunu Yai
Fast Food

Stand for
Yellow Taxis

Police &
Customs Post

Assane's Bar

Bush Taxi
Garage
(south & east)

Trust
Bank

Quantam

Ballanghar
Motel

Army
Barracks

0   200 m

Ballingo

Bambatenda Ferry & Soma

Despite the fact that this is an impoverished area, the sheer volume of produce on sale after the harvest can be staggering – lorry-loads of pumpkins in October and November, and great heaps of tomatoes in January. There are oddities like fetish items, and plenty of household goods on sale too. It's a good place to shop for fabric from Senegal and Guinea, including Fula indigo cloth, and wax cotton designs that have yet to make it to the Kombos.

Incongruous for its sheer size is Farafenni's new **hospital**, functioning since 1999, but only officially opened by President Jammeh in 2003; it has already made significant progress in reducing infant mortality in the poorly connected up-country villages in this region. If you need medical attention the outpatients department will see you.

You can enjoy sweeping views of the River Gambia near Farafenni at the fishing village of **Ballingo**, a twenty-minute drive out of town. It's reached via the laterite road that heads south opposite the hospital, passing through thinly wooded grassland distinguished by a few circles of mighty baobabs and silk cotton trees. The curve of mangrove-edged river at Ballingo is wide and shining, and there's a muddy beach of sorts on the riverbank, where it's possible to find secluded places to swim, away from the fishermen mending their nets and laying out mullet on millet-weave tables to dry in the sun. It's also possible to commission one of the boat-owners to take you out in the river by dugout.

Practicalities

Farafenni has two **bush taxi** garages, and if you're travelling from the north bank towns of Kau-ur (D20), Kuntaur (D30), or Lamin Koto near Janjanbureh (D45), you'll arrive at the central one. There are also direct minibuses from Soma, central Gambia's transport hub, via the River Gambia ferry (see p.51). Travelling from Barra via Kerewan by van (D45) or Peugeot estate (D60), you arrive at the smaller garage, on the Kerewan road. To travel from Farafenni to northern Senegal, first take a shared **yellow taxi** (D4) north up the Trans-Gambian Highway to the border post at Keur Ayip, where you can change for Nioro du Rip, Kaolack, and Dakar.

The best-known **place to stay** in Farafenni is *Eddy's Hotel* (☎573 5225 or ☎773 5611; rooms with showers and fan ❶; with AC ❷), formerly a thriving north-bank focus, but these days very rundown – the rooms, though a decent size, badly need refurbishing, and the generator often plays up. Still, the mango-shaded courtyard is a pleasant place to enjoy a drink. An alternative to *Eddy's* in better condition is the unpretentious *Ballanghar Motel* (☎773 5431; ❶), with eleven simple courtyard rooms with fan, in a quiet residential neighbourhood. There's no generator, so you're reliant on the vagaries of Farafenni's intermittent power supply.

While **food** is available at *Eddy's*, the wait can be so long it's better to head for one of the simple local restaurants on the main road. ⚑ *Sunu Yai*, centrally located on the east side of the road, doesn't look much and is deeply unassuming, but serves excellently baked and well seasoned chicken with chips, and allows you to bring along your own drinks. There are a few other small places nearby which offer standards like *domodah* and *benechin*. The best **bar** is in town is an unmarked place called *Assane's*, not far from the post office, which serves Gambian Guinness and cold Senegalese Gazelle beer. Bands sometimes play at the Community Centre next door to *Eddy's*.

You can get fuel in Farafenni, and for **money-changing**, there's a branch of Trust Bank (Mon–Thurs 8am–1.30pm, Fri 8am–11.30pm). Public **Internet access** is available at Quantum Associates on ✉qafarafenni@quantum.gm.

Bao Bolon Wetland Reserve

On the north side of the river, directly facing Kiang West National Park, is **Bao Bolon Wetland Reserve**, a vast complex designated a site of international importance by the Ramsar International Wetlands Convention. At 220 square kilometres it's The Gambia's largest protected area, distinguished by outstanding marshland flora, and home to rare West African manatees, African clawless otters, the strange marsh antelope called sitatunga, crocodiles and the occasional hippo.

Bao Bolon itself is a tributary of the River Gambia, meandering down from northern Senegal to meet the river in a broad shallow valley on the north bank, opposite Tendaba (which lies 8km downstream). Five other tributaries also feed in to the river in the area between the villages of **Salikene** and **Katchang**. The result is a riverside district that's a maze of pristine, briny creeks, fringed by unusually tall mangroves, some reaching over 20m. The creeks are as enjoyable as any in the country, but what makes this region unique is the fact that two other ecosystems, salt marsh and savannah woodland, are found in close proximity to the mangroves. Behind the mangroves is a large area of dazzlingly green waterweed; beyond this, the terrain is higher, rising to a quite dramatic citadel-like escarpment – location of the tiny fishing community of **Duntu Mallang**, surrounded by beautiful, ancient baobabs. Beyond this are occasional patches of delicate woodland amid broad, empty mudflats. The mudflats are driveable in the dry season from November to June, when the earth is baked to a salty crisp; after the rains, however, they become soft-going, with some parts impassable, and the terrain is green with reeds and grasses stretching as far as the horizon.

You get the best impression of the variety of remote habitats enclosed by the reserve by visiting by vehicle from the north bank of the river: there are **access tracks** from the Kerewan–Farafenni road at, from east to west, Katchang, Konti Kunda Niji, No Kunda, Njaba Kunda and Salikene. The reserve headquarters is a simple building at **Dai Mandinka**, 4km south of No Kunda (not to be confused with Dai Fula, a couple of kilometres east of Dai Mandinka) and the staff there may be able to help with guiding and with negotiating

Birdwatching in Bao Bolon Wetland Reserve

Bao Bolon Wetland Reserve is one of The Gambia's most rewarding areas for birdwatchers. The call of the African fish eagle is the reserve's most distinctive sound; other species to be found in the maze of creeks across the river from *Tendaba Camp* include the woolly-necked stork, striated heron, mouse-brown sunbird, goliath heron, the endangered brown-necked parrot and the whimsically named fairy blue flycatcher. African darters with strangely mobile necks sit on low branches and prosaically monikered Senegal thick-knees scrutinize passers-by from the mudbanks. The rare white-backed night heron, Pel's fishing owl and African finfoot are also occasionally seen.

a trip through the creeks by dugout *pirogue* with one of the fishermen from Duntu Mallang (this should cost no more than D500 per party). The closest hotel **accommodation** to the reserve is at Farafenni, or at Tendaba, across the river to the south. The reserve itself has nothing in the way of formal infrastructure for visitors, no vehicles available for hire, nor any other practical facilities. They're not used to taking any entrance fees here, either, and would prefer visitors to make all the arrangements they can at Abuko (see p.143). You'll have to make the trip in your own 4WD, or arrange a trip with a ground tour operator (see pp.49–51). Exploring this way, you'll have the opportunity to visit some of the twenty-odd villages in the reserve area, none of which receives many foreign visitors.

The usual way to visit, though one that shows you only a fraction of the reserve, is to take one of the highly enjoyable **pirogue excursions** organized by *Tendaba Camp*, likely to be advertised simply as a "creek trip" rather than a visit to Bao Bolon. Your *pirogue* takes you across the River Gambia first, then to the Kissi and Tunku creeks, where you can often see birds at very close range. If you ask the guide and keep your own eyes peeled, this is also a good place to look for monitor lizards – there are some big ones around, occasionally to be seen warming themselves on horizontal branches. Trips need to be timed carefully to make the best of the tides.

Kerewan

The promisingly large-looking settlement of **Kerewan**, marked on maps at the western end of Lower Baddibu District near Jowara Bolon, turns out on arrival to have virtually nothing to offer visitors. It's strictly a one-horse town, with no sign of the horse, no restaurants, no lodgings and no electricity. The wharf on the *bolon*, a kilometre out of town to the west near the bridge, is one possible access point to Kemoto, on the south bank of the main river. But, otherwise, the most exciting thing about Kerewan, or rather the **Yahya Jammeh's Bridge** over the *bolon* on the route to Barra, is the start of a decent tarmac highway back to the coast.

Travel details

Buses

Due to the state of the roads in the region, no buses are currently running

Bush taxis

Bintang to: Brikama (1hr 30min)
Bwiam to: Brikama (1hr 30min–2hr), Serrekunda (2hr–2hr 30min), Soma (2hr 30min–3hr).

Farafenni to: Kau-ur (1–1hr 30min); Kerewan (3hr); Kuntaur (3–4hr); Lamin Koto for Janjanbureh (3hr 30min–4hr 30min).
Kwinella to: Brikama (2hr 30min–3hr); Serrekunda (3–3hr 30min); Soma (1hr 30min–2hr).
Soma to: Bansang (2hr 30min–3hr 30min); Basse (3hr 30min–4hr 30min); Brikama (4–5hr); Sankulay Kunda for Janjanbureh (1hr 30min–2hr); Serrekunda (5–6hr).

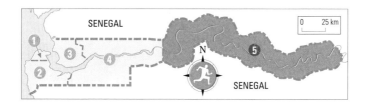

Eastern Gambia

CHAPTER 5 Highlights

✳ **Traditional villages** A visit to some of The Gambia's most remote up-river settlements is a great way to learn about tribal ritual and rural life in a harsh environment. See p.231

✳ **Wassu stone circles** Mysterious relics of ancient Senegambian culture, the Wassu stone circles are the most impresssive of The Gambia's prehistoric sites. See p.237

✳ **River Gambia National Park** The park's lush, jungle-covered islands are a high point of trips up-river by *pirogue*, offering a chance to spot chimpanzees and hippos. See p.240

✳ **Janjanbureh** Once a crucial river-trading centre, this island is now one of The Gambia's emerging ecotourism destinations, excellent for birdwatching, fishing and river-excursions. See p.241

✳ **Basse** Experience small-town, up-country life in Basse, a busy commercial crossroads beautifully located on a fine stretch of river. See p.250

△ Chimp, River Gambia National Park

Eastern Gambia

S cenically, **eastern Gambia** conforms to a stereotypical European view of Africa – a thin scattering of picturesque villages with grass-thatched huts, fenced with woven millet stalks or pickets of twisted branches, isolated in open countryside where sheep and cattle roam in search of pasture. Outside the villages, women bend over vegetable plots, pound grain under shade trees, or collect immense loads of firewood to carry home on their heads; under the *bantabas*, men discuss village politics or just lounge about. The massive, statuesque baobabs that dominate the landscape wherever there's a settlement – or wherever one used to be – bear witness to the ancient roots of these communities.

Up-country villagers eke out an existence with minimal resources, particularly on the **north bank** of the river, where paved highways are a novelty and few households have electricity. The living environment, and the climate, can be harsh: while the land adjacent to the River Gambia is thickly wooded and green all the year round, just a short walk away from the river the ground is blackened by bush fires or desiccated by the heat by the middle of the dry season, and only the hardiest trees and shrubs survive.

Culturally, there is much to discover about rural Gambia in this region, particularly if you know at least a few basic phrases in Mandinka, or have a good guide to translate – preferably both. **Tribal traditions** are in many ways more intact here than anywhere else in the country, and villagers are generally proud to share and explain elements of their culture, such as music and dance, with interested visitors.

Road travel along the **south bank** is far more comfortable in eastern than in central Gambia, partly because the tarmac sees very few heavy vehicles – as soon as you enter the region via the districts of **Jarra** and **Niamina**, the highway is almost empty of traffic of any sort and you'll often see neatly turned-out children walking long distances to and from school, right in the middle of the road.

One of the region's main attractions is the River Gambia itself, which at most times of year is still fresh water as far west as the rice-growing town of **Kau–ur** and some way beyond. As it flows through eastern Gambia, the river is not yet fringed by the mangrove forests that characterize its lower reaches; instead, the banks are wooded with palms and tropical evergreen trees, sometimes overshadowed by dramatic laterite escarpments.

On the north bank, close to the north bank town of **Kuntaur**, are the **Wassu stone circles**, an atmospheric remnant of Senegambian prehistory whose original purpose continues to puzzle archaeologists. Mid-river, east of Kuntaur, lies a series of islands, each covered with tropical forest, the closest The Gambia gets to jungle. One group of these, **Baboon Islands**, comprises the **River Gambia**

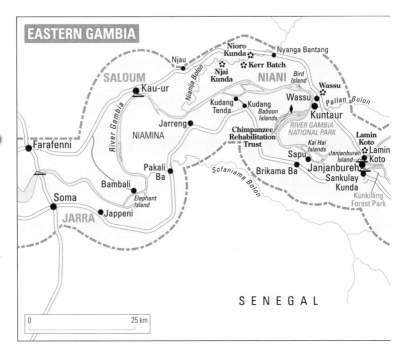

National Park, part of which is home to a chimpanzee rehabilitation project. The project has recently built some highly attractive accommodation for small groups of visitors who can enjoy the pristine river environment and observe the chimps at close range: it's not possible to set foot on the islands where the chimps live, but guests can get very good views from the wardens' boat. Others passing through the park on river trips may catch more distant glimpses of primates – not only chimps but also monkeys and baboons – as they cruise alongside the islands. This is also the most likely stretch of river for spotting hippos.

The usual starting point for boat trips in the region, and for short excursions to the stone circles, is **Janjanbureh Island** (also called MacCarthy Island). The island is becoming one of The Gambia's foremost ecotourism destinations, with the best choice of accommodation up-river; it's also home to the small, sleepy town of **Janjanbureh**, an old British colonial settlement.

The arc of land east of Janjanbureh is the tail end of the country, where the river makes its first winding inroads into The Gambia. On its south bank is the town of **Bansang**, impoverished and with a world-weariness that doesn't recommend itself to most visitors, but legendary among birdwatchers for its large population of bee-eaters. **Basse**, a riverside trading town further upstream, is a more appealing place, which, though small, has a distinctive energy. Well-connected, it's convenient as an endpoint for a long-distance trip up-river by *pirogue*, or as a stopover en route to Senegal's famous Niokola-Koba National Park. The area east of Basse is scattered with villages which are some of the remotest in this far-flung region, including **Fatoto**, just 10km from The Gambia's eastern tip, a quiet, unassuming village huddled around the country's easternmost river trading post.

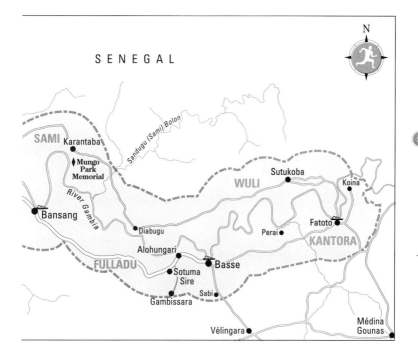

East to Janjanbureh: the south bank

Travelling up-country from central Gambia towards Janjanbureh and Basse along the south bank highway, the first districts you'll pass through after Soma are Jarra and Niamina. After the appalling state of the highway west of Soma, the conditions further east come as a great relief if you're travelling this way: as you leave Soma and continue through **Jarra district**, the potholed oyster-shell mix gives way to hot, black tarmac, with less frequent cracks and holes. On the way towards the village of **Jappeni** by road, you pass through a fairly wild stretch of bush where you're likely to see baboons and other monkeys. Jappeni itself is a good place to look out for marabou storks and wood ibis, which nest in trees in the village. The next sizeable village along the highway is **Kudang**, 18km to the northeast, set back from the river. Its wharf, Kudang Tenda, lies four kilometres north of the village along a bumpy track.

Heading up-river into **Niamina District**, the highway bears north to follow the river's meanderings. The first sizeable village you pass is **PAKALI BA**, 50km from Soma, a village by the Sofaniama *bolon*. It's an attractive village of traditional huts and compounds, marked by a ridge of small rocky hills – an unusual feature in this region of otherwise gently undulating savannah.

Pakali Ba is not the kind of place where tourists usually stop, but it has a vibrant local **story-telling tradition**. *Griots* here tell a tale about a local crocodile hunter called Bambo Bojang ("Crocodile Bojang"), related to the Bojang clan of the Katchikali crocodile pool in Bakau (see p.127), whose magical powers gave him immunity from crocodile attacks. Not surprisingly, he's now the patron saint of crocodiles; his descendants live in the area.

Niamina district is mostly flat, with open grasslands giving way to palm stands nearer the river, and palm beds, chairs and other furniture are handmade here. **Jarreng**, 12km northwest of Pakali Ba, is one of the handful of small towns in this area where you'll see an impressive – and very cheap – range of furniture laid out for sale beside the highway.

A few kilometres beyond the limit of Niamina in Fulladu West, and 110km east of Soma, is **BRIKAMA BA**, which is just another roadside village most days of the week. However, it springs into colourful life on Saturday, the day of its *lumo* (market), with stalls lining the highway and crammed into the backstreets, piled with fresh local produce, plus brightly-striped plastic kettles, flower-patterned enamel bowls, and other cheap household goods. Travelling traders weave through the crowds with trays of commodities on their heads, and livestock buyers size up bleating sheep and bellowing goats. There's a

△ Up-river scene

5

convenient and comfortable **place to stay** in this area – the National Agricultural Research Institute (NARI) rest house (T & F 567 8073, ask for the Station Manager; ❷) at **Sapu**, on the riverbank some 3km down the slope from Brikama Ba. With air-conditioning, fans and a kitchen, its seven rooms are often booked up.

The river in this area is broad and smooth, ringing with birdsong, with palm trees arcing over the water, and jungly vegetation behind. Across the river and connected to the south bank by a speedy GPTC ferry is the village of **BARA-JALI**, birthplace of ex-President Jawara, for which reason it was declared a national monument in 1985. Occasional bush taxis run from here to **Wassu**, the site of The Gambia's most famous stone circles (see p.237).

East to Janjanbureh: the north bank

The north bank of the River Gambia between **Elephant Island** and **Baboon Islands** (42km apart as the crow flies, but over double that by dusty road or winding river) is one of The Gambia's most fascinating areas – particularly for those with an interest in African prehistory and spirituality, as the country's greatest concentration of megalithic sites is found here. Most of these are in open bush between the rice-growing towns of **Kau-ur**, a small town at the point of one of the river's sharper bends, and **Kuntaur**, about 50km upstream. Just inland from Kuntaur, and very close to the main north bank highway, are the Gambia's most notable prehistoric remains, the **Wassu stone circles**. These famous, atmospheric stones are easily visitable within a day from Janjanbureh, 20km southeast of Wassu, and are a highlight of any broader exploration of archaeological sites in the region.

Kuntaur is the only sizeable north bank town east of Farafenni; most of the area's population are subsistence farmers living in traditional, isolated villages. There's a sense of the area being little-affected by the passage of time – village women still fetch water by hand from the river and its tributaries to tend their vegetable plots, and private vehicles are practically unknown. A few pockets of the area are home to ethnic groups little found elsewhere in The Gambia, such as the Fana Fana, a Wolof-speaking group distinct from the Wolofs of coastal Gambia and Senegal.

The main road from Farafenni that skirts the river's extravagant loops to Kau-ur and on to Kuntaur is newly surfaced, opening up this once-isolated region. Away from the river, the terrain is extremely dry for most of the year, with immense baobab and silk cotton trees looming over an otherwise almost featureless scrubby landscape. Around the villages in the growing season are swaying stalks of millet and grass-like couscous; after the harvest, however, the fields are bare except for golden stubble.

The bends of the river upstream of Elephant Island are particularly beautiful, the banks lined with gallery forest, resonating with bird calls all year round. Travelling long-distance by boat allows you to enjoy the scene to the full, and sharp-eyed visitors will spot families of **monkeys** staring from the treetops, and maybe even submerged **hippos**, their ears and nostrils just visible. Large well-wooded islands lie midriver, and the richest in foliage are **Baboon Islands**. These five islands make up the **River Gambia National Park**, part of which is home to an isolated population of West African **chimpanzees,** reintroduced to The Gambia under a rehabilitation programme which has recently started offering accommodation to small groups of visitors.

Elephant Island and Bambali

If you're travelling up-river by boat, the first stretches of water in which you might see hippos are a few kilometres east of the Bambatenda–Yelitenda ferry, where the estuarine part of the river ceases and the mangroves peter out. The no-longer appropriately named **Elephant Island** midstream appears to be the lowest grazing ground of The Gambia's small, threatened population of hippos, and there's a chance of catching a glimpse of them – or at least hearing them – anywhere between here and Janjanbureh.

On a north bank peninsula enclosed by a tight curve of the river between Farafenni and Kau-ur, the village of **BAMBALI**, 20km from the main road and right opposite Elephant Island, is sufficiently isolated to feel like an island community. Boat-trips between Tendaba and Janjanbureh (see p.52) sometimes stop at the jetty here. Visiting with a group, and walking up the broad red path to the village, you may, after shaking a few hands, be treated to a semi-impromptu drumming and dancing session from some of the village women – a display more full of joy and spontaneous energy than many of those given by professional troupes found elsewhere in the country. By opening their village to visitors, the community at Bambali has raised the money to buy a grain milling machine.

Kau-ur

KAU-UR, only 40km from Farafenni but well over an hour's drive away, is a small, conservative Wolof town, where the biggest activity is rice-cultivation. The extensive irrigated ricefields between the river wharf and the town are lush in the growing season, and are worked almost exclusively by women, while the men concern themselves with the cash crops – groundnuts, couscous, millet and maize. Despite the fertility of the region, the town doesn't manage to grow enough rice to feed itself all year round – nine months is the best they can hope for, sometimes only six if the rains fail – and the peanut works on the river wharf is long-abandoned. While the rice fields are fresh and beautiful before the harvest, at other times of year there's little in Kau-ur to detain visitors. The town itself, though not large, is spread out well away from the river, but the bush taxi garage, post office, telecentres and market, plus a few very basic shops are all very near the small central square. There's a petrol station on the Farafenni to Kuntaur highway.

Kuntaur

KUNTAUR, 56km east of Kau-ur, is also a **rice-growing** town, on a beautiful bend in the river. The town centre, set back from the river, is sleepy, torpid even, except on the day of its weekly market. It's an impoverished place, with the highest fertility rates in the country – women on average having seven children each. The main reason to pass through is to switch between river and road transport: it's the main transfer point for visitors to the Chimpanzee Rehabilitation Project (see p.240) and the start and endpoint for some of the Janjanbureh river cruises which pass Baboon Islands and the River Gambia's most outstanding stretches of riverine forest. You can also find transport from Kuntaur to the Wassu stone circles. With some hunting around, it's possible to hire a pick-up bush taxi, or a horse and cart, for the two-kilometre journey – the easiest day for this is Monday, the day of Wassu's *lumo*. If you find yourself stranded overnight, it's worth asking for directions to Kuntaur's *Agricultural Rest House* (no phone, ❶); it's basic and not geared up for tourists but anyone can request a bed here.

The area upstream of Kuntaur is one of the most likely places on the River Gambia to spot **hippos** – good news for wildlife enthusiasts, but bad news for local farmers, whose crops are often destroyed by these hungry creatures. It's bad news, too, for locals travelling to and from their fields by river: in January 2001, seven people lost their lives when a hippo capsized their canoe. Survivors reported that the hippo attacked the boat after one of the seven threw an orange at it in an attempt to scare it away.

The Wassu stone circles

The **Wassu Stone Circles** (daily 8am–7pm; D50), a national monument, are vestiges of a prehistoric society about which virtually nothing is known. Located on the edge of Wassu village, a little over 2km inland from Kuntaur, and 20km northwest of Janjanbureh, the site is The Gambia's second most-visited tourist attraction on the north bank, after Juffureh. Most visitors arrive here with some idea of what the circles look like, as part of the site features on the back of the 50-dalasi note. It's no Stonehenge, so adjust your expectations accordingly, yet it's an atmospheric place, even for visitors with no particular interest in prehistory.

The hardened laterite pillars, clustered in eleven loose rings around burial places, vary from mere stumps to veritable menhirs weighing several tonnes and standing three metres high. Carbon dating has pinpointed some of them to 750 AD, pre-dating the migration of the Mandinkas to this area; local oral history therefore contains no clues as to the stones' precise cultural origins. It's considered good form to leave rocks on top of the pillars – again, no one knows why.

The compound enclosing the standing stones contains a small **museum**, with detailed illustrations and explanations showing how the stones were quarried and rolled into place, and models of the burial sites beneath the circles. As this is a much-visited site in a relatively isolated area, visitors are often hassled by local kids; the museum's watchman tackles this by running at them with a large stick.

The Wassu stone circles are worth visiting at different times of year, if you have the opportunity, as the landscape changes radically with the seasons. After recent rainfall the stones are surrounded by billowing stands of long green grass. By the end of the dry season, however, they stand in near-desert – apart from a few fruit trees, the only remaining vegetation nearby is the areas of grass outside the compound that have escaped both the bushfires and the grass-harvesters.

Wassu itself is a small village that sees tourists regularly, but it's only really busy on a Monday, the day of its *lumo*, when the village's main thoroughfare (which is also the north bank highway) and the street behind it are clogged up with a jumble of stalls selling fabric, household goods, and foodstuffs.

Practicalities

Wassu is a standard stop on **group tours** of the area, by road or by boat, from or via Janjanbureh. To get there independently, your most likely starting point is Janjanbureh, a thirty-minute ride away by **bush taxi**. *Gelleh-gelleh* bush taxis leave from the Lamin Koto ferry ramp on the north bank of the river opposite Janjanbureh town; those heading to the village of Wassu or on to Kau-ur or Farafenni will drop you a few hundred metres from the stones. The best chance of transport there and back in a day is to go on a Monday, the day of Wassu's *lumo*. Approaching along the north bank from the west, Wassu is served by bush taxis from Farafenni and Kau-ur; however, if you'd like to explore any other stone circles in the area adjoining this route, you'll need a hired vehicle or private taxi.

Wassu has one **place to stay**, the *Berreto Village Camp* (no phone; ❶), sign-posted just off the highway, but it's not really recommended. This local drinking hole can accommodate a handful of guests; the atmosphere is friendly enough, and it's an easy walk from the stones, but it's very basic and there's no guarantee of security. Janjanbureh's accommodation options are a much better bet (see p.246). For simple **meals** in Wassu, a few places serve rice and sauce or *afra* along the highway in the village.

Kerr Batch and other stone circles

While Wassu is the most-visited and arguably the most impressive of the stone circle sites in this region, there are other circles to discover on the north bank, and even more if you pursue the quest into the Sine-Saloum region of Senegal. Many of these are hardly worth a second glance, but some are very striking. All but a couple stand in open bush, rather than fenced and groomed as at Wassu, giving them a wilder, more spiritual atmosphere. While these circles are sometimes still used as places of prayer and reflection, and even as burial sites, villagers are not precious about outsiders visiting them, and active interest from outsiders has led to organizations such as UNESCO supporting efforts to preserve the stones. In The Gambia, the sites are thinly scattered over a large area, more than 4000 square kilometres in extent. For visitors with limited time, the best area to investigate is the valley of the **Nianija Bolon**, between Wassu and the village of Njau, about 40km west of Wassu via the main north bank road.

The best-known site after Wassu, and the only other one for which there's an entrance fee (D50) is **Kerr Batch**, famous for its **lyre stone** near the centre of the site, a bizarre V-shaped megalith about 2m high. Legend suggests lyre stones indicate the co-burial of two people who died on the same day, and there are only a few examples in The Gambia; when this one toppled and broke a couple of decades ago, locals ham-fistedly patched it together with cement, leaving it looking rather forlorn. Kerr Batch, enclosed in a small compound, lacks the atmosphere of the unfenced circles but is worth visiting for its tiny but informative **museum** of rural artefacts from the Fula and Wolof tribes living in the Upper Saloum, Niani and Nianija districts. On display are beads, anklets, initiation masks, musical instruments and tools for cooking, fishing, hunting and farming; together they illustrate and explain the significance of the various trades in traditional Gambian society. Here you'll discover that Gambian leatherworkers double as town criers and mediators, and that blacksmiths are thought to have wizard-like powers because of their ability to control fire, a refuge for potent spirits. Kerr Batch is well signposted along the dust track from the main road at the village of **Nyanga Bantang**, 16km northeast of Wassu via the north bank highway. If you approach from another direction, it's useful to know that the local name for the place is Sinchu Demba.

Other standing stones in the Nianija valley include those on each side of the road at **Niani Maru**, 11km northwest of Kuntaur (a total of eight circles), and three more, including two concentric ones, 7km northwest of Nyanga Bantang at **Nioro Kunda**. The largest stones in the region (over 3m high and possibly weighing as much as 10 tonnes) are found in the two circles at **Njai Kunda**, near the village of Charmen, on the south side of the *bolon*, about 17km southwest of Nyanga Bantang.

To find the circles, you'll need an independent means of travel, and preferably a **guide** who can ask for directions and information in Mandinka, Serahule and Wolof. If you're not already travelling with a hired vehicle and guide from Kombo district, you could make enquiries at Janjanbureh's lodges. Without a guide, your best chance of information about the stones is to seek out a bright

Stone circles are subtle, mysterious, and a puzzle to archaeologists, and nowhere else in the world is there such a concentration of these as in the large area between eastern Gambia and the River Saloum in Senegal. The Gambia has around a hundred stone circles, mostly well over a thousand years old and very well preserved, in over thirty sites north of the river between Farafenni and Basse.

It's logical to assume a connection between The Gambia's wealth of megalithic sites (not just stone circles, but also isolated standing stones, tumuli or burial mounds, and cairns known as *tombelles*) and those of places as far-flung as Guinea-Bissau, Brittany, and the Orkney Islands, the similarities are so apparent. However, their original purpose remains uncertain. Possibly, the circles were used as clocks, or astrological calendars of some sort, or were merely there to mark and decorate **graves**. Some researchers have also suggested the stones might represent points of the compass, celestial bodies, or phases of the human life cycle, and might have been used as places of healing, insight and prayer.

The consistent appearance and construction of The Gambia's stone circles seem to suggest the work of a single, localized culture, its identity now completely lost. All are rings of between 10 and 24 **cylindrical pillars**, and all the pillars in any one ring are the same height, typically around shoulder height (elsewhere in the region, most stones are 60–310cm high and 30–115cm in diameter). Carbon dating has shown they were created over a period of around 1500 years between the third century BC and the thirteenth century AD, and they all enclose a **burial area** which in some cases pre-dates the circles by a significant period, suggesting the sites themselves were sacred. The **grave goods** found by excavation offer few solid clues: tombs have yielded iron arrows and spear heads, pottery vessels, and gold and bronze ornaments, all badly damaged by time. Such **skeletons** as have been discovered near the circles (notably at Sine Ngayebe in Senegal) appear to have been buried hastily, rather than neatly laid out in the manner of kings or chiefs, suggesting they may have been the victims of sacrifice or disease. Their appearance would have been similar to present-day Senegambians, and some have decorative notches between their two upper front teeth, a practice that persists today among some Jola tribes.

All the stones in the Senegambian stone circles are hewn from **laterite**, the deep russet-brown iron-rich sandstone that colours escarpments and outcrops all over the region, and is used as a road surface in lieu of tarmac. Laterite has a rough, spongy-looking surface texture that makes the stones seem even older than they are, as if bitten by rust over centuries. It's relatively easy to quarry and carve, gradually hardening after exposure to air, and it's a source of iron ore – the stones would have been cut using iron tools made from this raw material. Once carved into pillars, they were moved laboriously into position using wooden rollers, and held in place by a trench and retaining wall of small stones just below the ground. While most are still upright, centuries on, some have sagged backwards or fallen flat where the ground supporting them has softened.

Today, plenty of local **superstition** and spiritual belief still surrounds the stone circles, and their custodians will sometimes come to the circles to pray, bringing offerings of vegetables, candles or money. Some say that certain stones are luminous by night; others say that harm will befall anyone who tampers with the circles – which might partly explain why few exhaustive excavations have taken place.

youngster in the nearest village to each site, as few adults in the off-road areas speak fluent English.

The villages in the vicinity of the stone circles are quiet, appealing places to visit in their own right. The landscape along the Nianija Bolon is lush with tall rhun palms and reed beds, and the villages are small fenced settlements of

Chimpanzee Rehabilitation Project

The Gambia's **Chimpanzee Rehabilitation Project** (✉ crt@jdmar.freeserve.co.uk, ⊛ chimprehab.com, UK contact: ☎ 07881/687135, ✉ sarahlin@aol.com) is the longest-running project of its kind in Africa. It currently protects and monitors a population of 77 chimpanzees. These include animals that prior to their adoption were struggling to survive, let alone breed; now, however, their offspring, born on the islands, have in some cases produced young of their own. Once reasonably common, chimps had been hunted out of existence in The Gambia by the 1900s, and the islands are now the only part of the country where they're found in the wild.

Set up in 1969 by Stella Marsden, daughter of Eddie Brewer, the founder of Abuko Nature Reserve, the project's original purpose was to provide long-term care for a group of chimpanzees confiscated from hunters and traders by the Gambian wildlife authorities. The success of this endeavour led Stella to rescue and rehabilitate more West African chimpanzees that had been orphaned by poachers, or maltreated in captivity.

Animals discovered in distress in locations as far apart as Senegal and Germany are now brought to The Gambia to be nurtured back to physical and psychological health. After an initial period of assessment and care, they're integrated into the independent communities of chimps living on three islands within the River Gambia National Park. Here, in forest uninhabited by humans, they can rediscover their natural environment.

Until recently, the stretches of river nearest the project headquarters were completely out of bounds to visitors, but it's now possible for individuals and small groups to spend a night or two in the project's new, dedicated 🏕 **Visitor Camp** (contact details as above; packages including transport to Kuntaur available from The Gambia Experience (UK), ☎ 0845/330 2060, ⊛ www.gambia.co.uk; Hidden Gambia (UK) ☎ 01527/576239, ⊛ www.hiddengambia.com; Tilly's Tours (Kololi) ☎ 770 7356; full board including chimp-watching activities and boat tours ❽). Though expensive for The Gambia, the camp offers what is without a doubt one of the country's most remarkable wilderness experiences. It's situated in remote riverside woodland on a south-facing section of the south bank of the river, a gentle thirty-minute boat ride

---

mudbrick huts. Those along the track from the main road at Nyanga to Kerr Batch see a fair number of visitors passing through; beyond this, the villages see very few travellers.

The closest circles to the ones at Wassu are at **Pallan Mandinka** and **Jakaba**, near the Pallan Bolon. There's also a small circle at **Lamin Koto**, within easy walking distance of Janjanbureh, nine short, dumpy stones right beside the main road in the shade of a kuling tree, around 1km north of the ferry ramp.

River Gambia National Park

The beautiful stretch of river surrounding **Baboon Islands**, a collection of five small forested islands immediately southwest of Kuntaur, and the islands themselves, constitute the **River Gambia National Park**. The islands, which cover an area totalling a little under six square kilometres, include areas of swamp and savannah as well as forest.

While it's not possible for visitors to land on the islands, you can get good, close-up views of the forest fringes and the resident wildlife by booking into the visitor accommodation at the **Chimpanzee Rehabilitation Project** (see box above), and touring the park by boat in the company of one of their guides. Three of the islands are populated by chimpanzees introduced here by the trust; as well as seeing some of these (and hearing others) during your visit, you stand

from Kuntaur or a bumpy ten-kilometre drive from Kudang. Down at the water's edge is a rustic stilted lodge, used as a meeting place and dining room, and, perched on timber platforms high up on the riverside escarpment overlooking the islands, are four comfortable and attractive **safari tents**, each with romantic outdoor showers and stunning views. Guests can meet the project workers and follow the chimp feeding party which heads out by boat at 4pm each day, mooring at various points within fruit-throwing range of the islands. Excited by the mangoes, pumpkins, baobabs and *tapalapa* bread on offer, the chimps (from dominant males to tiny infants) cavort in the foliage at the water's edge, providing fantastic close-up views.

The feeding sessions may last little more than half an hour in total, depending on the animals' needs, but you can stay out on the water much longer than this by taking a boat tour of the peaceful, bird-rich river, puttering along close to the lush banks and visiting areas that are out of bounds to the standard boat tours that just pass through the main channel. Project guests can also head into the nearby village of Sambel Kunda by vehicle or horse-drawn cart, to visit the headquarters of the **Gambia Horse and Donkey Trust** (Ⓦ www.gambiahorseanddonkey.org), another of Stella Marsden's active concerns. This charity educates Gambians in efficient and sustainable horse and donkey management, and has an impressive success rate in improving working animals' productivity, health and well-being.

The chimp project is registered as a UK charity under the name of the **Chimpanzee Rehabilitation Trust**. While it receives many enquiries from individuals wishing to visit or to volunteer as assistants or researchers, the nature of the rehabilitation programme requires the chimpanzees to have **minimal contact** with people, so few requests can be accommodated. However, anyone can contribute by joining the chimp adoption scheme for £30 a year. Sponsors receive updates on the progress of their chosen chimp, with photos, twice a year, as well as a newsletter covering the community and its day-to-day life.

a good chance of spotting baboons, western red colobus and callithrix monkeys, hippos and numerous bird species including kingfishers, rollers, ospreys, herons and pelicans. West African manatees swim in these waters, too, though they're rare and seldom seen.

It's also possible to enjoy a more distant view of the islands from the river channel that's accessible to the general public; you'll pass this way if you take a **river tour** by boat to or from Janjanbureh (see p.247). When tourist boats enter the waters of the park, patrol boats collect a D100 per person entry fee (normally included in the cost of your tour). They also ensure that visitors don't anchor close to the islands, and it's essential that their directions are followed, both for the welfare of the island wildlife and for visitors' own safety: some of the primates behave aggressively when there are humans in sight. As your boat passes, you may be able to see families of chimps moving through the foliage or, with territorial screeching, shaking the branches.

Janjanbureh Island

Three hundred kilometres upstream from Banjul, and twenty square kilometres in area, **Janjanbureh Island** (also still known by its colonial name, MacCarthy

Island) is the only one of the River Gambia's wonderful, bird-rich islands easily accessible to tourists. A leafy retreat for visitors wanting to escape the tourist traps on the coast, the island is fast becoming one of the country's foremost ecotourism destinations, with excellent opportunities for exploring the river and viewing wildlife, and it offers the best range of accommodation in eastern Gambia. For most visitors, their stay is focused around one of Janjanbureh's bush lodges. The most-visited lodges are situated in beautiful riverside woodland, and make good bases for river-swimming, boat trips and wilderness walks.

If you're staying in the bush, you'd be forgiven for giving **Janjanbureh town** a miss. Also known as Georgetown, it's a characterful place, but backwaters don't come much further back than this. It lies at a crossroads of sorts, half way between Kau-ur and Basse and with river access to both the north and south banks. Once a crucial river trading post and administrative centre for the British, the town's present-day layout, and many of its buildings, date from the colonial period.

It's possible to visit Janjanbureh by two- or three-day group **excursion** by road from the coastal resorts, travelling by small coach, stopping at a couple of places of interest along the way, and staying at one of the lodges, usually *Bird Safari Camp* or *Janjang Bureh Camp*; a half-day river trip may be included. It's also possible, and highly recommended, to visit by double-decker *pirogue*, cruising upstream from Banjul, Bintang, Tendaba or Kuntaur, or downstream from Fatoto or Basse, possibly spending a few nights on board on the way (see p.52).

Some history

Over the centuries, Janjanbureh's midriver location and its mild, fertile terrain have provided a **safe haven** for runaway slaves, marabouts fleeing religious persecution, and traders looking for somewhere secure and well-connected to buy and sell groundnuts and other commodities. In 1823, when the **British** were ceded the island of Janjanbureh by the King of Niani for five cases of coins and a case of wine, it included no permanent settlements. Oral history suggests there were people already here, but little is known about them.

The British began to use the island as a base for trading, farming, and missionary work, and as a suitable point from which to defend the river against illegal slave traders. The first settlers included a group of Wesleyan missionaries, who established what is now West Africa's oldest remaining Methodist church (still visitable in the town centre), a number of traders from the embryonic Crown Colony of Bathurst (now Banjul), and an attachment of the West Indian Regiment, who, on the north side of the island, built a small mudbrick fort and named it **Fort George** after King George IV. These pioneers went on to construct Georgetown's wharves and warehouses, and trading in cloth, guns, iron, and local produce such as palm oil began in earnest.

Akus, the African slaves liberated by the British, arrived in the 1830s. Many of them were skilled artisans and labourers, and they helped develop the island's agricultural potential. They also benefited from Georgetown's unusually good **mission schools**: by the mid-nineteenth century, the town was firmly established as the best centre of education in up-country Gambia. The prestigious Armitage High School, founded in 1927 as a school for the sons of the Gambian aristocracy, and now the country's only government-funded co-educational senior secondary boarding school, is still highly respected.

When the trading and transport of **groundnuts** between the interior and the coast gathered pace in the 1930s, Georgetown was the hub of the business, its economy booming. By this time it was The Gambia's second town and an administrative centre for the Protectorate. In the 1960s, with the assistance of experts from China, **rice-cultivation** by irrigation was introduced, although the momentum of development didn't last. After Independence in 1965, Georgetown's fortunes changed. Much of the island's significance was lost in the 1970s after the completion of the south bank highway, and its fate was sealed by the closure of the riverboat service, leaving mainland towns like Bansang in a far better position for commerce. Georgetown's residents began to drift away to the Kombos now that the new road had made the distance much more manageable. Economic depopulation is still a problem in Janjanbureh: the island's youth are, on the whole, disillusioned about local career prospects.

With the growth of **ecotourism**, however, the community appears to be turning a corner. Although rice- and groundnut-cultivation are not wholly compatible with woodland conservation, the farmers here are beginning to appreciate the long-term merit of limiting the area of land farmed on the island, in order to safeguard the natural environment and its sizeable population of birds and mammals.

Arrival and orientation

Janjanbureh Island is connected to the mainland by two small vehicle **ferries** (see box on p.244). These take one truck or a couple of cars at a time, and when they're in good running order the crossings normally only take a few minutes. There are also a few small boats which operate as passenger ferries. The Lamin Koto vehicle ferry, the smaller passenger ferries and the *Janjang Bureh Camp* boat from the north bank of the river drop you right into Janjanbureh town.

The Sankulay Kunda ferry from the south bank takes you to the south side of the island. If you've crossed the river as a foot passenger then the cheapest way to get into town is to catch one of the island's few **bush taxis** (D5) along the 2.5-kilometre tarmac road – or just walk. The road leads through rice fields and pleasant countryside and eventually becomes the town's high street; it effectively connects the two ferry ramps.

Once you're in town, *Bird Safari Camp* is a boat ride away down the island to the west, using one of the small boats that normally wait at the *badala* (around D200 per group), or a bumpy drive by bush taxi (D75). *Janjang Bureh Camp* sits opposite the island on the north bank; if you're staying there, the boat to the camp from the rickety jetty east of the *badala* is free. All the other places to stay are in town, within easy walking distance. The town has a **post office**, a **Gamtel** office, and a hardware shop that doubles as a **telecentre**. Communications are unsophisticated here: neither *Bird Safari Camp* nor *Janjang Bureh Camp* has a phone on site (both use the landlines at their offices in town) and there's little or no mobile phone signal – mobile-owners here have been known to climb trees to make a call. There's Internet access at Gamspad, a skills centre at the east end of town.

Accommodation

Janjanbureh's **accommodation** options, mostly European-Gambian partnerships, are either bush lodges (well geared-up for tourists interested in exploring the natural environment, and comfortable but not luxurious) or simple guesthouses. Most are on the island itself; one is opposite the island on the River Gambia's north bank. Most of the places on the island are in Janjanbureh town, on the island's north shore. They're all are either right on, or very near, the riverbank, and close to unspoilt woodland. Some have generators, but a few rely on candles and lanterns by night, adding to the romance; none has hot running

Janjanbureh Island is accessible from both banks of the river. Most visitors cross from Banjul to Barra and then continue along the **north bank** highway, a distance of around 240km, most of which is newly paved or graded. Approaching via the main **south bank** highway, a 300km drive from Serrekunda, you'll have to tackle badly deteriorated roads for a significant part of the journey; at the time of writing, much-needed improvements to some, but not all, of this stretch were planned but unconfirmed.

The north bank route

Starting from Kombo district, you can join the **north bank route** by first taking the ferry from Banjul to Barra (see pp.102–103), and then following the north bank highway from there, travelling via Kerewan, Farafenni, Kau-ur and Wassu, to the Lamin Koto ferry ramp, close to *Janjang Bureh Camp* and right across the northern river channel from Janjanbureh town. One advantage of the north bank route is that you pass through some particularly interesting parts of the country, including the region east of Farafenni, where most of The Gambia's stone circles are concentrated. If travelling nonstop, you can cover the distance in four to five hours (not including the Barra ferry crossing).

Bush taxis cover the north bank highway from Barra to Lamin Koto. It may be necessary to take one vehicle to Farafenni (D60 or D75) and then change for Lamin Koto (D85). It's also possible to pick up transport at Kau-ur (D65) and Wassu (D20).

The **ferry** from Lamin Koto (8am–8pm; vehicles D45, foot passengers D2) brings you straight into Janjanbureh town in minutes – when it's running smoothly. As an alternative, hand-paddled iron tubs and engine-powered cruisers carry foot passengers across to the *badala* (wharf area) which doubles as the town's bush taxi garage, when there's demand.

The south bank route

Travelling from Kombo district to Janjanbureh by the **south bank route**, you follow the main south bank highway via Soma to the well-marked turning for the hamlet of **Sankulay Kunda** (this turning is west of Yori Beri Kunda and east of Sulolor Mandinka). After 3km, you reach the Sankulay Kunda ferry ramp; nearby are a telecentre and a couple of very basic eating places. The ferry (8am–8pm; vehicles D25, foot passengers D2) takes vehicles and passengers across the river channel to the southern side of Janjanbureh Island and is pulled by a cable – whenever the engine is out of order everybody on board is expected to help heave. Travelling nonstop from Serrekunda to Janjanbureh town takes a minimum of eight hours; you have to suffer the dusty and badly potholed stretches between Sotokoi and Soma on the way.

To travel up-country from Kombo district to Sankulay Kunda by **bush taxi** (D180), you can take a *gelleh-gelleh* minivan bound for Sankulay Kunda, Bansang or Basse from the garage at Bundung on the south side of Serrekunda or take a vehicle to Soma or Brikama and then change. Vehicles bound for Bansang and Basse will make the diversion to the Sankulay Kunda ferry for any passenger that requires this. Starting from Basse and heading west, the journey takes under two hours (D40); from Bansang, it's well under an hour (D10).

water, but you can ask for some to be heated for you. If you're travelling with a tent, you'll find some scenic potential pitches at *Baobolong Camp*, *Bird Safari Camp* or *Janjang Bureh Camp*.

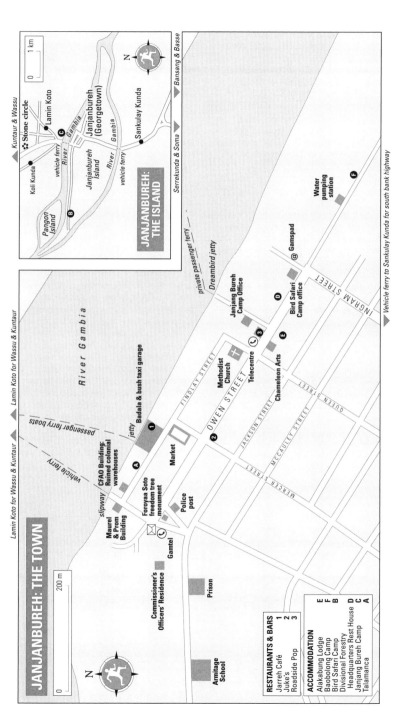

JANJANBUREH: THE TOWN

0 ___ 200 m

Lamin Koto for Wassu & Kuntaur

River Gambia

Lamin Koto for Wassu & Kuntaur

vehicle ferry
passenger ferry boats
slipway

CFAO Building:
Ruined colonial
warehouses

Maurel
& Prom
Building

Foroyaa Soto
freedom tree
monument

Gamtel

Badala & bush taxi garage

jetty

Market

Police
post

FINDLAY STREET

OWEN STREET

Methodist
Church

Telecentre

JACKSON STREET

Chameleon Arts

Janjang Bureh
Camp Office

Dreambird jetty

private passenger ferry

Bird Safari
Camp office

Ganspad

QUEEN STREET

MCCAULEY STREET

MERCER STREET

Water
pumping
station

INGRAM STREET

Commissioner's
Officers' Residence

Prison

Armitage
School

Vehicle ferry to Sankulay Kunda for south bank highway

Serrekunda & Soma

RESTAURANTS & BARS
Jarreh Café   1
Juke's   2
Roadside Pop   3

ACCOMMODATION
Alakabung Lodge   E
Baobolong Camp   F
Bird Safari Camp   B
Divisional Forestry
Headquarters Rest House   D
Janjang Bureh Camp   C
Talamanca   A

JANJANBUREH: THE ISLAND

0 ___ 1 km

Kuntaur & Wassu

Stone circle

Lamin Koto

Koli Kunda

Pangon Island

Janjanbureh Island

vehicle ferry

River Gambia

Janjanbureh (Georgetown)

vehicle ferry

River Gambia

Sankulay Kunda

Bansang & Basse

Serrekunda & Soma

Alakabung Lodge ☎567 6123. On the main street, a slightly rundown budget option with ten basic rooms with shower and fan in small thatched roundhouses. Gambian meals are available to order, but this can take some time. ❶

Baobolong Camp ☎567 6133 or 990 1667. Gambian-run lodge, a ten-minute walk east of the centre of town, a little off the beaten track, in a quarter with a village atmosphere. Spotlessly kept, its 37 brightly furnished rooms are in small houses around a compound. Meals can be provided when there's a group order, and even if you're not staying this is one of the best places in town to grab a cold beer. ❷

🏃 Bird Safari Camp ☎567 6108 (Georgetown office), ✉bsc@gamtel.gm, ⓦbsc.gm
. Bush lodge near the island's westernmost point, well away from the town, secluded in woodland that's excellent for short bird-walks. To get there, you take the dust track that leads westward from town, past the Armitage School and the colonial cemetery, through a grove of neem trees and some rice fields, and out into the bush. The eleven safari tents by the river are a little spartan, but with good private showers; there's also accommodation in spacious and comfortable self-contained thatched roundhouses, with West African-style beds. The rooms and tents all have electric light and fans, and there's also a river-water swimming pool (murky but, at the time of writing, due to be renovated). The food is decent but nothing special, and the overall atmosphere of the place can vary – it's an isolated spot, and everything goes into hibernation when it's not busy. At its liveliest, though, this is a great place to be, with exuberant after-dinner fireside drumming and dancing. Activities include drumming lessons, fishing, Gambian cooking sessions, village visits and excellent boat trips. ❹

Divisional Forestry Headquarters Rest House ☎567 6198 or 567 6199. Self-catering accommodation in the Forestry HQ compound in town, intended for visiting researchers, but others may stay if there's room. A gem of a place, set in a lush, wild garden by the river, with plenty of trees and a jetty perfect for diving off. The accommodation is in an attractive bungalow, with three bedrooms with fans and mosquito nets (room for six), a living room, a good kitchen and shower-room, and electricity from a generator. ❶

🏃 Janjang Bureh Camp ☎567 6182, or
   book through Gambia River Excursions,
Bakau, ☎449 4360, ✉contact@gambiariver.com, ⓦwww.gambiariver.com. Right opposite the island, in a beautiful grove of trees near Lamin Koto on the north bank of the river, this is Janjanbureh's most charming and friendly lodge. It's simple (no hot water or electricity) but comfortable, and very good value. The 27 thatched, whitewashed huts, rather like hobbit-houses, are all individually designed, curvy on the inside with interesting nooks and mini lofts. The buffet meals here are good, although they don't vary much. The lodge is often visited by monkeys, and its environs are excellent for bird-watching. Boat transfers across to town are free, and you can also hire a small motorboat or large *pirogue* by the hour or the day: possible trips include Sankulay Kunda (from D100 per group), right round the island (D1500), and to Kuntaur via the River Gambia National Park (D3500). When groups are staying, local drummers and dancers perform round a campfire after dark. ❷

Talamanca ☎992 1100. Primarily a bar, the rooms in this small riverside compound in town are basic (and noisy at times) but friendly and cheap. ❶

The Town

Janjanbureh town is laid out in a **grid system**, a reminder of its past as a British colonial administrative outpost. Much of the **architecture** in the old town dates from the late nineteenth and early twentieth century and there's a strong sense of buildings having been left to decay, whether in use or not, ever since Independence. Look carefully and you'll find the town's last-remaining **colonial lamp-post** (on the corner of Jackson and Mercer streets), once one of a network of functioning gas lamps, now sadly beheaded. There's also, on Owen Street, a single **timber-clad house**, similar to those found in Banjul, and very typical of the houses built in the 1830s by the Aku settlers.

The northeast quarter of the town resembles an open museum of the old trading days, with the tiled floors and ornate plasterwork of derelict warehouses disintegrating behind an onslaught of tropical vegetation. The **Maurel and Prom building** just west of the vehicle ferry ramp and the big roofless barn-like **CFAO building** are sometimes labelled "slave houses", but in fact both were built in the 1890s, and were probably stores for perishable goods. Just inland from the vehicle ferry ramp, in front of the police post, is the **Foroyaa Sooto Freedom Tree Monument**, a small triangular park with walls emblazoned with the Gambian colours. In the middle is a young, struggling bantang tree, planted to commemorate the Freedom Tree that used to stand in Fort George, near this spot. After the British ban on slave-trading in the early nineteenth century, MacCarthy Island became a refuge for runaway slaves from the surrounding area; the story goes that those who touched or hugged this tree had their names recorded by the British soldiers at Fort George, and were granted their freedom. These days, Janjanbureh is better known as a place of incarceration of another sort – it's the site of the country's main **prison**, a place so grim that a number of prisoners died of malnutrition in the early 1990s.

For local **crafts**, try Chameleon Arts, next to *Alakabung Lodge*, a colourful shop and artists' studio selling professional *koras* and *djembés*, jewellery and tie-dyed or painted handmade clothing. There are also a couple of places selling drums and crafts, but with rather limited stock, in the *badala* area.

By far the town's most appealing asset is the **river** itself. Locals will assure you that it's safe to swim here, since the level of human activity keeps crocodiles well away. **Fishing** enthusiasts will find plenty of good specimens in the water, and a trip by boat may well yield large catfish and even fierce-toothed, acrobatic tigerfish. You need the right bait, of course – apparently fly fishing is a non-starter, but live bait or balls of monkey dung work well. When deciding where to cast your line, remember that the River Gambia is tidal throughout the country. To arrange a fishing trip, or any other boat-trip, enquire at *Bird Safari Camp*, *Janjang Bureh Camp*, or *Baobolong Lodge*. Janjanbureh is in reach of stunning stretches of river, and Sapu, the Kai Hai Islands, the River Gambia National Park, Kuntaur (for Wassu) and Bansang all make good excursions. It's also a jumping-off point for long-distance **river-trips** to Tendaba and Basse (see p.51); this is a highly recommended way to experience the peaceful and scenically varied river environment.

Birdwatchers don't need to stray far from the camps to find an abundance of bird species. While the island itself and the north bank around *Janjang Bureh Camp* are excellent for bush walks, it's also worth making the short trip to **Kunkilling Forest Park and Tankandama Community Forest** on the south bank of the river opposite the east end of Janjanbureh Island, within ten minutes' drive of Sankulay Kunda (or 30min by boat from Janjanbureh town). This particularly fine patch of riverine woodland has recently been set up as a conservation area (tickets D100 from the Forestry Division HQ in Janjanbureh town, ☎567 6200). The park's observation platform, an impressive structure with a lofty open deck reached by a spiral staircase, is unique in The Gambia. White-backed vultures and red-necked falcons nest in the rhun palms here, while African finfoots forage through the roots of the screw pine trees. Other important tree species found in the forest include African mahogany, West African ebony and the rare dun palm.

Eating and drinking

Guests at *Janjang Bureh Camp*, *Bird Safari Camp* and *Baobolong Camp* invariably make their lodgings their base for **eating** and **drinking**, and non-residents may visit these camps for breakfast, lunch or the evening buffet (laid on whenever there's a group visiting), but there are also a few local-style options in town. *Juke's Bar and Bistro* is British-owned and serves cold JulBrew, soft drinks, some spirits and Gambian food until late; also open late for decent Gambian meals and drinks is *Roadside Pop*, near *Alakabung Lodge*. There's a clutch of simple eating and drinking places around the *badala* (wharf area) where the passenger ferries land and the

Birdwatching around Janjanbureh

Visitors to Janjanbureh's bush lodges are awoken by an enthusiastic dawn chorus, with the calls of hornbills and doves noticeable above the rest. Janjanbureh's woodland may yield sightings of yellow-crowned gonolek and pearl spotted owl; hammerkop, egrets and African crake frequent the rice fields; and the area around *Bird Safari Camp* is famous for swamp flycatchers. The island has plenty of conspicuous, chattering gaggles of glossy starlings, and Abyssinnian rollers are equally easy to spot. You could set out by boat in search of Pel's fishing owl, African finfoot (elusive but sometimes seen by the river), and carmine bee-eater, seen in silhouette on upper branches. Very occasionally, Egyptian plovers, more commonly associated with the Basse area, are found this far downstream between August and February.

bush taxis wait: they include *Jarreh Café*, a shack which serves tea, coffee, sandwiches and eggs in the mornings, and *Talamanca*, a small, noisy compound doubling as a drinking hole, with basic accommodation (see p.246).

East from Janjanbureh

Although eastern Gambia is, geographically at least, a gateway to the rest of West Africa, there's an increasing sense of remoteness the further east you go. The few travellers who take the time to explore the backroads of the districts beyond Janjanbureh will find a scattering of isolated Mandinka, Fula, Serer and Serahule villages, in a landscape which, on the **south bank**, is relatively lush with palms and towering mahogany trees; the **north bank**, by contrast, is austere, arid and breathtakingly hot.

The usual mode of transport for villagers in this region is by simple horse-drawn cart, or on foot. You'll see people covering considerable distances in the heat of the day, shading their heads with golf umbrellas. Only schoolchildren go bare-headed when the sun is at its highest, and women wear brightly patterned shawls over their turban-like *tikos*.

The first town east of Janjanbureh is **Bansang**, a small place on the south bank. The oldest hospital in up-country Gambia is located here, but it's otherwise insignificant, except to birdwatchers. Further east but on the north side of the river, and best approached direct from Lamin Koto, is a memorial to the great explorer **Mungo Park**, in a quiet riverside spot just outside the village of **Karantaba**.

The hub of the region is **Basse**, the eastern Gambian town with the strongest connections to nearby Senegal and the countries beyond. It's a long-established trading centre, located at a crossroads of road and river routes. Despite being right at the heart of an impoverished region, Basse is an energetic and characterful place that's very welcoming to travellers, and, after the vegetable harvest in the dry season, its produce market becomes one of the country's best.

With your own transport, or with time and patience, there's a rewarding **overland loop** to be traced from Janjanbureh, starting from Lamin Koto. You then follow the newly graded laterite road east past ancient baobab trees and mud-built villages of the north bank, all the way to the river ferry which connects the north shore to **Fatoto**, The Gambia's easternmost sizeable settlement;

Beaches
and boat trips

Rich in birdlife and sun-soaked for much of the year, The Gambia's tropical beaches and waterways count among the country's greatest assets. While much of the Atlantic coast is unspoilt and perfect for beachcombing and relaxing, one of the very best ways to discover the Gambian wilderness is to leave the ocean behind and head inland by boat. Cutting a swathe through the dusty West African bush, the River Gambia was once a magnet for intrepid explorers and ruthless traders; these days the river and the maze of mangrove creeks at its mouth attract adventurers of a different sort, including ecotourists, heritage tourists and birdwatchers.

▲ Sandel Bay near Kartong

Beaches

At barely 60km long, the **Gambian coastline** represents a tiny snippet of the African seaboard, but there's tremendous variety within this short distance. Many of the country's best hotels are situated on good, lively beaches where you can try freshly pressed juice, go horse riding, or just flop down on a sun-lounger. Away from the resorts there are plenty of appealingly remote stretches, from the traditional fishing centres of the southwest to the uninhabited strands in the north, great to explore on foot or by bicycle.

Exploring the mangrove creeks

At its salty western limits, the River Gambia is fringed by dense mangrove forests. Rich in biodiversity – fish, insects, birds and reptiles all breed and feed here, oysters cling to the roots and monkeys are regular visitors – these wetlands are rewarding to explore, preferably by a small, quiet boat which will allow you to enjoy the peaceful atmosphere to the full.

Numerous operators run trips into the **Tanbi Wetlands** (p.145) near Banjul, starting from the informal "marina" at Denton Bridge. Some boats just stick to the wider creeks, carrying substantial groups and providing treats such as buffets or champagne and caviar as they cruise to Lamin Lodge, a wonderfully rickety waterside bar and restaurant. Others cater specifically for people who want to go fishing or wildlife-watching. The creeks are home to ladyfish, barracudas, snappers and a host of watchful herons and egrets, candy-coloured bee-eaters and jewel-like malachite kingfishers. The best times for birdwatching are at dawn when the creeks are cool and the birds most active, or close to dusk, when the pelicans are winging their way to their roosts.

Further up-country, there are more creeks to discover. North of Banjul, **Niumi National Park** (p.201) is one of the best places in The Gambia to watch ospreys catching fish in their

▼ Callithrix monkeys

talons. To the south, visitors based at **Tumani Tenda**'s *Kachokorr Camp* (p.180), a community-run hideaway offering a refreshingly back-to-basics rural experience, or at **Makasutu**'s *Mandina Lodge* (p.179), a stunning creekside eco-retreat with rooms nestled in the bush or floating on the water, can ask a guide to paddle them along the waterways by dugout canoe, by far the most appealing way to explore. *Tendaba Camp* (p.217), a large, long-established lodge right on the river's southern shore, is

▲ Horse riding on Kololi beach

perfectly positioned for trips across the water into the spectacularly bird-rich creeks of the **Bao Bolon Wetland Reserve** (p.226).

Heading up-river

The River Gambia is the lifeblood of a region where navigable fresh water is scarce. While the lower reaches are salty and mangrove-fringed, the upper reaches, which supply the region's farmers with water, are bordered by lush tropical forest populated by monkeys, birds, crocodiles and hippos.

To the European adventurers who plundered this corner of West Africa between the sixteenth and nineteenth centuries, the river was of crucial strategic significance. Raiding parties combed its banks for commodities such as ivory, animal skins and, more menacingly, slaves.

Today, for African-American and Afro-Caribbean visitors, a pilgrimage up-river to **Juffureh's Museum of the Slave Trade** (p.197) and the ruined **trading post of Fort James** (p.199) offers a chance to retrace, in reverse, a journey that tore many thousands of captive Africans away from their homelands; symbolically, it's a powerfully emotional experience.

But perhaps the river's greatest asset, and the key to its future, is its embryonic **ecotourism** movement. The river banks are almost entirely undeveloped and, for those with a sense of adventure it's possible, by private arrangement, to travel by boat all the way from the coast to the up-country market towns of Basse and Fatoto over the course of a few days, enjoying the environment at its peaceful best, watching the ever-changing scenery unfold, and listening to the sounds of the river at dawn and dusk, the most magical times of all. The upper river is particularly beguiling, and one of the best ways to see it is by double-decker pirogue – a large version of a traditional West African boat.

Arguably the most beautiful part of the river is the **River Gambia National Park** (p.240), where the waters bend gracefully around uninhabited islands, thick with vivid greenery. There's a new and highly recommended place to stay here, the riverside *Visitor Camp* at The Gambia's Chimpanzee Rehabilitation Project. Another rewarding up-river destination is the island of **Janjanbureh** (p.241).

Spend a few nights at one of the friendly, quirky waterside lodges on or near the island and you can enjoy birdwatching, boating and high-spirited drumming and dancing around the campfire.

▼ Visiting the River Gambia National Park by pirogue

The Gambia's top five beaches

1. Sanyang p.163

With the softest sand, the coolest beach bars and possibly the most colourful of the southwestern fishing centres, the locals sometimes call this Paradise Beach. Watch the fishermen haul their brightly painted pirogues out of the water to sort through the catch, and then stroll along to one of the beachside restaurants to enjoy a plateful of the freshest ladyfish or butterfish around, hot from the grill.

2. Kartong p.163

The further you venture from the resort areas near the capital, the wilder and more beautiful the beaches become. Near the village of Kartong, close to the southern border, are a series of wide, empty bays fringed with palms, where you can walk for hours and see scarcely a soul except, perhaps, a fisherman on his way home, or a local herder, bringing his cattle down to the shore to lick salt.

3. Cape Point p.115

Cape Point is one of The Gambia's most family-friendly resorts, and here the broad, attractive beach is dotted with mature palm trees and thatched sun shades. Although unpredictable currents make it unsafe for swimming, it's perfect for beach volleyball and sandcastle-making, and there's a great variety of eating and drinking places nearby.

4. Kololi p.131

Right in the heart of The Gambia's busiest tourist area, but large enough to feel uncrowded even at the height of the season, Kololi's beaches are great for swimming or sunbathing. Until recently, tidal erosion was eating this area away but thanks to an ambitious sand-reclamation programme the beaches are back – and much better than before. Broad sands now extend all the way to Kotu, with juice stands and beach bars en route.

5. Jinack Island p.201

The Gambia's unspoilt northernmost Atlantic shores lie in a protected area, the Niumi National Park, home to an abundance of reptiles, insects and birds including pelicans, terns and fish eagles. With shallow water and pale sand backed by scrubland, dunes and baobab trees, the landscape is starkly beautiful. Time your visit to coincide with low tide to enjoy long, peaceful strolls along the waterline.

finally, you return via Basse along the south bank route. A shorter circuit takes you from Lamin Koto straight to Basse via the turning at Yarobawal, which leads to the Basse ferry, skirting The Gambia's easternmost reaches. Also highly recommended is a **river trip** from Janjanbureh via Karantaba to Basse, and possibly on to Fatoto. Throughout this region, the river is outstandingly peaceful, and empty apart from monkeys, birds and a few fishermen flinging out their nets from their dugout *pirogues*.

Bansang

If you're covering The Gambia by road from west to east along the southern highway, you pass the small town of **BANSANG**, 138km east of Soma and 16km southeast of Janjanbureh, on the way into into the tail end of the country. Few travellers stop in this small town, but it's famous with birdwatchers, since on its outskirts is a quarry that's one of the best places in The Gambia to see bee-eaters.

The highway bypasses the town, but an older road leads down through Bansang's

EASTERN GAMBIA | East from Janjanbureh

Birdwatching around Bansang

Birdwatchers head to Bansang specifically to visit the gravel quarry outside town, famous for its breeding colony of red-throated bee-eaters – it's common to see hundreds of these stunningly beautiful, brightly coloured birds there in a short visit. The best time is just before sunset, when many bee-eaters and other birds come to the pools for water. The site has been protected with fences by the local community (with assistance from West African Bird Study Association and the UK-based Gambia Birding Group), and you may be asked for a small entry fee.

town centre, hugging a magnificent bend in the River Gambia. Between the buildings are rare, urban glimpses of the river which manages to elude highway travellers all the way from Banjul to Basse. The opposite bank is a thick green ribbon of bushes, their branches hanging over the water, interspersed with mango trees. There's a hand-pulled vehicle ferry here, with room for two cars, and rudder-paddled boats for foot passengers. For elevated river views, the low hills behind the town, bristling with communications masts, are easily accessible. The town itself is a rather listless place, a ramshackle collection of oblong cement-block houses, with corrugated-iron roofs held down with old tyres and bricks.

To Gambians, Bansang is best known for its badly under-resourced **hospital** (☎567 4222), which was the only one up-river before the opening of the new sites at Farafenni and Bwiam. It's on the main highway, just east of a prominent HIV/AIDS awareness sign. In town, acute water shortages are commonplace and mains electricity remains a hollow promise.

If you're **staying the night** in Bansang, your best bet is the *Bansang Youth Centre* at the Basse end of town (☎991 0666 or 567 4614; ❶). This bright new community centre has decent rooms with private bathrooms – when the town's mains supply is down you'll be provided with buckets of water. The alternative is *Carew's Bar*, also known as *Boye's Bar* (☎567 4290; ❶) near the bus stop in the middle of town; this friendly place has basic accommodation in a few thatched huts, but no electricity.

Bansang is served by **bush taxis** to and from Serrekunda (D150), Soma (D70), Sankulay Kunda (D10) and Basse (D30).

Karantaba and the Mungo Park Memorial

Ten kilometres northeast of Bansang, the River Gambia sweeps north into a luxuriant loop, its westward course blocked by fortress-like laterite cliffs. Glassy green, it turns west again at the small north bank village of **KARANTABA**, 16km northeast of Bansang and 25km by road from Lamin Koto, before flowing on south through a sparsely populated landscape, far from the main roads on either bank. The riverbanks near Karantaba are a tangle of rhun palms and leafy shrubs, and if you're travelling this stretch by boat, you have a good chance of seeing little bands of red colobus and callithrix monkeys in the foliage, or larger troupes of baboons.

Karantaba features on tourist excursions cruising the river between Janjanbureh and Basse, or following the north bank along the road from Lamin Koto. Visitors come here to pay their respects to the memory of the great West African explorer, Scottish doctor **Mungo Park**. The point from which Park set out in search of the source of the Niger, in two separate expeditions in 1795 and 1805, is marked by a very plain twelve-metre obelisk on a concrete plinth close to the riverbank, a couple of kilometres upstream from Karantaba's wharf. It's helpful to ask local children to guide you there; it's a thirty-minute walk along a sandy path through thinly wooded bush.

Karantaba village is a collection of hamlets, each with a different ethnic make-up, and marked by huge, gnarled baobabs, testament to the great age of the settlement. On Wednesdays, the whole district, seemingly, congregates at Karantaba Wolof, the hamlet nearest the highway and 2km from the wharf, for the *lumo*, which is the oldest weekly market in this area. The action kicks off around 9am, when the first bush taxis lurch in, dangerously overloaded with buyers, sellers and produce, and the place is packed by noon. While it's not really a market for souvenir hunters, you can watch everyday scenes of up-country village commerce acted out, and it's possible to pick up good, cheap, freshly made food from the women serving spoonfuls of sauce out of enamel bowls.

Wednesday is the best day to visit Karantaba independently by bush taxi; these run infrequently along the newly graded laterite road from Lamin Koto, a forty-minute drive away to the west. The only Gambian north bank settlement larger than a small village in the 90km between Karantaba and the eastern border with Senegal is **Diabugu**, 25km southeast. This is a busy, purposeful little place set back from the the river, with a telecentre, some shops, and an impressive mosque in the midst of tightly-packed cement-brick compounds and thatched huts.

Basse

BASSE (Basse Santa Su, in full) is The Gambia's easternmost town, a surprisingly animated centre that gets its energy from its proximity to Senegal. It's 375km from Banjul, on the south side of the country, right on the riverbank, connected to the north by a small vehicle ferry, and it's been a busy trading centre since well before colonial times. This is a town that sees plenty of travellers from West Africa and elsewhere, so visitors blend easily with the cosmopolitan crowd. It's a polyglot place, with English, French, Wolof, Mandinka, Serer and Arabic in the mix; the traders here include well-established Senegalese, Guineans, Mauritanians and Lebanese. As a consequence, many travellers find it one of the Gambia's most relaxing towns. You need to be prepared, however, for shortages: of power, running water, and, at certain times of year, even food.

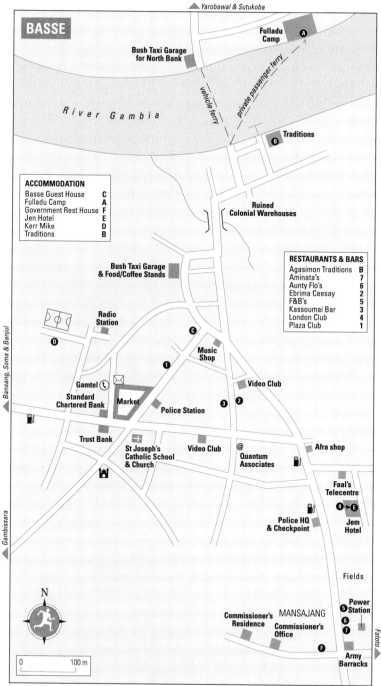

BASSE

▲ Yarobawal & Sutukoba

Bush Taxi Garage for North Bank

Fulladu Camp Ⓐ

River Gambia

vehicle ferry

private passenger ferry

Ⓑ Traditions

ACCOMMODATION

Basse Guest House	C
Fulladu Camp	A
Government Rest House	F
Jen Hotel	E
Kerr Mike	D
Traditions	B

Ruined Colonial Warehouses

Bush Taxi Garage & Food/Coffee Stands

RESTAURANTS & BARS

Agasimon Traditions	B
Aminata's	7
Aunty Flo's	6
Ebrima Ceesay	2
F&B's	5
Kassoumai Bar	3
London Club	4
Plaza Club	1

Radio Station

Ⓓ

Ⓒ

Music Shop

Ⓘ 1

Gamtel 📞

Standard Chartered Bank

Market

Video Club

Police Station

3 2

Trust Bank

St Joseph's Catholic School & Church

Video Club

@ Quantum Associates

Afra shop

Faal's Telecentre

4 ► E

Jem Hotel

Police HQ & Checkpoint

Bansang, Soma & Banjul

Gambissara

Fields

N

MANSAJANG

Commissioner's Residence

Commissioner's Office

Power Station

9

6

7

F

Fatoto ►

Army Barracks

0   100 m

251

Sabi & Vélingara (Senegal) ▼

Basse is the destination of long-distance **river cruises** from Tendaba via Janjanbureh (see p.52). The town is situated on a graceful, tree-lined bend in the river, which, even this far upstream, is affected by the tides, so you'll see it flowing east and west at different times of day.

One reason to stay in Basse is to break your journey if you're heading into Senegal to visit the Niokolo-Koba National Park. Even if you're not travelling that far, the riverine countryside around Basse lends itself well to off-the-beaten track exploring, and the riverbank in the town itself is one of the best places in the world to get a good view of a bird species much sought-after by birdwatchers: the **Egyptian plover**.

Arrival and orientation

Most of Basse's activity is centred round the area just south of the river wharf: this is the commercial hub where the market, bush taxi garage, banks, telecentres and post office are all located. Buildings stretch out along the route out to the west, and there's a small suburban quarter beyond the fields to the south, Mansajang.

Basse has only one **bush taxi** garage, roughly between the market and the river, and all bush taxis, including *gelleh-gelleh* from Serrekunda, Soma, Sankulay Kunda, Bansang and all other points on the south bank highway, arrive here.

The vehicle **ferry** from the north bank (daily 7am–6.30pm; vehicles D45, foot passengers D2) takes four cars or one truck at a time across the 100m wide river, and the screech of the ferry's ramp is one of the town's most familiar noises. The slipway on either side is steep, and the ferry loads on one side only, spinning around midstream, so if you have your own vehicle, prepare yourself to reverse sharply uphill to disembark. There are also small hand-paddled boat taxis for foot passengers (D2).

Basse has two **banks**: a branch of Trust Bank (Mon–Thurs 8am–12.30pm & 4-6.30pm, Fri 8am–noon, Sat 9am–1pm) and, opposite, a Standard Chartered Bank (Mon–Fri 8am–12.30pm & 4–6.30pm, Sat 9am–noon); neither has an ATM. The **post office** (Mon–Fri 8.30am–12.15pm & 2–4pm, Sat 2.30am–noon) is close by. The Gamtel office has no **Internet access**, but you can get online in the town centre at Quantum Associates (daily 8am–2.30pm & 8–11pm).

Accommodation

You're far enough up-country in Basse to appreciate a significant difference in climate between here and the coast; temperatures are more extreme, so it's wise to choose a **room** with either a good fan or blankets, depending on the time of year.

Basse Guest House ☎ 666 8283. The best of the cheap options, which isn't saying much. Its advantages are its central location, and its large communal living room area and balcony overlooking the busy street below. The rooms are basic, with fans (but intermittent power), no mosquito nets, and grubby shared washing facilities. ❶

Fulladu Camp ☎ 990 6791 or 985 0926, ✉ fulladucamp@yahoo.com. In theory, this is Basse's upmarket bush lodge, with a large compound in a great position by the river on the opposite side to the town (a small boat shuttles its guests across free of charge). In practice, it's

a place that, though friendly, has seen better days, with a ragged garden, a derelict pool and an inconstant water supply (the pump only operates in the evenings and early mornings). The rooms are in thatched roundhouses that look pretty from the outside but are extremely simple. When tour groups visit, there are lively drumming and dancing sessions in the evening; at other times, the place can be chronically quiet. Trips can be arranged to the Niokola-Koba National Park in Senegal, or up down the river. ❷

Government Rest House ☎ 566 8262. Pleasant and roomy, with air-conditioning and an

Basse marks the end of the tarmac road; east of here, the roads are laterite or dust. **Bush taxis** from Basse serve all points west along the main south bank highway, including Bansang (45min; D30), Soma (3.5–4hr; D100), Serrekunda (10–14hr; D200), plus the nearby pottery-making villages of Sotuma Sere and Alohungari. Transport to and from the villages lying on minor roads off the highway is most readily available on *lumo* days (Sunday in Fatoto and Sabi). If you're travelling from Basse to Vélingara in Senegal (20km from Basse), it's best to find a bush taxi going the whole distance: connections from the Gambian border post of Sabi are infrequent. If you're aiming for Senegal's Parc National de Niokolo-Koba, you'll need your own transport.

old-fashioned atmosphere, but quite a walk out of town in Mansajang. ①

Jem Hotel ☎ 984 3658 or 771 1911. Something of an institution in Basse, and notorious for the eccentricity of its owner, this place receives few guests but the rooms, though a little ramshackle, are a decent size. As elsewhere in Basse, power and water can be unreliable, and the whole place is noisy when the generator's running (even more so when the semi-dormant *London Club*, attached, grinds into life; see p.254). ①

Kerr Mike ☎ 993 1848. A bit out of the way on the western side of town near the football field, this is a typical urban compound with a block of concrete floored, corrugated-roofed rooms, shared latrines and bucket showers, and a small bar. It's slightly dilapidated, but worth considering if you're on a strict budget. ①

Traditions (also known as **Agasimon Traditions**) ☎ 566 8760. This riverside place has a garden compound with plenty of space to camp in the shade (and the use of decent outdoor washing facilities). In the main house are two guest rooms; they're huge and can be rather airless in hot weather. Camping ①, rooms ②

The Town

Basse's wharfside area has a slight ghost-town feel, with neglected colonial-era warehouses crumbling away under the elements and redevelopment progressing at a sleepy pace, but just inland from here, the commercial district is lively, colourful and noisy. Trade with Senegal from here is thriving, so the **shops** selling fabrics and household goods tend to be well-stocked; you'll find an abundance of pots and pans, bootleg cassettes, and excellent wax printed cotton and other textiles (cheaper here than in Banjul or Serrekunda). There are also groceries, pharmacies, and places where you can buy essentials such as batteries. The **produce market** is best well into the dry season, particularly January to June, when local women sell the vegetables grown in the town's community gardens: shiny aubergines, fluted bitter tomatoes, juicy-looking lettuce, pyramids of fat red chillies, bundles of mint and a great abundance of other foodstuffs. To one side you'll see shelled groundnuts and brilliant green cassava leaves being minced to a paste.

Highly recommended is a visit to the **craft shop** *Traditions* (☎ 566 8760, daily 8am–6pm), housed in a 1906 trading post on the river near the ferry, with a gloriously situated first-floor veranda overlooking the river. It sells a small but carefully chosen selection of West African art, crafts and traditional textiles, some using rich-coloured indigo and kola nut dyes, and others made from recycled fabrics and plastics. There's also a café here (see p.254), one of the best places in Basse to relax, with riverbank views.

The Basse area has a tradition of **dyeing and weaving**, and *Traditions* can arrange tuition with local artisans; you will also often find weavers working their strip-cloth looms in an open space not far from the post office. The local clay produces particularly good **pottery** of the rustic terracotta sort, called *dar* in

Birdwatching around Basse

The Egyptian plover, or crocodile bird, is a "holy grail" species for many birdwatchers visiting The Gambia. Basse is the best place in the country, and probably the world, to get a good view of this smartly plumaged, honey-beige and black-coloured bird, which regularly patrols the muddy riverbank near *Traditions* in small groups between August and February (particularly Nov–Jan); good vantage points are the wharf and the *Traditions* balcony. Vultures and carmine bee-eaters are also regularly seen in the area.

Mandinka; there's a compound in Mansajang, more or less opposite the Commissioner's Residence, with a small *dardula* (pottery works), where you can watch pots being made if you're here from around March to the end of the dry season. The Mandinka family here make *jibidas* (water cooler jars), colander-like rice steamers, storage pots and incense burners. Pottery-makers also work in compounds and community studios in the Serer and Serahule villages just west of Basse, including Alohungari and Sotuma Sere – their work is set out for sale beside the highway.

Eating, drinking and nightlife

All the **eating** and **entertainment** options in town have a definite local, rather than tourist, atmosphere, but Basse is very welcoming towards visitors. As well as the places mentioned below, there are a couple of unmarked *afra* grills in town, good places to stock up on protein if you're out late. There are also a great many women stationed along the main street, selling fruit, pasta sauce, or rice and fish from enamel bowls to passing travellers. By night, Basse feels like one big lorry stop, with long-distance drivers overnighting here and making the most of the abundance of good street food, then converging on the local "cinemas" and video clubs to watch the football.

Aminata's This cheerful little place serves omelettes for breakfast, Sierra Leonean specials such as *foofoo* and *supa kanja* (okra) for lunch and, on request, chicken, burgers or pizza, all at low prices. Daily 8am–11pm.

Aunty Flo's Popular with foreign volunteers working locally, this unpretentious spot has a switched-on Sierra Leonean owner who serves up great omelettes and stews. Mon–Sat 8am–10pm.

Ebrima Ceesay, International Coffee Maker A flyblown indoor local coffee and sandwich place, where the coffee is first class (if you like it local-style) and you can grab an egg or meat sandwich for next to nothing – great for breakfast.

F&B's Bar and Restaurant Quite a trek out of town beyond the fields but before Mansajang, and with service that gets mixed reports, the best reason to come here is to take advantage of its late opening hours. On offer are cheap, basic meals (rice, chicken, cow foot) and cold drinks. Daily 5pm–4am.

Kassoumai Bar An unmarked palm wine "ghetto" in the centre of town that sells soft drinks, beer and, of course, palm wine, in an unadorned concrete box of a space.

London Club At *Jem's Hotel*. A cavernous space with bizarre murals, this rarely functions as a nightclub now, except when hired for a naming ceremony or similar event – there's a permanent layer of dust on the bottles and fairy lights behind the bar – but you can still drink here.

Plaza Club Once the town centre's buzziest nightspot, great for reggae and West African music, this now opens on Saturdays only, with occasional special events on Fridays.

Traditions (also known as **Agasimon Traditions**) ☏ 566 8760. Although it's not quite the oasis it used to be before the present management took over, the upstairs balcony is still Basse's most relaxing hangout, with food such as sandwiches, omelettes and steak available on request. Daily 8am–6pm.

From Basse to Fatoto

Whether travelling through The Gambia by road or by river, there's a certain sense of completion to be achieved by travelling all the way to **Fatoto**, on the south bank, the easternmost sizeable village in the country, and the place where The Gambia stops, to all intents and purposes. It's an hour's drive from Basse

△ Market girls, Fatoto

Birdwatching around Fatoto

The banks of the River Gambia between Basse and Fatoto offer excellent birdwatching opportunities, especially if you're on the water, with various species of roller, glossy starling, plantain-eater and bee-eater conspicuous on perches high in the trees, or flying at speed over the foliage. Plovers are easy to spot on the banks and are impressive in flight, their backs and wings strikingly marked. You'll also see raptors soaring overhead or surveying the scene from the higher branches.

along a forty-kilometre laterite road, but it's also reachable by the little-travelled, but scenically impressive, north bank road, passing some of The Gambia's remotest villages on the way.

Travelling east from Basse along the south bank, the greenest spot in the landscape is at **Charmoi**, where the road crosses a *bolon*. On either side of the small bridge are mango trees, lily ponds and vegetable gardens, where some of the produce that fills Basse market with colour is grown.

The north bank route, from the Basse ferry to **Yarobawal** then heading east, takes you close to **traditional Fula settlements** and **Mandinka villages**, widely spaced and remote, where, in the rainy season, cereal crops sway and, in the dry season, livestock nibble at the brittle stalks while women pound millet under the shade trees or draw water from wells to sprinkle on vegetable plots. These fenced-off pockets of green are oases in a landscape that is arid in the extreme for eight months of the year. Life here is simple, and most settlements are small, attractive collections of mud-walled huts with a cone of thatch for a roof. Eventually you dip down through the grove of trees opposite Fatoto to the river, green and inviting with a sandy shore, a welcome vision of coolness after the heat of the interior. There's a hand-hauled chain ferry here, which can take two vehicles (vehicle D40, foot passenger D2) and runs on demand.

If you're travelling to Fatoto by river from Basse, you'll find more and more activity, wildlife-wise, the further upstream you are. The north bank, in particular, is very rich in birds, taking advantage both of the quiet, fresh water and of the abundance of vegetable gardens near the bank, occasionally seen through the acacias and shrubs that border the river.

FATOTO itself, spread out over an area of low, scrubby hills, has a forgotten-by-time atmosphere, its commercial area only just livelier than the derelict trading station by the river. On Sundays, the weekly market brings some much-needed colour to the place, with piles of everything from kola nuts, tomatoes and mint to cooking pots and flip flops. There are no hotels here, but you'll find a couple of places where you can buy rice and sauce, a few workshops and *bitikos*, and the *Konkodouma*, a place that calls itself a nightclub, but is really a "video club" which sometimes shows British football matches on satellite TV. Bush taxis between Fatoto and Basse (D35) are infrequent, but Sundays are busiest.

Travel details

This is a brief summary of journey durations; more thorough details are given throughout the chapter.

Bush taxis

Basse to: Bansang (45min); Brikama (10–12hr); Fatoto (1hr); Sankulay Kunda for Janjanbureh (1hr 30min–2hr); Serrekunda (10–14hr); Soma (3hr 30min–4hr).

Bansang to: Basse (45min); Brikama (9–11hr); Sankulay Kunda for Janjanbureh (1hr); Serrekunda (9hr 30min–11hr 30min); Soma (2hr 30min–3hr).

Lamin Koto to: Farafenni (2hr 30min–3hr); Kau-ur (2–2hr 30min); Wassu & Kuntaur (30–45min).

Kau-ur to: Farafenni (30min–1hr); Lamin Koto (2–2hr 30min); Wassu & Kuntaur (1hr 30min).

Kuntaur to: Farafenni (3–4hr); Kau-ur (2–2hr 30min); Lamin Koto (45min–1hr).

Sankulay Kunda to: Bansang (1hr); Basse (1hr 30min–10hr 30min); Soma (1hr 30min–2hr).

Wassu to: Farafenni (2hr); Kau-ur (1hr 30min); Lamin Koto (30–45min).

EASTERN GAMBIA | Travel details

257

Contexts

Contexts

History

T
he first known inhabitants of what is now The Gambia were a succession of ethnic groups who migrated to the fertile basin of the River Gambia from elsewhere in West Africa. European traders began to settle near the river from the mid-fifteenth century and the present-day borders of The Gambia were first drawn in 1889, in Paris, by British negotiators, with ruler and compass. Legend has it that the country's optimum dimensions were determined by measuring the extent of territory that could be defended by cannon-fire from a gunboat sailing up the river – hence The Gambia's long, thin and crooked shape.

Gambian prehistory

The **earliest people** of the Gambia valley may have been the Jola, who by tradition have a very limited oral history. The hundred or so Gambian **stone circles**, including the famous ones at Wassu, are compelling evidence of a civilization that lived near the river between 800BC and 1000AD, but hard facts about their ethnic origin have so far eluded archaeologists and ethnographers. The first known written record referring to the River Gambia appeared in the Carthaginian **Hanno**'s account of his voyage around the west coast of Africa around 470BC. His mission was to establish colonies on the Atlantic coast for the purpose of trade in ivory and gold, and it is thought that he made it all the way to Cameroon and back. Hanno's account, though geographically sketchy, was still being used as a reference by seafarers in the age of exploration two thousand years later.

Knowledge of the intervening centuries is very incomplete. The introduction of camels to Africa in the second century AD, facilitating long-distance desert travel, opened up West Africa to Arab traders in **slaves** and **gold**, who gave the indigenous Africans an appetite for commerce. Between the fifth and eighth centuries AD, the area that is now The Gambia was part of the ancient **kingdom of Ghana** (capital in present-day Mauritania, and from which the modern state of Ghana took its name), that was ruled by members of the Serahule tribe. Seven centuries on, control had transferred to **Mandingo** and **Susu** overlords from the Fouta Djalon plateau in Guinea, part of the Songhai empire. By the fifteenth century, most of the valley was under the control of small **Mandinka kingdoms** founded by immigrants from the Mali empire.

The dawn of the colonial era

The European settlers of the fifteenth and sixteenth centuries were mostly **Portuguese**. They set themselves up as trading partners with local headmen. Their larger game plan was to trace a route to the spice islands of the Far East, and in the process track down the fabled riches of the West African kingdoms and possibly find the source of the Nile. The River Gambia was assumed to be an open door to the interior of Africa. The first Portuguese adventurer to explore the mouth of the River Gambia was **Nuno Tristão**, sent to West

Africa in 1447 by Prince Henry the Navigator. Ten years later, other Portuguese explorers started to establish trading stations along the river, to purchase slaves and commodities in exchange for cloth, guns and other manufactured goods. The river was a highly rated trading area, with plenty of safe anchorages. The Portuguese landed on an island twenty miles up-river and named it St Andrew's Island after a sailor who died and was buried there. It was later renamed James Island. Some of the Portuguese traders made the district their home, marrying the daughters of chiefs. The descendants of these mixed unions often grew up to became local leaders and mediators.

In the late sixteenth century, when the Mali empire was in decline, the **British** first arrived in the area and started trading along the river. Other nationalities soon followed suit and, from the mid-seventeenth century, English, Dutch, French and Baltic merchant-adventurers shared and fought over trading rights from the small (but strategically invaluable) neighbouring bases of **Fort James** on James Island, mid-river, and **Albreda** on the north bank. In 1765,

The Transatlantic slave trade

There are no exact records of how many West African **slaves** were captured and shipped to the Americas between the seventeenth and nineteenth centuries. The figures are hazy partly because so many died in the process of capture, imprisonment and transportation, but estimates of the total range from several hundred thousand to fifteen million: around twenty thousand per year in the sixteenth century, rising to one hundred thousand per year in the eighteenth century, when the trade was at its peak. Of these, approximately one sixth are estimated to have been shipped out of the Senegambia area.

West Africans had been enslaving fellow Africans long before the arrival of the European traders, but the basis of these slaves' bondage sometimes included a get-out clause: if they had offered themselves as slaves through destitution, rather than being captured in war, they had a chance to earn back their freedom. For the slaves displaced by the Europeans, there was, prior to the abolition of the trade, absolutely no chance of return.

In The Gambia, the first European slave traders were **Portuguese**. Later, from the seventeenth century on, it was the **British** who held the greatest influence over the trade – though the French and Dutch were also heavily involved, and the Portuguese continued their involvement – and it was the British who banned the involvement of their own ships in the trade (but not the ownership of slaves) in 1808. Total **abolition** came in 1833.

The shipping of slaves from West Africa to the New World was just one leg of a **triangular trade** that began with slave ships sailing from Europe carrying cloth, iron bars, guns and other manufactured goods, to be exchanged for human cargo which was shipped to Brazil, the Caribbean and the southern American colonies to be sold to the plantation owners. The demand was a long-term one, as plantation owners found it a better investment to keep supplementing their labour force with fresh slaves rather than to treat those they already owned well enough for them to provide more than a few years' useful service, or to wait for these slaves' children to reach working age. The shippers were paid in cash, sugar, cotton or tobacco, which was then transported to Europe, where the cycle began again. In Britain, the economies of the ports of Bristol and Liverpool prospered as a result. Pickings from the trade were rich enough to justify the substantial risks posed by malaria, yellow fever and other diseases: many Europeans lasted less than two years in the tropics.

The Europeans tended to avoid the risky process of capturing slaves, relying instead on African intermediaries using whatever means necessary. Some slaves were undoubtedly taken by force, and villages were ransacked and burned to the

the British gained the upper hand in the area, instituting their first West African colony, the province of **Senegambia**, with its headquarters in St Louis on the banks of the River Senegal and its River Gambia base at Fort James. The colony was dissolved less than twenty years later, under the terms of the **Treaty of Versailles**. Most of the territory was handed over to France, but the River Gambia section remained under British control.

British interests in West Africa began to alter radically towards the end of the eighteenth century, as **slave trading** began to be not only less and less profitable, but also a positive hindrance to other trading enterprises. Even after the 1808 ban, the Gambian slave trade continued, illegally, for many decades, partly because the ban was a unilateral one that some French and Portuguese traders chose to ignore, and partly because the Gambians themselves profited so handsomely from the trade.

The British won lasting influence in the River Gambia area after the Napoleonic wars, and Captain Alexander Grant founded the city of **Bathurst**

ground by raiding parties. Once on board the slave ships, the captured Africans, already humiliated and traumatized, suffered such brutal treatment that mere survival was a challenge. Eighteenth century ship captains' logs suggest that if only a third of the lives on board were lost between Africa and the New World, that constituted a satisfactory result.

While first-hand reports from disinterested parties such as the explorer **Mungo Park** and humanitarian movements led by visionary campaigners like **Thomas Clarkson** and **William Wilberforce** played a significant part, ultimately it was economic factors that brought about abolition. By the early nineteenth century, the trade was barely profitable, and in 1805, when the US Congress imposed a new import duty of $10 per slave, the margins became almost unworkable.

West African tribal leaders held a significant position of power in the chain of transactions that led from Europe to Africa, to the American colonies and back to Europe again. They profited handsomely by exchanging hostages captured in intertribal disputes for commodities that would otherwise have been beyond their reach, particularly guns. Enough was at stake for a delegation of chiefs from The Gambia and other territories to visit London and Paris around the time of abolition in order to argue fiercely against banning the trade. It was not until 1895 that Gambian chiefs and rulers finally agreed with the British to abolish inter-tribal slave trading and the keeping of house slaves.

Today, there is a vocal movement calling for financial **reparations** to Africans for the slave trade. In the United States, this takes the form of African-American civil rights activists suing major corporations for damages on behalf of their ancestors, claiming that such corporations' financial strength was built at the expense of the slaves who laboured on the plantations. In West Africa, campaigners demand that the United States government pay reparations to every African state whose population was stripped by the transatlantic trade. So close to the heart of some Gambians is this issue that the former British High Commissioner Eric Jenkinson was questioned on the subject in a Gambian press interview shortly after his arrival in 2002. His reply was that the concept of redress was "more of an intellectual concern than a real issue", a neat dodge of an extremely sensitive issue.

More positively, **educational programmes**, monuments, commemorative days and ceremonies are now bringing together communities which, at this remove, feel a complex mixture of abhorrence, bewilderment and guilt at the events of the past. In The Gambia, the preservation of Juffureh, Albreda and James Island as a combined **heritage site** plays a crucial part in the healing of old wounds.

(now Banjul) in 1816. This defensive post was named after Henry, 3rd Earl of Bathurst, who governed the region from Freetown (Sierra Leone) as British colonial secretary at the time. In the 1820s, Britain declared a **Protectorate**, the "Settlement on the River Gambia" and Alexander Grant acquired a small up-river island, which he named **MacCarthy Island** (later Janjanbureh), and built Fort George to defend it. In the following decade, **groundnuts** (peanuts) were introduced to the area for the first time and became the Settlement's most important cash commodity after beeswax, ivory and skins, soon accounting for one third of its total export income. Around the same time, the protectorate gained a new, willing labour force in the parties of **freed slaves** who were

The Soninke-Marabout Wars

Mandinka civil war along both banks of the Gambia River began in the **1850s**. Local holy leaders – the **marabouts** – influenced by the great Muslim expansionist Omar Tall, called for the overthrow of the traditional Mandinka kings known as Soninkes, whose adherence to Islam was greatly tempered by indigenous religion and alcohol. The marabouts aimed to install a puritanical Islam and to capture local states (best described as manors) and trading networks.

Most of the "wars" consisted of battles, skirmishes and feuds between villages, which disrupted trade and agriculture year after year. Serer and Jola mercenaries were bought in on both sides to bulk out the limited armies. The main areas of unrest were: **Kombo**, south of the tiny British enclave at Bathurst, where a wild young marabout called **Fodi Kabba** spread serious anarchy; **Baddibu** and **Niumi** on the north bank, where a renegade Soninke-turned-marabout, **Ma Ba**, caused massive destruction; and **Fuladu**, up-river on the south bank, where **Fula marabouts** from the southeast, outside the region, swept the local Mandinka aside with great savagery.

By the mid-1870s, the whole of the Kombo district was under maraboutic control. Religious imperatives had been forgotten as purely political and economic considerations pitted one leader against another. Acting under financial constraints laid down in London the **British** avoided interference whenever possible, refused requests for protection from besieged Soninke leaders and only went into battle to defend the Colony or British subjects. Only when there seemed to be a risk that the fighting might jeopardize British commercial interests did the governor try to impose a truce.

But in the **1880s**, the British were unable to avoid being drawn into the conflicts. In Baddibu the wars had become an internal affair between competing marabouts, and they spilled over into French-occupied **Senegal**. The French, in hot pursuit on behalf of their Sine-Saloum chiefs (the French were much more actively involved in protection than the British) chased the marabout army back into "British" territory as far as Barra. The British were forced to arrest the marabout in question, **Said Mati**, to forestall any further French advances. Mati's removal led to a power vacuum in Baddibu, which the French began to fill with their own appointees. The British had no choice but to enter into binding protection agreements with as many Gambian chiefs as possible.

A period of relative peace ensued, but in the Kombo and Foni regions Fodi Silla and Fodi Kabba kept up **continued resistance** against the now-expanding British. With the country's borders fixed and support at last from London, the British moved against **Fodi Silla** in 1894, occupying all the towns of Kombo – Gunjur, Sukuta, Brikama – and pushing Silla into Senegal, where he was captured and exiled to St-Louis.

Fodi Kabba pursued the struggle, killing a travelling commissioner and his entourage at Sankandi on the border in 1901. The British and French moved swiftly and in concert, "pacifying" the region in imperial style and killing Fodi Kabba, a campaign which marked the end of the Soninke-Marabout Wars.

moved from the slave ships and plantations via Freetown to The Gambia and settled in Bathurst and Georgetown. The Gambia's first **Legislative Council** was introduced in 1843, and the Protectorate was given its own colonial administration, based in Bathurst, rather than being governed from Freetown.

In the second half of the nineteenth century, while the British hesitated and focused their attentions elsewhere, the French were battling their way deep into the Soudan (present-day eastern Senegal, Mali, Burkina Faso, Niger and Cote d'Ivoire), actively engaged in a mission to conquer. From 1850 to 1901 the whole of the Gambia region was in a state of social chaos as the **Soninke-Marabout Wars** repeatedly flared up between renegade Muslim leaders and Mandinka kings, and the British were forced to consolidate the region or else lose it to France.

Britain's establishment of "The Crown Colony and Protectorate of the Gambia" was formally agreed at the Paris conference of 1889. The **Colony** comprised St Mary's Island and the capital Bathurst, the district of Kombo St Mary, and MacCarthy Island, where Wolofs predominated. The **Protectorate** was the rest of present-day Gambia, at the time ruled by headmen and chiefs and populated by Mandinkas. Britain's decision to claim this territory stemmed less from commercial ambitions than from **imperial strategy**. The intention was to pawn off the country in exchange for some better French territory. Gabon was one chunk favoured by the British – they'd already turned down the offer of the Ivory Coast sea forts. But the temporary expedient of holding the river became permanent when, having failed to agree on an exchange, the British succeeded merely in delimiting a narrow strip of land on each side of the River Gambia, burrowing into the heart of French territory: France acquired most of Senegal at the Paris conference, and Casamance was later transferred to France from Portugal. Yet Britain wasn't fully reconciled to its responsibilities along the River Gambia until after World War I – thus, in practical terms, The Gambia's era of effective colonialism lasted only forty years, from the 1920s to the 1960s.

Colony and Protectorate

The imposition of **British hegemony** lacked both cohesion and commitment. Beyond the limits of the Colony, in the up-country Protectorate, the country's headmen and chiefs, some of whom were appointed by the Crown, were allowed to rule their people little disturbed by the two "travelling commissioners" to whom they were answerable. Two or three African representatives from Bathurst were nominated to the Legislative Council after 1915, but there was no representation of the 85 percent of the population who lived in the Protectorate.

The main relationship between the people and the government soured over the issue of **taxes**. The Gambia's first **currency**, the penny and the tenth-of-a-penny, was introduced in 1907, followed by pounds and shillings ten years later. Two-thirds of Gambia's revenue was accounted for in the salaries of the colonial administration. The remainder was insufficient to develop the country's infrastructure, education or health systems. "Benign neglect" is about the best that can be said of the administration's performance – only the most rudimentary infrastructure was set up during this time. One of the few positive developments was the establishment of the **Medical Research Council** in Fajara in 1913, for the study of tropical diseases. When the **Armitage High School** in Georgetown, a boarding school for the sons of village chiefs, was founded in 1927, it was one of The Gambia's few educational institutions. There were virtually no paved roads and, until the 1930s, only one public passenger and cargo river boat service, the *MV Lady Denham*, operated on the River Gambia.

Things started to improve only after World War II, though the government was gravely embarrassed by the **Yundum egg scheme**, a plan to mass-produce poultry and eggs, which ended in fiasco when fowl pest resulted in a loss of £500,000. **Groundnuts** had been a successful export crop since the middle of the nineteenth century, and the country was self-sufficient in food (remaining so until the 1970s). There were minor advances in transport, education and medical services, and traffic and trade increased on the river. By 1961, the country had five doctors and 37 up-country primary schools.

Financial pressures on the Colonial Office in the 1950s, and mounting international demands for decolonization were as much instrumental in the **push to independence** as Gambian nationalism. Britain was at least as anxious to rid itself of its financial liability as the country's own senior figures (barely yet leaders) were to take power. From Britain's point of view, there was no reason to delay the country's return to independence – except, perhaps, a measure of concern over the fate of such a small and unprotected nation. Colonial civil servants were in broad agreement that The Gambia would be forced to merge with Senegal, but chose to defer the move.

The road to independence

In a manner similar to that of many other countries in West Africa, The Gambia's progression to independence was not a heroic one – the men who led the country into the neocolonial era were not so much nationalists as ambitious politicians.

The **Bathurst Trade Union**, founded in 1928, mounted successful campaigns for workers' rights, but the first **political party** wasn't formed until shortly before the Legislative Council elections of 1951. Through most of the 1950s, the Gambian parties were reactive, personality-led interest groups rather than campaigning, policy-making, issue-led organizations. All the early-1950s parties – the Democratic Party, the Muslim Congress Party and the United Party – were Wolof, and Colony-based (that is, based in Bathurst, rather than up-country) and highly sectional. Gambia had to wait until 1960 before a party with a genuinely grassroots programme emerged. This was the Protectorate People's Party, quickly relabelled **People's Progressive Party** **(PPP)**, led by an ex-veterinary officer from MacCarthy Island Division, **David Jawara**. The PPP looked to the people of the Protectorate for support, but was distinctly anti-chief. Instead it spoke for rural Mandinkas and others in their resentment against corrupt chiefdoms, and for disenfranchised and younger Wolofs of the Colony.

The administration had overhauled the constitution in 1951 and finally, after consultation with senior Gambian figures, produced a complicated new constitution in 1954. This gave real representation to the up-country Protectorate peoples for the first time, but precipitated sharpened demands for greater responsibility for Gambian ministers in the government. It also put extraordinary power in the hands of the chiefs, who were, for the most part, supporters of the colonial status quo. To avoid a crisis, another constitution was formulated in 1959 which abolished the Legislative Council and provided for a parliament – the **House of Representatives.**

In the run-up to the 1960 elections, the Democratic and Muslim Congress parties merged as the **Democratic Congress Alliance** (DCA), but couldn't shake off the popular impression that their nominees were all puppets of the British administration. As a result, the DCA took only three seats, while the United Party of PS N'Jie (with whom the governor had recently fallen out) and David Jawara's PPP took eight seats each. The British governor, in a move to placate the Protectorate chiefs, offered the post of prime minister to PS N'Jie, to the consternation of Jawara, who became education minister. But the 1959 constitution gave rise to further indecisive election results. More talks in 1962 resulted in yet another constitution, providing for a 36-seat House of Representatives with 32 elected seats and just four chiefs nominated by the Chiefs' Assembly, and granting universal suffrage to all citizens of 21 years and above.

The balance of power now shifted against the United Party. Jawara and the Democratic Congress Alliance found room for co-operation and, in the **1962 elections** – which were to determine the political configuration for full self-government – the two parties contested seats in concert to squeeze out the UP. The results of this electoral alliance were highly successful for the PPP, which won seventeen out of the 25 Protectorate seats and one of the seven Colony seats. The DCA, however, managed to gain only one seat in the Colony, and couldn't shift the UP from its urban power base. As a result, with the support of the DCA's two elected members, Jawara had an absolute majority in parliament. Jawara and his party were to remain in power for the next 32 years, until the 1994 coup.

After the 1962 elections, Jawara entered into a coalition with the experienced PS N'Jie of the United Party to form the first fully **independent government**. Independence Day came on February 18, 1965, when The Gambia was admitted to the **Commonwealth** as an independent constitutional monarchy and began five years as a parliamentary democracy, with Queen Elizabeth II as titular Head of State and Jawara as Prime Minister.

Independent Gambia

In 1966, Jawara was knighted by the Queen in London, and PS N'Jie backed his United Party out of the coalition government to lead the opposition. Four years later, on April 24, 1970, following a referendum, The Gambia became a **republic** with prime minister Dawda Kairaba Jawara (now using his Muslim name) its president. In contrast to the many other African countries operating as single-party states, The Gambia opted for a multi-party democracy with a five-year parliamentary term. However, at every election, the PPP continued to win the vast majority of seats, and at every election N'Jie claimed that the vote was rigged. Despite the corruption allegations, the PPP, with its roots in the Mandinka villages, managed to establish credible support across the country.

The first fifteen years of independence were peaceful, and the groundnut economy fared better than expected due to high prices on the world markets. In 1971 the Central Bank of The Gambia was established and launched the new **dalasi currency**. In 1973, with the Gambian population exceeding 500,000 for the first time, Bathurst was renamed Banjul with much patriotic pride, and in the same year a record groundnut harvest earned a balance of trade surplus of D25.2 million, increasing the per capita income of the population by half .

However, by 1976 prospects for the government were less favourable. Two new opposition parties had formed: the somewhat Mandinka-chauvinist **National Convention Party** (NCP), led by dismissed vice-president Sherif Mustapha Dibba, and the more left-wing **National Liberation Party**. Groundnut prices fell in the late-1970s, and The Gambia experienced a string of disastrous harvests. This economic recession, and political opposition to the government – perceived increasingly as incompetent and corrupt – partly account for the conditions that led to the formation of two new **Marxist groupings** in 1980 and an **attempted coup** in October of that year. Senegalese troops were flown in under a defence agreement and the leaders of the **Gambia Socialist Revolutionary Party** and the trans-national **Movement for Justice in Africa-Gambia** (MOJA-G) were arrested and their organizations banned.

The Senegambia Confederation

A far more serious coup attempt on July 30, 1981 (while Jawara was at the wedding of Prince Charles and Diana in London), resulted in a force of three thousand Senegalese troops arriving with a group of SAS soldiers from Britain, to put down sporadic, bloody fighting around Banjul. The trouble lasted a week and may have cost as many as a thousand lives.

The insurrection shook the government and immediate steps were taken to maintain Senegal's support. The subsequent **Senegambia Confederation**, ratified on December 29, 1981, assured The Gambia of Senegal's military protection while ostensibly assuring Senegal of The Gambia's commitment to political union. **Treason trials** in the wake of the attempted coup led to long jail terms, but the increasing importance of tourism and international opinion meant there were no executions.

In 1982 the constitution was amended once again to make the president electable by the people rather than by members of parliament, and Jawara scored another conclusive victory in the subsequent **presidential election**, receiving a personal vote of 137,000, with Sherif Mustapha Dibba, who was in detention at the time, receiving 52,000. A 1984 cabinet reshuffle brought in some popular reformist MPs, and in the following year public opinion led to the dismissal of several ministers after allegations of corruption. The government also launched an **Economic Recovery Programme** designed to attract foreign aid.

After Dibba's release, the NCP mounted a serious challenge at the 1987 general and presidential elections. However, it was a new opposition grouping, the **Gambia People's Party** (GPP), led by the respected former vice-president **Hassan Musa Camara**, that made the most impact on the government. President Jawara's own vote was reduced from 72 to 59 percent, but though his party's share of the vote was also reduced, the PPP still managed to win 31 of the 36 elected seats in the House, with the NCP holding the remaining five. Supporters of the GPP, particularly in its Fula- and Serahule-speaking strongholds upriver, were left frustrated, as were supporters of the new socialist party, the **People's Democratic Organization for Independence and Socialism**, a party with close ties to the banned MOJA-G. Meanwhile, government and services were known to be plagued by corruption and mismanagement, the education system was in desperate need of improvement, and malnutrition was widespread up-country, as a direct result of a public expenditure squeeze and cutbacks in subsidies to farmers. At the 1986 Independence Day celebrations in

Banjul, a teenager named Baboucar Langley staged a solitary protest before the presidential platform on behalf of the Gambian farmers forced into poverty by government policy, declaring that "the people are dying of starvation". He was arrested and sentenced to 18 months' imprisonment.

A new **coup plot** – really a long-running, conspiratorial rumble – was uncovered in February 1988. The conspiracy involved both Gambian leftists and Casamance separatists from Senegal. It was suggested at the trials that the Senegalese opposition leader, **Abdoulaye Wade**, had been involved in planning it.

Throughout the end of the 1980s and the first years of the 1990s, with the Economic Recovery Programme still grinding through its measures, the country began to face up to the causes of its hardships. Senior ministers, bankers, customs officials and heads of the Produce Marketing Board (GPMB) and the Utilities Corporation responsible for the intermittent electricity supply were all investigated for corruption, and President Jawara routinely "cleaned out" public offices. However, accountability was not enforced with tough sanctions, and a prevailing sense of stagnation and recycled rhetoric hung over Banjul.

On the broad economic front, the **liberalization of groundnut sales** removed the GPMB's monopoly and allowed farmers to sell their harvest to the highest-bidding private trader. Although this risked forcing down the price in remote areas, the net effect was to keep more of the crop from being smuggled to high-paying Senegal. Tourism, too, benefited from the sale of the state's hotel interests and an increased profile abroad, with more than one hundred thousand tourists visiting every year.

But the wider future was marred by the **breakdown of the Senegambia Confederation** (officially dissolved on September 30, 1989), as a result of Senegal's frustration at the slow pace of moves towards union. Senegal, in its latent conflict with Mauritania, withdrew the troops which provided The Gambia's security (and indeed President Jawara's personal security), saying they were needed at home.

The end of the Senegambia Confederation left a huge question mark over The Gambia. It had been the national controversy for the best part of a decade, supported by the mostly urban Wolof but generally mistrusted by the Mandinka, whose dominant position in the country was always threatened by a powerful Senegal. For The Gambia's opposition parties and ethnic minorities, the breakdown of the confederation represented an opportunity lost.

Attention was focused in 1990 on **Liberia**, with numbers of Liberian refugees making their way to safe haven in The Gambia and Jawara sending a small detachment of Gambian troops to support the West African ECOMOG forces trying to maintain the peace in Liberia – the country's first overseas military expedition. Administrative failures resulted in the soldiers not being paid, and a dangerous confrontation was narrowly averted when they returned to Banjul. The chief of the armed forces resigned, admitting he'd lost the confidence of his men, and was replaced by a Nigerian officer. It was a warning of changes to come.

President Jawara was **re-elected** for a sixth term in April 1992, a month before his 68th birthday, after being persuaded to stand, despite his professed wish to retire. He polled 58 percent of the vote; his nearest rival Mustapha Dibba 22 percent. Jawara softened his stance against MOJA-G and the Gambian Socialist Revolutionary Party, announcing an amnesty for all members of the previously proscribed organizations. He also began again to make noises about corruption in public life. In 1993 The Gambia's population passed the one million mark, and in the same year the country became the first African state to abolish the death penalty.

Military rule

The **corruption** issue boiled up quickly through the end of the 1994 dry season. In April there were demonstrations in Brikama – the country's third largest town, close to the coast but not benefiting from tourism – over the unaffordable cost of public utilities. Then, on July 22, after returning ECOMOG soldiers complained of abusive treatment by Nigerian commanding officers at Banjul airport, their widespread anger and demands for unpaid salaries coalesced through the day into a successful **coup** led by **Lt Yahya Jammeh**, a Jola from Foni district, with the support of a hastily assembled **Armed Forces Provisional Ruling Council** (AFPRC). Jawara and some of his cabinet fled to the sanctuary of an American ship docked at Banjul, and received asylum in Senegal, but others were arrested.

Jammeh, only 29 years old and an uncharismatic figure in regulation dark glasses, made a poor impression on the international community. Casual observers had long harboured the illusion that Jawara's Gambia was one of the few admirable political cultures in West Africa. Indeed, it appeared hard at first to find an altruistic justification for a coup in The Gambia. Though the country's human rights record was not unblemished, the fundamental fairness of its multiparty system had not seemed open to question. Opposition parties were consistently frustrated at elections, but the evidence for vote-rigging was limited: Jawara won because he commanded a popular following, albeit also a largely Mandinka one.

However, the AFPRC managed to convince sceptics that, fair or not, the political system was shoring up a Gambian state riddled with **corruption** from bottom to top: President Jawara himself was said to have spent the equivalent of the annual health care budget in a six-day shopping trip to Switzerland just weeks before the coup. Jammeh insisted his administration, which included some civilian members, would seek the return of stolen state property.

His announcement, however, that the AFPRC would not step down to an elected civilian government for four years was greeted with disbelief. After an unsuccessful counter-coup, in which several soldiers were killed, and a reported threat by Jammeh to the safety of citizens of any countries that might be planning the forcible reinstatement of Jawara, the British Foreign Office warned tourists that The Gambia was unsafe to visit. Nearly all the tour operators and charter airlines pulled out, and **tourism** plummeted to twenty percent of normal levels, precipitating a genuine crisis. The response was pragmatic: Jammeh brought the date of transition forward by two years, which led to the withdrawal of the Foreign Office's advisory notice and the tour operators' resumption of holiday bookings.

The Second Republic

Jammeh's first few months in office convinced him he had considerable grassroots support: most Gambians noticed no downswing in their fortunes since his coup, and the country at large anticipated some results from the AFPRC's efforts to return looted Gambian funds. They were to be disappointed: rumours circulated that the AFPRC itself was not squeaky-clean; ministers previously sacked by Jawara for corruption were given posts by Jammeh, and the story quickly spread that Jammeh had engineered the counter-revolt himself in order to eliminate potential rivals. Throughout 1995, a number of high-ranking officers fled the country, and there was a rash of accusations and counter-accusations of corruption and theft from the public purse on a grand scale. The finance minister died in suspicious circumstances; a new secret police service, the National Intelligence Agency, was created, with sweeping powers of arrest and interrogation; and the death penalty was reinstated. Meanwhile, Jammeh sponsored several showy architectural projects designed to mark his regime out as a force to be reckoned with: Senegalese architect Pierre Goudiaby was commissioned to design a triumphal arch for Banjul, and to build a striking new international airport.

Jammeh's first real test came in 1996, as the country prepared for the return of an elected government and the electorate began to realise that it would almost certainly be headed by Jammeh himself, in civilian clothing. A **constitutional review commission** was established to hear the views of Gambians and to usher in a new republic. But it was manipulated by the AFPRC to give Jammeh and his coterie every advantage over all opposition elements: the age for presidential candidates was set at 30–65, thus making the youthful Jammeh eligible and ruling out many senior politicians of the Jawara era; political parties which had been active in the Jawara era were all banned from competing; and the timing of the presidential and parliamentary elections were set such that Jammeh's opponents had virtually no opportunity to campaign, while the AFPRC had effectively been on the campaign trail throughout the country since soon after coming to power.

The **presidential election**, which eventually took place on September 26, 1996, was flawed in every respect. Jammeh retired from the military and his 22 July Movement, which was to be dissolved, was replaced by a new party, the aptly acronymic **Alliance for Patriotic Reorientation and Construction** (APRC) – the AFPRC out of uniform. They managed to hog the media spotlight, with The Gambia's new TV station almost entirely neglecting the opposition; meanwhile the military intimidated the minor parties. Jammeh took 55 percent of the vote, while lawyer and human rights advocate **Ousainou Darboe** of the **United Democratic Party** received 35 percent. In the legislative elections, which took place in January 1997, the severely limited resources of most of the opposition meant they could only field candidates in a proportion of the country's 45 constituencies. The vote itself, however, was observed to be fairer than the presidential poll, with less intimidation of rival candidates. Jammeh's party took 33 seats, five of them unopposed, while the opposition was lucky to secure 12 seats spread among three parties and two independent MPs.

Early parliamentary sessions in the **Second Republic** were undignified affairs, with opposition members prevented from asking difficult questions by the Jammeh-appointed speaker of the house, and repeated complaints that the president seemed unable to abide by the country's new constitution in his dealings with parliament. Jammeh, meanwhile, continued to consolidate his power base and in 1998 further reduced his cabinet.

Discontent rose violently to the surface in 2000 after the torture and death in custody of a student. In demonstrations in protest, fourteen people were shot dead by police in the Kombos. A few weeks later, the opposition leader **Ousainou Darboe** of the UDP and twenty of his supporters were charged with the murder of an APRC activist, though they were later released on bail. Soon after, nine people, including several soldiers, were charged with treason following an alleged coup, just one of a series of conspiracies and attempted coups.

Jammeh's second term

In the **presidential elections** of October 2001, Jammeh won a second five-year term, with a victory over Ousainou Darboe. Despite rising tensions beforehand, the polls were given a clean bill of health by foreign observers. Claims of fraud continued to be made by the opposition, however, including the claim that Jola voters were brought in from Casamance in Senegal. The opposition boycotted the January 2002 parliamentary elections, claiming APRC harassment of UDP candidates and, amid widespread voter apathy, the APRC scooped a victory.

Ousainou Darboe and **Yankuba Touray** – Tourism Minister and APRC mobiliser – continued to lock horns, and in November 2002 new amendments to the Criminal Procedure Code were drafted, denying bail to anyone on a murder charge, and allowing Darboe to be re-arrested. Then in December 2003, Touray himself – one of Jammeh's few close associates to remain in power since the 1994 coup – was dismissed from office and arrested for embezzlement on his return from a trip to Switzerland.

Jammeh, while rewarding his fellow Jolas with positions in the government and civil service, also tried to connect with the **Mandinka farming majority** in the up-country divisions, spending two weeks on a "Meet the people" tour, during which his main message was that Gambians should get back to the land. However, regular coup rumours suggested there was serious division in the army's upper command, between the Mandinka majority and Jammeh's frequently refreshed inner circle.

Jammeh continued to make noises about the abuse of office and regularly called for **corruption** to be curtailed. Early in 2004 several Central Bank officials were tried on fraud charges, but the IMF is deeply sceptical of Jammeh's good faith and has not been able to carry out an audit of the bank's foreign exchange business. Meanwhile, the fragmented opposition declared that Jammeh's words rang hollow when there was widespread evidence that he was the main perpetrator of corruption.

The **alien registration scheme**, introduced in 2003, whereby all foreign residents were required to pay D1000 (around £25/$40, a considerable amount in local terms) per family member per year – was broadly popular with Gambians, and resulted in the exodus of a large section of the work force, but left some local industries, such as small-scale fishing, teetering on the brink of collapse.

Jammeh's second term saw him making regular **attacks on the media**, invariably calling for "responsible journalism" when facing press or radio criticism himself. **Censorship** included the closure and hypertaxation of radio stations and the arrest of newspaper staff. 2003 saw **arson attacks** on *The Independent* newspaper and Radio FM1 as well as on the home of the BBC's correspondent.

Then, in December 2004 came a turning point, with the murder of the respected journalist, editor of *The Point* newspaper, **Deyda Hydara**, shot in his car, at night, just two days after he had criticized new laws drastically curtailing the freedom of the press. Nobody in Jammeh's close circle was directly implicated, but the campaign group Reporters Without Borders found that threatening letters had been received by Hydara and other outspoken critics from a group calling themselves the Green Boys – hardline young activists from the APRC (green having always been associated with the 1994 coup). The Network of

African Freedom Expression Organisations (NAFEO) called Jammeh's government "the most violent violator of press freedom in West Africa". There was no doubt in the mind of any Gambian with a radio, or sufficient education to read a paper, that Hydara had been murdered for his views, and that the country had entered a new, and dangerous, phase.

The Gambia's future

At the end of March 2006, a presidential communiqué announced that loyal agents had thwarted an **attempted military coup** led by a close Jammeh associate, **Colonel Ndure Cham**. Jammeh, who was visiting his military friends in Nouakchott at the time, returned hurriedly from Mauritania. Dozens of senior military figures were arrested and many others fled the country. In the wake of numerous previous "coup attempts", a cynical nation widely supposed that the March coup attempt was another deliberate distraction and roundup of possible nuisance elements well in advance of the 2006 presidential elections. Only a few months earlier, the mayors of Serrekunda and Banjul had been arrested and numerous military sackings had also preceded the coup attempt, while rumours circulated about the danger of mentioning unpaid salaries – an issue frequently deemed to be raised only by troublemakers. In the aftermath of the coup attempt, five suspects being transported from Banjul to Janjanbureh prison in the east of the country disappeared when, according to their guards, they "escaped" after their vehicle careered off the road.

As the country waited for the 2006 rains to break, attention focused on two landmark events. The first was Jammeh's long-desired **African Union summit**. Held in early July, in and around the half-built Sheraton Hotel in Brufut, and at enormous expense (£12 million/€18 million) for the country, the AU convened to trade platitudes while Gambians looked on in bemusement. The question of how many African presidents would actually fly to Banjul was a hot topic around Banjul during the run-up. No friend of most of today's West African leaders, who see him as a mercurial representative of the bad old days (Jammeh backed the brutal late dictator of Nigeria, Sani Abacha, and the imprisoned former warlord of Liberia, Charles Taylor), the Gambian leader has had more success cultivating ties with the Maghreb. He is particularly close to Morocco (Jammeh's wife is Moroccan), and to the governments of Mauritania and Libya. Libya's Colonel Gaddafi travelled to the summit overland from Senegal, in a convoy of seventy vehicles, but many heads of state spurned the event. Jammeh arranged surprise cameo appearances by President Mahmoud Ahmadinejad of Iran and Venezuela's Bush-baiting President Hugo Chavez, in a purely grandstanding move, the relevance of which to Africa's pressing problems few observers could fathom.

The second big event of the year, the **presidential elections** due by October 2006, was once again being manipulated by Jammeh, who pulled the poll forward to September, ostensibly to pre-date 2006's Ramadan, but possibly also to jump the gun on a high-profile, and potentially embarrassing lawsuit over unpaid fees, brought by a US public relations firm that had been engaged to boost Jammeh's image. Also, at this time of year, disgruntled rural farmers would be busy in the fields, and less inclined to put tools down to make the journey to the polling stations.

On the eve of the AU summit, the Gambian government received bad news: the country's eligibility for development funds from the US **Millennium**

Challenge Corporation had been suspended, the MCC citing a "disturbing pattern of deteriorating conditions . . .growing human rights abuses, increased restrictions on political rights, civil liberties and press freedom, as well as deteriorating economic policies and anti-corruption efforts".

Jammeh's reputation among his peers at the AU summit was further dented by the growing evidence that, for many years, he has backed one of the two main **separatist rebel factions** in the Senegalese Casamance region, just across the border from his own Foni district. There were several bouts of fighting between rival groups in the Mouvement des Forces Démocratiques de la Casamance (MFDC) in northern Casamance in 2006, including around the small tourist resort of Kafountine and near Djibidione, just a few miles across the border from Jammeh's headquarters at Kanilai. In recent years, it has become clear that banditry and control of the lucrative local cannabis crop have become more important to most MFDC fighters than the political principles at stake. Meanwhile, refugees from the fighting tend to flee to The Gambia, with rumours circulating that large numbers of displaced Senegalese Jola have been registered to vote in the Gambian presidential elections.

It was against this background that, just days before the opening of the AU summit, Senegal's **President Abdoulaye Wade** made a flying visit to Banjul, signalling his displeasure with Jammeh by insisting on meeting him in the airport itself for three hours of terse discussions before flying back to Dakar. Stability in The Gambia is now being measured in terms of stability in Senegal and Guinea-Bissau – Jammeh's position directly linked to the MFDC and another rebel group seeking the overthrow of the francophone-leaning government in Guinea-Bissau.

Relations with Senegal have always been strained, the larger country experiencing The Gambia as an irritating thorn in its side. Disputes break out frequently over border regulations and trans-Gambia ferry fares, often resulting in a virtual closure of the borders, disrupting normal trade and business for weeks on end. Senegal continues to push hard for The Gambia to build a bridge over the river to speed up communications between northern Senegal and its southern, Casamance region, but there are no signs that Jammeh has any interest in committing to such a huge project when even the one main road up-country is barely surfaced.

While poor regional relations and the failure to obtain development funds are embarrassing for the government, they cause huge hardship to the Gambian people, especially in the impoverished countryside. As this book went to press just before the September 2006 presidential elections, the biggest issue of concern to most Gambians was the question of when they would be paid for the **December 2005 groundnut harvest**. Their harvest had been bought from them on credit by government-controlled buying agents. As planting of the 2006 crop commenced, groundnut farmers were still owed about £20 million (€30 million) – a gigantic figure for a small population used to wages of a euro a day. In the wake of the costly AU summit, the upfront costs of presidential campaigning, and the financial disaster of the MCC walkout, it was hard to see how the groundnut debt would be paid.

Meanwhile, as his trusted circle tightens still further, Jammeh manipulates and pressurises the judiciary, harasses and intimidates the opposition and, ignoring constitutional niceties, uses the resources of state for his campaigns. His widely feared security service made hundreds of arrests in 2006 – of journalists, lawyers, MPs and army officers, members of Jammeh's own family, senior figures in the National Intelligence Agency itself and the prominent human rights lawyer, Mariam Denton – all, including the widescale sacking of civil servants, part of a pre-election softening-up process that the country recalled only too well from 2001. Then, in July 2006, the head of the **independent electoral commission** was sacked, a move which would provoke an outcry in the media in most countries. But in The Gambia the media has been almost silenced.

On state-owned TV and radio, in the pages of the state-controlled *Daily Observer*, in every sphere of public life, President Dr Alhaji Yahya AJJ Jammeh, 41, is almost the only visible figure. Few "cabinet" ministers have high public profiles, such is the turnover of those who get close to the president.

In **the opposition**, neither Ousainou Darboe of the UDP/NRP nor Halifa Sallah of the National Alliance for Democracy and Development seem likely to step aside for the other to lead a united opposition front against Jammeh. And former president Dawda Jawara, back in the country, with a house in Fajara, keeps his head down and seems unlikely to get involved again in politics.

The **anger and bitterness** levelled at Jammeh has reached new depths. Formal cabinet structure for government has been largely abandoned in favour of rule by presidential prerogative, or bullying, with cash inducements and lightly veiled threats in common use. More than ever, the "Smiling Coast" looks like a country in serious financial and political trouble, propped up by tourism. There is little chance that the limited abilities of Jammeh's government will be enough to avert disaster for themselves or for the Gambian people. The best prognosis would be a strong showing for the opposition in the forthcoming elections, a period of reflection for the president, and very clear signals from regional neighbours and the international community that the game is up, and Gambians want to move on.

Society

The Gambia's population of around 1.5 million is a multi-ethnic, multi-lingual mosaic of peoples, originating from all over West Africa and beyond, and coexisting remarkably peacefully. In a continent where inter-racial rivalry and oppression have been the root cause of problems ranging from routine discrimination to full-blown genocide, Gambians are proud of their reputation for tolerant acceptance of all races and religions.

Closely contained in a tiny, densely populated landmass, Gambian society is very tightly knit. Gambians are born, married and laid to rest in **village communities**, where people live outdoor lives in extreme proximity to each other. **Islam**, practiced by ninety percent of the population, is a significant unifying force, but, whatever their religion, all Gambians observe traditional **rites of passage** in virtually the same manner. The birth, initiation, marriage and death of every individual are marked and celebrated by family and community events, often involving music, dancing and the consumption of vast quantities of food.

Peoples of The Gambia

The Gambia's racial and cultural categories are unevenly spread, and overlap with neighbouring communities in Senegal and beyond. While it's common for families of the same ethnic origin to be concentrated in a particular home patch, the boundaries between these territories are fuzzy and bear no relation to political boundaries. West Africa's national borders and divisional boundaries were, after all, drawn up by Europeans, and ethnic distribution was barely acknowledged in the process.

The most enduring and meaningful ethnic indicator is **language** – a person's first language is still important as an index of social identity. Children adopt their father's tribal identity, in name at least, and his first language as their first language (although in practice, if their mother is from a different tribe, children grow up speaking two tribal languages equally fluently).

Distinctions between ethnic groups would be simple for outsiders to pinpoint if all those who speak the same language and share a common culture also had obvious similarities in physical appearance. The term "tribe", though commonly used by Gambians about themselves, tends to imply homogeneity. But tribes have never been closed units, and language, appearance and culture have always overlapped. While it's possible to make broad generalizations about each group's characteristic build and facial features, these distinctions are becoming more and more dilute as Gambians become increasingly mobile, with rural youngsters moving from their home villages to find work elsewhere and marrying outside their tribe. Intermarriage between Gambians of different tribes has always been reasonably common, and Gambians believe that this, and the unifying force of Islam, are the keys to their success as a peaceful multi-ethnic society. Over the last few generations, as the country has become more outward-looking, tribal identities have broken down and have been replaced to some degree by broader **class distinctions** based on wealth and influence rather than language and culture.

Even so, an individual's ethnic identity is still a matter of personal pride, and a significant means by which Gambians define and categorize their friends and acquaintances. Loyalty towards "brothers and sisters" of the same tribe is deeply felt, and there is much joking banter between members of rival tribes, even those who are great friends, whereby "tribe-ist" insults are traded and quickly retracted in good-natured style. This habit of categorizing people according to their ethnic group partly explains why Gambians will refer to and address white people by the blanket label "toubab", even after they've known the individual concerned for a long time.

The Mandinka

The **Mandinka** make up 42 percent of the population and are by far the most populous tribe in the up-country rural areas. They dominated the Gambian political scene from 1962–1994, when President Jawara, himself a Mandinka, rewarded extended family members with positions of power and influence. Post-coup, Mandinka influence has diminished in inverse proportion to the increased influence of the Jola, Jammeh's own tribe.

Traditionally, Mandinka are devout Muslims, who make a living as farmers (particularly groundnut-farmers) and fishermen. They tend to take real pride in displaying their material wealth, and prefer houses built of cement blocks to traditional constructions of mud-bricks and thatch; Mandinka villages therefore generally appear more established than those of the rural Fula or Jola. Men, if they're dressing up (that is, every Friday, or for traditional celebrations and occasions), wear formal West African Muslim attire: an embroidered brimless cap, and a *haftan*, like a long shirt, often in pastel-coloured damask with intricate embroidery round the neck, over damask trousers and pointed-toed, backless white shoes. Women wear a *tiko* or head-tie with hand-tailored dresses and ruffled sleeves and bodices, nipped waists and plunging backs: the classic West African styles that were originally inspired by the fashions of eighteenth-century France, as worn by colonialists' wives.

Mandinka have a strong musical tradition that culturally they share with their Malian cousins, the Bambara and Mandé; they're particularly famous for virtuoso *kora* playing. Mandinka celebrate Muslim festivals and family celebrations with great gusto, when the music also includes danceable drumming and *balafon*. Many ceremonies are marked by the appearance of the *kankurang*, or devil-dancers (see p.288).

The Fula

The Gambia's second largest ethnic group, the **Fula** people, are widespread within West Africa, particularly in Senegal and Mali, and within this broad range they have various names including Fulani, Fulbe, Peulh and Peul. Their cultural homeland is in northern Senegal, and their traditional occupation of cattle-herding, always searching for good grazing, explains their broad dispersal. They are well-adapted to life in the Sahelian semi-desert and are skilled at keeping cattle healthy in relatively harsh environments, sometimes keeping cattle for other tribes on commission.

The Fula's nomadic lifestyle means that they tend to avoid cement-block buildings, preferring instead simple round mud-brick houses, roofed with thatch. Most Fula are Muslim, and they tend to have lighter skin and straighter hair than most other tribes. Traditional dress for Fula women includes huge gold earrings, and they sometimes tattoo their gums and faces (especially round the mouth) with dark dye. Herders are always men and boys, and traditionally wear tunics made of rough-weave undyed cotton and conical hats. Fula music is

△ Simba dancer

desert music, with mournful tunes played on herders' flutes (made from wood, bamboo or millet stalks) and the rasping, violin-like *riti*. As well as work songs, love songs and lullabies, they compose songs in praise of cattle, sung to them as they graze.

The Wolof

The **Wolof** are descended from the aristocratic founders of the Jolof Empire. Today, theirs is the language most often heard in the Kombos; they also dominate Dakar and coastal Senegal. The up-country villages on the north bank of the river east of Farafenni are populated by Wolofs with long family lineages known as *Fana Fana*. Almost all Wolofs are Muslim, and earn their living in the Kombos as traders and businesspeople, or up-country as farmers. Many Wolof-speakers in the urban area are not ethnically Wolof, but people from other tribes who have adopted Wolof as their first language. In fact, while the Wolof are in many ways a highly respected group, other ethnic groups have begun to object to the "wolofization" of Gambian culture – the Wolof are a minority, but their influence has become extremely pervasive.

Traditionally, Wolof society was rigidly hierarchical, although today status is defined far more by wealth or education than by caste. Wolofs are typically fine-featured, with high cheekbones and very dark skin. They tend to have expensive tastes and are snappy dressers, the men in flowing robes and the women in gorgeous flowing *mbubas* (traditional gowns, often a voluminous tunic-like dress with an embroidered or embellished neck, worn over a *wrapper* or wraparound skirt) with elaborate hairstyles, towering head-ties and killer heels.

The Wolof are superb drummers and dancers, and the lion-like *simba* or *zimba* dancers (see p.68) are a favourite feature of Wolof festivals. Wolof music such as *mbalax, ndagga* and *sabar* drumming dominates the Senegalese music scene and is hugely popular in The Gambia, with Youssou N'Dour one of its most celebrated exponents.

The Jola and the Manjago

Related to the Diola of Senegal and Guinea-Bissau, the **Jola** are mostly concentrated in southern Gambia, near the border with the Casamance district of Senegal. The origins of the tribe are obscure, but the Jola seem to be the earliest known settlers in The Gambia. The tribe is currently in meteoric ascent, in profile, confidence, and influence, since President Jammeh is a Jola and he has favoured many of his kin with prestigious positions in public life.

Unlike the Wolof social hierarchy, Jola **society** is segmented and flexible, with no lower castes. Even those Jola who are Muslim tend to be heavily influenced by traditional animist beliefs and practices. Jola wrestlers, for example, famous for their strength and skill, would not consider entering a tournament without first visiting a sacred crocodile pool and seeking *jujus* and magical potions from a marabout.

Traditional dress for Jola men is shirts or waistcoats with huge baggy trousers, while women wear long strings of beads crossed from each shoulder to the opposite hip. Unusually for a West African tribe, the Jola do not have a strong oral tradition: they have plenty of traditional music, but no *griots* to act as praise-singers and historians. They are a bellicose tribe, and their celebrations (see p.214) include a great deal of noise and eccentric bravado.

Traditionally, the Jola are farmers, hunters, fishermen and palm wine-tappers. Most palm wine-tappers are **Manjago**, a subsection of the Jola tribe originally from Guinea-Bissau, who are usually animist or Christian rather than Muslim. As well as running palm wine "ghettoes", the Manjago gather palm nuts for oil, and keep pigs. Because their practices run so contrary to Muslim tradition, their compounds are often semi-isolated on the fringes of villages.

The Serahule, Serer and Aku

The **Serahule**, **Serer** and **Aku** are the least numerous of The Gambia's West African ethnic groups, together accounting for less than fifteen percent of the total population.

Resident up-country in eastern Gambia, the **Serahule** are related to the Soninke of Mali and Burkina Faso, and are thought to be one of the oldest ethnic groups in West Africa. Traditionally they are Muslim farmers and potters. Many are also gold- and silver-traders, and Serahule women often wear gold hoop earrings wound with red thread.

The **Serer** are best known as fishermen, and are originally from the valley and delta regions of the River Senegal. They, along with the Jola, were among the first ethnic groups to settle in The Gambia, and there are Serer boatbuilders and fishing communities around the mouth of the river, particularly in and around Barra on the north bank. Some communities are nomadic, following the migration of fish up and down the river.

The **Aku** are the descendants of freed African slaves, repatriated to Africa in the nineteenth century. Some Aku are descended from Europeans, who had children with African women. There was once a large population of Aku in Georgetown (now Janjanbureh), but they have since migrated to the Kombos; the sizeable and long-established community in Banjul is still active. Most Aku families have very English names, like Roberts and Jones, passed down the generations from the days when slaves were given the surname of their owner and master. While most are Christian, some are Muslim, and have Muslim first names and English surnames. The Aku language is a mixture of English and creole.

During the colonial era, the Aku's good English, relatively high standard of education, and experience of European customs all stood them in good stead to take up positions in local government, and they became part of the local elite. Aku were dominating the political scene at the time that Jawara took over the reins of government; subsequently their influence faded as Jawara favoured Mandinka for positions of power. While Jola have taken over from many Mandinka under Jammeh's regime, there remains a strong Aku presence in the Gambian civil service.

The Mauritanians and the Lebanese

Concentrated in Banjul but also found running businesses in up-country towns are the **Mauritanian-Gambian** shopkeepers, traders, teachers, tailors and jewellery-makers, conspicuous in their ankle-length robes (usually sky-blue) and cotton turbans. They are Muslim, and to outsiders look more Middle-Eastern than African; they're known for being enterprising in business, and usually speak French, Hassaniya Arabic and Wolof.

The **Lebanese-Gambians** are a prominent feature of the commercial and social scene, running import-export businesses, foreign exchange bureaux, hotels, restaurants and retail enterprises. Most are Muslim, including some Shi'ites; some are Christian. Lebanese migrants first moved to West Africa in the late nineteenth and early twentieth centuries, settling and often intermarrying with Africans, and a second wave arrived during the Lebanese civil war of the 1970s and 1980s. They tend to have a love-hate relationship with other Gambians, who admire their business acumen, but object, jealously, to their chanelling their Gambian-earned profits out of the country to relatives in Lebanon.

The Gambian village

The Gambia is a nation of villagers. Even the larger towns – Serrekunda, Bakau, Brikama, Banjul – are essentially overgrown **villages**, or collections of villages that have merged into one. While colonial Banjul, Janjanbureh and parts of Bakau were planned to a degree, with streets laid out on a grid pattern of sorts, all other Gambian settlements have evolved organically, growing out from a central meeting place, market and mosque.

There's little room for privacy in this country, where Western-style family houses are rare, except in the expat enclaves – instead, most people live in a compound with their extended family, which may number thirty individuals or more, sharing rooms with curtains for doors, where every sound can be heard. While some might see such a way of life as claustrophobic, Gambians choose to appreciate it as a support mechanism. The Gambia has no social security system – no unemployment benefit, or care homes for the elderly – so it is the responsibility of every working Gambian to house and give financial support to every member of the family who is not earning. In areas where agriculture is foundering and there are few employment opportunities, one wage-earner may be supporting as many as fifty others, including babies, children and elderly relations. Non-earners are, in turn, expected to pull their weight in the daily routines of domestic maintenance, which are highly labour-intensive and time-consuming, as few Gambians are able to afford private transport or domestic machinery, many are without mains electicity, and many have to leave their compound every day to fetch water from a shared well or pump.

Every Gambian village has at least one notable **natural feature** to define its location – a creek, an escarpment, a ring of huge and ancient baobabs or silk cotton trees, a sandy bay, or a stretch of the River Gambia that's good for fishing. Often the village will be named after this feature, or after the founder of the village, or after the primary occupation of the villagers. It's not unusual up-country for a whole village, or even a whole area, to be populated by just one ethnic group. In the Kombos, however, it's more usual for villages to be mixed, but known, say, as a Fula village, if Fula are in the majority or if it was a prominent Fula who founded the village.

A Gambian **village** is a microcosm of rural life: a self-contained unit where people eat, sleep, care for their families, farm, trade, worship, share information and make political decisions. Gambian **villages** have not one central focus, but several: the **bantaba**, a meeting place for the men of the village; the **water supply**, in isolated areas a well or wells, where women go to draw water but also to catch up on local gossip; the **market**, the commercial heart of any village; and the **mosque**, the village's spiritual focal point. Each extended family lives in a compound, a collection of huts or a brick-built block enclosed by a fence or wall. Compounds often contain fruit trees, and there may be larger orchards, plus fields and vegetable gardens, on the outskirts of the village. Some villages are enclosed by a wall or a fence of wooden stakes or woven millet stalks.

Larger villages may have several *bantabas,* which are always shaded, often by a huge, centuries-old baobab or silk cotton tree. Baobabs and silk cotton trees are spiritually significant to Gambians and it's rare to come across a village without at least one spectacular specimen; a ring of baobab trees out in the bush generally marks the place where a village once stood. They act as village notice boards as well as meeting places. The *bantaba* is usually a platform of planks or logs, though some are made from scrap metal. Male villagers of all ages while away hours in conversation sitting here in the shade, playing cards, checkers or *warri* (see box on p.282) and drinking *attaya*, while their wives and sisters are working in the compound or in the fields. They justify this division by arguing that men are the decision makers, so need to discuss; and that men's work – such as clearing fields before planting, rethatching huts and building new ones

In The Gambia, where illiteracy is high and many people don't have regular access to television, radio and the Internet, leisure-time social interaction often revolves around music, storytelling and games, particularly board games and cards.

Gambian children grow up without manufactured toys, so instead play chasing games, noughts-and-crosses-type games using sticks or counters, or make do with whatever they find, bending models out of wire or pushing old bicycle tyres around with sticks. On street corners in urban areas you may see men playing backgammon or checkers under shady trees, with a social gathering of onlookers monitoring the game. Outside bars, young Gambians battle it out in table football games, while the bar game of choice is pool.

Warri, the game of holes and seeds, is an ancient game for two that's played all over Africa. The game has a handful of seeds, cowries or pebbles as playing pieces, and a board, but since this just consists of two opposing rows of six small hollows, a "board" can easily be hollowed out on the beach. It's a game that's simple to grasp but, at the same time, mathematically highly complex in its endless chain of cause and effect – financial analysts love it.

Crazy eight is the classic Gambian card game, though, again, it's not unique to The Gambia. Like *warri*, it's deceptively simple, but highly strategic. If you're new to the game it might all seem childishly simple – but after a few rounds of being beaten hollow by a Gambian 6-year-old, you may think again.

– is just as laborious as women's – pounding grain, cooking, childcare, planting, weeding and watering – but more seasonal.

Until recently, many up-country villages lacked a reliable source of clean water, and had to make do with open wells which are vulnerable to contamination. Few villages are built close to the banks of the River Gambia, because of the malaria risk, and only those settlements closest to urban centres had mains water. A major advance occurred during the 1980s and 1990s when a series of foreign-funded aid programmes brought potable water to practically every village, in the form of **hand-pumped tripod wells** or **solar-powered boreholes**. Women who previously had to face a long walk to the nearest clean water supply, followed by an even harder walk back with buckets or basins of water balanced on their heads, have had their lives transformed. However, some Gambian women say that they preferred the old days, when they had a good excuse to spend time away from the compound, chatting with friends.

Gambians typically practise subsistence farming, so village **markets** tend to offer a limited quantity and variety of produce: fruit, vegetables, spices, fish and meat. It's the women who grow the vegetables for market, sell them (often through a third party) and do the shopping, and markets are therefore a social focal point for Gambian women. They are also eating places: women sell rice and sauce or bread and fish balls or fritters from enamel bowls. The market may be an open-sided brick- and cement building in which each trader has a rented pitch, or it might just be a gathering of women sitting under a shade tree with their produce laid out on pieces of fabric. Some villages also have a once-weekly *lumo*, a larger market held in a separate marketplace, often on the edge of the village, at which goods from all over the region and further afield are sold – including fabric, clothes, furniture, livestock and household goods. If the village has a **shop**, it won't have windows, but is more likely to be a storeroom with a counter, possibly caged off with chicken wire. All but the smallest villages have a general grocery store (*bitiko* in Mandinka) with a very rudimentary stock of household commodities.

The stature and style of the village **mosque** is a key indicator of the age and affluence of the village. The humblest mosques are mud-brick huts with a Muslim crescent symbol on the roof, but some mosques are large cement-block buildings painted white and green, decorated with patterned airbricks, and with one or more minarets from which the imam's call to prayer blasts out five times a day. The buildings may also be decorated with verses from the Koran, but all other decorations are abstract, since representations of living things are forbidden in Islamic art.

Mosques are normally found near the village centre; if a village mosque is small but the population is wealthy, the villagers will upgrade by building a new mosque large enough to house the entire congregation for Friday prayers. It's considered a great honour to take part in the building of a new mosque and every devout villager will make a point of wielding a shovel at some time during the construction process. Women must be dressed appropriately in the vicinity of a mosque, with covered head, arms and legs; they don't normally join the men inside the mosque for Friday prayers, but pray outside, or at home in their own compounds.

The Gambian compound

Domestic **compounds** are shared living spaces consisting of a collection of huts or a block of rooms within a yard. They may be enclosed by beautifully woven palm-frond or millet-stalk fences, rows of bound-together rhun palm stalks, or barricades of wooden stakes, often just gnarled, twisted and unfinished branches planted upright in the earth as a readymade feast for termites. Hedges are rarer, while sturdy walls of cement blocks are regarded as a status symbol. The purpose of the compound boundary is just to mark out a space, not to keep anybody in or out: children are free to play wherever they choose, and generally roam about in gangs in the vicinity of their compound and beyond; it's normal for villagers to drop in on their neighbours uninvited, and small domestic animals – chickens, sheep and goats – are free-ranging. Many Gambian compounds are built around mango or orange trees, which give the compound colour and shade, as well as an abundance of fruit in season; pawpaws and bananas are also commonly grown.

Inside the compound fence is the courtyard, usually of vigorously swept bare earth, where domestic life is lived out. The day starts just after dawn, between 6.30 and 7am for most of the year. The first meal of the day is often a type of porridge made with millet and sometimes served with rich creamy sour milk, like crème fraîche. Either within the compound, or outside under shade trees, women stand for several hours a day pounding grain (millet, sorghum or couscous), using long heavy wooden mortars in large bucket-sized wooden pestles. Some compounds have a roofed-over kitchen that also acts as a store and smokehouse (for preserving fish and corncobs), and others just have an outdoor cooking area. Women tend pots over open fires for a considerable part of the day, most Gambian specialities being slow-cooked stews, and everybody eats together outside, sitting or squatting round communal bowls laid on mats, one for the men and another for the women. In the evening, if the family owns a TV, they may bring the set outside for everyone, neighbours included, to gather round.

Mud-brick huts with roofs thatched with grass or palm fronds are very common in rural villages, and are practical, as they are cool by day and warm on cold nights. However, many villagers opt for cement-block rooms with corrugated iron roofs if they can afford them, as they require less maintenance, even though they make buildings roastingly hot in the sun and deafeningly noisy in the rain. Hanging just over the doorframe inside each hut or room is a collection of domestic *jujus*, which may be verses from the Koran bundled up in pieces of cloth, shells, or other fetish objects blessed by a marabout to bring good fortune upon the house.

It's not unusual for the huts or rooms in a compound to be used only for sleeping and storage, but, if a visitor arrives, they may be ushered into a room to take a seat in the best chair in the compound and, at meal-times, to eat there alone. Women often share their huts or bedrooms with their children; if a man has several wives, they take it in turns to spend the night with him, on a strict rota. The men's houses are generally at the front of the compound, so there's no chance of anybody visiting the women unnoticed. If the compound is home to craft-workers, such as potters or batik-makers, then one area will be set aside for their work.

Plumbed-in sanitation is very rare in rural villages; instead, there's a fenced-off area at the rear of the compound with a long-drop latrine and a "shower" area for washing with bucket and soap.

Village social structure

Gambian society is patrilineal and stratified, with clearly defined roles for members of each generation, and a structured system of meetings and consultations for dealing with problems and challenges. Traditionally, the **village elders** were the decision-makers, although central government, the police, the armed forces and the judiciary also have an official role to play which affects Gambians at village level.

The **chief** of the village, or *alkalo*, is typically a male (one current exception is the *alkalo* of Juffureh), and is usually the eldest descendant of the founder of the village, but may be appointed by election. Once appointed he holds the post for life unless unusual circumstances preclude this. Anybody visiting a village for the first time should start by introducing themselves to the *alkalo* and offering him a gift, such as some kola nuts or a token amount of money. He may be able to offer assistance in the form of local information or a place to stay: *alkalos* are duty-bound to find accommodation for stranded travellers who request their help. The *alkalo*, who takes care of disputes but has no judiciary power and is answerable to the *seyfo* or district chief, is also responsible for the distribution of land within the village.

Equal in stature to the *alkalo* is the imam, the resident **Muslim leader** who leads prayers at the mosque and presides at religious rituals. It is his voice, either live or recorded, that calls out from the minarets of the mosque at prayer times, five times a day. The imam is also sometimes a marabout, a charismatic Koranic teacher who can offer votive prayers and make *jujus* for people with specific requests. The imam sits on the village council of elders in an advisory capacity.

Each village has a **village development committee** which coordinates village development projects and mobilizes young people to act as a labour force. In villages where the majority are illiterate, news of committee decisions is passed around the village by traditional announcers, like town criers, who go around beating drums and singing out messages.

The **head of the compound** is legally responsible for everyone living in his compound, and is required to mediate in any family disputes. Groups of extended families who are part of the same clan live in neighbouring compounds, and are overseen by the **head of the clan**, who is usually the most senior of the compound heads.

Religion

Islam has a very tangible influence over many facets of Gambian society – in people's names, their manner of dress, eating, drinking and washing habits, marital practices, their adherence to special observances such as Ramadan and the Hajj, and even the manner in which they greet each other. Despite this, Islam has not extinguished traditional beliefs; even the most devout Gambian Muslims practise a brand of Islam that blends the teachings of the Koran with **animist beliefs** that long predate the arrival of Islam in West Africa. Today, most Gambian Muslims are **Sunni**, and the imams are their spiritual guides and leaders.

Far out-numbered by Muslims, but nonetheless conspicuous in the urban areas are the **Christians** of various denominations.

Islam

Islam was introduced to West Africa via North Africa, and existed in pockets in the region since the time of the great Empire of Ghana in the eleventh century, but it was not until the nineteenth-century *jihads*, or holy wars, that Islam became the majority religion and a unifying force within the region. One important reason why Islam was so readily accepted was that the Muslim scholars provided services that were compatible with traditional animist beliefs, such as offering prayers for people, and making amulets and charms. Islam also brought writing to The Gambia: children were taught the Arabic alphabet by Koranic teachers, and basic literacy among Muslims was generally much higher than among non-Muslims.

The presence of Islam in The Gambia has countless manifestations in everyday life. The **mosque** is one of the focal points of every town and village, and the **call to prayer**, which in some districts can be an ear-shattering chant broadcast through crackly speakers, and in others the most beautiful, ethereal music, is heard in every neighbourhood. The prescribed routines of the faithful punctuate the days, with five prayer times daily; the weeks, with everyone dressed in their finest for Friday prayers at the mosque; and the years, with the observance of **festivals** and the holy month of **Ramadan**.

Many Gambians have traditional **Muslim names**, or Gambianized versions of them, such as Modou for Mohammed, or Fatou for Fatima. **Islamic phrases** colour everyday speech: the universal greeting that all Gambians use is an Islamic one, "Salaam aleikum/Maleikum salaam", meaning "Peace be upon you/And upon you", and common interjections include "Insh'Allah", meaning "If Allah wills it", the equivalent of "God willing", and "Alhamdoulila" meaning "thanks be to Allah". It's common for young children to receive an Islamic **education** by studying under a marabout – before secular state schools became widespread in the up-country areas, this was the only education available to many families.

Gambians are very proud of the sense of morality, discipline and cleanliness engendered by their faith, and some (though not all) view the Islamic sanctioning of **polygamy** as a great privilege – many Gambian men aspire to having more than one wife. Like Muslims everywhere, their holy book is the Koran, believed to be the word of God as revealed to the prophet Mohammed, and containing the religious laws and doctrines of Islam. Muslims are required to follow the tenets known as the **Five Pillars of Islam**: recognition of Allah and the prophet Mohammed, daily prayer, fasting during Ramadan, alms-giving, and making the Hajj (pilgrimage to Mecca). Other Muslim practices include abstention from **alcohol**, commonly but not always strictly followed in The

Animist beliefs are bound up in a complex web of **superstitions and taboos** that are often taken very seriously, even by devout Muslims and Christians. Some are so secret they're never discussed. The following are a few that are commonly held:

A **water jar** should never be left empty in one's compound, as the dead may wish to drink when they pay a visit.

Pouring **cold water** on the ground first thing in the morning brings good luck for the day.

Seeing a **snake** in a dream is a sign of pregnancy.

Seeing a **horse** in a dream means a new wife is on the way.

If you are **laughing** in a dream, you will soon be crying.

If you sit in a **doorway**, evil spirits may strike you.

Somewhere in the River Gambia lives the ninki-nanka, a **dragon-devil**.

Every family has a **totem animal** they should never harm: for the Jobartehs, it's the chameleon, for the Mbyes, the monitor lizard, for the Ndeys, the rabbit, and for the Jammehs, the goat.

It's bad luck to buy or sell **soap** at night.

Don't answer a **call at night** for it may be a devil.

It's bad luck to **whistle** after dark.

Owls are the carriers of messages from evil spirits.

Throw **newly cut hair** away because if a bird finds it and makes it into a nest, you will have a constant headache.

Anything that happens on a **Saturday** will soon happen again, so avoid visiting the sick on this day.

It's bad luck to do anything on a **Wednesday**.

If a **pig** crosses your path and you don't mention it to anyone, you'll have good luck.

Gambia. The Gambian brand of Islam is not fundamentalist or fanatical, and Gambian Muslims are tolerant of non-believers.

Animism

West African **animism** is based around the conviction that natural phenomena, such as trees and animals, plus specially created objects, such as idols and fetishes, have spiritual power. Every ethnic group has their own distinctive version of similar beliefs. Most Gambians, though professing to be Muslim or Christian, also believe in the existence of non-abstract supernatural forces, some harmful and some beneficial, and that witch doctors, herbalists, diviners and marabout*s* have powers over these forces. These spiritual guides can also act as mediators between the living and the dead, enabling people to communicate with their ancestors, revered in all African societies.

Practically every Gambian wears at least one *juju*, or sacred amulet, a piece of leather into which is stitched a fetish object, such as a sliver of bone, feather, or wood, or a piece of paper inscribed with specific verses from the Koran prescribed by a marabout for their spiritual potency. Thus *jujus* may be either semi-Islamic or non-Islamic. They may be decorated with beads or cowries and worn on arms, legs, neck, or waist, and are thought to enable the wearer to control the supernatural. Their effect may simply be to protect against evil spirits, but particular *jujus* may be made for more specific purposes. For example, stitching somebody's hair into a *juju* may cause them to fall in love with the wearer, and making a *juju* with the fur of a black cat is thought to make the wearer invisible. *Jujus* may also secure a promotion or a bank loan, cure mental illness or impotence or make rivals get ill, die or disappear. Certain prayers or requests require the sacrifice of an animal. Others require the supplicant to bathe in sacred water, notably water drawn from a sacred crocodile pool (see p.127).

Christianity

The European settlers and their missionaries first brought **Christianity** to The Gambia, and there are now over one hundred thousand Christians of various denominations in the country. The spread of Christianity increased a little when freed slaves, many of whom had converted to Christianity, migrated to The Gambia and settled there in the early nineteenth century.

Most Gambian Christians live in the Kombos, and can be seen piling into churches in their best clothes on Sunday mornings. **Missionary movements** are as active as ever, but their missions are now less about conversion and more about exchange of skills and ideas. Gambian Muslims tend to show devout Christians a great deal of respect, and there is a long-standing relationship between The Gambia and the evangelical Christian-run Mercy Ship organization which provides crucial medical care and services to various nations, by rota, from a floating hospital.

Rites of passage

In The Gambia, an individual's passage through life is marked by a series of cornerstone rituals that bestow blessings and confirm the individual's position and role in their family, their clan or extended family, and in society at large. These rites of passage, and the social structures that underpin them, are mutating as Gambian society becomes more outward-looking, but Gambians are generally extremely proud of their cultural heritage and are reluctant to give up the ways of the past.

Naming ceremonies

Whereas in the Western world, **pregnancy** is usually a time of great excitement, anticipation, and exhaustive discussion with friends and relatives, Gambians treat the matter with shyness and discretion and do not talk about the baby before the birth, from a deep-seated superstition that to do so could endanger the baby's life.

Once the baby has been born, invariably at home, the mother remains indoors for a week, throughout which a fire is kept burning in her compound. When the baby is exactly a week old, a **naming ceremony** is held (*kulliyo* in Mandinka, *ngente* in Wolof). In preparation for this, the mother dresses in new clothes, has her hair elaborately plaited, is showered with gifts and is generally treated like a princess. The women of the compound spend the whole day, from the early hours, preparing food for the guests. The ritual part of the naming ceremony takes place in the morning, when a marabout or an elder cuts a lock of the baby's hair, says a silent prayer and whispers into the baby's ear the name that has been chosen by the parents, while a chicken, goat or sheep is slaughtered. A *jali* or *griot* then proclaims the name to everyone in the compound. The Mandinka nearly always name their first-born sons Lamin; otherwise names tend to honour relatives and friends on the father's side of the family. Kola nuts and specially prepared food are distributed among the guests, and the lock of hair is buried while everone present wishes the child health and long life.

At the end of the day the celebration turns into a major party. All Gambian family celebrations of this type involve music, dancing and plenty to eat and drink (though rarely any alcohol unless the family are non-Muslim). This sometimes lasts for several days, particularly if the guests have travelled some distance for the occasion. The type of music played depends on the tastes of the family but traditional bands of singers accompanied by *balafon* and drums, paid for by the family and their guests, are very popular.

Births are such regular occurrences in The Gambia that anyone staying in a village for a few weeks will almost certainly experience at least one naming ceremony, and whenever you hear drumming in the distance in the crowded urban areas, there's a good chance that the neighbourhood is welcoming another baby into the world.

Initiation ceremonies

The **circumcision of boys**, shortly before reaching puberty, marks an important step in the transition from childhood to adulthood. These days it's no longer common for boys to go through the lengthy process of "bush school" and they may instead be circumcised by a medical practitioner at a clinic, but in rural areas ancient tribal practices persist.

Traditionally, the ceremony itself (*sunnaro* in Mandinka, *jonga* in Wolof, *futampaf* in Jola) is accompanied by a lengthy period of elaborate ritual, much of which is secret – the initiates are forbidden from telling anyone the details of what happens and what they are taught. The process begins when the initiates are rounded up to be taken away for their period of preparation. Among the Mandinka it is the *kankurang* that does the rounding up, a devil dancer who comes in various guises but is usually dressed in a costume made of leaves and the red bark of the camel-foot tree, a piece of which he clamps between his teeth. He also waves a cutlass, intended to scare off any malign spirits that may attempt to prey on the initiates while they are most vulnerable.

The boys are circumcised in the bush by the village blacksmith, and while they are healing they undergo a period of private instruction at "bush school" at the hands of a marabout or a tribal elder. Over the course of a few days or weeks they learn all about sex, tribal lore and the essentials of good conduct such as respect for one's elders. Gambians are increasingly fearful that with urbanization, secular education and the popularity of foreign media, the current generation of teenagers is exposed to influences that could subvert the tradition of showing unquestioning respect for age and experience – and that irrevocable moral decline is just around the corner.

The villagers make elaborate preparations for the return of the initiates from the bush, and the occasion may be marked by more ritual elements, including the planting and watering of trees and the slaughtering of sacrificial animals, plus more socialising and masquerade dancing from the *kankurang* (in Mandinka communities) or *kumpo* (Jola). The newly initiated, dressed in white hoods, are the guests of honour.

Female circumcision, though much more controversial, is still widespread in The Gambia, and is legal, although it has been outlawed elsewhere in sub-Saharan Africa. Referred to by its detractors as female genital mutilation, female circumcision is an act prescribed by African, not Muslim, culture, and it is currently performed on around eighty percent of Gambian girls, either in babyhood or aged 10–12 years. The operation takes different forms, and can involve clitoral or labial removal. The operation, which in remote rural areas is carried out by a female elder, is extremely painful (unless carried out under anaesthetic, which is rare). Complications that may arise include excessive bleeding, septicaemia, sexual dysfunction, difficulty giving birth, and severe psychological scarring. The practice persists because there are strong cultural associations between circumcision and feminine virtue in traditional Gambian society, and, in a social structure in which being a single woman is a difficult option, mothers do not like to contemplate the possibility of their daughters becoming unmarriageable outcasts just because they neglect to perform the operation. Girls, too, often too young to fully understand the situation, feel that they don't want to be left out of a celebration in which they would receive special attention and be treated as women for the first time. Men, meanwhile, are not usually the ones to put pressure on for the operation to be performed: many, when questioned, do not express any particular preference either way.

Marriage

In traditional Gambian society, all marriages are **arranged** by the couple's parents, although the marriage cannot take place against the will of either party. In the urban areas, it's now becoming much more common for couples to marry by personal choice, and they may or may not stick to other elements of marriage ritual; even so, parental wishes hold sway over many young people's choice of partner.

Traditionally, the first overture leading to marriage negotiations is the sending of a gift of kola nuts from the man's family to the woman's parents. The father of the bride-to-be discusses the matter with his wife and their daughter, and if everyone agrees then consent is signalled by sharing the kola nuts among their relatives, friends and neighbours. Expensive gifts pass from the man to his in-laws-to-be before the marriage takes place, including luxuries such as more kola nuts, cash, new beds, jewellery and new clothes, to a total value that is a matter of negotiation. If the bride's parents don't think the gifts offered are up to scratch, they may start considering offers from other suitors. Gifts given to the woman remain hers even if the couple later split up. Her parents, in turn, provide her with a dowry, consisting of all the utensils and equipment she needs to set up home.

Typically, a woman is much younger than her husband: in up-country villages, men in their 30s marry girls in their teens, because it can take years for a man to be able to afford the price of a wedding, and, as in so many other cultures, virgins are thought to make the best brides.

A legal **ceremony** may take place at the mayor's office, but is not necessary. If this does happen (usually in the urban areas) it's followed by a procession of cars all driving from the office to the woman's compound with horns blaring at top volume. In villages, the marriage is made official either in her compound or at the mosque, in a ceremony that the husband and wife don't actually attend. The imam blesses the union with prayers in the presence of both families, and after this formal ceremony, everyone joins in a great celebration with music, dancing and feasting. Guests all contribute to the cost of the food and fees for the musicians but, if the groom is particularly short of cash, the celebration may take place some months after the ceremony.

The woman does not always go to live with her husband straight away, particularly if she is young; she may sometimes stay with her parents until after the birth of her first child. The time of her transfer to her husband's compound is another cause for festivity, when her hair is specially braided, she is formally received by her new family, and there's more celebratory music and feasting.

Islamic tradition allows a man up to four wives, if he can afford to support them all, and there's a certain kudos attained by having more than one wife in The Gambia, so **polygamy** is not uncommon. The rise of the women's movement has given women more freedom to express their feelings on polygamy but not all of them, by any means, are negative. In an unmechanized society where daily household chores such as fetching water, cooking, washing and cleaning can be extremely laborious and time-consuming, a co-wife with whom to share the graft may be a boon. Nevertheless, there's no escaping the feelings of rivalry and betrayal that polygamy can stir up, and women generally have absolutely no say in the matter of their husband marrying again. It's not unusual for husbands and wives to live apart after a few years of marriage, with the children living in the husband's compound, cared for by a second wife. Divorce is, however, almost unheard of, and would cast great shame upon the woman involved, and leave her at a serious financial disadvantage.

Funerals

Gambian **funerals** are cathartic occasions marked by much loud vocalization of grief, particularly from the female relatives of the deceased. The person who discovers a death immediately emits a loud wail. Elders then start to make funeral arrangements without delay, and send word to relatives and friends.

Funerals are not normally private occasions, and the bitter reality of short life expectancy in The Gambia means that death is too familiar an occurrence to be surrounded by taboo. The body is washed, wrapped in a white shroud, and then either rolled in a mat or placed in a coffin. It is then taken by the men of the family to the mosque for prayers, while the women remain in the compound. After prayers, the burial takes place, and charity is given to the family of the deceased, customarily money or food. The family observe a forty-day period of mourning, marked by their neighbours and the village elders offering them charitable gifts on the third, seventh and fortieth days after the burial.

According to traditional Muslim practice, a widow must remain in **mourning** for four and a half months, during which time she is supposed to wear mourning dress (basically anything plain and modest) and not leave the compound. The idea behind this is to determine whether any child she later gives birth to is the child of her late husband. Widowers do not have to observe any such practice.

Wildlife and nature

The Gambian landscape includes a wide variety of habitats for such a small territory. The landscape is dominated by Sahelian scrub and Guinea woodland savannah, with extensive mangrove wetlands concentrated near the mouth of the river and along its lower reaches, and narrow strips of tropical forest along the banks of the creeks further east. Wildlife, especially the country's avifauna, is plentiful and conspicuous, and animal-lovers visiting Africa for the first time will be dazzled by the variety of species – though don't expect too many sightings of large mammals: this isn't east Africa.

Habitats

The Gambia's defining feature is the **River Gambia**, which winds gently across the country from east to west, through a virtually flat valley punctuated by occasional low cliffs of red laterite. The valley is so shallow, and the tides so pronounced, that the river's waters are salty from the Atlantic for over 200km upstream in the dry season (slightly less in the rainy season), and there is noticeable tidal movement throughout the country. River-bank habitats change dramatically from east to west, from the **jungle** of palms and tropical evergreen trees in the freshwater reaches to the thick low forests of **mangroves** closer to the estuary. Around the estuary, muddy mazes of creeks and salt flats are the dominant features. Increasing salinity upstream causes problems for Gambian farmers, who are trying to introduce salt-adapted strains of rice in order to exploit the areas of transition between salt and fresh water.

The classic up-country Gambian landscape is flat **grassland savannah** thinly scattered with acacias, thorn trees and baobabs – lush and green in the rainy season, and straw-blond, or blackened by bush fires, in the dry season. In rural areas many Gambians view trees as a waste of good groundnut-farming space: deforestation is rife, and soil erosion a major problem, particularly in the mid-to-late dry season when the rice, millet, couscous and sorghum crops are all cleared and hot winds skim off the topsoil as dust. Fortunately, small pockets of forest survive here and there, where community forest husbandry schemes are in operation.

The Gambia's **beaches** are sandy, with shallow waters, backed either by dunes or by soft laterite cliffs. Once firmly bound by forests of palm trees, deforestation now endangers the coastal environment, and sand-mining has had the disastrous effect of exacerbating natural tidal erosion. Erosion stripped the coastal reaches of sand in the 1990s, and it's likely to take many years for them to recover.

One of the most striking silhouettes on the Gambian horizon is that of the **baobab tree**, sometimes nicknamed the "upside-down tree" because it looks as though it's been uprooted and replanted the wrong way up. Baobabs live for centuries and have a timelessly majestic presence in The Gambia; massive when mature, they are rarely cut down because they have spiritual significance – some tribes used to bury deceased *jalis* in hollows inside their stubby trunks. Baobabs are leafy only during the rainy season; by November they are hung with velvety pods like large oval Christmas tree baubles. The seeds ripen in January and contain a sherbet-like substance that's a source of tartaric acid, and can be chewed to stave off thirst or made into cordial or sorbet. The trunk contains water which can be tapped in the dry season, and the bark is sometimes stripped to make rope. There are particularly wonderful baobab specimens in up-country villages on the north bank of the river.

Equally huge and impressive features of up-country villages are the mature **silk cotton trees** which produce kapok inside long, pointed pod-like fruit. Silk cotton trees, with their elaborately pleated exposed roots and shade-giving foliage, have similar spiritual significance to baobabs, and village *bantabas* are often built beneath them.

On the coast, in the Kombo districts and in well-watered areas there are various varieties of palm, of which the **rhun palm** is the most distinctive, for its oddly top-heavy looking trunk and fan-like leaves. **Oil palms** and **coconut palms** have more feathery leaves. Palm oil is made by boiling away the husks of the palm fruit that grow in clusters at the top of the trunk; the palm-nut kernels, meanwhile, provide palm nut oil. The trees are tapped for palm wine, the tapper shinning up each tree using a brace that loops round his waist and the tree trunk, making an incision at the top of the trunk and inserting a funnel to allow the sap to run into a bottle over the course of a day or so. Palm trees everywhere are used for timber, and the fronds for roofing and fencing.

The **mangrove** is a useful, saltwater-adapted tree, and mangrove forests are as crucial to wetland ecosystems as rainforests are to inland ecosystems. Mangrove creeks act as nurseries for breeding fish, crabs, shrimps, oysters and other aquatic creatures, and, as a consequence, constitute rich feeding grounds for many birds and animals. With their complex aerial salt-filtering roots and salt-excreting leaves, they are natural processors of nitrates and water pollutants.

Other distinctive Gambian trees include the **flame tree**, stunningly florid in the rainy season, the small, flat-topped thorny **acacias**, and the **African locust bean trees**, whose pods are, like many seeds and leaves, used in natural remedies. Mature **kola nut trees** are found in the older villages: kola nuts have ritual significance in many West African societies as a traditional gift (see p.73). Village **orchards** are planted with grapefruit, orange, banana, pawpaw (papaya) and cashew trees, and mango trees are encountered everywhere, welcome as much for their deep shade as for their fruit.

Wildlife

The Gambia's **birdlife** is astonishingly diverse, and the 560-plus bird species have relatively few predators. Characteristic sights are pied crows, urbanite magpie-like birds that are common throughout the Sahelian region; electric blue Abyssinian rollers perched conspicuously on telephone wires and on bare branches; the marvellous, lurching flight of hornbills swooping across the road in forest areas; and unmistakable gaggles of noisy, glamorous long-tailed glossy starlings just about everywhere. The Gambia is also a regular haunt of Palearctic migrants – migratory species from Europe and Asia that overwinter in the tropics. For more details on bird species found in The Gambia, see p.17.

Because the country has such a rich and varied bird population, a number of ornithological studies have taken place here. By monitoring the behaviour of selected bird species, ecologists are able to keep up to date on changes to the Gambian ecosystem, and formulate environmental policy recommendations. For example, if a bird that usually frequents up-river areas is seen near the coast, this can indicate a change in the sea level and in the salinity of the River Gambia.

The large mammals most often seen out on the road or in the bush are **monkeys** and **baboons**. The country has three species of monkey – callithrix, patas and western red colobus – and an up-country population of Guinea baboons. **Callithrix**, the most numerous, have grizzled golden-green fur, a dark grey face and paler grey hands and feet, and are unique to West Africa, though very similar to the green vervet monkeys found elsewhere in Africa. Male **patas** are sandy coloured with russet crowns and tails, white limbs and shaggy grey shoulders; the females are plainer in colour. The **western red colobus** is an extremely attractive monkey with rich russet and grey fur, a dark tail, and a blue-black face. All three species are a similar size in adulthood, the males slightly larger than females, with a head and body 60–80cm in length, and long, slender limbs and tails. African monkeys don't have prehensile tails, nor do you see them brachiating (swinging from branches), but they're impressive leapers and swift runners. The patas, largely terrestrial, is the world's fastest monkey, capable of speeds of up to 30mph (50kph) on the ground – which will come as no surprise to anyone who's had their lunch stolen by one. All three species live in troops of one or two dozen family members, the babies clinging to their mothers' fur. They are well adapted to woodland savannah habitats and range widely in search of food. They're most commonly found on forest fringes – they rarely stray too far from the safety of the trees – but they do sometimes raid crops, causing havoc for the farmers. It is the up-country **Guinea baboons**, though – larger than the other primates, with dog-like faces – that are the real rogues when it comes to crop-raiding.

Small **antelopes** are quite common in The Gambia, but they're shy and well camouflaged, so hard to spot. **Bushbuck** and **Maxwell's duiker** are occasionally seen grazing near the *bambo* pool at Abuko, and it's sometimes possible to spot the rare and semi-aquatic **sitatunga** on the banks of the river in the Kiang West area. Small herds of the impressive, horse-sized **roan antelope** sometimes enter the Gambia from Senegal in search of pasture.

Most of the big game was hunted to extinction a century ago (the last Gambian elephant was shot in 1913), and some species, such as zebra and rhino haven't lived in this part of Africa in historical times. Today, despite long-term conservation efforts such as ex-president Jawara's much-vaunted "Banjul Declaration", the faunal heritage continues to diminish while the human population expands, causing a chronic shrinkage in wildlife habitats. A very small population of **leopards** remains, nocturnal and rarely seen, though tracks are occasionally spotted in the Niumi and Kiang West national parks.

The Gambian **hippo** population is thought to have dwindled to fewer than a hundred animals. Although strictly protected, like all wild animals in The Gambia, hippos are persecuted because of their danger to rice fields and threat to human life. The Gambian fear of hippos is well-founded for, despite their placid appearance, they are dangerous if threatened, causing more human deaths in Africa than any other creature apart from the mosquito, and they regularly devastate crops. Sightings are now rare, and the likeliest place to see one, or at least a pair of ears and nostrils, is by taking a boat through the River Gambia National Park (see p.240). The mid-river islands here are also home to a population of rehabilitated **chimpanzees**. The Gambia no longer has an indigenous

CONTEXTS | Wildlife and nature

chimp population, though native chimps still live in Niokolo-Koba national park in Senegal, the western boundaries of which reach practically as far as The Gambia's eastern extremity.

Fearsome-tusked **warthogs** (known locally as **bushpigs**) are still relatively common in Gambian woodlands, but overhunting – by farmers, sportsmen, and for the tourist restaurant trade – may be changing that already. Other woodland mammals include the curious, termite-eating **aardvark** and clans of **hyena** which prowl by night; neither species is seen often.

Nile crocodiles are seen in the river and its creeks from time to time, particularly in the coolest months (December and January) when they often bask on the banks. They are mercilessly hunted because they occasionally attack children and domestic animals. There are also a few West African **dwarf crocodiles** – a miniature species that grows to less than a metre in length – at Abuko, where they live in the forest and are active by night.

Lizards are common everywhere, especially **rock agamas**, the brightly coloured males typically seen performing vigorous push-ups on sunny rocks. Some places positively swarm with them, no doubt in proportion to the insect supply. Large lizards (all African lizards are harmless) include two species of monitors, of which the grey and yellow **Nile monitor** grows to an impressive two metres. Nile monitors live near water, and are often seen dashing across the road or through undergrowth, or occasionally draped motionlessly over a mangrove. The slightly smaller Bosc monitor is more often found out in the bush, poking through the undergrowth. Both species have characteristic long, forked tongues with which they constantly check their environment. **Chameleons**, unmistakable for their prehensile tails, swivelling eyes, and rapid colour-changing abilities, may be spotted in trees or bushes by the sharp-eyed – or more often squashed flat on the road ahead. Their tongues stay firmly inside their mouths – until a suitable insect alights within striking range, when the tongue is hurled out and its sticky pad yanks the insect back into the waiting maw. Watching a chameleon hunt is an engrossing experience. Finally for lizards, in most areas, at night, house **geckos** come out like translucent little aliens to scuttle usefully across the ceiling and walls in pursuit of moths and mosquitoes.

The Gambia has around forty species of **snake**, all of which are elusive and most of which are harmless. The nine that are dangerously venomous, including the **puff adder**, the **spitting cobra** and the **green mamba**, will only strike if threatened, and walking heavily will usually scare them away (they're highly sensitive to vibration). Impressive looking, but harmless to humans, is the black-and-tan, rodent-eating **rock python** and the smaller, stocky **royal python**, which shelter in burrows. The best place to see snakes at close range is to visit the reptile farm near Kartong (see p.170).

Two species of dolphin, the **Atlantic humpbacked dolphin** and the slightly larger **bottle-nose dolphin** patrol the Atlantic coast and the shallow waters of the Gambia estuary in schools of between half a dozen and five hundred animals. A rare inhabitant of the coastal mangrove creeks is the **West African manatee**, a vegetarian mammal, superbly adapted to a life drifting in shallow salt water and, with its joined rear limbs and large breasts, thought a likely source of the mermaid tale. One aquatic animal you probably won't see, but may hear about, is the **ninki-nanka**, a large and likely mythical water beast, that many Gambians claim exists, somewhere. Older people insist that seeing it will ultimately cause your death. A team of crypto-zoologists mounted a search for the ninkinanka recently, but found nothing conclusive. Beached **whales** may account for some such stories.

Gambian waters are rich in tropical **fish** including barracuda, tigerfish, tarpon and *bonga*, plus small sharks and rays. Particularly numerous in the mangrove creeks are **tilapia**, a genus found all over Africa. On any creek trip, you'll also see numerous **mudskippers**, 10–15cm (4–6in)-long fish that appear to be in the evolutionary process of becoming land-dwelling amphibians. Their front fins have become flippers, almost stumpy legs, and at low tide you can see literally thousands of them skittering over the mud.

On the invertebrate front, **spiders** and **scorpions** and various other bugs, including fascinating **praying mantises**, are encountered less often than you might expect. Not that you won't find an astonishing variety if you're intent on looking: the search is usually very rewarding. **Butterflies**, well over a hundred species in total, are numerous and colourful, especially in the rainy season, when they flutter in clouds at the edge of forests and in sunny clearings.

Books

West Africa has produced quite a few world-class authors, but The Gambia doesn't have a vibrant contemporary literature scene of its own and Gambian fiction is rarely available outside the country. The in-print choice of books about The Gambia is also pretty limited and books about Africa that touch on The Gambia are not much easier to find. A few publications that may be useful to travellers visiting The Gambia, such as the various hand-stapled Mandinka and Wolof language manuals, are sold in hotel shops, at the airport and in Timbooktoo, the country's only well-stocked bookshop, in Fajara. Books marked with the ⚑ symbol are highly recommended.

Travel and literature

Jens Finke *Chasing the Lizard's Tail: By Bicycle across the Sahara*. Entertaining and insightful travelogue, recounting Rough Guide author Finke's solo journey from Morocco to The Gambia, with vivid descriptions of pre-coup Banjul, where his travels came to an abrupt end.

⚑ **Mark Hudson** *Our Grandmothers' Drums*. Rich, absorbing story of the author's stay in the village of "Dulaba" (Keneba) in the Kiang West area; Hudson immersed himself in traditional rural Gambia by befriending a group of village women, and become an honorary member of their *kafo*, or working cooperative. Occasionally shaky on anthropology, but frank and revealing on the intricacies of Gambian women's lives.

Elspeth Huxley *Four Guineas*. This account of Huxley's trip through the four Anglophone colonies on the eve of independence is full of credible conversations – and the occasional lapse into racist angst. Probably only available in libraries, or secondhand.

⚑ **Rosemary Long** *Under the Baobab Tree*; *Together Under the*

Baobab Tree. Cheerful and chatty autobiographical accounts of a Scottish writer's new life married to a Gambian, running a tourist guesthouse on a shoestring in the Kombos in the early 1990s, with plenty of homespun wisdom about grass-roots Gambia as seen through expat eyes.

Mungo Park *Travels into the Interior of Africa*. A bestseller in its time, this is the Scottish explorer's own account of his two journeys in search of the source of the Niger.

⚑ **Ann-Britt Sternfeldt** *The Good Tourist in The Gambia*. Brief but refreshingly thoughtful and honest guide to responsible tourism in The Gambia, showing how to enjoy the best of the country's attractions while supporting local businesses and appreciating the natural environment.

Bamba Suso et al *Sunjata*. The legend of the founder of the Mali empire, which once reached as far as present-day Gambia. The Penguin edition presents two strikingly different Gambian versions of the epic.

History and politics

A.E. Afigbo et al *The Making of Modern Africa*. A detailed, illustrated guide in two volumes, putting West Africa in the wider African context up until the first big changes after independence.

Adu Boahen *Topics in West African History*. An excellent introduction to basic themes in West African history by one of Ghana's most respected historians.

🏃 George E. Brooks *Landlords and Strangers*. The history of West Africa prior to the peak of the colonial era, drawing on oral records and written documentation to trace the significance of climate and inter-cultural communication in the region's development.

Basil Davidson *Africa in History*. Lucidly argued and readable summary of Africa's dominant nineteenth- and twentieth-century events.

🏃 Ada Dinkarala et al *Historic Sites of The Gambia*. Solid background information on topics as diverse as slave-trading, forts, shell-mounds and stone circles.

Cheikh Anta Diop *Pre-Colonial Black Africa*. Diop asserts that Western civilization had its origins in Africa. First published in the 1950s, this book encouraged a whole generation of students to reinterpret the past from an African perspective.

Harry A. Gailey *A History of the Gambia*. Published in 1980, and largely superseded by his later *Historical Dictionary*, but one of the few books available.

Arnold Hughes and David Perfect *A Political History of The Gambia, 1816–1994*. The history of the country prior to the 1994 coup, focussing on The Gambia's coming of age as a multiparty democracy.

Arnold Hughes and Harry Gailey *Historical Dictionary of The Gambia*. Definitive coverage of the country's history from pre-colonial times to the present, with short biographies of key figures and entries on events, institutions and cultural topics.

Patrick Marnham *Dispatches from Africa*. Although published in 1980 and now inevitably dated, this journalism remains devastatingly sharp. Includes an essay on The Gambia.

🏃 Mungo Park *Travels into the Interior of Africa*. Absorbing account of the youthful Scottish explorer's two journeys (1795 and 1797) along the Niger.

Society and culture

Thomas D. Blakely et al *Religion in Africa: Experience & Expression*. Thorough examination of religion in Africa and the diaspora.

🏃 Simon Broughton et al *The Rough Guide to World Music, volume 1: Africa and Middle East*. This authoritative work, published in a new third edition in September 2006, discusses the Gambian *kora* masters in the context of West Africa's musical heritage, and includes features on Senegambian stars, CD reviews and playlists.

Samuel Charters *The Roots of the Blues: An African Search*. Charters' serendipitous journey (The Gambia, Senegal, Mali) aimed to find the blues' roots in West Africa. While he failed, his other discoveries make great reading.

R.J. Harrison Church *West Africa.* A traditional geography reference – excellent and unexpectedly absorbing.

Thomas A. Hale *Griots and Griottes: Masters of Words and Music.* A comprehensive look at *griots* – male and female – of Niger, Mali, Senegal and The Gambia and their roles as historians, genealogists, diplomats, musicians and advisors.

Patience Sonko-Godwin *Ethnic Groups of the Senegambia Region.* A brief and graspable social history of the region.

David E. Maranz *Peace is everything: the world view of Muslims and Traditionalists in Senegambia.* A wonderful book, though a dense read, that paints a complex and positive view of Islam. Good, too, on Muslim brotherhoods.

Claudia Zaslavsky *Africa Counts: Number and Pattern in African Cultures.* Includes a chapter on *warri* games.

Natural history

Clive Barlow et al *Field Guide to the birds of The Gambia and Senegal.* Excellent, authoritative bird bible for the region, by a renowned British ornithologist resident in The Gambia.

Stella Brewer *The Forest Dwellers.* The story of Brewer's chimpanzee rehabilitation project, now located in the River Gambia National Park.

Jonathan Kingdon *The Kingdon Field Guide to African Mammals.* Beautifully illustrated, and very detailed, the essential companion for real enthusiasts.

W. Serle and G. Morel *A Field Guide to the Birds of West Africa.*

Comprehensive guide for the whole West African region, with specially commissioned illustrations.

Rod Ward *A Birdwatchers' Guide to The Gambia.* Detailed information on some of the country's prime ornithological sites, accessibly presented.

Silva & Schaltz *A Photographic Field Guide to the Birds of the Gambia and West Africa.* Excellent pocket guide, with CD-Rom (see www.vogeldocumentatiefonds.nl).

John Willliams *A Field Guide to the Butterflies of Africa.* Great fun to have with you if you can carry an extra book, though it is fairly selective.

Fiction

T. Coraghessan Boyle *Water Music.* Lengthy, meticulous – and at times outrageously funny – fictionalization of Mungo Park's explorations. Boyle's vision of the West Africa of two centuries ago is utterly captivating: if you take just one book, take this.

William Conton *The African.* A rags-to-premiership story by a

Gambian writer from the colonial era: still a classic, this was a bestseller in 1960s Gambia.

Ebou Dibba *Chaff in the Wind; Fafa.* In *Chaff in the Wind*, this highly accomplished Gambian author, describes life in 1930s Gambia. *Fafa* is the tale of a remote trading post on the River Gambia.

Alex Haley *Roots.* An entertaining American saga to read on the beach – only the first few chapters are set in Kunta Kinte's semi-mythical Gambian homeland, but village life is vividly described.

Lenrie Peters *The Second Round.* A readable, if downbeat semi-autobiographical account of an African doctor's experience of culture shock when he returns home after working abroad. This Gambian author has also published several collections of poetry.

Tijan Sallah *Kora Land.* Verse with an uncompromising take on West African politics and social manoeuvring, from a Gambian poet and essayist who tackles themes such as corruption, poverty and injustice.

Music

N owhere in the world has quite the same rhythm, melody and musical colour as West Africa. Throughout the region, every rite of passage is marked by a musical celebration of some sort, but music is also an integral part of everyday life, embroidering urban and village landscapes with a rich background texture of drumming and song.

Gambian music overlaps and interweaves that of Mali, Guinea and above all Senegal. Music is the Senegambians' main creative outlet, and is far more significant (and widespread) in traditional society and daily life than any of the visual arts. Improvisation around familiar themes plays a big part in Gambian musicians' creative processes, since a great deal of Senegambian music is based on well-known ancient songs, tunes and rhythms passed down from generation to generation by the *jalis*, the hereditary caste of musicians and storytellers whose music accompanies traditional dances. Storytelling, music and dance are intricately connected all over West Africa.

The Gambia's musical heritage is as rich as its ethnic make-up, and each tribe has a distinctive set of traditional instruments: the flutes and rasping *riti* violins of the Fula, the pounding *boucarabou* and driving percussion of the Jola, the thunderous *sabar* and rippling *tama* drums of the Wolof and the Mandinka's melodious **kora**. Arguably the country's most distinctive music is the traditional repertoire of the Mandinka *jalis*, sung solo to tunes on the *kora*, but the music you're most likely to hear on the radio or on cassette, blaring out of workshops, bars and bush taxis everywhere, is *ndagga* and *mbalax* **dance music** from Senegal.

Traditional music and dance

The Gambia's Mandinka *jalis* are, like the Manding *jelis* and *griots* elsewhere in West Africa, the custodians of folk history, which they convey through rhythm and song. Largely untouched by Western influences, their music is all sweet melodies, hypnotic rhythms and ancient stories, and has a lilting quality. The title of *jali* is possessed only by certain very old families, notably the Kontehs, Kuyatehs, Jobartehs and Susos. Traditionally, the **kora** and many other instruments are played exclusively by them.

A *jali*'s reputation is built upon humility and correct behaviour as well as his knowledge of history and family genealogies. Originally, the job involved singing the praises of the noble and wealthy (no occasion – a wedding or naming ceremony for example – would be complete without a *jali*), but now they're just as likely to have business or civil service patrons. Some *jalis* are also philosophers or satiricists who deliver social comment in musical form.

Jalis call on a great **repertoire** of songs, but if you listen to several artists, you'll start to recognize lyrical variations on common melodic themes. Classics like "Sundiata Faso", "Tutu Jara", "Lambang", "Koulanjan", "Duga", "Tara", "Alla l'aa ke" and "Sori" are heard time and time again. A *jali*'s skill lies in the improvised flourishes and ornamentation (*birimintingo*) that he brings to the recurrent theme or core melody (*donkili*).

While *kora* music is generally quiet and contemplative, Gambian **percussion** – drums, xylophone-like *balafon*, and all manner of simple instruments

Traditional Senegambian instruments are made from indigenous materials such as wood, calabash, animal skin, millet stalks and horn, and each one has **spiritual significance** as something alive, possessing its own language – this is why the skin of the goat (the most talkative of animals) is used for drums and lutes. Some instruments are used **seasonally**, for example at harvest time, and some instruments are gender- or generation-specific.

Drums

Drums are the most basic and familiar instruments played by all Gambian ethnic groups; they feature at most events, whether ceremonial, ritual or social, and have multiple functions including issuing announcements and warnings.

Boucarabou Three or four drums of different pitches played simultaneously by one Jola drummer.

Djembé The classic West African drum, originally from Guinea but played all over the region. Made from a goblet-shaped hollowed-out wood core over which a goat skin is tensioned with cords. Played with the hands.

Mandinka drums Three conical drums of differing height played together by three musicians.

Sabar Tall, freestanding cylindrical Wolof drums, played with hand and stick in drum bands of up to twelve players.

Tama Small, hourglass-shaped talking drum, tensioned with strings which run from top to bottom. When squeezed between the upper arm and the body and struck rapidly with a stick, it produces an amazing series of high-pitched tones.

Other percussion

As well as the main percussion instruments below, a wide range of simple instruments is used to beat out complex syncopated rhythms, including rattles, bells, whistles and, universally, clapping hands.

Balafon Rosewood and gourd xylophone with between 17 and 27 keys, known to have been around since the fourteenth century.

Kiring and **tombolong** Small or large hollow log with closed ends and a long slot from end to end, played with sticks for a hollow sound.

Sheikeire Calabash covered with beads or shells, shaken or struck.

Water drum Calabash in a basin of water, played with a stick, often by women.

Stringed instruments

Bolom (or bolombato) Percussive harp-lute with three or four strings, a skin-covered calabash base tensioned with cords and an arched neck that used to be played for warriors going into battle. It's now an instrument played by men who are not of a *jali* family.

Kontingo Small, oval lute with five strings.

Kora Mandinka, Manding and Mandé *jali* harp-lute made with a large decorated half-gourd covered with a skin. The 21–25 strings, usually made from fishing line, are attached with leather thongs to a rosewood pole put through the gourd. The player plucks and strums the strings to produce a melody, bass line and embellishments all at the same time. The top of the body has a large sound hole, doubling as a collection point for money from the audience. It's played at waist level, standing or seated.

Riti Fula violin with one to four strings, played with a bow.

Xalam A single-string *jali* lute with a half-gourd, skin-covered soundbox.

Wind instruments

Flute Made from terracotta, wood, millet stalks, bamboo, horn or calabash, and played by the Fula and Jola tribes.

to shake, chime or rattle – are played at top volume. Every ethnic group has its own brand of exuberant percussion. The **dances** associated with Gambian drum music – high-stepping, arm-flapping, stomping solos that elicit shrieks and applause the faster they go – are an expression of individuality and, at the same time, of community solidarity. It's a tradition that The Gambia shares with other West African countries, and which resonates far beyond Africa's shores: the principles of West African music and dance inhabit the collective cultural memory of African descendants throughout the diaspora. Within Senegambian rhythms are the foundations of music and dance made famous by Western stars of funk, jazz, soul and hiphop. See a Fula dance and you understand exactly where breakdancing comes from.

Modern music

Modern music in The Gambia is essentially Senegalese, largely because of Senegal's cultural domination of its tiny neighbour. Gambian musicians have always had great difficulties breaking into the international music scene. The country has poor infrastructures for professional musicians; The Gambia has yet to pass any copyright laws, so any profits from recordings are swiftly eaten away by pirating. Most Gambian musicians scrape a living from tips for live appearances, or from teaching. As a result, it's difficult to state categorically who are the greatest Gambian musicians. Few are well known outside their homeland – in fact, there are many master musicians whose music is never heard outside their own compound.

Heading for Senegal to expand their musical influence further takes cash and commitment. Those musicians who can afford it go to Dakar, the nerve centre of the Senegambian music scene, a city that swaggers to the rhythm of the music it gave birth to, **mbalax**. The city's soundtrack seeps out of the roadside stalls, bars and clubs: the call of the *tama* (talking drums) and *sabar* (tall drums), and the nasal keening of the *gewels* or *gawlis*, traditional Wolof singers and counterparts of the *jalis*. Everybody who is anybody in Senegambian music either hails from Dakar, or gravitates here, drawn by the magnetism of big audiences and serious money. In West African terms, the Dakarois recording industry is a sophisticated machine, which holds an overwhelming sway over Gambian musicians' livelihoods.

The *kora* is usually a solo instrument, accompanied by solo voice, but in the 1990s, young *jalis* breathed new life into traditional *kora*-playing by setting up semi-acoustic ensembles combining amplified *koras* with percussion and other instruments, and playing in an up-tempo, tumbling, danceable style. One of the *jalis* at the forefront of this movement was Jaliba Kuyateh, one of The Gambia's most popular live performers, who makes regular appearances at festivals and other important events.

Recently Gambians have been experimenting with new styles, mostly American and Jamaican influenced. A whole generation of Gambian youth, particularly in the urban areas, sways along to **reggae** – Bob Marley Day is a major celebration for many – and homegrown **ragga**, **rap** and **hip hop** acts are fast gaining ground on the more traditional bands. Local names to look out for in the CD stalls include Dancehall Masters, Da Fugitivz, Egalitarian, Hamaleh G, Smokey, Njie B, Mystic MC and Freaky Joe; for now, it's rare to find recordings by these artists outside The Gambia, but it's only a matter of time. Unlike their American counterparts, the lyrics of Gambian rappers and hip hop stars tend to be positive, philosophical and observational, steering clear of bitter ghetto-speak, and they receive plenty of airtime on the nation's most popular commercial radio station, West Coast Radio.

Discography

Much of the music you'll hear in The Gambia is by Senegalese stars, who regularly work with Gambians, and outnumber them in the list of artists below. This selection of recordings, all available internationally, includes the best of *mbalax*, *kora*, and the region's irresistible take on Afro-Latin jazz.

Tata Dindin *Salam – New Kora Music* (Network Medien, Germany). While this talented *jali* is known for his innovative compositions and technique (he sometimes even plays his *kora* with his teeth, Hendrix-style), this recording finds him in traditional, meditative mode.

Pa Bobo Jobarteh & Kairo Trio *Kaira Naata* (Real World, UK). Evocative kora from this young Gambian *jali*, recorded live on the beach and in other low-key locations: plaintive melodies, with bird calls and ocean waves between tracks.

Ifang Bondi *Gis Gis* (Warner Basart, Netherlands). This band have been pace-setters in the Gambian music scene since the 1960s (when they were known as the Super Eagles); here they combine Fula, Mandinka, Jola and Wolof influences in smoothly produced, modern-edged sound.

Cheikh Lô *Bambay Gueej; Lamp Faal* (World Circuit, UK). Youssou N'Dour's brilliant protegé stirs up a warm, potent mix of Cuban guajira, soukous, reggae, urban funk and makossa jazz, with addictive results. *Lamp Faal* includes complex new rhythms and flavours inspired by a residency in Brazil.

Ismaël Lô *The Balladeer* (Wrasse, UK). Lô represents the gentler style of Senegalese music, with whimsical ballads woven around harmonica and acoustic guitar melodies.

Baaba Maal *Mi Yeewnii / Missing You* (Palm Pictures, UK). Known as The Nightingale for his clear, high-pitched voice, Senegal's second biggest star has an electrifying onstage energy. He also has a contemplative side, and this acoustic album, produced by John Leckie (producer of Radiohead's *The Bends*) finds him in sweet and soulful mode.

Youssou N'Dour *Set* (Virgin, UK); *The Guide (Wommat)* (Sony, UK). Two classic recordings from the region's greatest cultural ambassador. N'Dour's huge body of work is patchy, varied and fascinating, continually reworked to cater to the separate demands of his markets at home, in France and in the English-speaking world. You're likely to hear his voice at least once every day, anywhere where music is played in The Gambia. *Set* is the aficionado's favourite; *The Guide* includes *Seven Seconds*, the duet with Neneh Cherry that catapulted Youssou to international fame.

Orchestra Baobab *Specialist In All Styles* (World Circuit, UK). Genius producer Nick Gold gives the veteran band the *Buena Vista Social Club* treatment with this, their first album for fifteen years. The Casamance meets Cuba in a fresh, danceable, instant classic.

Yan Kuba Saho *Yan Kuba: Kora music from The Gambia* (Latitudes,

USA). Spirited and atmospheric recording made in Serrekunda with vocals and *konkondiro* (percussive tapping on the body of the *kora*) from Saho's wife Bintu Suso.

Mansour Seck *Yelayo* (Stern's, UK). Seck, the childhood friend and mentor of Baaba Maal, is a supreme singer and guitarist; this is Fulani music at its best.

Thione Seck *Orientation* (Stern's, UK). Seck was one of the creative geniuses who, back in the 1960s, co-invented *mbalax*. This Dakar-meets-Bollywood-style musical travelogue marks a fascinating change of direction.

Jali Nyama Suso *Gambie: L'Art de la Kora* (Ocora, France). Classic 1970s recording from the late *kora* master who in his prime was one of the country's most influential artists.

Various *Kairo – Sound Of The Gambia* (Arch Records, UK and The Gambia). Showcase collection of established Gambian talent, including some of the nation's greatest virtuoso singers, drummers and *kora* players.

Various *The Rough Guide to the Music of Senegal & Gambia* (World Music Network, UK). Compelling introduction to the best of the region's music.

Language

Language

Language

W est Africa is the most linguistically complex region in the world. The Gambia alone, though the second smallest country in the region, has dozens of languages and dialects, of which six – English, Mandinka, Wolof, Fula, Jola and Serer – are in common daily use.

Many Gambians speak several languages – their own tribal language, at least one other and English. English is the country's official language, and it dominates the media, but it's not the *lingua franca*; Gambians rarely use it between themselves, preferring **Wolof** in the Kombos and **Mandinka** up-country. English is, however, the only language permitted in schools, so as education standards rise it's likely to become more widely spoken and understood. At present, an individual's fluency in English usually corresponds directly to their level of education and their degree of interaction with foreigners. Naturally enough, English is much more commonly spoken in the tourist areas than anywhere else in the country, and some Kombo-dwellers, even those with little formal education, have also picked up German, Danish or Swedish. Most Gambian languages include a peppering of words and phrases adapted from English, French and Arabic, including the universal Arabic greeting *Salaam aleikum – aleikum salaam* used by all ethnic groups. Gambians that trade with or travel to Senegal generally speak good French.

None of the Gambian languages had a written form before the arrival of the Europeans, and it's only recently that linguists have made any attempt to standardize spellings – definitive rules do not yet exist.

Pronunciation and grammar

Most Gambians speak Mandinka or Wolof (often both) more fluently than English, even if neither is their mother tongue. A little of these therefore goes a long way in making yourself understood.

Mandinka is not difficult to get your tongue around, though grammatically it's likely to feel unfamiliar. A characteristic of spoken Mandinka is the omitted final vowel, lending a "clipped" quality to the language. Wolof grammar is different again; as a beginner you're best off learning a few phrases by ear. In both languages, a double consonant makes the sound harder, as in English, and a double vowel spelling lengthens the sound, as indicated below.

Vowel sounds

a short, as in "cat"	aa long, like the vowel sound in "cart"	o short, as in "sock"	oo long, like the vowel sound in "sort"
e short, as in "bet"	ee long, like the vowel sound in "bear"	u short, as in "sugar"	uu long, like the vowel sound in "food"
i short, as in "fit"	ii long, like the vowel sound in "feat"		

Mandinka consonants

ny – like the "ni" in "onion"

ng – like the "ng" in "sing"

kh – like the "ch" in "loch"

Wolof consonants

x – like the "ch" in "loch", but throatier

Greetings

No interaction in The Gambia ever begins without at least the most basic of **greetings**, so learning a few simple ones will make your encounters with local people far more rewarding. Responses to greetings are normally ritualized, and effectively evasive rather than specific.

Universal greeting (exchanged by all Gambians)

Salaam aleikum	Peace be upon you	Aleikum salaam	… and peace be upon you (response)

Mandinka greetings

Kayira be	I wish you peace	Dookuwo be nyaadii?	How is the work?
I be kayira to?	How are you? (to one person)	Domanding, domanding	It's coming along (lit: small, small)
Ali be kayira to?	How are you all?	Ila musoo lee?	How is your wife? (lit: where is…?)
Kayira dorong	Peace only (in response to any of the above)	I keemaa lee?	How is your husband? (lit: where is…?)
A be nyaadii?	How are things? (lit: it is how?)	Dindingolu lee?	How are your children? (lit: where are…?)
Suu moo lee?	How is everyone (lit: where are the people of your compound)?		
		I be jee	They're well (lit: they are there, response to any of the above)
I be jee	They're well (lit: they are there)	Tana taala	No problem with him/her
Kortanante?	No problem? (general, further greeting)	Tana teela	No problem with them
Tanante	No problem	I saama	Good morning (response identical)
I nimbaara?	Well done, good work (lit: you at work; said to one person if they're working, or even just chatting)	Somandaa be nyaadii?	How's the morning?
		Somandaa be jang dorong	Fine (lit: the morning is here only)
Ali nimbaara	(said to several people)	I tiinyang	Good afternoon
I nimbaara, nimbaara	I'm working (response to either of the above)	I tiinyang	Good afternoon (response)
		Tilibuloo be dii?	How's the afternoon?

I be jee	Fine (lit: it is there)	Wulaaroo be dii?	How's the evening?
I wulaara	Good evening (response identical)	I be jee	Fine (lit: it is there)
		Fo waati koteng	Goodbye

Wolof greetings

Nakam?	Hello (how's things?) (colloquial)	Jaama nga fanaan?	Did you spend the night peacefully?
Nanga def?	How are you?	Jaama rek	Yes thank you (lit: peace only)
Mangi fii rek or: mang fi	I'm fine (lit: I'm here only/I'm here)	Naka suba si	How's the morning?
Jaama ngaam?	Do you have peace? (formal greeting)	Suba sangi fii rek	Fine (lit: the morning is there only)
Jaama rek	Peace only	Jaama nga endu?	Are you having a peaceful afternoon?
Alxamdu lillaax	Thanks be to God/ thank goodness	Jaama rek	Yes thank you (lit: peace only)
Naka waa ker ga?	How are things in your compound?	Naka becheg bi	How's the afternoon?
Nyung chi jaama	Everybody's fine	Beche bangi fii rek	Fine (lit: the afternoon is there only)
Ana waa ker ga?	How are the people in your compound? (lit: Where are the people in your compound?)	Naka ngoon si	How's the evening?
		Ngoon sangi fii rek	Fine (lit: the evening is there only)
		Naka guddi gi	How's the night?
Ana waa England/ Angleterre?	How are things in England? (lit: Where are the people of England?)	Guddi gangi fii rek	Fine (lit: the night is there only)
		Nyu endu chi jaama	Have a good day
Ana ... ?	How is...? (lit: Where is...?)	Nyu fanaan chi jaama	Have a good night
		Jaama rek	Yes thank you (lit: peace only)
Nyung fa	They're fine (lit: They're there, response to either of the above)	Naka ligey bi?	How's the work?
		Ligey bangi fii rek	Fine (lit: the work is there only)

Fula greetings

| Nambata? | How are you? | Jamtan | I'm fine |

Jola greetings

| Kassumai? | How are you? | Kissindi? | How is the family? |
| Kassumai kep | I'm fine | Cocobo | They're fine |

Serer greetings

| Nafio? | How are you? | Memehen | I'm fine |

L

LANGUAGE | Greetings

Basic questions in Mandinka and Wolof

Almost as important as asking someone how they are and how everything's going at home, is, if they're a stranger, to ask their name, where they're from, where they're living or staying and where they're going. This is not nosiness, but common politeness. Again, the responses don't have to be too specific.

Mandinka	Wolof	
I tondii?	Naka nga tudda?	What's your name?
N too mu Kebba le ti	Kebba laa tudda or: Mangi tudda Kebba or: Sama tuur Kebba la	My name is Kebba
I kontongo dung?	Naka nga santa?	What's your surname?
N kontongo mu Suso le ti	Suso laa santa or: Mangi santa Suso or: Sama santa Suso la	My surname is Suso
I bota mintoo le?	Foo jogee?	Where do you come from?
M bota England le	England laa jogee	I come from England
Sii	Toogal	Sit down (take a seat)
I ka taa mintoo le?	Fooy dem? or: Fan ngaay dem?	Where are you going?
I ka taa marisee le to bang?	Ndax marse ngaay dem?	Are you going to the market?
N ka taa Basse	Basse laay dem	I'm going to Basse
I be sabatiring mintoo le?	Foo dekka?	Where are you staying/living?
haa	waaw	yes
hani	deedeet	no
tumandoo	xej na	perhaps
abaraka	jerejef	Thank you (thanks, blessing)
abaraka baake	jerejef bu baax	Thank you very much
amiin	amiin	You're welcome (lit: amen, response to a blessing)
abaraka	sa waala	You're welcome (lit: blessings, response to thanks)
… lee?	Ana … ?	Where is…? (used for people, and moveable things) Where is…? (used for people,
Naam	Naam	Yes, I'm here (when called)

Mandinka and Wolof words and phrases

Basic expressions

Mandinka	Wolof	
Hekatu	Baalal ma	I'm sorry
M mang mandinka moy baake	Man deeguma wolof	I don't speak (lit: hear) much Mandinka/ Wolof
M mang a fahaam	Xamuma	I don't understand
A fo kotenke	Waxaat ko	Please repeat
I ye English moy le bang?	Deega nga English?	Do you speak English?
I mang English moy bang?	Deeguloo English?	Don't you understand English?
domanding dorong	tuuti rek	a little bit
dukare	ngir yaala	please (for God's sake!)
naa dyaateeye	su la neexee	if you like
nna haaji te jee	Suma yoon neeku chi	I don't mind/care
tanante/problem taala	amul solo	no problem
M mang i kumandi jang	Ooyuma la fii	I didn't invite you
M mang lafi … la	Buguma …	I don't like/want…
M mang a long/M maa long	Xamuma ko	I don't know him
M mang i long/M mee long	Xamuma la	I don't know you
M mang lafi ila deemaaroo la	Buguma sa ndimbal	I don't need your help
M bula/Fata m ma	Baay ma, waay!	Leave me
A manke ila haajoo ti	Du sa soxla	It's none of your business
Moo le ka m batu	Am na ku may xaar	Someone's waiting for me
Ali taa/A cha!	Dem leen!	You go/Clear off! (to children)
Ila nying motoo ye n nyaabo	Buga naa sa woto	I like your car
I mang nyong soto	Amuloo morom	You have no equal
Ila nying parewo nyinaata	Sa mbuba rafet na	Your dress is lovely
Fo waati doo	Be benen yoon	Till the next time
N ka taa le	Mangi dem	Goodbye (lit: I am going)
I si i kontong/Ali si i kontong	Nuyu leen	Pass on my regards (lit: you (all) greet them)
Suumoolu kontong	Nuyul waa ker gi	Say hello to them
I saa moy	Dinenyi ko deega	they will hear
Fo nyaato	Be si kanam	see you soon
M be naa la nyaato	Dinaa nyow chi kanam	I'm coming back later

Getting around

Ali nga taa	Nyu dem	Let's go
Loo (jang)	Taxawal (fii)	Stop (here)
Naa (jang)	Kaay (fii)	Come (here)

Mandinka	Wolof	
… be mintoo le?	… mungi fan?	Where is…? (used for places)
Gunjur siloo be mintoo le?	Yooni Gunjur fan la neeka?	Where is the road to Gunjur?
Post-office siloo yitandi n na	Won ma yooni post-office bi	Show me the way to the post office
Jana?	Nale?	That way?
Jee?	Fale?	There?
Jang?	Fii?	Here?
Kilometre jelu?	Nyaata kilometre?	How many kilometres?
bulubaa	ndeyjoor	right
maraa	chaamong	left
sutiyaa	jegeng	near
jamfa	sori	far
muntuma	kanyi?	when?
tariyaa/tariyaata baake	gaaw/gaaw torop	fast/it's very fast
domang domang	ndanka ndanka	slowly

Shopping and ordering food

I lafita mune la?	Lan nga buga?	What would you like?
I ye banaanoo soto le bang?	Amuloo banana	Do you have any bananas?
… sotota le bang?	… am na?	Is… available?
M mang kodoo soto	Amuma xaalis	I don't have any money
N lafita banaanoo la	Buga naa banana	I want some bananas
Banaanoo sang n nye	Jaay ma banana	Sell me some bananas
Jelu le mu	Nyaata la?	How much (money) is it?
N so jiyo la	May ma ndox ngir yalla	Please give me some water
M be … dii leela	Dinaa la jox …	I will give you …
dalasi luulu	juroomi dalasi	five dalasis
A koleyaata!/A daa jawuyaata!	Dafa seer!	It's expensive! (lit: difficult)
A koleyaata baake!	Dafa seer torop!	It's much too expensive!
A daa talaa!	Wanyi ko tuuti!	Lower the price!
I be m faa la!	Hey! yangi may rey!	Hey! you're killing me!
a kaanyanta	doy na	enough
faa	fees	full
lafaa	dolil	more/again
domanding	tuuti	a little
(soos) jamaa	(soos) bu bari	a lot (of sauce)
(buk) jamaa	(buk) yu bari	many (books)
a beteyaata	baax na	OK/that's all
I ye mune soto?	Loo am?	What do you have? (eg food)
… naati n nye	Indil ma …	Bring me…
A diyaata (baake)	Neex na bu baax	It's (very) delicious/nice! (for food/drink/places)

Mandinka	Wolof	
A beteyaata (baake)	Baax na torop	It's (very) good! (for anything: good taste/quality/quantity)
nyinyaata	rafet	Nice/beautiful
beteyaata/beteyaata baake	baax/baax torop	Good/best
(a daa) diyaata	yomba na	Cheap (its price is easy)
a daa mang koleyaa	seerut	Inexpensive
manee	doy waar	Funny
N kontaanita baake	Kontaan naa	I'm very happy
M bataata baake	Soona naa torop	I'm very tired

At a celebration or festival

I ye a kata baake	Jeem nga bu baax	You've done well (congratulations)
Ala maang na sali siyaa la	Yal nenyi feekee dewen	May you witness many more feasts (salutation at a religious festival)
Ala maa deenaanoo Yal na xale bi guda fan siimaayaa la		May God let the baby live long (salutation at a naming ceremony)
Bisimila	Bisimila	You're welcome to come in (bisimila is also said before eating, like saying grace)
Domori waatoo siita	Waxtu leeka jot na	It's time to eat
I lafita mune domo la?	Loo buga leeka?	What do you want to eat?
jansoo	ndooli	gift marking a ceremony

Numbers

Mandinka	Wolof	
kiling	beena	1
fula	nyaar	2
saba	nyet	3
naani	nyenent	4
luulu	juroom	5
wooro	juroom beena	6
worowula	juroom nyaar	7
sey	juroom nyet	8
kononto	juroom nyenent	9
tang	fuka	10
tang ning kiling	fuka ak beena	11
muwang	nyaari fuka	20
tang saba ning luulu	nyeti fuka ak juróom	35
keme	teemeer	100
wuli (kiling)	(beena) juni	1000

Vocabulary

Mandinka	Wolof	
somandaa	suba	Morning
tilibuloo	becheg	Afternoon
wularoo	ngoon	Evening
suutoo	guddi	Night
tubaab	tubaab	White person (vocative)
tubaaboo	tubaab	White person (referring to one)
moo fingo	nit ku nyuul	Black person
naaroo	naar	Arabic/Lebanese
buunyaa	mayee	tip
dukoo	duku	bribe
presentoo	mayee or: present	present/gift
bii	tey	today
saaying	léegi	now
saama	eleg	tomorrow
waati doo	benen yoon	next time
taapalaapa, senfuur	mbuuru	bread
maanoo	maalo or: chep	rice
suboo	yaapa	meat
nyee	jen	fish
nyoo	dugub	millet
tiyoo	jerte	groundnut (peanut)
tulusee	diwtiir	palm oil
jiyo	ndox	water
tendoloo	senge	palm wine

Glossary

Al-Haji – name given to a man who has made a pilgrimage to Mecca, or their descendant; the female equivalents are Ajaratou or Haja

alkalo – village chief

APRC – Alliance for Patriotic Reorientation and Construction, the political party led by President Yahya Jammeh

ba – big, as in tenda-ba (big wharf)

baa – river

badala – waterfront, beach

balafon – traditional West African xylophone

bambo – crocodile

banabana – wandering street vendor

bantaba – village meeting place and men's communal siesta platform, found in every village and in many compounds

banto faro – river flood lands

bengdula – craft market

bitiko – small shop

bolon or **bolong** – creek

boubou or **mbuba** – voluminous Wolof dress

brother – friendly term of address for any male

bumster – beach boy, hustler, tourist tout

bush taxi – shared public transport

butut – one-hundredth of a dalasi

car – minibus

chop – local-style meal

chop-shop – local restaurant

dalasi – Gambian currency

dash – bribe

djembé – Guinean drum

duma – lower

fanal – paper and bamboo lanterns, usually in the shape of ships, traditionally paraded at Christmas and New Year

fodeh/foday – teacher or marabout

Food and drink terms

afra – barbecue, or grilled meat stall

attaya – chinese green tea, brewed in ritual style

benechin – literally "one pot", a spicy stew of rice with chicken, meat or vegetables

bonga – common Gambian fish

bui – baobab cordial

chakery – dessert made from yogurt, sour cream, couscous, nutmeg, vanilla and fruit

chawarma – Lebanese-style mutton or lamb kebab, usually served in pitta bread.

daharr – tamarind juice

domodah – rich peanut sauce, sometimes including meat or fish

foofoo – pounded cassava

kinkiliba – dried leaves used to make an infusion

mbahal rice – rice with dried fish, groundnuts and spicy peppers

minties – black mints, a Gambian weakness, sold in *bitikos* everywhere

plasas – sauce made from cassava leaves and okra

senfour – Gambian bread, lighter than *tapalapa*

sisay yassa chicken *yassa*, chicken with onion, garlic, chilli and lime

tapalapa – Gambian bread, like French bread but chewier (literally "thin stick")

wonjo – bright red cordial made from sorrel flower pods

Fula – ethnic group, traditionally cattle herders

futampaf – Jola tribal intiation ceremony

Gamtel – Gambian telecommunications company

garage – bush taxi park

gelleh-gelleh (Mandinka) or **tanka-tanka** (Wolof) – bush taxi, a converted van with forward-facing seats

gewel (Wolof) traditional musician and oral historian

ghetto – unofficial bar where palm wine is sold by Manjago palm tappers

griot – traditional musician and oral historian

haftan – man's traditional long shirt

Hajj – Muslim pilgrimage to Mecca

harmattan – cold dusty wind that sometimes blows across West Africa from the Sahara between December and March

imam – Muslim religious leader

jakalo – bush taxi, a converted van with a truck back where passengers sit on benches

jali – (Mandinka) traditional musician and oral historian

juju or **grisgris** – magical amulet

JulBrew – Gambian lager

Jola – ethnic group (President Jammeh's tribe)

kafo – traditional "youth club" or working association of men or women of one age group

kankurang – Mandinka masquerade dancer, appearing at circumcision ceremonies and festivals

kerr – place or compound

kola – the nut of the kola tree, chewed as a stimulant and exchanged as a ritual gift

kora – traditional harp-lute

Koriteh – Muslim festival marking the end of Ramadan

koto – old

kuliyo (Mandinka) or **ngente** (Wolof) – naming ceremony

kumpo – Jola masquerade dancer, who wears a costume that looks like a haystack with a pole sticking up from his head, and dances by whirling around upside down

kunda – place or home

kuta – new

Lamin – first name given to most Mandinka first-born sons

lapa – thin

lumo – weekly (or regular) rural village market

Mandinka – a West African ethnic group, The Gambia's largest tribe

Manjago – a West African ethnic group, traditionally non-Muslim palm-tappers

Maolud Nabi – the Prophet's birthday, an Islamic festival

marabout – powerful Koranic teacher thought to have magical powers as a mystical healer and granter of wishes

mbalax – dance music, from Senegal

nakko – garden

ndagga – dance music, from Senegal

nding – small

nyamo – spiritual strength, conferred by *jujus*

pagne (pronounced "pane") – dress-length of cloth

PPP – People's Progressive Party (the political party of ex-president Jawara)

pirogue – traditional canoe, used for fishing or transport, sometimes a hand-paddled dugout, or sometimes a larger boat with an outboard engine

Ramadan – lunar month of fasting prescribed by Islam

riti – Fula violin

sabar – traditional Gambian drum, played with a stick

santo – upper

saliboo – a gift given to celebrate a religious festival

sept-places – Senegalese bush taxi, an estate car taking seven passengers

Serahule – ethnic group, traditionally silver traders and potters

Serer – ethnic group, traditionally boat builders and fishermen

seyfo – district chief

simba or **zimba** – Wolof lion dancer

sister – friendly term of address for any female

soft – fizzy drink

su – home

sunnaro (Mandinka) or jonga (Wolof) – circumcision ceremony

sai-sai – scoundrel

tama – talking drum

Tamharit – Islamic New Year

tapa – stick

tenda – port, wharf, riverside

tesito – self-reliance, a slogan of Jawara's government, now adopted by development projects

tiko – woman's head-tie

Tobaski – Muslim festival celebrated by the ritual slaughter of a sheep

toma – namesake, a special friend

toubab or tubab – white person

Vision 2020 – APRC political programme

warri – traditional board game

wax – African-style printed cotton

Wolof – ethnic group, dominant in the Kombos

LANGUAGE | Glossary

Travel store

UK & Ireland
Britain
Devon & Cornwall
Dublin **D**
Edinburgh **D**
England
Ireland
The Lake District
London
London **D**
London Mini Guide
Scotland
Scottish Highlands &
   Islands
Wales

Europe
Algarve **D**
Amsterdam
Amsterdam **D**
Andalucía
Athens **D**
Austria
The Baltic States
Barcelona
Barcelona **D**
Belgium &
   Luxembourg
Berlin
Brittany & Normandy
Bruges **D**
Brussels
Budapest
Bulgaria
Copenhagen
Corfu
Corsica
Costa Brava **D**
Crete
Croatia
Cyprus
Czech & Slovak
   Republics
Dodecanese & East
   Aegean
Dordogne & The Lot
Europe
Florence & Siena
Florence **D**
France
Germany
Gran Canaria **D**
Greece
Greek Islands
Hungary

Ibiza & Formentera **D**
Iceland
Ionian Islands
Italy
The Italian Lakes
Languedoc &
   Roussillon
Lanzarote **D**
Lisbon **D**
The Loire
Madeira **D**
Madrid **D**
Mallorca **D**
Mallorca & Menorca
Malta & Gozo **D**
Menorca
Moscow
The Netherlands
Norway
Paris
Paris **D**
Paris Mini Guide
Poland
Portugal
Prague
Prague **D**
Provence & the Côte
   D'Azur
Pyrenees
Romania
Rome
Rome **D**
Sardinia
Scandinavia
Sicily
Slovenia
Spain
St Petersburg
Sweden
Switzerland
Tenerife &
   La Gomera **D**
Turkey
Tuscany & Umbria
Venice & The Veneto
Venice **D**
Vienna

Asia
Bali & Lombok
Bangkok
Beijing
Cambodia
China
Goa

Hong Kong & Macau
India
Indonesia
Japan
Laos
Malaysia, Singapore
   & Brunei
Nepal
The Philippines
Singapore
South India
Southeast Asia
Sri Lanka
Thailand
Thailand's Beaches &
   Islands
Tokyo
Vietnam

Australasia
Australia
Melbourne
New Zealand
Sydney

North America
Alaska
Baja California
Boston
California
Canada
Chicago
Colorado
Florida
The Grand Canyon
Hawaii
Las Vegas **D**
Los Angeles
Maui **D**
Miami & South Florida
Montréal
New England
New Orleans **D**
New York City
New York City **D**
New York City Mini
   Guide
Orlando & Walt
   Disney World® **D**
Pacific Northwest
San Francisco
San Francisco **D**
Seattle
Southwest USA

Toronto
USA
Vancouver
Washington DC
Washington DC **D**
Yosemite

Caribbean
& Latin America
Antigua & Barbuda **D**
Argentina
Bahamas
Barbados **D**
Belize
Bolivia
Brazil
Cancún & Cozumel **D**
Caribbean
Central America
Chile
Costa Rica
Cuba
Dominican Republic
Dominican Republic **D**
Ecuador
Guatemala
Jamaica
Mexico
Peru
St Lucia **D**
South America
Trinidad & Tobago
Yúcatan

Africa & Middle East
Cape Town & the
   Garden Route
Egypt
The Gambia
Jordan
Kenya
Marrakesh **D**
Morocco
South Africa, Lesotho
   & Swaziland
Syria
Tanzania
Tunisia
West Africa
Zanzibar

D: Rough Guide
DIRECTIONS for
short breaks

Available from all good bookstores

Travel Specials

First-Time Around
the World
First-Time Asia
First-Time Europe
First-Time Latin
America
Travel Online
Travel Health
Travel Survival
Walks in London &
SE England
Women Travel

Maps

Algarve
Amsterdam
Andalucia & Costa
del Sol
Argentina
Athens
Australia
Barcelona
Berlin
Boston
Brittany
Brussels
California
Chicago
Corsica
Costa Rica &
Panama
Crete
Croatia
Cuba
Cyprus
Czech Republic
Dominican Republic
Dubai & UAE
Dublin
Egypt
Florence & Siena
Florida
France
Frankfurt
Germany
Greece
Guatemala & Belize
Hong Kong
Iceland
Ireland
Kenya & Northern
Tanzania
Lisbon
London

Los Angeles
Madrid
Mallorca
Malaysia
Marrakesh
Mexico
Miami & Key West
Morocco
New England
New York City
New Zealand
Northern Spain
Paris
Peru
Portugal
Prague
The Pyrenees
Rome
San Francisco
Sicily
South Africa
South India
Spain & Portugal
Sri Lanka
Tenerife
Thailand
Toronto
Trinidad & Tobago
Tuscany
Venice
Vietnam, Laos &
Cambodia
Washington DC
Yucatán Peninsula

Dictionary
Phrasebooks

Croatian
Czech
Dutch
Egyptian Arabic
French
German
Greek
Hindi & Urdu
Italian
Japanese
Latin American
Spanish
Mandarin Chinese
Mexican Spanish
Polish
Portuguese
Russian
Spanish

Swahili
Thai
Turkish
Vietnamese

Computers

Blogging
iPods, iTunes &
music online
The Internet
Macs & OS X
PCs and Windows
Playstation Portable
Website Directory

Film & TV

American
Independent Film
British Cult Comedy
Chick Flicks
Comedy Movies
Cult Movies
Gangster Movies
Horror Movies
Kids' Movies
Sci-Fi Movies
Westerns

Lifestyle

eBay
Ethical Shopping
Babies
Pregnancy & Birth

Music Guides

The Beatles
Bob Dylan
Classical Music
Elvis
Frank Sinatra
Heavy Metal
Hip-Hop
Jazz
Book of Playlists
Opera
Pink Floyd
Punk
Reggae
Rock
The Rolling Stones
Soul and R&B
World Music
(2 vols)

Popular Culture

Books for Teenagers
Children's Books,
0-5
Children's Books,
5-11
Conspiracy Theories
Cult Fiction
The Da Vinci Code
Lord of the Rings
Shakespeare
Superheroes
Unexplained
Phenomena

Sport

Arsenal 11s
Celtic 11s
Chelsea 11s
Liverpool 11s
Man United 11s
Newcastle 11s
Rangers 11s
Tottenham 11s
Poker

Science

Climate Change
The Universe
Weather

AFRICA

IT'S CLOSER THAN YOU THINK

THE AFRICA CHANNEL

WHERE AFRICA COMES ALIVE!

An All New, All-English, 24/7 Destination Channel For The World Traveler In You.

www.theafricachannel.com

AFRICA CONFIDENTIAL

The inside track on Africa – politics and business
www.africa-confidential.com

KENYA: Africa Confidential was the first to name the European companies and Nairobi politicians who are defrauding Kenya of billions of dollars.

CONGO-KINSHASA: Inside the mining business with exclusive information from confidential investigations and expert analysis on the elections.

SOUTH AFRICA: What's at stake in the trial of ex-Deputy President Jacob Zuma and the widening investigations into the US$6 billion arms deal?

EQUATORIAL GUINEA: How did Africa Confidential break the story of the failed coup and find the wonga list naming Mark Thatcher?

UNITED STATES/NIGERIA: What links Vice-President Dick Cheney to a corruption probe into a US$10 billion gas plant in Nigeria?

ZIMBABWE: Which leading supplier of military equipment to President Robert Mugabe dined at 10 Downing Street and has indefinite leave to remain in Britain?

If you're serious about Africa, you should be reading Africa Confidential.
Get the real facts about the people and the politics shaping the continent today.
Africa Confidential, serious about Africa since 1960.

Save a massive 20 per cent on a year's subscription to Africa Confidential, the world's leading fortnightly bulletin on Africa, by taking advantage of this special one-off price of only £400 or US$800.
Reply quoting the code below by email to info@africa-confidential.com or by telephone with credit card on 44(0)207831 3511. Or photocopy this page, fill in your details and fax back to 44(0)207831 6778.

Subscriptions Priority Order Form

☐ Yes, I want to subscribe to Africa Confidential at this special discounted rate of £400 or US$800.

☐ Please invoice me for one year's subscription @ £400 + VAT or US$800.

☐ Please send me a sample copy of Africa Confidential.

Name:_____

Job Title:_____

Address:_____

_____

_____Post/Zip Code:_____

Company Name:_____

Department:_____

Tel:_____

Fax:_____

Email:_____

Credit card payments: Visa   Amex   Mastercard

Card number:_____

Name on card:_____

Expiry date:_____

Africa Confidential, 73 Farringdon Road,
London EC1M 3JQ, Britain
tel:44(0)207831 3511 fax:44(0)207831 6778

☐ Tick this box if you would like us to contact you about other publications and services.

45DM092AFC

Avoid Guilt Trips

Buy fair trade coffee + bananas ✓

Save energy - use low energy bulbs ✓

    - don't leave tv on standby ✓

Offset carbon emissions from flight to Madrid ✓

Send goat to Africa ✓

Join Tourism Concern today ✓

Slowly, the world is changing.
Together we can, and will, make a difference.

Tourism Concern is the only UK registered charity fighting exploitation in one of the largest industries on earth: people forced from their homes in order that holiday resorts can be built, sweatshop labour conditions in hotels and destruction of the environment are just some of the issues that we tackle.

Sending people on a guilt trip is not something we do. We know as well as anyone that holidays are precious. But you can help us to ensure that tourism always benefits the local communities involved.

Call 020 7133 3330
or visit **tourismconcern.org.uk** to find out how.

A year's membership of Tourism Concern costs just £20 (£12 unwaged)
- that's 38 pence a week, less than the cost of a pint of milk, organic of course.

Fighting Exploitation in Tourism

TourismConcern

Afridisiac?

If you're planning a trip to Africa, or would just like to learn more about it, *Travel Africa* magazine is the ideal read for you.

Published in the UK four times a year, each edition comprises atleast 128 pages of travel ideas, practical information and features on Africa's attractions, wildlife and cultures.

The magazine is supported by an extensive website with our full back issue archive and a Safari Planner to help you plan your next adventure.

Explore Africa in your own home. Subscribe today.

Small print and
Index

A Rough Guide to Rough Guides

Published in 1982, the first Rough Guide – to Greece – was a student scheme that became a publishing phenomenon. Mark Ellingham, a recent graduate in English from Bristol University, had been travelling in Greece the previous summer and couldn't find the right guidebook. With a small group of friends he wrote his own guide, combining a highly contemporary, journalistic style with a thoroughly practical approach to travellers' needs.

The immediate success of the book spawned a series that rapidly covered dozens of destinations. And, in addition to impecunious backpackers, Rough Guides soon acquired a much broader and older readership that relished the guides' wit and inquisitiveness as much as their enthusiastic, critical approach and value-for-money ethos.

These days, Rough Guides include recommendations from shoestring to luxury and cover more than 200 destinations around the globe, including almost every country in the Americas and Europe, more than half of Africa and most of Asia and Australasia. Our ever-growing team of authors and photographers is spread all over the world, particularly in Europe, the USA and Australia.

In the early 1990s, Rough Guides branched out of travel, with the publication of Rough Guides to World Music, Classical Music and the Internet. All three have become benchmark titles in their fields, spearheading the publication of a wide range of books under the Rough Guide name.

Including the travel series, Rough Guides now number more than 350 titles, covering: phrasebooks, waterproof maps, music guides from Opera to Heavy Metal, reference works as diverse as Conspiracy Theories and Shakespeare, and popular culture books from iPods to Poker. Rough Guides also produce a series of more than 120 World Music CDs in partnership with World Music Network.

Visit www.roughguides.com to see our latest publications.

Rough Guide travel images are available for commercial licensing at www.roughguidespictures.com

SMALL PRINT

Rough Guide credits

Text editor: Helena Smith
Layout: Jessica Subramanian
Cartography: Jasbir Sandhu
Picture editor: Jj Luck
Production: Aimee Hampson
Cover design: Chloë Roberts
Photographer: Emma Gregg
Proofreader: Stewart Wild
Editorial: **London** Kate Berens, Claire Saunders, Geoff Howard, Ruth Blackmore, Polly Thomas, Richard Lim, Alison Murchie, Karoline Densley, Andy Turner, Keith Drew, Edward Aves, Nikki Birrell, Helen Marsden, Alice Park, Sarah Eno, Joe Staines, Duncan Clark, Peter Buckley, Matthew Milton, Tracy Hopkins, David Paul, Lucy White, Ruth Tidball; **New York** Andrew Rosenberg, April Isaacs, AnneLise Sorensen, Amy Hegarty, Sean Mahoney, Ella Steim
Design & Pictures: **London** Simon Bracken, Dan May, Diana Jarvis, Mark Thomas, Harriet Mills; **Delhi** Umesh Aggarwal, Ajay Verma, Ankur Guha, Pradeep Thapliyal, Sachin Tanwar, Anita Singh

Production: Sophie Hewat, Katherine Owers
Cartography: **London** Maxine Repath, Ed Wright, Katie Lloyd-Jones; **Delhi** Rajesh Chhibber, Jai Prakash Mishra, Ashutosh Bharti, Rajesh Mishra, Animesh Pathak, Karobi Gogoi, Amod Singh, Alakananda Bhattacharya
Online: **New York** Jennifer Gold, Suzanne Welles, Kristin Mingrone; **Delhi** Manik Chauhan, Narender Kumar, Shekhar Jha, Rakesh Kumar, Amit Verma, Amit Kumar, Rahul Kumar
Marketing & Publicity: **London** Richard Trillo, Niki Hanmer, Louise Maher, Jess Carter; **New York** Geoff Colquitt, Megan Kennedy, Katy Ball; **Delhi** Reem Khokhar
Special projects editor: Philippa Hopkins
Manager India: Punita Singh
Series editor: Mark Ellingham
Reference Director: Andrew Lockett
Publishing coordinator: Megan McIntyre
Publishing Director: Martin Dunford

Publishing information

This second edition published November 2006 by **Rough Guides Ltd**,
80 Strand, London WC2R 0RL
345 Hudson St, 4th Floor,
New York, NY 10014, USA
14 Local Shopping Centre, Panchsheel Park,
New Delhi 110017, India
Distributed by the Penguin Group
Penguin Books Ltd,
80 Strand, London WC2R 0RL
Penguin Putnam, Inc.
375 Hudson Street, NY 10014, USA
Penguin Group (Australia)
250 Camberwell Road, Camberwell,
Victoria 3124, Australia
Penguin Books Canada Ltd,
10 Alcorn Avenue, Toronto, Ontario,
Canada M4V 1E4
Penguin Group (NZ)
67 Apollo Drive, Mairangi Bay, Auckland 1310,
New Zealand
Cover concept by Peter Dyer.

Typeset in Bembo and Helvetica to an original design by Henry Iles.
Printed in Italy by Legoprint S.p.A.
© Emma Gregg and Richard Trillo 2006
No part of this book may be reproduced in any form without permission from the publisher except for the quotation of brief passages in reviews.
344pp includes index
A catalogue record for this book is available from the British Library
ISBN 1-84353-703-6
ISBN 13: 9-78184-353-703-8
The publishers and authors have done their best to ensure the accuracy and currency of all the information in **The Rough Guide to Gambia**, however, they can accept no responsibility for any loss, injury, or inconvenience sustained by any traveller as a result of information or advice contained in the guide.
1   3   5   7   9   8   6   4   2

Help us update

We've gone to a lot of effort to ensure that the second edition of **The Rough Guide to Gambia** is accurate and up to date. However, things change – places get "discovered", opening hours are notoriously fickle, restaurants and rooms raise prices or lower standards. If you feel we've got it wrong or left something out, we'd like to know, and if you can remember the address, the price, the time, the phone number, so much the better.

We'll credit all contributions, and send a copy of the next edition (or any other Rough Guide if you prefer) for the best letters. Everyone who writes to us and isn't already a subscriber will receive a copy of our full-colour thrice-yearly newsletter. Please mark letters: **"Rough Guide Gambia Update"** and send to: Rough Guides, 80 Strand, London WC2R 0RL, or Rough Guides, 4th Floor, 345 Hudson St, New York, NY 10014. Or send an email to **mail@roughguides.com**

You can also check Gambia updates and make comments at the authors' update **blog http:// theroughguidetothegambia.blogspot.com**

Have your questions answered and tell others about your trip at **www.roughguides.atinfopop.com**

SMALL PRINT

Acknowledgements

From Emma Gregg: Very special thanks to the following people in the UK: Nathan Pope, for his support, love and enthusiasm; Craig Rix of *Travel Africa*; Richard Trillo, whose idea it was; and all the team at Rough Guides, especially Claire Saunders and Helena Smith for their extremely professional input. Thanks also to The Gambia Experience for travel arrangements.

In The Gambia, I would like to thank my good friends: Clive Barlow of Birds of The Gambia, for ornithological expertise; Stella Brewer-Marsden OBE and David Marsden; Francis Glynn and everyone at GTS, for ideas and assistance; all at Gambia Tourism Authority and the Ministry of Tourism; David Talfryn-Griffiths, for introductions; Peter Losen and his team at Gambia River Excursions and *Janjang Bureh Camp*; Geri Mitchell, Maurice Phillips, Lesley, Zoe and everyone at Safari Garden, for guidance, support, understanding, and amazing generosity; Suelle Nachif of the African Living Art Centre, for inspiration; May Rooney of PRSP; Patrick Sothern and his team at West African Tours, for their highly professional assistance and warm good humour; Mark Thompson and everyone at *Bird Safari Camp*; Foday Trawally and Ann Rivington at *Madiyana* on Jinack Island, for the nights watching shooting stars; Lawrence Williams, James English and their team at Makasutu, for great company and outstanding hospitality.

I'd also like to thank the following for their generous assistance during my research for both editions of this Rough Guide: Abi at Geri & Maurice's; Adama Bah at Village Gallery and Gambia Tourism Concern; Ablay Bayo at Tanje Village Museum; Matthew Belford of Banjul Breweries; Debbie Burns of Cityscape, for help with maps; Ebrima Colley, for excellent language tuition; Baba Ceesay and Momodou Joof at NCAC; John Baldwin of *Kaira-Du-La Lodge*; Farid and Fouzia Bensouda of *Coconut Residence*; David Clamp at VSO; Modou Diouf and Moriba Kuyateh in Brikama; Famara Drammeh at Abuko; Modou Lamin Faye at *Kambeng* and *Jokor* in Brikama; George Foster at *Jokor*; Modou Gaye at Cityscape; Derek & Jenny Hewitt in Farafenni; Charbel Hobeika of Gambia Tours; Karen Hobbs; Ous Jagne at Timbooktoo; Mawdo Jallow at Bao Bolon Wetland Reserve; Khadija Jammeh; Jette Jarra of *African Heritage*; Malick Jeng; Amadou Johnson of Fulladu Camp; Will Knowles of Madox Microlights; Mark Longster and Tracey Day; Mama of *Mama's* in Kololi; Alagi Mbye of Maali's Music School; Evamaria Minuth; Hu Morris in Kau-Ur; Abdoulie Njie; Farma Njie of Discovery Tours; Sheikh Tejan Nyang; The Professor of Fajara; RM Tours; Lamin Sanyang at Kiang West National Park; Ann Slind at *Traditions* in Basse; Kawsu Sillah at *Kairoh Garden* in Tanji; Sulayman Sonko of Tumani Tenda; Helen Stott; Foday Suso; Tony Tabbal; and especially Ibrahim, Kalifa, Numo, Alhaji, Jerreh and Ben of West African Tours.

Finally, thanks to the following fellow travellers: Simon & Nicole Angling; Chris & Alexa; Nick Clark; Ludovic Dumont; Patrick Dyke; Harold Goodwin; Sallie Grayson; Kathryn Haylett; Dan, Mandy and Manuel Huertas; Baba Ishangi; Joe & Nina; Nigel Killikelly; Sarah McLaughlin & Simon; Marianne Harstad; John Shettel, Angie Silva; Martine Stone; Mark Stratton; Phil and all Geri's yoga class. Warmest thanks go, too, to all the other Gambians and Gambiaphiles I met in The Gambia and in the UK while researching and writing this Rough Guide. Without their inspiration and appreciation the book would never have been possible.

From Richard Trillo: Huge thanks to Jerreh Gibba of West African Tours for his enthusiastic and indefatigable assistance and driving skills in Kombo and around the country, to Patrick Sothern of West Africa Tours for generous assistance with transport, and to Geri Mitchell and Maurice Philips at Safari Garden Hotel. Many thanks to the kind hospitality of Adama Gaye in Dakar. And to Phoebe Trillo for travelling with me and making the research such an enjoyable experience.

Readers' letters

Many thanks to the following readers who sent us updates on the first edition.

Josef Alter, Michael Asher, Jim & Margaret Clark, Michael Franke, John Gibbons, Sue Hardy, Gail Hopkins, Lukas Jonkers, Nina Mueller-Effinger, Jo Page, David Somers, Ward Tanghe, Steve Turton, Jan Vercammen.

Photo credits

All photos © Emma Gregg except the following:

Cover
Back image: Fishing boat © Alamy

Title page
Beachgoers relaxing at Kololi © Jon Hicks/Corbis

Full page
Women walking along roadside © Jack Sullivan/
   Alamy

Introduction
Basketware at Senegambia Craft Market
   © International Photobank/Alamy
Terminal 3, Tendaba Airport © Richard Trillo

Birds of The Gambia
Little bee-eater, striated heron, intermediate
   egret, marabou stork, hooded vulture, palm
nut vulture, African jacana, whimbrel, Egyptian
   plover, Senegal thick-knee, Senegal coucal,
   verreaux's eagle owl, pied kingfisher, giant
   kingfisher, little bee-eater, red-thoated bee-
   eater, northern carmine bee-eater, violet turaco,
   Abyssinian ground hornbill, bearded barbet,
   yellow-crowned gonolek, purple glossy starling,
   exclamatory paradise whydah © Nigel Blake
Pink-backed pelican, African pygmy kingfisher,
   fine spotted woodpecker, village weaver,
   northern red bishop © Vogel Documentatie
   Fonds
Hammerkop, western reef heron, black-headed
   plover, Abyssinnian roller, grey plantain-eater,
   rose-ringed parakeet, red-billed hornbill,
   beautiful sunbird, red-cheeked cordon-bleu
   © Gerard Mornie

SMALL PRINT

Index

Map entries are in colour.

INDEX

335

INDEX

341

R.C.L.

MAI 2007

G

Map symbols

maps are listed in the full index using coloured text

━ ━ ━	International border	✈	Airport
─ ─ ─	Chapter division boundary	★	Bus/taxi stop
═══	Major tarred road	⛽	Petrol pump
═══	Minor road	◉	Accommodation
───	Major clay road	▣	Eating/drinking
········	Unpaved road	ⓘ	Tourist office
─ ─ ─	Path	@	Internet
‖‖‖‖	Steps	⊠	Post office
─ ─	Ferry/boat route	ⓒ	Telephone
───	Waterway	⛳	Golf course
───	Wall	⛴	Ferry crossing
♦	Point of interest	▬	Building
♦	Custom post	➕	Church (town maps)
♠	Park headquarters	⊞	Cemetery
❖	Stone circle	☐	Park
❦	Baobab tree	▨	Mangrove
⛫	Mosque	░	Beach/sand
♜	Fort		

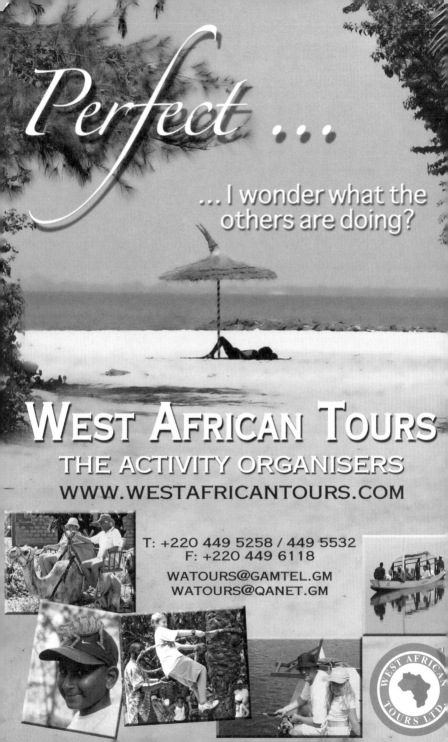